Learning for All 2

Policies for Diversity in Education

D0023710

Learning For All

The other volume in the series:

Volume 1 Curricula for Diversity in Education
Edited by Tony Booth, Will Swann, Mary Masterton and Patricia Potts

This reader is one part of an Open University integrated teaching system and the selection is therefore related to other material available to students. It is designed to evoke the critical understanding of students. Opinions expressed in it are not necessarily those of the course team or of the University.

If you would like to study this course, please write to The Central Enquiries Office, The Open University, Walton Hall, Milton Keynes MK7 6AA, for a prospectus and application form. For more specific information write to The Higher Degrees Office at the same address.

Learning for All 2

Policies for Diversity
in Education

Edited by
Tony Booth, Will Swann,
Mary Masterton and Patricia Potts

London and New York
in association with
The Open University

First published 1992
by Routledge
11 New Fetter Lane, London EC4P 4EE

Simultaneously published in the USA and Canada
by Routledge
a division of Routledge, Chapman and Hall, Inc.
29 West 35th Street, New York, NY 10001

Typeset in 10/12 pt September by Leaper & Gard Ltd, Bristol
Printed and bound in Great Britain by Mackays plc, Chatham, Kent

British Library Cataloguing in Publication Data
Policies for Diversity in Education. –
    (Learning for All)
    I. Booth, Tony   II. Series
    371.9

    ISBN 0–415–07185–2

Library of Congress Cataloging in Publication Data
applied for

Contents

Figures

FIGURES

Tables

TABLES

Contributors

Paul Abberley is a Senior Lecturer in Sociology in the Department of Economics and Social Sciences, Bristol Polytechnic, and a member of the Avon Coalition of Disabled People.

Derrick Armstrong is a Research Associate in the Department of Educational Research, Lancaster University.

Len Barton is Professor of Education at Sheffield University.

Tony Booth is a Senior Lecturer in Education at The Open University.

Margaret Boushel was Principal Assistant for Children and Families in the Social Service Department of the London Borough of Islington. She is now a Lecturer in Social Work in the School of Applied Social Studies at Bristol University.

Veronica Broomhead is a parent of a child with special needs and founder member of Special Parents for Special Children.

Denise Buchner is a teacher of the deaf in Swaziland.

Jenny Corbett is a Senior Lecturer in the Department of Education Studies, Polytechnic of East London.

Mairian Corker is Head of the Centre for Deaf People and Speech Therapy at the City Literary Institute, London.

Sheila Cunnison is an Honorary Fellow at Humberside Polytechnic.

Philip Darley is Project Director at Delta, an Adult Education Project focusing on Personal Development and Relationship Building.

Shirley Darlington is Assistant Secretary (Equal Opportunities) at the National Union of Teachers.

Claire Debenham is Professional Assistant (Special Educational Needs) in the London Borough of Newham.

Liza Dresner was an under-5s worker for the London Borough of Islington. She is now raising an under 5 at home.

John Fish is an education consultant and was formerly Staff Inspector for Special Needs with Her Majesty's Inspectorate.

David Galloway is a Reader in Education in the Department of Educational Research, Lancaster University.

Christine Gilbert is Deputy Director of Education and Head of Resources in the London Borough of Harrow.

Chris Goodey is a part-time tutor in social science for the Open University.

Anna Gorbach was an under-5s worker for the London Borough of Islington. She is now a nurse.

Elizabeth Grugeon is a Senior Lecturer in Language in Primary Education at Bedford College of Higher Education.

Veronica Hanson was formerly Special Needs Liaison Officer for the Wales Pre-School Play Groups Association.

Michael Hart is Head of Learning Support at Whitmore High School, Harrow.

Paul Howard is Head of the Schools Support Service in the London Borough of Newham.

Tim Jewell is Principal Psychologist in the London Borough of Southwark.

Linda Jordan is Chair of the Education Committee in the London Borough of Newham.

Tony Kerr is Principal Educational Psychologist in Avon.

Roger Kidd is Head of the East Riding Learning Support Service in Humberside.

Tim Lee is a Research Fellow in the Centre for Applied Social Policy at the University of Bath.

Nancy Marlett is an Associate Professor in the Rehabilitation Studies Programme at the University of Calgary.

Micheline Mason is a disability equality trainer and campaigner.

Mary Masterton is a Course Manager at The Open University.

Mary Newton is Head of the Learning Support Service in Staffordshire.

Chris Onions is a freelance child psychologist and educational adviser.

Margaret Peter is Editor of the British Journal of Special Education.

Patricia Potts is a Lecturer in Education at The Open University.

Richard Rieser is a Geography and Humanities teacher.

Katheryn Riley is a Senior Research Fellow at the Institute of Local Government Studies, University of Birmingham.

Linda Shaw works at the Centre for Studies on Integration in Education.

Mårten Söder is Professor of Sociology at the University of Uppsala, Sweden.

Tim Southgate is Head of Ormerod School in Oxfordshire.

Will Swann is a Lecturer in Education at The Open University.

Simon Trotter is Assistant Director – Special and Pupil Services in the London Borough of Newham.

Maureen Turnham is a Lecturer in a College of Further Education.

Judy Watson is Head of English at a secondary school for girls in Kent.

Acknowledgements

We should like to acknowledge the assistance of Caroline Fawcus and Teresa Kennard in the production of this book and its companion volume *Curricula for Diversity in Education*.

Material used in Chapter 9 is from *Special Children* magazine, published by the Questions Publishing Company Ltd, 6–7 Hockley Hill, Birmingham B18 5AA. Subscriptions and back issues are available from the above address. While the publishers have made every effort to clear copyright permission, in some cases they have been unsuccessful and would be grateful to hear from the owners of the copyright of the following extracts: 'A curricular response to diversity at Whitmore High School', adapted from Gilbert, C. and Hart, M. (1990) *Towards Integration: Special Needs in an Ordinary School*, Kogan Page; 'Provision for the under fives', Katherine Riley, from *Local Government Policy-Making*, vol 16, No 1, June 1989, pp. 38–44; 'My Story', Judy Watson, from Reiser, R. and Mason, M (eds) (1990) *Disability Equality in the Classroom: A Human Rights Issue*, Inner London Education Authority, pp. 53–56; Internalised oppression: how it seems to me', Richard Reiser, Inner London Education Authority, pp. 29–32; 'Disability as a social construct: the labelling approach revisited', from Söder, M. (1989) article of the same title, *European Journal of Special Needs Education*, 4(2), pp. 117–129; and 'Integration, disability and commitment: a response to Mårten Söder', from Booth, T.A. (1989) article of same title, *European Journal of Special Needs Education*, 6(1), pp. 1–15.

Introduction

Tony Booth

Learning for All is a series of two books concerned with the education of children and young people who experience difficulties in learning or who have disabilities. They cover the age range from pre-school through to further education though they concentrate on the years of compulsory schooling. The first book carries the title *Curricula for Diversity in Education*, with this second book being titled *Policies for Diversity in Education*.

The books are readers for an Open University course with the same general title – *Learning for All*. The great majority of the contents of these books is being published for the first time. They are intended as a new contribution to the field.

The books are a continuation of a project in which we have been engaged for many years. This is reflected most closely in a previous series of books, *Curricula for All* (Booth *et al.* 1987, Booth and Coulby 1987, Booth and Swann 1987), and with a pack for teachers: *Teaching for Diversity* (Potts and Booth 1987). Within our project, the resolution of difficulties in learning is seen as part of the task of creating an education system that is responsive to all learners, irrespective of their gender, skin colour, background, level of attainment, abilities or disabilities.

Difficulties in learning arise when students are unable or unwilling to respond to what they are expected to learn. We are more concerned, then, with making curricula appropriate for the diversity of learners than with the identification of students with learning difficulties. The number of students with learning difficulties in any group will vary with the nature and quality of teaching. A group in a special school for students designated as having severe learning difficulties may all be actively engaged in learning, an A-level History group may all have lost the thread of the industrial revolution.

Teaching and learning take place within interacting contexts which are at varying removes from students and teachers. For example, there are the size and composition of groups, the organisation and morale of schoolworkers and students, the location, history and community of a school, the resources that are available to, and those that are used by, schools and within a student's family; the nature of government legislation, the attitude of teachers and others to educational law. All such contexts create enabling and constraining pressures on teachers and students and hence contribute to the production and resolution of difficulties in learning.

Workers in schools and colleges experience a perpetual stream of pressures and distractions. Yet the demands made on teachers conflict over time and between local and central government, school governors and parents. Such outside pressures are a poor foundation on which to construct an approach to teaching and learning.

Currently, the 1988 Education Act is providing the biggest challenge to relationships between teachers, pupils and curricula in state schools. While some of its intended effects seem inescapable, since it changes the balance of power between central and local government and the schools, its intentions will inevitably be transformed as it works its way through the digestive tract of the education system. Its effects will be modified, too, because from its inception it contained contradictions which meant that it was impossible for it to be consumed as a whole. Apart from the fact that a so-called National Curriculum was designed to apply to only part of the education system, the National Curriculum introduced an entirely new core syllabus for 14–16 year olds which entailed their own forms of assessment only shortly after the 16+ GCSE had replaced O-level and CSE examinations. Other contradictions involve the unrealistically complex and time-consuming approach to assessment of 7, 11 and 14 year olds and the specification of core subjects, such as Modern Languages, for which teachers are in short supply, without the diversion of resources to train teachers to teach them.

It is very likely that the degree of specificity of the National Curriculum, as well as the belief that the ten attainment levels are comparable between attainment targets or subjects, will be modified over the next couple of years. So will the unprecedented faith of central government that teachers obey educational law without incorporating it into their own belief structures and existing practice.

Our reasons for action, in education as elsewhere, must be personally owned. We argue that the way we teach, the conditions for learning we create, have to be based on a set of carefully considered principles which form a more permanent framework within which all the competing pressures can be interpreted and assessed. We see the 1988 Act as a significant force, which is recognised in the subject matter of several of the chapters in these books, but it cannot supersede our own responsibility for decisions about the way children and young people are educated.

We are interested in supporting the development of an education system which recognises, values and provides for diversity. It is one which seeks to reduce the formidable pressures within our society, and hence our schools, to value students according to their competence or appearance. It would be absurd for us to pretend a concern for the welfare of those who experience difficulties in learning or have disabilities if we were to regard them as less than equal members of schools and society. An education system which values the diversity of its students as a human and cultural resource is one in which education takes place together in common, comprehensive schools and colleges; in which there is the minimum of separation on the basis of competence and appearance. Similar principles happen to form the starting points, too, of the National Curriculum Council guidance on 'special needs in the National Curriculum' called, co-incidentally, *A Curriculum for All* (NCC 1989). The ways such principles inform and are informed by the details of policy and practice, by the joys, troubles and conceits of experience in education, provide the unifying themes of our books.

Many authors have made contributions to the books and while we have sought chapters which illustrate the themes of our course there is not a unanimity of perspective. In our negotiations with authors, in the process of drafting and redrafting chapters and in the final editing, we have tried to keep jargon to a minimum. We see the books as contributing to the development of the education system as a whole rather than being preoccupied with a group of pupils and schoolworkers who carry the label of 'special needs'. We avoid talking of 'children with special needs' because it misleadingly implies a dividing line between ordinary and extraordinary, or special, students and curricula. Never-theless some of our contributors use that language and we have not paraphrased it. We are aware too that classification systems in bookshops and libraries tend to reinforce the notion of 'special needs' as a separate sector of education.

We have reflected the variety of contexts for learning in our choice of chapters for the two books. Policy issues are frequently neglected in a consideration of difficulties in learning and we have tried to give them a thorough examination in this book. However, we have not made an artificial split between policy and practice. Policy is made both in committee rooms and classrooms. Nor do we take a narrow view of the curriculum. The curriculum is what students learn at school and college. There is the written Word, in National Curriculum folders and school development plans, and the curriculum as constructed together by pupils and teachers. There are also lessons, intended and unintended, which do not appear on any syllabus but are picked up in classroom, corridor and play-ground. These may be among the most memorable and long-lasting.

THE CONTENTS OF THIS BOOK

This book, *Policies for Diversity in Education,* is about attempts to plan and coordinate educational practice in colleges, schools and classrooms, in education authorities and nationally. It is also about the recipients of those policies: for example, parents and children affected by the process of educational assessment in the preparation of Statements or by professional diagnoses. It is concerned too with the attempts of these 'recipients' – parents of children who experience diffi-culties and adults with disabilities – to take a full part in defining services and educational provision.

It is a large book, but we have tried to retain coherence, particularly within sections. It contains thirty-six chapters, nine of which have been previously published. Each chapter is preceded by a brief italicised editorial introduction describing its contents and where necessary providing background information.

Part 1, 'Inclusive schools', looks at the way some schools have developed so that they can include a wide range of pupils who experience difficulties in learning or who have disabilities and can provide an appropriate education for all their pupils. It starts off with accounts of the history, organisation and curricula in two schools, one primary and one secondary, which are attended by a number of students with disabilities. The stories provide an opportunity to reflect on the extent to which present practice depends on accident or design. These are followed by a chapter on school development plans required of schools under the 1988 Education Act, which argues that they can be used to plan how to fit current demands and future developments in a school, within a clear philosophy for comprehensive, primary and secondary schools.

Two chapters, both written by the head teachers of the schools concerned, provide experiences of the changing fortunes in special schools. The first of these is about a school for pupils with physical disabilities, which actively sought to support most of its students within mainstream schools and then transformed itself into a centre for the intensive education of young children with cerebral palsy and spina bifida along the lines of Conductive Education. The second is about the closure of a school for pupils categorised as having moderate learning difficulties and their subsequent support within mainstream schools. The school reopened as a base for students categorised as having emotional and behavioural difficulties who were transferring into the county from residential school.

Part 1 ends with the report of an action research project by Sheila Cunnison, challenging gender attitudes and stereotypes and examining the relationship between these and difficulties in learning and discipline in a primary school.

Part 2 is called 'Integrating services for the under fives'. Its themes are the attempts to produce coherent sevices across health, social services and education and the integration of children with disabilities into mainstream provision. There is a review of local initiatives and central government inertia, a case report of the efforts by a group of workers within a social services department in a London Borough to get a policy off the ground in the face of cuts and local resistance and the successful development of integrated playgroups in Wales.

The first two chapters in Part 3, 'Life after school', examine the concept of 'transition' into adult life, for young people who have disabilities and those who have experienced difficulties in learning at school. The first provides an international perspective, drawing on innovative work in the USA and in European countries to provide recommendations for the way services can be coordinated and opportunities maximised. The second chapter cautions against an uncritical view of 'transition' in which the formidable obstacles within the structure of society to the employment and participation of young people may be disregarded.

The next two chapters are about policies towards adults with severe learning difficulties. The first looks at the extent to which a further education college adapts to and includes a group of young people on a course called 'life preparation', the prejudices that exist within the college and the selection procedures which exclude people with multiple disabilities and 'challenging behaviour'. The final chapter in Part 3 describes the experience of two women who have spent much of their lives in 'mental handicap' hospitals as they come to terms with supported living in the community.

Part 4 is called 'The experience of families'. The first chapter reports and discusses how parents of children with Down's Syndrome experience the interventions of professionals. It is argued that many professionals behave towards parents as if their children are not fully human. The next reports on the experience of a family of Asian origin of the Statementing procedures and special school placement for one child. This is followed by a research study on the assessment of young people who are referred to educational psychologists for advice leading up to a Statement because they are said to have 'emotional and behavioural difficulties'. Lastly, there is an account of the organisation set up in one county where parents work cooperatively with professionals to advise other parents on the difficulties of their children and to contribute to policy change.

Part 5, 'Integration and disability', opens with the accounts of two teachers with disabilities of their experience of their own education, their working lives and their disabilities. These are followed by a report of the background issues which led to the setting up of the 'Integration Alliance', an organisation of people with disabilities and parents of children with disabilities who are campaigning for integration in education. Three more theoretical chapters complete the section. The first looks at the social creation of impairment and disability and argues that the concept of oppression is essential for an understanding of the experience of disability. The next argues that the concept of labelling has been misunderstood and that proponents of integration believe that they can avoid the negative consequences of disability and thereby deny the experiences of people with disabilities. The final chapter is a response to the previous one and argues that people who advocate integration are a varied group and that they have differing responses to labelling and disability.

Part 6 looks at 'Aspects of national policy'. It starts with a detailed analysis of the effects on special education policies of local management of schools, the devolution of powers and changes in funding for education brought about by the Education Reform Act. The next chapter provides an opportunity to compare aspects of funding in the UK with the way services for children with severe disabilities and difficulties in learning are funded in Alberta, Canada.

The following three chapters deal with centres of influence in the system. The first describes the hectic process by which the National Curriculum Council produced its guidelines on special educational needs called 'A curriculum for all'. Next, there is an account of the involvement in special education policy of the National Union of Teachers which perceives the meeting of special educational needs as an aspect of equal opportunities. Then there is a study of the contributions to education policy of the National Deaf Children's Society and the principles that underlie them. The final chapter in Part 6 is concerned with the variety of responses to young people who are felt to disrupt the running of schools.

The last section of the book asks the question, 'Local authority?', in recognition of the increased difficulties faced by education authorities with curtailed powers and budgets in coordinating policies in education. Cornwall has the lowest rate of segregation out of the mainstream in England, and the first chapter in Part 7 contains interviews with people working in education in Cornwall who provide the 'Voices behind the statistics'. Then there is a description of the review of special provision in the County of Avon. This is followed by an account of integration policy in the London Borough of Newham which represents a more concerted attempt to control policy from within the council chamber. An aspect of this policy, the development of a support service from the resources previously allocated to a special school for pupils seen as challenging in their behaviour, provides the subject for the next chapter. The theme of support services is continued with a description of the changes that have taken place in the special educational needs support service in Staffordshire and their problems of survival in the era of devolved budgets. Reports of aspects of the working lives of educational psychologists are provided by a principal educational psychologist in Southwark. The book ends with a series of memos that were exchanged between two education officers, where they attempt to define with parents of children who experience difficulties in schools the work that is to be done by the more junior of them, a new recruit to the office.

REFERENCES

Booth, T. and Coulby, D. (eds) (1987) *Curricula for All: Producing and Reducing Disaffection*, Milton Keynes: Open University Press.

Booth, T., Potts, P. and Swann, W. (eds) (1987) *Curricula for All: Preventing Difficulties in Learning*, Oxford: Basil Blackwell.

Booth, T. and Swann, W. (eds) (1987) *Curricula for All: Including Pupils with Disabilities*, Milton Keynes: Open University Press.

National Curriculum Council (NCC) (1989) *A Curriculum for All: Special Needs in the National Curriculum*, London: National Curriculum Council.

Potts, P. and Booth, T. (1987) *Teaching for Diversity*, Milton Keynes: Open University Press.

Part 1

Inclusive schools

Chapter 1

Under the walnut tree
The Grove Primary School

Tony Booth

In this chapter Tony Booth provides a portrait of the Grove Primary School. He describes the history of the school and its place in the community and the way it adapted as it included, first, children with visual disabilities, and then children with physical disabilities when a nearby special school closed down. He illustrates the curriculum of the school with the example of three lessons each of which includes all pupils in a shared experience as a basis for a range of group and individual activities and discoveries. The complexities of organising and supporting the learning of pupils is discussed as well as the implications for pupils and staff of 'moving on' from the Grove.

> The children just work in groups and we work on a range of things . . . I don't think of people having different abilities I think about them as having different shaped minds.
>
> (Mary Hilton, class teacher)

1 PROLOGUE

One of the first people to see an almost finished version of the TV film we made about the Grove school, albeit without commentary, sat through the first part and then remarked – 'but this could be any school, it could be the school down the road – why am I watching this?' After my feelings of ruffled pride had subsided I realised that she had grasped what we were trying to portray: an ordinary primary school and its curriculum. We had chosen to avoid holding up the school as spectacular practice, disembodied from the lives of real teachers and pupils. Nor did we wish to pretend that the fortuitous circumstances, on which many changes at the school had depended, were really part of a carefully plotted rationality. Hence the reasons for the current shape of the school may have seemed more mundane than some would like to envisage as the driving principles of educational change.

The Grove school *is* unusual in some respects. It contains several pupils with disabilities together with the staff and facilities to support them. But we did not wish an early concentration on these children to detract from a portrayal of a fundamental purpose of the school: providing a challenging, relevant and flexible curriculum for all its pupils.

The Grove is also atypical in having new buildings with wide corridors as well as good staffing levels and a large playing area. Some people used to seeing children educated in cramped old buildings may resist reflecting on the lessons of the Grove. I am convinced that, if they allow themselves to do so, they will find matters of educational principle which transcend the particular state of school buildings though I have no wish to diminish their sense of injustice and their demand for adequate facilities for all.

This chapter is the 'book' of the film, drawing on interviews gathered during the making of the programme as well as on other sources of information concerning education in the area. Such a task is eased considerably since for me the Grove school is 'the school down the road'. Although it gives a much fuller picture of the school and the issues it raises than the television programme it is transparently still a partial account. As I have fleshed out some of the details of one particular school I have been very aware of how the lifting of one corner of the education system reveals interconnections with the whole.

In reading the stories of the school it may seem that the corners have been rounded and that the tone is sepia; that the daily irritations, arguments, mistakes and messiness of school life are not emphasised. You will have to keep these in mind as background, and sometimes foreground, noise.

I have borne in mind three themes in producing this account. I will portray the school and the pupils and workers in it as having a past and a future. I will sample the curriculum in the school and consider the extent to which it facilitates the inclusion of all pupils. I will examine, more specifically, the way pupils with disabilities are supported in the school and the consequences this has for the way it is organised.

2 THE INHERITANCE

The old days

The school is in Cambridge, a mile from the centre and at the heart of an estate built by the council in the early 1960s. It is physically and psychologically set in its community in a way that makes government rhetoric about parents playing the educational market seem as remote as the inner city life of Cambridge University. The present chair of the governors – a postman and city councillor – feels he has been involved in the school 'from day one'. He was rehoused before the school was built from what was then an undesired residential area across the tracks on the other side of town: 'over the bridge' on Mill Road. He recalls moving into his factory built home:

> When I was due for a house this was the place all the houses were coming up
> ... my wife and I moved over here and we watched our house come off two

lorries. It's sort of a glorified prefab, but it's a smashing house and I wouldn't change it ... it was right in the middle of a field ... and as you can imagine there ain't no fields hardly now ... I've seen it grow from a few houses to one of the most densely populated parts of the city ... It was a desert when I first moved over here and it's not now. It's a good place to live.

Thelma Jopling is the longest serving member of staff. She has been at the school since it started in 1963 and has a pupil in her class whose mother was taught there. She, too, recalls the Manor Farm, the only remnant of which is the old walnut tree, now locked into a central courtyard at the school. She has mixed views of the past. She regrets the eroding of formalities and discipline:

It was quite different from what it is today. The children all wore uniform ... everybody walked along the corridors and they all went to assembly without making a sound ... It was ... very much more formal ... there isn't as much control as there was. They're much more free to charge about, to say what they like and go where they like. Some of that's a good idea ... but I think perhaps it's gone too far.

The desks in her classroom were in rows facing the blackboard. Physical punishment was an option:

The first headmaster used to keep a slipper in his office, which was occasionally applied but very rarely. We used to slap children. Yes, definitely, if a child misbehaved itself a slap on the leg was quite in order. I don't think it did them any harm really.

However, some of the attention to form was an irritant. Hours were spent ensuring the perfection of entries in the registers:

Every register had to be marked carefully in red and blue ink, no biros. If you made a mistake you had a little bottle of ink eradicator in your drawer so that you could get rid of any sign of it. You had to add up every day's total and every week's total. We used to spend hours and hours adding the totals up in our registers. It was dreadful ... I don't know what they'd think of registers today ... not that I ever knew what we added them up for. We just knew we had to do them.

Including pupils with visual disabilities

The loosening up of classroom structures has been part of the changes taking place in most primary schools in the UK. A further radical change in the character of the school was initiated with the inclusion of pupils with visual disabilities at the end of the 1970s. The local authority ended its policy of sending pupils with visual disabilities to residential special schools – a move affecting about twenty pupils. The secondary age children were included in the neighbouring Manor Community School and the Grove was chosen to include those of primary age. The children were drawn from all over the county and even from adjacent counties when parental pressures persuaded their local administrators to make a mainstream arrangement for their child. Carol Jones, who is now the coordinator of special needs support but was then a class teacher, took a particular interest in these developments:

> I've always been interested in children who find difficulties in school in one way or another ... I was a class teacher here and I had one of the visually impaired children in my class when they first came to The Grove.

She made a study of the integration of the visually impaired in Cambridge for her MA degree. It is on this study that my knowledge of this provision depends (Jones 1983). The area educational psychologist had reviewed out-of-county placements and reported to her how he had been affected by his contact with pupils and their families:

> I ... was struck by the unfairness of the Hobson's choice of provision offered: your child receives education in a residential school or nowhere.
>
> (Jones 1983: 13)

In pressing for integrated non-residential provision he was aware of the by-product of reflected lustre:

> If we were going to get a unit going in Cambridge, it would be one of the first of its type in East Anglia. Let's face it, there was kudos for us in getting and having it here as well.
>
> (Jones 1983: 14)

The Grove was chosen for primary pupils because it had a sympathetic head teacher and had space, was on a single level site, was close to both an appropriate nursery and secondary school and because it was conveniently placed on the special transport routes. This was an important factor in keeping down transport costs of far-flung pupils. By the time the pupils with visual disabilities were being included at the secondary school there was a strong feeling that this concern with parsimony was over-zealous. Teachers were concerned that only a part of the saving of £7,000 that the local authority made in sending each pupil to a mainstream rather than a residential special school was being used to support their mainstream education.

Interpretations of integration

The meaning of integration was interpreted differently at the Manor and the Grove. At the former, the teacher with responsibility for the visually impaired wanted the pupils to participate in lessons to the maximum extent possible. At the Grove the first full-time specialist teacher believed that both he and the pupils should be based for most of the time in the Unit which would provide 'the opportunity to develop skills in a slowed situation':

It's a kind of cloistered environment in here, but I think on the whole, it's necessary for them to learn in that situation, then they've got to go out into the hurly-burly and practice those skills.

(Jones 1983: 24)

Teaching, then, was seen as the responsibility of the specialist teacher with the class teacher playing only a minimal role in providing an environment for the repetition of training and the 'cultivation of social relationships'. In fact there was a clash of philosophies between the head and the specialist teacher which was eventually to lead to the latter leaving the school. The head saw the integration of pupils with disabilities in the following terms:

The idea of integration is that you give children, whatever their special needs are, the same range ... of options and experience that a normally sighted child would have, the same sort of choices socially, emotionally, academically.

(Jones 1983: 21)

The fire

All developments at the school were interrupted in June 1982 by a dramatic event. Thelma Jopling remembers it vividly:

I shall never forget it, I think it was one of the most momentous times of one's life ... I was woken at seven by someone ringing to say the school was on fire ... We came up here and it was true. The whole of the hall and the administrative area of the school, plus a couple of classrooms, were just gone. Everything was just a smoking ruin with the big girders of the hall roof standing out against the sky; with all the smoke and the fire brigade and water, I just burst into tears. I suppose the thing I remember most is standing by the hall and Peter Cowell, the chairman of the governors, he put his arm round me and said 'It'll all be rebuilt, don't you worry, it'll all be rebuilt.'

The school community stepped into action over the next couple of days:

Parents came in their hordes and cleaned up ... at that time councils were looking for ways of cutting back and numbers were down and we thought, well if the school's closed for more than a day or so, we'll never reopen ... so on the Tuesday we opened with everybody in different rooms. It was really quite amazing, but the atmosphere and ... the way everybody worked together was incredible, it's never been like it before or since.

In fact the fire was to contribute to a transformation as well as a renaissance of the school.

Including pupils with physical disabilities

Shortly after the fire the specialist teacher for the visually impaired left the school and the head approached Carol and suggested that she become qualified to take his place:

> The head said to me 'Look, you've been doing all this reading ... this is a career move you could make' ... I was never interested in moving up the normal hierarchy of deputy heads and heads so I ... went away and had a year's secondment at Birmingham University.

Carol became the coordinator for special needs on her return but was interested in using the role to support a very different model of integration where, instead of developing a separate 'empire' in the school, support was to be provided in the mainstream.

But the largest change was prompted by a drama unfolding in parallel at another school. The Roger Ascham had been purpose built as an open air school and had opened in 1928. At the start it had served as a rehabilitation centre for pupils who were recovering from illness, often tuberculosis, and the open air regime of the day meant the classrooms were established as a set of separate pavilions which could be exposed to the elements on four sides. It had also taken in a group of pupils labelled as 'mentally defective' who were carefully separated from the 'physically defective' group by having different starting and finishing times to the school day as well as a separate lunch break. By the early 1980s the school had evolved from providing a vigorous and bracing regime for 'delicate pupils' to catering for children with physical disabilities. In a new age the facilities seemed inadequate and a campaign had started from within the school to get them brought up to date. The local authority administrators and advisers, however, were considering a different option. They decided to recommend the closure of the school and the transfer of the pupils to centralised resource bases to be established in mainstream schools.

A fierce battle followed, with the head and the chair of the governors of The Roger Ascham School orchestrating a campaign to retain their school. By and large, the parents of the Ascham pupils were opposed to the move. Nevertheless, the local authority gambled on the eventual agreement of the officials advising the Secretary of State in the Department of Education and Science that the school closure would be ratified and pressed ahead with their building plans. The fire may have been fortuitous for the local education authority in two ways. It provided a reason for sorting out the future of Roger Ascham pupils as well as a 'sensible' location for those of primary age range. In part because the Grove was already involved in a building programme following the fire, it was selected again as the base for primary provision.

It might have made sense to locate new provision for secondary pupils with physical disabilities at the Manor school, to which 90 per cent of pupils from the Grove transfer when they leave. However the Conservative County Council of the time were keen to close the Manor school and hence discouraged further development there. There was also a suggestion that the staff of the Manor felt they had been 'sold short' when the provision for the integration of pupils with visual disabilities had been established at the school. There was a report, too, that the head of Roger Ascham, anxious to fight the closure of his school, had spoken to the Manor staff and had painted 'a wholly negative picture', asking them how they would cope with incontinency and 'children drooling at meal-times'. Impington Village College, a school about three miles distant, was chosen instead as the place for new purpose-built facilities attached to the school and known, with a nice touch of continuity with the 'open air' past of some of the pupils, as 'The Pavilion'.

The local authority's gamble paid off. Agreement from the Department of Education and Science was finally obtained and The Roger Ascham School closed in 1987, a year after the new buildings at the Grove were ready and a very few children had transferred. Two years later the ex-chair of the Roger Ascham governors was still pursuing the issue and was left with the dubious satisfaction of obtaining a confession from the Department of Education and Science that they had not handled the matter reasonably.

The final phase of the rebuilding programme of the Grove included a swimming pool for the use of all the pupils, and this had its gala opening in 1989. In these days of delegated budgets it is carefully referred to as hydrotherapy provision so that it continues to be funded by the local authority's central funds. Ironically, the building of a pool had been a cherished dream of the head of Roger Ascham who had launched an appeal thirteen years earlier to acquire a prefabricated pool. It was obtained but never erected and in the end was left to rot.

Staff changes

The new pupils brought with them a huge increase in staff. Before the fire there were 10.5 teachers (ten full-time and one half-time) and one support teacher. To support the wider inclusion of pupils with disabilities, there were to be, eventually, an additional fourteen welfare assistants and three specialist support teachers phased in with the pupils. The area education officer agreed that the number of class teachers would be increased to thirteen to keep classes to a maximum of twenty-five pupils, to assist the process of integration. The number of welfare assistants to support the twenty-five pupils who were the subject of Statements, was way above the norms for the rest of the country (DES 1989). The staff became even more overwhelmingly female in composition than it had been before the fire; only the caretaker, one class teacher and the new head teacher were male.

In a further account of developments Carol noted the additional strain that new appointments might add to staffroom relationships when 'a new stratum is added to the existing hierarchy of the school' (Jones 1987). The support teachers who came into the school were all paid on a B allowance. This was at a time when teachers who had previously held posts of responsibility were placed on a common 'main professional grade' leaving them feeling demoted. This provided opportunities for rivalries and jealousies concerning the pay of support teachers who were regarded by some as not 'real' (i.e. class) teachers. The view of the relative status and contribution of staff is complicated in integrated settings where class teachers are expected to develop a new level of expertise in orchestrating the educational experience of a more diverse group of pupils.

The large group of welfare assistants introduced a further dynamic. Here was a new group of staff, with a wide variety of experience but no national career structure, getting a low rate of pay. Initially the welfare assistants were paid on a lower rate than they would have received in special schools but the governors fought for, and achieved, parity. This was undermined when NALGO negotiated a new pay increase for welfare assistants in special schools which did not include those in the mainstream.

In addition to support provided by education budgets there was a school nurse, and speech therapy, physiotherapy and occupational therapy sessions.

Graham Else had joined the staff as head, in 1985. Because of the fire his introduction to the school had been unusual:

> My first impression of this school when I came to visit was the building site. It was just a pile of rubble at the front and I was escorted round the school ducking my head to avoid timbers.

He was undaunted by the prospect of including pupils with disabilities and was keen to see them fit into a pattern of 'ordinary classroom' practice.

3 CREATING THE CURRICULUM

According to Graham there are implicit rules which operate at the Grove about the way classrooms should be organised:

> We don't have any ... policies that say 'Thou shalt not ability teach' as it were but ... you would have to be a fairly brave teacher at the Grove to start to stream or ability set.

A class group contains pupils of diverse experience and attainment, working together. Under the regime Carol and the other teachers have developed therefore, all the pupils with disabilities are ordinary members of mainstream classes and the support they need usually comes to them. They may come out of their classes to use the special facilities of the physiotherapy room or for speech therapy or for a quiet Braille lesson, though even in these cases they may be accompanied by friends without disabilities.

The amount of support available to the pupils is striking and means that any child who needs close personal attention from a teacher or welfare assistant can receive it. It also means that classrooms are unusual places in that they may have anything up to four adults present.

In this school, the responsibility for planning the lesson rests with the class teacher. The support teachers and the welfare assistants negotiate within this plan though in practice the direction lessons take may be unpredicted. As Mary Hilton, a class teacher, indicated:

> I'm the one who delivers the curriculum and it's my ultimate responsibility ... but that doesn't mean that other adults don't contribute to the curriculum, in fact children do, to a large extent as well.

I have selected three lessons to give a flavour of the curriculum in the school, the way staff work together and the diversity of pupils in each class.

Sue Williams's class: the naming of rats

Sue Williams has a class of 5 and 6 year olds. She is in her second year of teaching and has only known the Grove as it is now. She did not apply specifically for a post at the school but was selected for interview from the Cambridgeshire pool of probationary teachers when she finished college. At first, whenever there was another adult in the room she felt she was being assessed:

> I found it hard to settle in ... at the beginning of the year ... having another adult in the room still felt like my supervisor sitting there jotting down notes ... They were very ... friendly and non-judgemental ... I still felt ... very uncomfortable.

She found that as the year progressed she got used to her colleagues as well as to the pupils:

> By the end of the year you're sort of thinking I don't want to change. I want to stay with the same people really ... Like an old shoe it really fits by then.

But she did not keep her class for the next year and this year she had two different pupils with disabilities. A whole set of new relationships had to be formed.

> There were suddenly two, sometimes three adults in the room and it had to start all over again.

The class, like other classes in the school, is grouped around tables and there are activity areas and a computer on one side. In the lesson I have selected, the class rat was being introduced. She explained how this formed a 'common ground' for the pupils:

> All the children have come into contact with small furry animals ... we all looked at the rat, held the rat and we all talked about it ... they're all capable of sitting and drawing it ... others would be capable of looking into what it eats, exactly how much it weighs.

The groups work on different aspects of the rat theme, drawing, model making and house building with a geometric building set. The three adults move around lending assistance, asking questions, encouraging the pupils.

Brendon is being helped with colouring in a drawing of the rat by his welfare assistant Elsie Chandler, identifying the parts of the rat's body and relating them to his own.

Before coming to the Grove, Elsie had spent many years working in special schools with children categorised as having severe learning difficulties. She does not feel that her particular experience and role in the classroom are a challenge to the position of the teacher:

> They've studied for a long time to get their qualification and that higher salary. I haven't, but I hope I can contribute to the classroom and my years of experience will be of some use to the teacher.

Although Brendon has considerable physical and visual disabilities, Elsie sees his social development as requiring the most support:

> He gets tremendous things out of being in that class. He socialises ... which was very difficult for him when he first came to the school ... He will be alone if you let him so we try to encourage him to sit at the table with the other children as much as possible.

Sue adds:

> He's beginning to ask now who he wants to sit next to and to prefer to be near some children rather than others ... He'll build with stickle bricks and can be left to build ... without an adult hanging over him.

A careful balance has to be found between encouraging and taking over his learning. In Elsie's words:

> You must build up a relationship with the child that you are there to help them but you're not there to interfere with what they're doing ... If the child you're working with can be left to carry on an activity on their own then you can work with the other children in the class or sometimes you can work as part of a group where you involve the other children in what you're doing with the child you're key worker with.

Katie is blind, though she is much more vocal and independent than Brendon and expertly organises her social life and work around the classroom. Caroline Brett, her welfare assistant and a qualified nursery nurse, helps her to make a playdough model of the rat. Later, the model will be thermoformed, a process in which a permanent plastic record is made of the model's shape. Caroline has been learning Braille for a year and supports Katie in recording her work.

Sue moves round taking up requests for help and spending time with the construction group predicting the shapes required and then testing out how they will fit together to form the ideal rat home. She matches her expectations to her assessment of the capabilities of the pupils:

> One child might bring ... basically a blob with four sticks off it and I say 'That's wonderful' ... whereas if another child brings me the same thing I say 'Well what are they meant to be? ... er hasn't the thing got a tail?'

The lesson ends with the results of the efforts of one group of three pupils who have recorded an opinion poll on the rat's name:

> Can I have Gemma, Liam and Simon here? ... (leave it on there now). I want you all round the table. Daniel just bob down at the front so we can see ... bob down people at the front ... Right, Katie, do you want to stand up so you can see? [Katie is led to the front so that she can feel the count.]
>
> I wanted them to think about the maths with voting for it, I mean all this stuff about democracy, try to hammer some idea of democracy into their infant minds ... I wanted them to just be thinking how a majority decision might carry something.

Sue recognised the respective roles of members of the group who had gathered and recorded the votes: Simon who was interested in the maths, Gemma 'who was more concerned with making sure it was Elizabeth that got voted in' and Liam who was the clerical assistant: 'He was really enjoying going round with the list saying so and so, come and get your vote and ticking it off.'

After carefully counting up the columns it takes an effort for Sue to persuade some of the citizens that the rat should be given the name which received the most votes. Nevertheless, finally, the new class member is named Elizabeth.

Thelma Jopling's class: a trip to Wicken Fen

Thelma's class of 9 and 10 year olds are preparing for a field trip to the Upware Centre at Wicken Fen, staffed by the local authority, where the pupils can learn about the plants, animals and the artefacts of fenland life. There are three other adults present though only one of them, Pat Sherwood, a welfare assistant, would be there on most days. Paula Crankshaw is a parent and a local authority appointed governor who helps in the class regularly on a Wednesday afternoon. Carolyn Stirrat is a student, on her final student placement at the school. Most of the time she has had full responsibility for the class.

Thelma explains how she, too, has made the adjustment to a new method of working:

> We've had to come to terms with a lot of differences. Having wheelchairs and other equipment in our classrooms ... but most of all ... having other adults in the classrooms ... I always thought they would be critical or get in the way ... but I think it's great, it's marvellous. I wouldn't like to go back now, not to

having someone else in there. If I look around and there's no Pat or there's no somebody else, I think oh heck, I've got to manage on my own.

The preparation for the trip has been considerable and Thelma is using the lesson to encourage the pupils to develop their skills of independent study:

> They've seen a film on fenland life and wildlife in particular. We've done quite a bit of talking about how the fens have changed since they've been drained ... the people at Upware Field Centre who we shall go to are very good at showing them badger footprints and fox droppings and ... we'll see at least ten or fifteen different varieties of birds ...
>
> I wanted them to see if they could find out something about some of the birds and animals that they might see ... some of them are getting to the point where they can work quite well on their own but there are one or two now who still need a lot of individual help.

She moves round the room offering assistance, asking questions, giving an opinion. She asks one boy about his drawing of a woodpecker:

Thelma: A hole in the trunk of a tree ... usually where?
Child: The wood is soft or has started ...
Thelma: Why do you think it chooses a place like that to dig its hole?
Child: Because it's easier to peck out.
Thelma: Yes of course it is, yes. Wouldn't be any good choosing the hardest part would it? Right, and look how long it gets ...
Child: Get's deep. How big's that? About two of them?
Thelma: Half a metre ... about this long ... deep into the tree. That's a long way to dig out with your beak. Think yourself lucky you're not a woodpecker.

Pat has been coming into Thelma's class for the last three years. She is attached to the class, nominally, in order to assist James. James, however, needs very little support with his learning, though much physical help. Most of her time is spent with pupils who struggle with the content of the books or find it difficult to focus on an interest or make a start with a piece of work:

Pat: That's just flowers so there isn't a fox there at all. So we'll have a look at this one ... can you draw that?
Child: You draw it for me.
Pat: No, I can't draw, you're supposed to be drawing it anyway, not me. I told you. I can't draw a straight line.
Child: Yes you can, if you really tried.

Pat indicates the shift in the balance of classroom culture that having more than one adult in the classrooms can bring:

> The more adults there are the better it is really because you can get something

going ... we're not always strait-laced and very serious ... we can be silly ... and I think the children appreciate it as well.

Paula has been helping in various classrooms for several years:

Being rather a more mature parent, I'd lost track of how they teach our children, I thought, well, the best way to find out is to get in the school.

She is totally integrated into the activities of the class and is used to offering help where it's needed:

Perhaps reading to a child that can't understand the text of a book ... any problems you know. 'Please miss can you help me do this? How do you spell this?' ... and of course I get the perks of going on the outings, which I thoroughly enjoy and I must admit, I've learnt a lot, not being a native of Cambridge, about the environment I live in.

Carolyn, the student, feels she is beginning to understand how to involve everyone in the curriculum:

I've learnt that you've got to expect different things from each child ... every single child is going to produce something different, is going to approach something in a totally different way. It's been very frustrating at times ... you've wanted to get moving, to get onto a different area or topic for example ... some children have only ... grasped the first ideas and other children are raring to go. So I've found ... work tends to involve a lot of investigations from the children – getting them into groups they find out their own information and then take that to their own level.

This has also involved her in learning skills that are not part of the usual training:

I feel a lot more confident about standing up in front of a class of children and not worrying about what other people are doing in the classroom. I've also got used to assigning different jobs to different adults.

Despite her nostalgia for the formality of the past Thelma has grown attached to the informality of the present. She tries to provide a welcoming atmosphere for parents as well as pupils and is concerned that there are still some parents who 'think school is a place to be wary of and teachers are a race apart, which is sad really':

I don't think the children feel like that because they're very happy to chat to you and want to know all about your family which I think is lovely ... I think they like to think you're an ordinary person ... that you might be a grandma or you might be a mum ... I think their relationship in that way is better than it used to be.

Mary Hilton's class: the rock collection

In Mary Hilton's class of 10 and 11 year olds, Tim Lister, a parent of one of the pupils, has brought in his rock collection.

Mary explains:

> It comes at the end of some work we've been doing on earth science. We've looked at the solar system and we've looked at the earth in space and we've worked our way down to making collections of rocks and stones and then we found this terrific bonus really that Tim Lister was an amateur collector of rocks – being a dad of somebody in the class was too good to be true ... so we asked him in with his collection.
>
> The ultimate aim ... is to get the children to be collectors because a lot of science work starts there.

David Lister was pleased, though a little light-headed, about having his father into the school. However, it would be wrong to assume that all pupils are eager for their parents to participate in lessons. When I asked a small group of children if they would like their parents coming into the classroom there was silence. A particular question to one of them was met with the response: 'No, he would show me up.'

Tim Lister explains where each rock was found or obtained and what it is, then passes it round for the pupils to inspect. There is a Stone Age hand-axe 'found in some rubbish being thrown out of a shed':

Child:	They've chipped it, they chipped it into shape.
Tim Lister:	Right, these two, these two bits came from jumble sales and market stalls, that bit cost me 5p. It looks like ordinary rock but if you look at it closely you can see that there are specks of gold in it here.
Child:	Crack it open ... it might be a whole lump of it in the middle.
Tim Lister:	I doubt it ... I've brought along some fool's gold and you can see the difference between the real gold and the fool's gold ... Now this somebody found in their fire ... They thought it was coal ... but when you feel the weight of it you will realise why it didn't burn.
Child:	That's heavier than that too.
Tim Lister:	It's got a lot of magnesium and chromium in ...

[The collection contains a vast black fossilised mammoth's tooth (my favourite specimen), with the root and grinding ridges very well preserved.]

Tim Lister:	That one's a rhinoceros tooth ... and this one's even got a bit of the jaw still attached.
Child:	That's digusting.

Kim Watson is a welfare assistant. Her time is largely devoted to supporting Madeleine. Madeleine has severe athetosis, a form of cerebral palsy in which there is little control of voluntary movement. She has no speech of her own. Kim finds her 'a delight' and 'very easy to work with'. She describes how she supports Madeleine by making the materials accessible for her:

> She's got very good understanding, so she understands all about sedimentary and igneous rocks ... We tried to get her to touch the rocks, so she can feel the sensations as well ... she hasn't got particularly good eyesight from a distance.

Madeleine communicates in a number of ways. Those who know her well are adept at picking up the meaning behind the shifts in her gaze. She also operates a computer and a light-talker through a knee switch. The latter is a machine preprogrammed with a large selection of words, the order of which can be controlled and then converted into speech. Madeleine speaks with a clipped male American voice.

The speech therapist at the school is responsible for planning the development of Madeleine's communication. Madeleine is currently learning a new programme in her light-talker, and according to Kim she is doing this 'a lot quicker than the adults around her'.

The support teachers

There are two specialist support teachers for the visually impaired: Carol and Heidi Lorenz, and two for children with physical disabilities, one of whom – Marilyn Hamilton – had worked at The Roger Ascham School for nine years. She applied for the post as soon as the Grove was ready to accept pupils with physical disabilities, a year before The Roger Ascham School closed: 'I was very apprehensive about it because I was used to having my own class of children and I knew here I'd just be a support teacher.'

Marilyn has considerable expertise in information technology and has responsibility for computer education and software in the school. She is the link teacher for transfer of pupils with disabilities to secondary school and supports older pupils in their classes. She has to be prepared to adapt the curriculum, at times, at very short notice:

> We do have some planning meetings for the curriculum but often ... you go into the classroom not always sure what is going on ... it's my job then to make sure that the child can join in with what the other children are doing, whether they need certain equipment ... or have the work modified slightly.

Heidi, one of the two specialist teachers of the visually impaired, sees herself, like other support teachers, as a link person 'between a class teacher, the assistants and the parents'. She argues that the class teacher has the main responsibility for a child's learning while she supplements aspects of the curriculum commonly acquired through vision. She explains how Katie's experience can be extended in and after the lesson on the rat:

you'd find other animals ... we've got a rabbit out in the courtyard and so you'd compare the size of the rabbit to the size of the rat, talk about weight differences, talk about coat textural differences, talk about differences in appearance and talk about them in a very visual way because those are the words that she's going to hear around her.

She sees her job as 'primarily involved with enabling the children with visual impairment to have the same access to the curriculum that the other children have'. Besides the direct teaching of pupils, much time is spent in finding and adapting materials including Brailled and taped books, models, and raised maps and diagrams. Manni is learning to play the violin and has to have the tunes on tape:

Braille music isn't introduced until much later on because it's very difficult and also it gets in the way ... of the fluency of what you are playing.

Although materials are produced by the Royal National Institute for the Blind (RNIB) *or* through special schools, usually these are inappropriate:

they do have a transcribing unit at the RNIB regional centre but you have to give them six months advance [warning] of books that you want ... infants [like Katie], they'll crack through a book in a couple of days and so we have to transcribe those or put it on tape for her to take home ... so that she knows what's going to happen the next day.

All this support has to be given to pupils without undermining their independence or making them feel they have no privacy:

as many opportunities as possible are taken for the adult to move back out of the situation or just to set an activity going with that child and three or four others and then to move out of it to be around in the vicinity if needed ... but not ... to be an adult getting in the way of the normal interaction with the peer group.

Physiotherapy

Physiotherapists, as speech therapists, are in short supply. When I visited, the school speech therapy post was vacant and the physiotherapist was ill. In her absence physiotherapy sessions were taken by Mary King, a physiotherapist who had retired after working at The Roger Ascham School over a period of forty years. She now works voluntarily at the Grove on two days a week as a welfare assistant in Mary's class. She had worked with both Madeleine and Andrew when they were at Roger Ascham. Unlike many of her colleagues she supported their move wholeheartedly:

I was delighted ... It's always been my aim to get these youngsters integrated into society ... Madeleine's parents were very apprehensive and they're just thrilled to bits that Madeleine has so many friends . . . the able-bodied children are gaining so much for themselves and again they will grow up with an understanding of disability and not have the fear of it which so many adults have.

Mary King was aware that at first Andrew didn't see Madeleine, his classmate, 'as a human being'. After a couple of months, however, he was able to romp with Madeleine in their physiotherapy sessions. Mary King sees this physical contact as something the children with disabilities can miss out on, particularly if, unlike Andrew, they don't have brothers or sisters.

Andrew always uses a wheelchair to get around although he does possess callipers and crutches. He has got feeling on his thighs and down to his knees. In the particular session I observed, Mary was encouraging Andrew to stand and play a modified hockey game with crutches:

> It's very important he keeps on his feet for as long as possible for all sorts of reasons . . . It strengthens the bones . . . he's getting his feet in a good position and stretching up the back of his legs but unfortunately his hips have dislocated some time ago . . . it does aid the digestion too.

Andrew also had a period of hanging backwards with his knees hooked over a large covered polystyrene wedge, to help to arrest the curvature of his spine. Andrew's mother remarked particularly how the physiotherapy activities at the Grove, together with the swimming and horse riding, were helping him to develop physical courage.

One of the other pupils at the school had just returned from the Petö Institute in Budapest where Conductive Education, a particular form of integrated group physiotherapy and education, has been pioneered. Mary is interested in Conductive Education and regards it as an 'excellent method of treatment' but feels that it has drawbacks:

> In Hungary you can't go to school unless you can walk, so for years physiotherapy and walking becomes the be-all and end-all and it can lead to terrible disappointments.

She trained on the Bobath method herself. She regards it as a right for 'every child to stand and walk if they want' but also argues that for children such as Madeleine, 'speech and hand control is so much more important than walking'. With Madeleine the emphasis is on allowing her a period free of the involuntary jerky movement of her body. Mary also commits the heresy of arguing that the warmth and interest of the therapist may be as important as technical skills and is particularly keen to pass on her skills to the other welfare assistants:

> I've seen some people with really very little technique who can achieve wonders with children because they've got the knack for bringing out the best in them . . . the welfare assistants here are so good that I think they are getting the best out of the children.

4 FAMILY VIEWS: MADELEINE AND ANDREW

There are four children who are the subject of Statements in Mary's class. Besides Madeleine, there is Andrew who has spina bifida and who is also in a wheelchair, Liam who has cystic fibrosis, and Paul who has mild hemiplegia.

Madeleine Norman lives in a fen village, Witchford, near Ely and has further to travel to school than any of her classmates – though a child in a different class travels in from Essex because there is no integrated provision in his locality. Madeleine's mother regards Cambridge as 'really local ... it's only twenty minutes'.

The journey time is this short because Madeleine is last in the taxi and first out. Before travel arrangements were sorted out at the Grove, and when she was at The Roger Ascham School, the journey took much longer.

> When she first started the Roger Ascham she went on a minibus ... she was first on and last off ... that was an hour and a half each way ... We refused to let her go on the minibus because she was only four and a half and I said 'No, she's not being out of my house from eight in the morning until five at night' ... so we took her in ourselves and then after about a year and a half she just came home on the minibus ... Then I had David and she did have to go in on the minibus but she was a lot older by then ... but now we've got the taxi it's worked out very well.

Madeleine's parents were part of the majority group of parents who opposed the closure of The Roger Ascham School, as her mother explained:

> We were very unhappy about the closure but it has worked out well for Madeleine. We never thought she'd work in an ordinary primary school because of having no speech so we were very worried ... she got on really well straight away ... she needed the extra stimulus. At Roger Ascham she was in a class of eight. She was the most handicapped but the brightest, so she wasn't getting any stimulation from the other children. As soon as she got in a class of twenty at the Grove she came on quick at her work ... The Grove seems a really special school somehow ... there's not one thing you could say that you don't like about it.

It had never been an aspiration of theirs to have Madeleine attend her local school although it was suggested to them in the heat of the battle when Madeleine was about to start school:

> I've never thought anything about it really because we've had no choice. Although they did try to persuade us to send Madeleine round to the local primary school in Witchford but that was only because they were secretly trying to close Roger Ascham and I said no because I knew there were twenty-five children starting and there were no facilities. It's all split level there, they wouldn't have been able to cope with a wheelchair ... They were trying to say no new children were going in to the Roger Ascham.

Andrew Bennish, too, lives outside the immediate vicinity of the school in a 1930s estate of semi-detached houses but he has only half a mile to travel each day. Usually, he wheels himself in his wheelchair. He is in England for a year with his family while his father is on sabbatical from his university in Texas. He first attended The Roger Ascham School in 1981–2 when he was two-and-a-half then again in 1984–5 when the battle over the closure was at its height. His parents recalled their feelings about the dispute and closure. Andrew's father:

> The main advantage of Roger Ascham school was that it was comfortable and the kids didn't stand out as being particularly odd and there was a lot of support.

Andrew's mother:

> The staff there were great ... feelings were running very high and I just felt sorry for the people ... they had just finished this adaptive learning centre the previous year ... a flat where the teenagers can learn to take care of themselves and this was going to be totally left behind ... I remember I was there when they opened it and all the excitement ... you've seen something that was good and worthwhile close down ... and yet I kind of felt it was probably the best thing in the long run.

In between these two periods at Roger Ascham, Andrew attended a special school for children with physical disabilities and severe learning difficulties in Texas. Children with disabilities are entitled to an education in Texas between the ages of 3 and 21, and at nursery age – in the absence of universal nursery provision – this is likely to be in a special school. From the age of 5, at his parents' request, he was 'mainstreamed' in his local school and at that time he was the only pupil in a wheelchair. His parents felt that Andrew viewed himself as 'an ordinary kid who happened to use a wheelchair instead of walking'. Andrew's father:

> He does just about everything ... he wrestles with his brothers and ... we play baseball in the States and he's been the team manager but he can also hit the ball and catch a little bit and he tries running the bases in his wheelchair.

When the family returned to England in 1989 they heard about the Grove, and its arrangements for children with disabilities, through friends. They decided to send Andrew there along with his two brothers. Andrew's father:

> I didn't know how much they would stand out with American accents and thought it would be nice if they were all at the same school to support one another.

It came as a surprise to his parents that at first Andrew found the presence of other pupils with disabilities disturbing. In particular, it took him some time before he could acknowledge that someone with such a severe disability as Madeleine 'had a right to be there'. His feelings were undoubtedly complex. He had not considered himself as part or a member of a group of people with disabilities and this must have involved a major realignment of his view when he became a potential recipient of special support at the Grove. Andrew's mother:

> He's spent very little time in hospital compared with other disabled kids so he doesn't see himself as part of that group. He's been very healthy.

He has now made friends with Mathew 'who has a similar disability to him', although most of his time is spent with boys without disabilities, 'but his best friend in school is Andrew Baylis who is not handicapped ... mainly he's with non-handicapped kids'.

He also had to adjust to an unfamiliar open style of education. In his school in the States there was a much more formal approach: pupils had to complete a certain number of highly specified assignments each week. Andrew's mother:

> Three or four years ago the state of Texas mandated changes very similar to what the National Curriculum is going to do to you. School is much more regimented than I remember it being for my generation. One of Andrew's teachers said last year it's gotten to the point that if ... she wants to read them a story she can't because there's no free blocks of time any more ... So it was more of a grind ... and also there are the standardised test scores and schools are compared and there's a real drive for each school to excel on these tests ... which the National Curriculum is going to have as well so my advice would be: *don't let them publish the test scores.*

5 HOLDING IT TOGETHER

It has become customary in the last ten years or so to be open about the way schools are managed; to think of them as having 'a senior management team' and even 'middle management'. Such ideas can still have a strange ring to those who think of a school staff as consisting of a community of colleagues. Nevertheless, schools have always had a power structure. At this school the senior management team is seen by the head to be himself, the deputy head, the special needs coordinator, and the infant and junior coordinators.

Governors

The staff don't see the chairperson of the governors as part of the senior management team of the school, though the governors, following the 1986 and 1988 Education Acts are, in theory and in law, the most powerful force in the school. However, it is difficult to see how an unpaid group with limited time can gain the information and control they would require in order to exert their power. Peter Cowell, like other governors up and down the country, is feeling the strain:

> What used to be a pleasant enough pastime ... is now becoming a sort of part-time job ... with the pressures on education ... with the paperwork involved

now and the rules and regulations . . . it really is a full-time job. Fit that in with the council work and my own job and life can get hectic.

He is delighted about the way the school has developed and sees his job on the governors as ensuring that the school gets as large a share of resources as possible:

> I've seen it burnt half down and rebuilt and I've seen it blossom into a school that encompasses children with special needs and I've seen it develop into something wonderful . . . I try to make sure they get the best of everything. I hassle and I shout and I scream and I push to make sure that whatever is going they get their share of . . . It's no good trying to integrate if they don't give you the extra staff to do so . . . the governors are forever insisting that we need the staff to do it properly.

There is a county councillor on the governing body as well as a city councillor and this does help to ensure that the needs of the school are brought to the attention of the local authority officers, though under local financial management this has reduced significance. There can be little doubt that at present the school is well staffed.

The governors have an involvement in the school which is far broader than funding. One meeting was held when the schools and parents were just managing to fight off the attempt by the County Council to stop any provision of hot school meals. This would have made a considerable impact at the Grove where most children have a school lunch and it is a communal occasion. A parent governor reported on the hardship this would involve for his son, who has a disability:

Parent governor: I wrote to the chairman of the education committee and to my local county councillor asking 'How was my child meant to get home for a hot mid-day meal when he has to be transported twenty miles? And if children were to come home would the authority please transport them back in the lunch hour?'

Second governor: Have you had a reply?

Parent governor: No.

There was also the question of organising a room for Carol. Carol had been sharing a base with fourteen welfare assistants but needed a place where she could meet staff and parents in private. The governors decided to make the room, which had been set aside for the part-time speech therapist, available for Carol's use and rearrange the use of two other rooms between the speech therapist, the nurse and the school doctor.

The head

Graham Else, the head teacher, has overall responsibility for trying to ensure that the complex interrelationships at the school run smoothly: for balancing class numbers, and matching teachers and class groups:

> We're into the chemistry of children's relationships with each other, children with teachers, teachers with support staff whose expertise is working with particular age groups ... what we have to do is try to balance these various interests ... and come up with something that's workable. It will never be perfect and even this year we have had an area of the school where we've made amendments to the personnel working with the children.

As part of the effort to keep class sizes down to twenty-five he teaches a class for an afternoon each week and says that this is the most satisfying aspect of his week. The class is taken on that morning by Claire Marrian, one of the support teachers.

In planning the school he starts with the premise that all pupils must be involved in everything and believes that this has become such a strong element of the school culture that pupils ensure that it is reproduced:

> I think that teachers will often take cues from other children. Children will not let their friends be left out of anything and I think even if a teacher didn't have a particularly clued up attitude to integrating everybody into all activities other children would soon make it quite clear that this was so.

The special needs coordinator

However, most of the responsibility for ensuring that the support systems operate effectively is delegated to Carol. In her role as the special needs coordinator she regards herself 'as a full-time teacher of the Grove *first*' rather than as a specialist without a concern for the development and well-being of the whole school. She feels this is essential to ensure that 'anything that is to do with special needs is central and not peripheral'. She continues to do some class teaching and besides being involved as support teacher she feels that she should tackle all the tasks done by the welfare assistants:

> I get involved in everything, because there's a theory that the dirtiest jobs are always done by those who are least well paid ... and I always feel anything anyone else has to do I should be able to do as well – physio backup, taking kids to the loo, supporting them in the swimming pool, going horseriding with them.

She chairs a weekly support staff meeting. I attended a meeting where staff aired their perennial concerns: movement around the school, the skills (or the absence of skills) of turbo wheelchair drivers, home transport, the visits of camera crews, etc. However, most of the support Carol gives to other staff takes place with individuals:

a lot of counselling comes in with colleagues ... it's the kind of job that gets you on the raw really ... there's a lot of talking through with teachers and welfare assistants, how you work in harmony as a team.

There's also the constant balancing of human resources to ensure that activities have the support they require. Officially most of the welfare assistants are contracted to work with particular pupils, though in practice resources are used more flexibly. Staff themselves make sure that assistance is where it's needed:

Before I can even get my coat on to see if there's nobody in the playground someone else has gone out or ... taken a child to lunch or whatever.

Considerable care goes into selection of welfare assistants:

We go to a lot of trouble ... to get that indefinable something ... someone who is going to fit in with the team and we mean that in a very wide sense: everyone at the Grove.

Defining separate roles

Despite the possibilities for conflicts between types of staff over status or salaries Carol feels that:

There is no kind of conflict or jealousy operating at all ... but it's something you've got to work at and when you've got it to cherish it really.

Teachers take overall responsibility for the running of the classroom, but otherwise there is no clear demarcation between the work of welfare assistants and the work of teachers, however carefully and diplomatically the staff may wish to tread in their self-descriptions. While, by and large, the teachers may have more flair at creating a place for learning and a greater facility at organising the classroroom, these skills can overlap. How could this be otherwise when qualified teachers can be appointed as welfare assistants and have been at the Grove and other schools in the city? As Carol says:

The aim is to work with everybody under the direction of the class teacher. If there's a conflict then a child who needs to go to the loo, who has to have callipers taken on and off, that would have to be seen to first, and then they would be helping somebody with their maths ... I saw one of our welfare assistants today taking groups of children to do a traffic survey outside school.

However, as Carol makes clear, although welfare assistants do not have to *prove* themselves as effective teachers, support teachers do:

It's a different problem for support teachers and for welfare assistants. Support staff who are teachers have to feel they have a credible role in the school. It's important for them to be involved in all the staff meetings and to interact with all the staff as an equal.

Carol is a teacher governor. Carol and Heidi are on the Parent–Teachers

Association Committee. Support teachers take assemblies, take part in curriculum development discussions, attend full staff meetings. Welfare assistants are not expected to attend such meetings unless there is an item on the agenda that is of specific concern to them. The conventions here are not made explicit and are open to change. The present boundaries are the result of conscious decisions, unquestioned assumptions and some conflict.

The coordination of the health professionals raises different issues because they are assigned to the school by the health authority rather than being appointed by the school to fit in with the team. In Carol's words:

> It's a huge gamble because you get designated a certain number of hours for physiotherapy, speech therapy, occupational therapy and people come into the school who you have no control over ... you have to hope you get people who share our concept of: 'Wouldn't it be great to do physio when the kids are in the PE lesson? Wouldn't it be interesting to do this speech therapy in his or her own classroom?' ... We've been very fortunate at the Grove, to date, really, in that we've always worked with cooperative people.
>
> At present we're very short indeed which means for a considerable number of children their physiotherapy routines are being carried out by welfare assistants or people like myself with no training whatsoever.

6 A SCHOOL FOR ALL?

How successful are the staff at supporting the diversity of their pupils? This is a complex question and there are no easy answers. In the time-scale of this study of the school it was only possible to sample practice and gain an appreciation of some of the principles that staff are attempting to apply.

The workers in this school appear to operate the same model of disability as most of the pupils. It can appear both highly sophisticated and also quite natural. For the adults it may involve unlearning or at least holding back on the assumptions they have made about people with disabilities. The pupils, with fewer and less deep assumptions, may be in need of less sophistication to counter any preconceptions and feelings they may have about disability.

The support and special equipment is continually evident in the classrooms as is the disability of some but not all the children who are the subject of Statements. Nevertheless, for Mary, for most of the time, as for many others in the school, the category 'child with disability' is submerged:

> It isn't something that's uppermost in my mind unless it affects the way they think ... for instance Manni, when we were doing poetry on darkness, asked me why people are frightened of the dark. He lives in a dark world ... so I was brought up short against his disability, but normally I never think about it.

All pupils?

While there is a carefully considered acceptance of pupils with disabilities in the school this does not mean that the school encompasses all children in its communities irrespective of the difficulty they experience. There are no pupils with Down's syndrome or the partly overlapping group categorised as having severe learning difficulties. Children with Down's Syndrome do attend other primary schools in Cambridge. This is not a matter of deliberate policy at the Grove but reflects the channelling of pupils along conventional lines before they reach school age. Carol Jones feels 'she would be very sad if the school said no to a child in the local community'. If pupils categorised as having 'severe learning difficulties' were included at the school this would entail new negotiations at transfer to secondary school.

On two occasions since Graham Else has been head, pupils have been transferred to special schools because of concerns about their behaviour, which he recalls with ambivalence:

> I think you always feel a sense of failure when ... we've got some children within our provision for whom we are really saying they are not suitably placed ... I think when you resource for special needs you are never going to resource it for all ... we felt with these two particular pupils that we were not giving them the best deal they deserved ... and I had to balance in my mind – was their continued presence compatible with the efficient education of the other children? ... we're not certain even now that the deal they are getting is significantly better than the deal they were getting here.

Carol felt particularly uncomfortable about one boy who also had a visual disability who now attends Wilburton Manor School for pupils categorised as having emotional and behavioural disturbance:

> I particularly regretted that we had to make what was for me a painful decision and I did bow to majority opinion on that because I had seen so many staff demoralised after a long period of quite bad physical as well as verbal abuse ... I asked that we should be involved in all his reviews and that the move for this child will be, I hope, a temporary one ... but so far we haven't been involved in anything.

Countering all discriminations?

Staff and pupils have become sensitised to the way pupils with disabilities can become valued members of the school community. What of other possible sources of devaluation? There is a clear wish to avoid divisions into 'high and low achievers'. There is less formal discussion of the way differences of gender, class or skin colour may form the basis for subtle judgements of value. The acceptance of cultural and religious diversity has not been eased by the broadly Christian nature of assemblies which the 1986 Education Act requires schools to offer their pupils in a daily act of worship. The approach to gender in a school with a predominantly female staff and a male head which includes a large group of female welfare assistants in a subordinate position requires careful thought. As Margaret Clark has demonstrated in an Australian study, even those teachers selected because they have a reputation for equitable treatment of boys and girls may categorise behaviour of their pupils in a way that appears to be to the disadvantage of girl pupils (Clark 1989).

At one point, one member of staff appeared to place a low value on the pupils' backgrounds. She spoke of the absence of academic drive in the pupils as well as the way their lives gave them preoccupations which might be incompatible with school work.

> I think our children at the Grove do have considerable difficulties to do with social pressures. They have very strong peer group pressures, particularly by 10 ... A lot of them don't have particularly happy home lives ... several children in my class actually go home and cook the evening meal for younger brothers and sisters because Mum and Dad are both working or perhaps just only Mum ... there is only a single parent family anyway and Mum might well be working at night ... those sorts of pressures do create problems for them and their priorities are different. They are not necessarily academic priorities when they come to school.
>
> I always feel that tension at the Grove very strongly – that there are several other sets of interests and priorities running concurrently with the curriculum ... I've always imagined in a more, for want of a better word ... 'middle-class school', there isn't that terrific tension all the time. I could be wrong but I suspect that it's easier in a sense to convince middle-class children of the value of what you're trying to do.

Here are the familiar prejudices about class, women who work, and about family structures which differ from a moral norm. Yet, it is not a straightforward matter to relate utterances to actions. There are conventional 'wisdoms' about pupils which may emerge from our mouths at times of stress or otherwise. Nevertheless, their availability may tell us that they have the potential for guiding action.

All schoolworkers?

Differences in value can be ascribed to schoolworkers as well as to pupils. Like any staff there are subgroupings within the staff at this school. Thelma relates the development of these to the expansion in staff numbers:

> It's too big to be a totally united staff ... there isn't room for all the welfare assistants to be in the staffroom with the teaching staff which is a pity really because it splits them up and makes them different.

Another teacher suggested that it is not the size of the staffroom but the number of chairs in it which restricts its use. But it is questionable, though, whether the staff in this school, as in most other schools, could ever have been described as totally united. Thelma divides the staff into the traditionalists, who include herself, the progressives, and the group in between 'who sit in meetings and say little'. Even these divisions may not hold up when practice in classrooms rather than positions in staffroom debate is observed.

It is still possible to ask whether the welfare assistants feel that participation in all aspects of school-life is as open to them as they would like. They can attend staff meetings though there have been occasions when this has been discouraged, subtly.

There are other staff too to be considered, office staff performing an ever more central role in the running of locally managed schools, and cleaning and care-taking staff.

7 MOVING ON

One of my motives for depicting the past of the school has been to counteract the tendency for case studies to convey a picture, frozen in time. Over the last twenty-seven years of its existence the Grove school has been transformed and it is changing still. All schools are under severe immediate pressures from recent legislation. The teachers at this school are not obsessive about the 1988 Education Act and this in itself is likely to reduce its impact, but the introduction of the National Curriculum, the prospects for testing, and the immediate demands of local financial management are all exerting influence. Graham Else feels that the increased role of teachers in formal assessment of pupils will 'eat into their contact time' and may have a negative effect on pupils:

> the whole business of labelling children which could be one of the less tasteful results of the standardised attainments tests, is a huge worry and would be counter to the kind of ethos we have in this school where removing labels is really what we're all about.

He also believes that the National Curriculum challenges the school's grouping policies:

> Some of the attainment targets will lend themselves to having a group which is fairly close together in terms of ability.

Carol Jones is very aware of the problems that may result from the dual system of funding the school:

> Special needs will still be funded centrally, but I think on a declining budget, so I'm really quite pessimistic about how we will maintain, particularly, our low pupil–teacher ratio.

Leaving and joining

But while some predictions of change prompted by government policies are uncertain for some pupils and teachers, for pupils and schoolworkers who join or leave the school the change in their lives is clear cut.

Pupils

The vast majority of pupils from the Grove move on to the Manor Community College. A small group go to Chesterton, about three-quarters of a mile away outside the council-built estate. A very few attend Impington Village College, a legacy of Henry Morris, who wished to establish village colleges at the heart of a village community, and Walter Gropius, its architect – this is about three miles away, outside the city, but one of only two schools within a reasonable distance which has a sixth form. (Cambridge has a system of further education and sixth-form colleges.) All the pupils with visual disabilities transfer to the Manor school and all the pupils with physical disabilities move on to Impington. To quote Graham Else:

> We do have a problem when it comes to the children with physical disability for whom the Authority has made provision in a comprehensive school which is three miles outside the city boundary. This causes us headaches with liaison ... the children ... will have built up peer group relationships here over a period of years ... to find that they've got to start ... again with a completely new set of relationships in a new school in another part of the county. We feel that is not as ideal as it might be.

There have also been problems about the entry criteria for pupils that the head of Impington has tried to apply. Parents of children who left The Roger Ascham School to attend the Grove were given an undertaking by the local authority officer involved that, when the time came, a place would be available for them at Impington. However, it appears that the head teacher of Impington had a misconception about the attainments of children with physical disabilities: she thought they would all be able to read and write reasonably well. She now wished to exclude those with very low literacy levels.

Madeleine is one of the pupils who is utterly undaunted by the move to secondary school. Marilyn, a support teacher, also has responsibility for liaising with secondary schools for pupils with physical disabilities and she has taken Madeleine on a 'couple of brief visits to use her light-talker and ... ask some questions'. In the summer term she will go back on a more regular basis 'so that she can be involved with a few classes there and find her way around'.

Madeleine's mother 'was overwhelmed by the size' of the school when she visited Impington, compared to the secondary school she had attended herself, although she felt 'the unit was nice'. She didn't feel it would concern Madeleine however: 'She'll probably be all right, she never minds any change but I don't like any change at all.'

Staff

At some point schoolworkers leave the school too. The jobs of assistants attached to particular pupils can be precarious. Some of them are on a fixed team attached to the school, but others are 'named' for particular pupils. When pupils leave in the fourth year they may be reattached to new entrants in the infants but there is still a problem when overall numbers of pupils with 'Statements' decrease.

Other schoolworkers may plan to leave in order to further their careers. Heidi is aware of the problems this might cause if she ever wanted to move on, in a field where most job opportunities are in special schools:

> I came from a special school background . . . I think I'd find it difficult if not impossible to go back to working in a totally segregated setting, but unfortunately there aren't enough other places like the Grove in existence and so quite where I go from here I don't know.

Thelma is retiring at the end of the school year:

> I've decided it's time really . . . I want to do other things and it's horrible to say this, but I'm the oldest person left . . . I'd like to see more of my grandchildren, I'd like to go to the University of the Third Age . . . probably do a bit of supply to earn a few pennies . . . I shall be choosy where I go and when I go . . . I think it's time to go now.

Thelma would 'dearly like' Carolyn to take over from her and this is a sentiment that Carolyn shares:

> I'm hoping to stay in the Cambridge area . . . I'd like actually, to stay in this school if possible . . . I'm certainly going to apply for a post here.

ACKNOWLEDGEMENT

I wish to acknowledge the kind cooperation of the staff and pupils of the Grove Primary School.

REFERENCES

Clark, M. (1989) 'Anastasia is a normal developer because she is unique', *Oxford Review of Education* 15 (3), 243–55.

Department of Education and Science (DES) (1989) *Report by HM Inspectors on Educating Physically Disabled Pupils*, London: HMSO.

Jones, C. (1983) 'Forging a link: the integration of visually-impaired children at the Meadow Community College, Cambridge', Unpublished dissertation for the MA in Applied Research in Education, CARE, UEA/Cambridge Institute of Education.

—— (1987) 'Working together: the development of an integration programme in a primary school', *Cambridge Journal of Education* 17 (3), 175–7.

Chapter 2

A curricular response to diversity at Whitmore High School

Christine Gilbert and Michael Hart

Source: Adapted from Gilbert, C. and Hart, M. (1990) *Towards Integration: Special Needs in an Ordinary School*, London: Kogan Page.

In this chapter Christine Gilbert, who was the head teacher, and Michael Hart, the head of learning support, describe the changes that took place at Whitmore High School as staff rethought the way curricula might be made responsive to the diversity of pupils at the school. A unified support system was devised from the resource available for supporting English as a Second Language teaching, pupils defined by the local authority as delicate, pupils with physical disabilities and pupils who experienced difficulties in learning. A switch from withdrawal teaching to in-class support led on to approaches to teaching which fostered curriculum development to responses from subject departments to find teaching approaches which recognised and responded to pupil differences in mixed groups.

1 INTRODUCTION

Whitmore High School is a co-educational 12–16 comprehensive in the London Borough of Harrow which has a system of first, middle and high schools, and then tertiary colleges. There are 1,000 students on roll and these come from a fairly mixed catchment area reflecting a range of social and economic backgrounds. The borough has operated a system of open enrolment for some time and Whitmore's popularity has entailed a rise from eight to nine form entry in recent years. Dating from the 1940s, much of the building is of single-storey construction and there is adequate specialist accommodation. Although not an attractive building, much staff and student effort goes into creating a welcoming and pleasant environment.

The existing school was established as a comprehensive in 1974 when the separate girls' and boys' secondary moderns on the site were amalgamated. However, the school still retained a strong secondary modern 'ethos' and its academic status was not high. In January 1983 a new head teacher was appointed who believed it was important for the school to find more effective ways of valuing all of its pupils. She was keen to establish an ethos in the school which ensured that children were perceived as individuals with different styles of learning. She saw mixed-ability teaching as a major way of encouraging this perception. Her appointment led to a review of existing curricular and pastoral patterns of organisation, their suitability for a 'truly comprehensive intake' and, indeed, Whitmore's provision as a comprehensive school.

Locally, the school's image was not good and Whitmore was undersubscribed. This exacerbated the problem of falling rolls. In 1983 it was one of the three schools in Harrow identified for possible closure by the Education Committee on the basis of unpopularity. This had the very positive effect of making many of the staff receptive to the ideas for change initiated by the new head. Most were keen to be involved in establishing a whole-school philosophy and policies to implement it. The school embarked on a process of self-evaluation and planning which led to changes in various aspects of Whitmore's curriculum and organisation. The innovative developments which have taken place in special needs provision since 1984 and the improvements in effective teaching and learning need to be set against this background.

When the head joined the school the support provision had three strands: a remedial department, a unit for 'disruptive pupils' and an English as a Second Language (ESL) teacher. A year later the local authority asked the school if they would consider setting up a 'delicate unit'. The term 'delicate' is a carry-over from the open air schools and is disappearing from use. In terms of the nine pupils who initially came to the school it was felt that the label 'delicate' seemed to be the 'catch-all' term for children who would not fit conveniently into any of the other categories used by the Psychological Service. Trouble over attendance at school, severe anxiety and obsessive behaviour, speech problems, difficulties with social relationships and emotional problems requiring psychiatric help were some of the symptoms which presented themselves.

In 1987, Whitmore became the local education authority (LEA) secondary school base for pupils with physical disabilities. Encouraged by the head, the staff at the school began to look at alternative ways of using the support they could muster to respond to the difficulties the pupils faced. They set up a single Learning Support team which, by September 1989, had seven teachers and three welfare assistants, with two more due. By and large support was to be delivered within mixed-ability teaching groups across the curriculum.

Theoretical background

Fullan (1988) has described educational innovations as being dependent on three dimensions of change which he outlines as materials, teaching approaches and beliefs with the latter stressed as the most significant. Each of these, he considers, is important for the successful implementation of a curricular programme and they are best seen as part of an evolving process rather than a single event.

At Whitmore we felt that integration could only be effective if pupils were provided with an appropriate curriculum to meet their needs. The 'curriculum' is interpreted here as including all aspects of learning within the classroom: the content of lessons, the range of resources, the style of presentation, the variety of pupil activities and the use of teachers' time. The school's involvement with the Open University's materials *Teaching for Diversity* (Potts and Booth 1987) offered staff a theoretical framework to discuss how the curriculum might develop, which at the same time accorded with the school's principle of valuing all pupils.

These in-service education of teachers (INSET) materials emphasised the belief that learning difficulties arise when there is a mismatch between the learner's interests and abilities and the curriculum that is provided. Instead of underlining the deficiencies of pupils and expecting them to fit into existing provision, the curriculum needed to be responsive to the diversity of pupils in any one classroom and the levels of attainment that each of them had reached. By the end of the course participants recognised the value of this approach not only for the pupils being newly integrated into the school and those who had previously been withdrawn to remedial groups, but also for the effective learning of all pupils. Three main areas for development emerged from the course:

- Extending the types of task with which pupils were presented.
- Experimenting with different forms of classroom organisation.
- Enhancing the format of stimulus materials and ways of presenting them to pupils.

The contrast was made during the course, for example by Weedon (1987), between teaching styles in the primary sector where classrooms might contain a variety of simultaneous activities and in the secondary sector which often consisted of lessons directed at the whole class, with few opportunities for differentiation of the mode of learning. Above all, secondary schools frequently provided a repetitive diet of lessons led from the front of the room with a high level of teacher talk, use of the blackboard, copying of notes and completion of exercises aimed at pupils in the middle of the apparent ability range. Those who failed within one classroom because the style or the level of the activity was inappropriate for them were likely to meet repeated failure in most subject areas due to the similarity of the teaching strategy adopted. There was a need, therefore, to vary the teaching style and to explore ways of arranging lessons so that a variety of types of pupil responses could be built into the planning process for the whole class.

Changes at Whitmore can be seen as evolving from two main sources. First, there were developments within the school which arose independently of the work of the Learning Support department. These reflected the need to review the school's curriculum, by giving greater priority to course planning and the development of strategies to encourage pupil learning. They were linked to the appointment of new staff who brought fresh ideas from experiences in other schools and who had a commitment to mixed-ability teaching. Some of the developments stemmed from the school's involvement in a Technical, Vocational and Educational Initiative (TVEI) project; teachers' participation in locally and school-based in-service training; and national developments, such as the introduction of GCSE, which were changing teachers' expectations of what were appropriate teaching methods for secondary schools.

Second, the Learning Support department in the school altered its method of working by transferring its staffing resources to the provision of in-class support and also to the development of collaborative approaches to help to improve the curriculum. These two changes, outlined in more detail in this chapter, were encouraged by the practice of some schools in Scotland in the late 1970s as a reaction to an HMI report (Scottish Education Department 1978).

2 IN-CLASS SUPPORT

The amalgamation of all the support staff into one department in September 1985 produced the impetus to make in-class support the usual means of providing extra help to all pupils in the school who experienced difficulties. At the meeting at which it was decided to do this, staff envisaged that a small amount of teaching by withdrawal of pupils would still be necessary. In practice this kind of arrangement became very rare, with class teachers welcoming the extra in-class support in all areas of the curriculum.

Many reasons were put forward both by Learning Support and subject teachers for the preference of in-class support rather than the withdrawal of pupils from lessons and these are listed in Table 2.1.

Three main benefits can be seen in this list. First, the support teacher's work is

Table 2.1 Why learning support is provided in the classroom at Whitmore

- Pupils are helped to cope with the real demands of the mainstream classroom.
- Help is available to all pupils in the classroom, such as for those needing it occasionally and those for whom extension of the work is required.
- Support is provided across all curricular areas rather than concentrating on a few skills.
- There is an increase in discussion between the class teacher and the support teacher. Materials and methods may be suggested.
- The stigma of withdrawal is removed.
- It is possible to avoid the low expectations that the pupil and the remedial/support teacher may develop in a withdrawal situation.
- Much less time is needed for assessment/testing. At the start of the year, support can be provided very early on before some initial difficulties have become major problems.
- Class teachers may welcome a chance to talk to another non-threatening colleague, especially if they feel isolated in their classroom all day. Some may be reassured of their own capacity to cope with all abilities.
- Some cross-curricular fertilisation may be possible as support teachers become more familiar with the syllabuses of different departments.
- Sometimes the presence of two teachers in the classroom may have a calming disciplinary effect.

focused directly on the types of difficulties with which pupils may be faced in the classroom throughout the school day, i.e. the context is relevant and meaningful.

In-class support opens up channels of communication between the subject teacher and the support teacher. Schools which operate a withdrawal system often set up elaborate systems of representatives for special needs within each subject department as a means of establishing liaison with the remedial or Learning Support department. By focusing extra support in the classroom, opportunities for discussion about pupils are opened up and, where the support is provided in a wide range of subjects, a system of representatives is no longer necessary because all staff are involved. At Whitmore such a system was also rejected because of the danger that it might continue to project the idea that special needs was the responsibility of only some teachers rather than the part of a whole-school policy.

The adoption of in-class support has helped to break down the suggestion that there are few pupils who require extra support while the remainder of the class have no difficulties. The majority of the time spent on assessment by remedial teachers in the past has in reality been an attempt to ration out limited resources of extra help. By contrast, support teachers working in mainstream classes are able to adjust how they allocate their time as a response to needs that arise in the specific lesson. The support teachers can overcome the danger that stigma of failure is merely transferred from the withdrawal situation into the classroom, by demonstrating that all pupils may need to seek help.

The degree of success in realising these potential benefits depends upon sensitive handling by the staff involved. The role adopted by support teachers will vary from one classroom to the next and also as their relationship with the subject teacher and the class develop. Initially, for example, the support teacher might focus on the one or two pupils most obviously in need of help and only gradually work with others in the room. Alternatively, it may be the case that the pupils experiencing the greatest difficulty are sensitive about being singled out and it is preferable for the support teacher to work with everyone in the class and only gravitate towards them once the support teacher's presence in the room has been accepted. Similarly, the expectations of subject teachers will determine the breadth of the support teacher's role. Whereas one subject teacher may be comfortable having a colleague moving around the room, another may prefer the support staff to work with a particular group of pupils on one or two tables. Invariably, over a period of time the expectations of teachers and pupils increase.

Table 2.2 shows a continuum which represents the different roles of the support staff. It raises a central question of this method of working. How much subject content can the support teacher or welfare assistant be expected to know when they are operating in many areas of the curriculum? In some instances their knowledge may be little more, or even less, than that of the pupils. This can sometimes be turned to an advantage as the support teacher can more closely perceive the difficulties of the work from the students' perspective and indicate to the class teacher when an explanation has not been completely clear. There are

Table 2.2 A continuum showing the possible roles of support staff

Level	Focus of attention	Involvement with lesson planning
1	Sits and helps one pupil	No previous knowledge of the lesson
2	Provides help to other pupils	Talks about lesson/pupils afterwards
3	Moves freely around the classroom helping other/all pupils	Makes occasional contributions to lessons
4	Takes control if mainstream teacher is away	Obtains information about lessons to come. Makes suggestions for possible future lessons
5	Joint planning, teaching and marking of lessons for all pupils in the class.	

other situations where the support teacher can read up the appropriate topic to a sufficient level to be at ease helping in the classroom, while not at the same time being afraid to admit to pupils that it might be better to consult with the subject teacher. It is a realistic and encouraging message to convey to pupils that teachers do not always have all the answers. There are, however, times when a support teacher feels totally out of depth in a particular subject and it is therefore important to bear this in mind when the support timetable is worked out. Similarly, it is useful to take advantage of the support teacher's strengths when planning the timetable.

In practice it has been possible at Whitmore to provide support in every area of the curriculum. Indeed, at any one time virtually all departments can expect to receive some help from the Learning Support department. The initial tendency to concentrate on the practical areas of Home Economics, Graphical Communication and Science was followed by support in subjects such as English, Mathematics and History, and later with pupils with physical disabilities arriving at Whitmore subjects such as PE also welcomed extra support. It is probable that the early requests from practical subjects reflected the greater ease of accommodating another adult in the classroom due to the size of rooms and the amount of pupil movement which normally occurred in the rooms. Having established the principle in those areas, other departments became more enthusiastic.

The type of support varies in different subjects. In some lessons the support teacher, working at levels 1 to 3 on the continuum in Table 2.2, may be helping pupils to write their answers, perhaps by spelling words, acting as a scribe, suggesting how to start an answer, going over the task several times until it is clear, providing more opportunities to discuss orally what is required, bringing an electronic typewriter to the lesson or just gently coaxing the pupil into making an attempt at the task. It may be that in some circumstances this help is better provided by the subject teacher, which then releases the support teacher to provide assistance to other pupils in the classroom. In other lessons the main requirement may be literally another pair of hands, for example with pupils who are paralysed down one side of the body, by holding material for cutting or assisting with setting up science equipment. At other times the support teacher will be joining in the lesson more actively, maybe by reading part of a textbook, participating in a PE lesson or acting a role in a French conversation. A further contribution may be the provision of appropriate resources – adapted apparatus for Science or Home Economics, practical equipment for Mathematics, enlarged worksheets for pupils with visual impairment, a tape recording or dictaphone for a pupil experiencing considerable literacy problems or perhaps a computer for a disabled pupil in a Design lesson. Most often, the main requirement is for someone to assist with little details which when overlooked lead to feelings of failure and subsequent reluctance to attempt work. Staff have learnt, for example, when it is more appropriate for them to write down students' homework tasks clearly rather than leave them with the frustration of later interpreting their own writing which may be hard to decipher. Similarly at times the quiet word of encouragement, the lending of a pen or pencil, being aware of possible anxieties in situations where pupils have to find others to make up groups or just being available to explain a piece of work after the lesson are some of the small ways in which staff can smooth a potentially difficult situation.

3 A TEAM-TEACHING APPROACH TO CURRICULAR DEVELOPMENT

When in-class support was introduced as the norm by the Learning Support department, it was agreed between members of the department and senior staff that one of its main purposes was to assist in the development of the school's curriculum to make it more accessible to pupils experiencing difficulties in learning. The collaborative approaches in the Open University 'Teaching for Diversity' course were to act as a model with support teachers spending part of their time operating at the team-teaching level shown in Table 2.2 as level 5.

The head of Learning Support was especially keen not to be over-ambitious by, for example, offering to work on curriculum materials throughout the whole of the school at the same time. It seemed important to set up a programme that had a reasonable chance of being successful and would be within the capabilities of the support staff and the time available.

It was agreed to focus on one subject department at a time. Initially this was to be the English department, as a response to their enthusiasm for the method, and subsequently it involved most other departments in the school. The arrangement was to be for a set period of time, and although the first plans had considered a term to be a reasonable length of time, in practice this was changed to periods of six months or a year. With each department, Learning Support and the subject teachers were paired up to teach all of the lessons of one or two classes, so in the first arrangement five English classes were taught by a pair of teachers for six months. The rest of the support teacher's timetable during this period was to be spent either on a certain amount of mainstream teaching or general in-class support as outlined in the previous section of this chapter.

The first pairings involved classes in three of the four year groups of the school, though the subsequent pairings in other departments tended to concentrate on pupils in the first two years in the school. The team-teaching arrangements were established with a joint meeting of all teachers involved, at which the expectations and ground-rules were decided. Table 2.3 shows the list of questions which formed the basis for the discussion and this list was also frequently used by support teachers working in class with other teachers on a less formal basis.

There were no predetermined 'right' answers, with different decisions being made with each set of teachers. However, it was always accepted that while discipline and most classroom responsibilities would be shared, the subject teacher would have the main say in the content of the curriculum. Wherever possible, planning and presentation of the lessons were joint activities and it was usually considered advisable to involve the support teacher in leading at least part of one of the first lessons at the start of the term. The importance of joint planning led to teachers often setting aside substantial amounts of time out of school hours or occasionally during lessons when pairs of teachers happened to have non-teaching periods at the same time. Once the team-teaching arrangement was established, there were some joint meetings of all the teachers involved but the main planning of lessons fell to the pairs of teachers to organise and then report back to the whole group.

A difficult decision revolved around the possibility of one teacher being away and whether they should be covered. If the teacher was not covered, what message would this convey about the value of what was being attempted? On the other hand, could someone covering a lesson be of real use in contributing to a team-teaching situation? Perhaps colleagues losing a non-teaching period might also be resentful when there already was one teacher for the class. Only over time

Table 2.3 Questions for discussion between support and subject teachers

It may be useful to iron out some of the issues below to avoid any misunderstandings later on:

- What are the aims of this method of working?
- Who has overall responsibility for the class?
- Who is responsible for any discipline problems?
- Who will do the preparation, presentation and marking of work?
- When is there time for planning and evaluation of lessons?
- What arrangements will be made if one of the staff concerned is away?
- Is it necessary to explain the arrangements to pupils in any way?
- Is the support teacher helping particular children or the whole class?

was the issue resolved with a decision that either teacher would be covered if absent. The remaining teacher would take over leading the lesson and decide whether or not to ask the teacher who was covering to stay.

Much easier to decide were questions about the aims of the arrangement. Each department had usually identified their perceptions of the benefits of team-teaching, with emphasis on the development of materials and approaches to meet the demands of mixed-ability classes. Other specific aims were often added, such as attempts to improve methods of assessment, the introduction of new schemes of work, preparation for GCSE coursework, etc. Generally it was explained to classes that the pairs of teachers would be working on new materials as a reason for the presence of the extra member of staff, though after in-class support became the norm there seemed to be less need to make much of an issue of what was happening. Invariably the decisions described above made it clear that the purpose of the collaborative approach was an improvement in the teaching of all pupils, although it was recognised that at times the ones experiencing particular difficulties might require greatest attention. Nevertheless, one aim was to structure lessons so that the needs of the full range of ability were built in to the planning and delivery mechanisms of the lessons.

As the system developed and feedback from those involved could be evaluated, several benefits emerged which went beyond those described in Table 2.1. These are shown in Table 2.4.

Table 2.4 Benefits of collaboration/team-teaching

- Joint planning of lessons. Two teachers interact to produce better ideas than each individually.
- Extra materials, perhaps newly made, may result.
- There may be experimentation with types of teaching that might be less successful with one teacher or which teachers on their own might be reluctant to try, e.g. oral work, drama, video recording, groupwork, games.
- Both teachers can observe the lesson from the pupils' viewpoint when the other teacher leads the lesson.
- Joint evaluation of lessons may improve the following lessons.
- Continuity is possible when one teacher is away.
- Variation in voice and style of presentation may occur.
- Discussion of marking and assessment is possible.
- By involving a whole department, discussion of more general issues may result for all those participating in the arrangement.

The results of two teachers working together may be effective without the production of new materials or different styles of teaching. A teacher who can observe the class dynamics while a colleague is leading a lesson may identify a small alteration, for example the need to change students' seating arrangements to improve the organisation of a lesson. This might involve a suggestion such as gathering the class around the teacher's desk for a demonstration rather than talking to a widely dispersed class, rearranging tables either to encourage or discourage talk between pupils, or perhaps moving pupils who marginalise themselves by sitting outside the teacher's main line of vision.

Similarly discussion might focus on how work is marked. What kind of feedback is to be given to pupils whose work is poor by comparison with the rest of the class but whose achievements by their own previous standards are significant? The value of comments by teachers, words of encouragement and the setting of goals for further improvement may stem from the interaction of subject and support teachers as they each bring a contrasting perspective to the task of assessing pupils.

The setting of homework is a similar area for joint discussion. Apart from decisions about suitable content of homework tasks to reflect the range of attainment in any class, questions may be raised about how homework is set. When is the best time to set it during the lesson? Is it beneficial for some pupils if the teacher writes instructions on the blackboard or even notes the homework in their books for them? How long is a reasonable period to allow before homework is handed in? Should there be just one common homework for the whole class? Again, either teacher may be able to raise quite routine issues which may affect the smooth running of the class but which also can alter the responses of those who are often labelled as having difficulties in learning.

Two examples illustrate the process of team-teaching and its possible benefits:

English

A pair of teachers working with an English class were aware of the need to make tasks accessible to all pupils, including those who might find work involving large amounts of writing difficult. One such task from the scheme of work involved pupils in writing a long story, divided into chapters and planned out in detail in advance. For several pupils this would be potentially very demanding, especially in order to overcome the 'blank-paper syndrome' faced by pupils when starting out on such a task.

Several attempts at planning the lesson resulted in a decision to prepare a simple 'snakes and ladders' style of boardgame on which the squares recorded events which might occur on a fictitious journey. Pupils were asked to note down the events described on any squares on which they landed. After a few minutes several of them became aware that they had the outline for the chapter headings of a long story. With this starting-point all pupils went on to plan and write their own fictional account of a journey.

The task and the means of introducing it were not especially original but it did achieve its aim of making all pupils feel able to attempt the task, while providing an interesting way of introducing the piece of work. The important factor was the realisation of the potential difficulty by the teachers and the ensuing exchange of ideas until a suitable method of teaching was agreed upon.

Religious education

An approach adopted in Religious Education lessons illustrates the introduction of alternative styles of teaching. Pupils usually begin their studies in this subject with a series of lessons in which they examine the diversity of religious backgrounds in the class and then investigate some factual information about each religion. The pairs of Religious Education and Learning Support teachers wanted to find ways of involving all pupils and they were aiming to produce a high quality piece of work from each pupil, rather than a series of brief notes gathered in each lesson.

Interaction between teachers, including an inter-departmental discussion, led to a decision to ask pupils to produce a large-sized introductory booklet about one religion. Pupils were to work in groups so that all the major religions were researched in each class. The task was to be introduced by the demonstration of a booklet on one religion, which was made by a member of staff, and by structuring the task to ensure that each booklet would include certain key facts – for example, the founder of the religion, name of its holy books, place of worship and the main festivals. Pupils used a range of research materials to produce their group booklet, after which they were asked to present their main findings in front of the class. This presentation which allowed practice of a valuable skill in itself, was videoed and replayed the following week, at the end of which all members of the class had to complete a worksheet which entailed finding out the key facts about each of the religions. This final task involved examining each other's booklets to find the appropriate answers.

Pupils who might in many circumstances have experienced learning difficulties benefited from the variety of media in which the information was presented, the opportunity to contribute at their own level within their group, the assortment of available books at different levels and the motivating factor of producing work for an 'audience' which included the whole class.

Avoiding problems

Team-teaching may lead to some friction or dissatisfaction which would counteract its advantages if not properly handled. There are potential problems when two teachers share a classroom, hence the need to discuss the list of questions presented in Table 2.3. Pupils may not always respond equally to the two teachers though this is usually something that resolves itself over a period of time, especially as similar arrangements are a regular occurrence in the school.

The more frequent worry is that, having stimulated interest in curriculum development and the benefits of collaborative work, the subject teachers will feel less competent when teaching on their own. In practice this is usually more of a worry than a reality using the system at Whitmore. First, the subject teachers will only have been working collaboratively with one or two classes and will have taught the rest of their classes on their own. Second, any materials produced and many of the methods used can be repeated with other classes. Third, it is possible to continue in-class support at a different level (see Table 2.2) with a department once the Learning Support department's key focus has been transferred to another curriculum area. Fourth, the real benefits of any curriculum change are only felt once the teachers concerned have 'ownership' of the ideas. This process is therefore more likely to become a regular feature of classroom practice once it is no longer possible to ascribe the changes to the presence of the support teacher.

4 WHOLE-SCHOOL CHANGES

The impetus for change in the curriculum has sometimes arisen as a result of the collaborative work described in the previous section. At other times it has emerged through the regular decision-making process of a particular department, following discussions about how to improve the learning of all pupils. When this happens, it is apparent that 'ownership' of the ideas trialled in the Open University pack has been shared more widely than among those who originally took part in the course.

The reorganisation of the teaching methodology in Mathematics was one outcome of participation in the Open University course. Discussions about mixed-ability teaching, individualised schemes and pupil cooperation encouraged a Mathematics teacher to explore further with his department the possibility of adopting new approaches in the subject. Until then, were placed in 'settled' classes shortly after arriving at Whitmore, based mainly on the results of a written test administered in the first few weeks. There tended to be little movement upwards or downwards between the sets although this was possible for a small number of pupils each year. Most lessons consisted of class teaching with predominantly blackboard exposition and exercises presented for all members of the class to complete. Pupils were expected to cope with the same materials and tasks despite the fact that even within one set there was always a range of attainment levels and varying competencies on different aspects of mathematics. Because each set tended to work at a different rate, there were soon differences in the curriculum being presented across the year group and these gaps made movement between sets even more difficult. Pupils inevitably became aware of their ranking in the subject and many of those in lower sets quickly became disenchanted with the subject, labelling themselves as failures in a form of self-fulfilling prophecy.

The Mathematics department investigated alternative approaches and visited schools adopting other systems. This had the support of the head teacher who had given a firm lead in the introduction of mixed-ability teaching throughout the school. The outcome of the investigation was a decision to replace the existing system with a scheme of work based on two commercially available banks of mathematics resources, SMILE and SMP. The principle change was that these materials depended on an individualised method of learning. Each class worked on one Mathematics topic for a set period of time but every pupil worked at their own level within that topic. A short test was used to start pupils at an appropriate level in the topic, after which there was a range of materials to be covered before moving on to the next level. The materials included a substantial amount of practical equipment and visual resources in order to encourage students' ability to work independently. Some cooperation between pupils was also possible, especially as the layout of several classrooms was rearranged to reflect the changing teaching style.

The curriculum change in Mathematics was part of an evolutionary process with subsequent decisions, for example, to include a certain amount of whole-class and group teaching where this was more appropriate. Nevertheless from an integration point of view there were clear advantages. There was a reduction in the labelling of pupils as failures and increased opportunities to recognize the appropriateness of different tasks to reflect varying levels of attainment. The subdivision of Mathematics into topics allowed pupils to work at different levels on each area of Mathematics that was studied.

The successful introduction of this approach to the teaching of Mathematics entailed a considerable investment of time and effort from all members of the department. They needed to become familiar with the two banks of materials, selecting those resources which would make a new coherent programme of study. Practical decisions included organising a system so that all pupils could have easy access to the materials in the classroom and establishing methods for monitoring and recording pupil progress.

Initially the Mathematics department intended reverting to setted classes for the second year group in the school (13–14 year olds), but subsequently they decided to extend the individualised scheme with mixed-ability classes to include both of the years in the lower-school (12–14 year olds). A further change was that, although some setting continued in the upper-school as a response to the perceived need to prepare pupils for different examinations at GCSE, the degree of setting became less precise. Interestingly, some of the self-fulfilling expectations then recurred in the upper years with the lowest sets becoming less interested in the subject and more difficult to teach.

A different development evolved in the Science department as a result of the reorganisation initiated by a new head of department. Before her arrival Science lessons tended to consist of whole-class demonstrations by the teacher and experiments carried out by all members of the class at the same time. There were exceptions to this arrangement with programmes, for example, on electronics which allowed pupils to proceed at their own rate through a sequence of experiments, and at times individual teachers set up lessons with alternative approaches. A series of Science experiments might be set up as a 'circus' arrangement with pupils moving around the room completing each experiment before moving on to the next one. The advantage for pupils who frequently encountered difficulties in class was that often in the whole-class situation, they would not complete an experiment in one lesson only to have to move on to another one in the next lesson, whereas a 'circus' style of teaching allowed pupils to spend as much time as was needed on any one task before moving to a new one. The disadvantage of such schemes was the considerable amount of preparation necessary for the teacher if this style of teaching was to be more than an occasional variation.

The new head of Science introduced a more innovatory system of teaching which allowed pupils to use workcards and move through a series of experiments on one topic at their own pace. Trolleys of materials provided the necessary resources for several weeks' work with pupils being given a checklist of tasks they needed to complete. This list included extension tasks which most pupils would be expected to complete but which could be omitted at the teacher's discretion in order to steer a pupil through the core aspects of the materials. An additional feature was the use of a test given before and after the topic was studied in order to find out the extent to which pupils had progressed on each area of Science, with the same questions being used on each test, and the award of certificates for achievement.

Like the Mathematics scheme, the change of approach in Science with the transfer of responsibility for learning passing much more on to pupils, presented a few difficulties. These were sometimes organisational but they also consisted of questions about the teacher's role. There was a danger of Science lessons becoming automatic work without adequate time for reflection and checking by teachers that the material had been adequately understood. As in Mathematics, there was still a place for teachers to introduce experiments clearly, draw together the results with groups of pupils or the whole class and ensure that when marking work they probed orally to discover if the task's outcomes had been completely absorbed.

One significant feature of both the Science and the Mathematics changes was the advantage they produced for the system of in-class support. It was easier to avoid highlighting pupils' difficulties by giving them different work from the rest of the class in a situation where variety was built in to the standard set-up. Furthermore it became far simpler for support staff to move around classrooms to help all pupils when the lesson was not focused on the class teacher directing operations from the front of the classroom. Similarly a whole-class style of lesson can waste the support teacher's time while s/he listens to the class teacher, whereas the approaches presented in Mathematics and Science allow a full involvement for the majority of a lesson.

Developments in Mathematics and Science merely illustrate two areas of whole-school change. Other changes were happening in most other subjects of the curriculum, for example with a less didactic style in Graphical Communication; closer attention to worksheet presentation in Home Economics; increased oral work in Modern Languages with a new teaching scheme and a major reduction in setting; greater practical experience in Music; and more experimental and decision-making work in History.

Some changes were encouraged by the introduction of GCSE with greater opportunities for coursework, resulting in the abandonment of upper-school setting for English and dual entry of far more pupils for both English Language and Literature 100 per cent coursework examinations. For pupils with special needs the GCSE has presented new opportunities for coursework investigations in subjects such as Sociology which can involve negotiated structuring between pupil and teacher. Coursework demands may, however, create difficulties for some pupils if they are not helped to organise themselves for extended pieces of work. A side-effect of this has been that the recognition of these difficulties encouraged subject staff to value the provision of in-class support in the upper-school years. Whereas any extra help with older pupils remained at a low level under the original withdrawal/remedial model, the trend is for support to be increasingly welcomed across the full age-range of the school.

A further development which has allowed experimentation in teaching methodology has been the introduction of a modular course, entitled 'Society and the Individual' for all pupils in their final two years in the school. This non-examination course for all pupils established as part of the school's involvement in the TVEI Project has led to a diversity of lessons that includes work based on simulations, games, visits and tasks out of school, drama, videoing, word processing, photography and so on, with a strong emphasis on the development of groupwork. Active learning is emphasised with teachers producing detailed lesson plans for six-week modules which can be used with a complete sequence of teaching groups. Pupils who might have failed in a more didactic style of lesson within a General Studies/Social Education course, which this one replaced, have responded well to the variety of activities.

Finally, a Community Work upper-school course has enabled several pupils to be part of groups which are involved in contributing to the local community by visiting the elderly, assisting at playgroups, teaching handicapped children to swim and other projects. It has been noticeable that Whitmore pupils who may have experienced difficulties in more formal school situations have often flourished during these sessions. The added trust by the school and the working environment beyond the school are two contributory factors to this success.

Each course in the school is open to all pupils. It is necessary to encourage the expectation amongst all departments that they should make provision for the full attainment range. This prevents the establishment of 'sink' classes and motivates teachers to re-examine their practice in order to improve their provision. Better teaching in terms of resources and methodology is to the benefit of all pupils. It is significant that many of the recommendations of Marjoram (1988) in *Teaching Able Children* include very similar advice to that found to be beneficial for the integration of pupils with a range of special needs.

5 CONCLUSION

At Whitmore the presence of pupils with Statements had offered an initial reason for providing a system of in-class support. This introduced one mechanism for encouraging discussion about the provision of an appropriate curriculum for all pupils. In turn, these discussions have contributed to the evolving process of introducing new curricular developments. Integration may be seen in this context as beneficial not only to the pupils coming in but also to the community of which they become part.

REFERENCES

Fullan, M. (1988) 'Research into educational innovation', in R. Glatter, M. Preedy, C. Riches and M. Masterton (eds), *Understanding School Management*, Milton Keynes: Open University Press.

Marjoram, T. (1988) *Teaching Able Children*, London: Kogan Page.

Potts, P. and Booth, T. (1987) *Teaching for Diversity*, Milton Keynes: Open University Press.

Scottish Education Department (1978) *The Education of Pupils with Learning Difficulties in Primary and Secondary Schools in Scotland: A Progress Report by Her Majesty's Inspectorate*, Edinburgh: HMSO.

Weedon, C. (1987) 'A room of their own: workbases at Ballingry Junior High School', in T. Booth, P. Potts and W. Swann (eds), *Preventing Difficulties in Learning*, Oxford: Basil Blackwell.

Chapter 3

Planning school development

Christine Gilbert

Christine Gilbert is the deputy director of education in the London Borough of Harrow and in this chapter she outlines an approach to writing a development plan for a school. She sees such planning as complementing the development of a 'Curricular response to diversity' described in Chapter 2 for the school at which she was previously head teacher. The chapter looks at the advantages of writing a school development plan, at the details of the planning process and at elements of the procedures adopted and plans devised at both Whitmore High School and Vaughan First and Middle School. The case studies are presented as working examples not paradigms. Christine Gilbert argues that a development plan and the process of producing it, will depend on the particular history and culture of the school.

1 INTRODUCTION

Schools have been bombarded over the last few years with a multitude of changes and may have seen the increasing emphasis on the need for development planning as yet another pressure. This chapter seeks to set out the advantages of school development plans, to explain the planning process which underpins them, and to illustrate this practically with extracts from the plans of two schools in the London Borough of Harrow. Both these schools are using school development plans to meet the needs of their pupils by adopting a more collaborative approach to school management. They see development planning as a way of encouraging a more coherent, practical and positive response to diversity amongst their pupils. The process leading to the production of each school's school development plan (the SDP) has sharpened debate about curricular and organisation strategies and what constitutes good educational practice.

Harrow is not an authority with a tradition of institutional development planning, but it chose to focus its local management of schools (LMS) training for governors, heads, LEA officers and advisers, on the importance of school development plans. An agreed school development plan (SDP) which has long-term vision and the needs and interests of children at its core was seen as the force which should drive the operation of LMS. Such a plan should involve all the partners in the school and focus on the curriculum, so that educational priorities are the base for resource decision. The team devising the local authority's training programme saw the SDP as a concrete way of encouraging a school to be clearer about its purpose and the direction in which it wanted to move. Development planning of this sort commits the school to improvement and to constructive competition against itself rather than against the nearby school. The two schools described later in the chapter have used their SDPs as a support in responding effectively to change and as a valuable way of approaching LMS.

The advantages of development planning

Many schools already make their planning explicit by producing an SDP, but in many others the production of a formal planning document has not been a priority. Some schools have plans which are explicit in that they are shared and exist in written form; others have plans which are implicit and not committed to paper. All schools do, however, have plans of one sort or another; they have, for instance, always made certain decisions about resources. It is easier to ensure plans are shared and understood if they are written down. A school development plan has the potential for bringing together coherently and practically:

- the school's aims and values;
- its policies, achievements and needs for development;
- LEA and national priorities and initiatives.

In coordinating these different elements within the SDP, the school sharpens its sense of direction and disciplines itself to manage development and change. The plan presents a longer-term vision as well as the details of priorities within the coming year.

At a series of Harrow conferences, teachers, governors, and officers and advisers identified the advantages of SDPs as shown in Table 3.1. These advantages become more and more obvious to schools as they become accustomed to using SDPs as planning tools.

2 THE PLANNING PROCESS

Develoopment planning focuses the school's attention on four fundamental questions:

- Where is the school now?
- Where is it going?
- How is it going to get there?
- How will the school know if it has got there?

Hargreaves *et al.* (DES 1989) have produced a concise and very useful document offering advice to governors, heads and teachers on planning for

Table 3.1 Perceived advantages of development plans

---

1 They are based on the aims and values of the school and as such focus
   attention on children's learning and achievement.
2 Translating aims and vision into short- and long-term goals and action plans,
   makes them understood more readily and more of a reality in terms of practice.
3 An agreed SDP encourages the school to reflect, to be self-critical and to
   devise strategies for improving teaching and learning.
4 They are a vehicle for linking all the different aspects of planning already going
   on in any school, e.g. those relating to
     ● curriculum and assessment,
     ● overall management and organisation,
     ● professional development,
     ● resources and finance,
   and for integrating them more rationally and systematically.
5 An SDP makes INSET planning easier and relates staff development more
   effectively to what the school needs and wants.
6 In giving schools back control of their direction, SDPs reduce stress and
   encourage confidence in moving forward.
7 They encourage the development of a shared language for discussion about
   the work of the school.
8 SDPs offer a framework for reporting on the school.
9 They make relationships with other partners in the education service easier and
   clearer.

---

school development. Four essential processes in development planning are
described (DES 1989: 5):

● Audit: a school reviews its strengths and weaknesses.
● Plan construction: priorities for development are selected and then turned into
  specific targets.
● Implementation: of the planned priorities and targets.
● Evaluation: the success of implementation is checked.

This is best illustrated by the following diagram (Figure 3.1) which is based
loosely on the Department of Education and Science (DES 1989) model:

Audit

Effective planning needs to start from where the school is, at a particular time,
and so form an analysis of the immediate context. This entails establishing a clear
picture of current provision and the deployment of resources. Such an audit, or
review, aids the identification of strengths on which to build and weaknesses to
be overcome. It also provides a sound base for the selection of development
priorities.

To some extent every school already makes some audit of curriculum and
resources in planning staffing and timetables for the coming year. It is also now

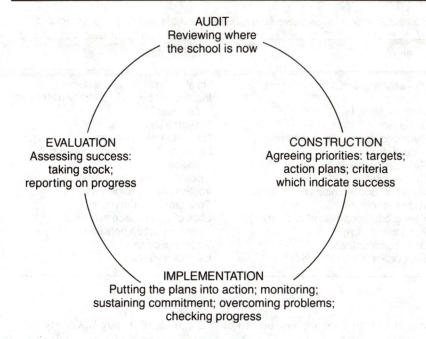

Figure 3.1 The planning cycle

incumbent on governors to publish an Annual Parents' Report which must include a review of both the school's curriculum and of the governors' deployment of resources in a given year. This report must also contain information about the governors' work in strengthening the school's links with the community. Reviews about different aspects of provision might also be available in the reports of local advisers or inspectors or HMI. The secondary school referred to later in this chapter has regular review built into its structures for self-evaluation.

Audit can also take place at a less formal level. When the staff of Vaughan First and Middle School, described later in the chapter, embarked on development planning the staff had a brainstorming session to produce lists of the strengths and weaknesses of the school (see Table 3.2).

Although these lists may lack coherence, such an approach to review can take place very quickly and can generate useful information to add to that produced by more formal approaches. It might be carried out on one aspect of the school's work or offer a more general perspective. It can also be carried out easily by the different partners in the school community and could be of particular value in involving children in reviewing the work of the school.

The starting point for action stemming from the school's audit must be the aims and values of the school and these may need to be agreed anew. The governing body has the responsibility for establishing the values and ethos of its

Table 3.2 How staff perceive strengths and weaknesses of Vaughan School

Strengths	Weaknesses
Pleasant and clean environment	No sinks in some classrooms
Displays	Insufficient pupils to make two classes
Well resourced	per year
Good stock	Only one hall
Relationships between staff and	Not welcome to visitors
children	Large number of children with special
Relationships with parents	needs
Open school	Special needs coordination
Variety of opportunities for children	Intolerance amongst children
Wide curriculum	Poor dinner supervision
Year group cooperation in planning	Lack of quiet space in school
the curriculum	Communication between staff
Daily communication	Team building
Supportive governing body	Lack of continuity

school and for deciding how best to meet the needs of its pupils. Clearly this is best done with the head teacher and staff and shared with parents, pupils and the wider school community. Any school audit should also take account of external pressures such as local or national policies and initiatives.

Plan construction

The construction of a school development plan entails selecting priorities for development, agreeing objectives and then devising action plans to meet these. These action plans become working documents in implementing the SDP. Clear targets will offer not only guidance for action, but also a focus for evaluation.

The overall plan includes details for the year ahead, and to encourage the continuity and coherence of the school's development, priorities should also be outlined for the next three or four years. The difficulty for most schools, even those with a long tradition of development planning, is not usually the identification of priorities but which to select for Year 1 and which to defer to Years 2, 3 or 4. The general tendency is to try to do too much and thereby not tackle any priority in sufficient depth.

Advice from the Department of Education and Science suggests that the SDP might include:

- the aims of the school
- the proposed priorities and their time-scale
- the justification of the priorities in the context of the school
- how the plan draws together different aspects of planning

- the methods of reporting outcomes
- the broad financial implications of the plan

(DES 1989:10)

Whatever the shape of each school's plan, if it is to have any real meaning for the school it is important that head, staff and governors – and beyond that parents and pupils – feel ownership of it and some authorship too. Considerable time should therefore be given to agreeing the procedures for consultation and decision-making. Those adopted by one secondary school are detailed later in the chapter.

Implementation and evaluation

Although there is overlap between each of the four elements in the planning process, these two are inextricably linked. Evaluation should not only enable the school to take stock at the end of a year, it should also help shape and support developments in the course of implementation. Effective implementation is likely to entail explicit support from senior staff and even governors in sustaining team commitment and motivation. Progress checks are also necessary and named staff should be given responsibility for ensuring these are carried out regularly. Such checks might show for instance that a time schedule needs modification or that additional resources of one sort or another were necessary.

At the end of development work on a particular target area, advice suggests that the succcess of implementation should be checked in the following way:

- giving somebody responsibility for collating the progress checks
- allowing time for the team to discuss and analyse the extent of the success
- noting changes in practice as a result of the plan
- writing a brief report on target implementation
- collating the reports on each of the targets to create a final report on the priority as a whole with indications of what helped and what hindered progress
- working out the implications for future work
- assessing the implications for all those not involved in the implementation and for the school as a whole.

(DES 1989: 16)

Towards the end of each annual planning cycle there also needs to be some formal evaluation of the year's SDP. This often involves the senior member of staff, who has overall responsibility for the SDP, collating reports on each of the identified priorities. Such evaluation moves the planning process back to the review/audit stage and so the cycle begins again.

3 WHITMORE HIGH SCHOOL

Whitmore is a 12–16 co-educational comprehensive school with 1,000 pupils on roll (see Chapter 2). These come from a fairly mixed catchment area reflecting a range of social and economic backgrounds. The school has twenty-eight pupils on roll who are the subject of Statements under the 1981 Education Act; these come from across the LEA rather than the school's immediate catchment area and are integrated into mainstream, mixed-ability classes. The school has sixty-four teachers, three of whom are funded from the LEA's Special Needs Budget, and one from Section 11 funds. Dating from the 1940s, the building is ugly and traditional, though much effort goes into creating an attractive environment for learning. The school is considerably oversubscribed with a regular 350 applicants for its 250 intake places.

A school development plan has been produced in Whitmore for several years, although it is generally agreed that it is only over the last three years that priorities have been shared, and remembered, by the staff and really informed the school's direction. Three 'B' allowances are now advertised and allocated on an annual basis to give impetus to a particular aspect of development. As a result of their work in shaping plans, staff confidence in what they are trying to achieve as a comprehensive school has been a great strength in managing the educational changes generated nationally over recent years. The latter have been built into plans for the school's development. They have not been allowed to divert staff from establishing a school which could be considered truly comprehensive.

Whitmore has a long tradition of consultation and staff involvement and endeavours to ensure a coherent whole-school approach. Its formal consultative structure encourages the review and development of all aspects of the school's work and rests on the premise that teachers need to work collaboratively and with mutual support for the school to move forward positively. This tradition in the school enabled the formal process of development planning to be introduced easily and has enhanced the school's capacity to manage change. Joint planning and review is facilitated by a programme of staff meetings (departmental, year and whole staff) held each Monday when the school closes slightly earlier than usual. There are also meetings for heads of department, heads of year as well as for various cross-curricular committees and task groups, most of which originate from priorities identified in the SDP.

A focal point of the school's consultative structure is its management board, which is the central policy and decision-making group. It is made up of senior staff, governors, the attached adviser and elected staff representatives. Under LMS, the school received a fully delegated budget in April 1990 and at that time added to the number of governors on its management board rather than set up a separate sub-structure of governor committees. The consultative structure is presented diagrammatically in Figure 3.2.

The management board offers advice to the governing body, but also makes

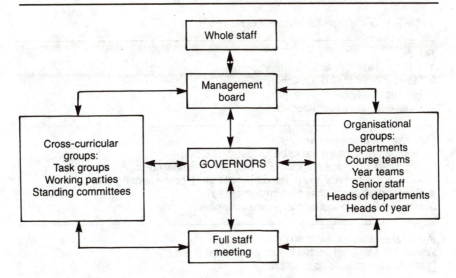

Figure 3.2 The consultative structure at Whitmore High School

many decisions through the power delegated by the governing body to the head teacher. Although the head has the right of veto over board decisions, this power has not been exercised since the management board was established in 1983. The board ensures the establishment of a clear and working consensus within the school community.

Constructing the plan

The plan for the following year is constructed during the summer term. At the first stage the management board is provided with a brief paper from senior staff and meets to agree the time-scale and general approach to the production of the annual SDP. For some time now, an agreed set of questions (see Table 3.3) has formed an important stimulus to both individual and group review and an aid to prioritising developments.

A small task group is also set up at this meeting of the management board to collate the responses to these questionnaires coming from individuals and teams later in the term. The group is chaired by the deputy head responsible for overseeing the production of the plan, and consists of no more than three other people one of whom is the INSET coordinator.

At a full staff meeting fairly soon after this meeting, the SDP features as the major item on the agenda. Its purpose and the procedures to be adopted are discussed. The questionnaires are distributed, one for each member of staff and others for team leaders, together with dates for their return and the timetable for production of the SDP.

Table 3.3 SDP consultation questionnaire

Review
1 What were last year's priorities and plans?
2 How far have they been achieved?
3 How do you know?
4 What else has been achieved?

Plans for the coming year
1 How do the above need to be further developed?
2 What new priorities (school/LEA/national) are now emerging?
3 What are your priorities (a maximum of three) for the coming year?
4 How and when will these be implemented?
5 How will you monitor and evaluate your plans?

INSET (in-service education of teachers)
What INSET will be needed to carry out these plans?
Please be as specific as possible.

Resources
What are the resource implications of your plans? (This includes some analysis of
the need for time, staff, rooms, equipment and money.)

Planning for the longer term
Look again at sections B, C and D with relevance to your priorities for the following
three years.

A few days following the staff meeting, at a regular meeting of senior staff, heads of department and heads of year, consideration is given to local and national developments. This is often a review of issues which have emerged in the course of the year. Experience at Whitmore has shown that such discussion is best conducted with team leaders rather than at a full staff meeting. They are then able to inform debate in their teams where the size of meetings is likely to involve more staff in discussion. In smaller schools, of say twenty or fewer staff, this scene-setting could be conducted effectively in a full staff meeting.

In the period before half-term, the different teams meet to review and plan ahead. This has been standard practice for departments and year groups for some time, but it has now been adopted by many of the other teams too, for example the Design Technology cross-curricular team and the Equal Opportunities group.

Although priorities have to be limited to no more than three, the questionnaire outlined above is used only as the basis for discussion. Teams tackle it in different ways. Some approach it as a discrete exercise and answer the questions in just one or two meetings. Others use it as part of their formal team review and tackle different aspects of it over four or five meetings.

Once completed, the questionnaires are returned to the coordinating task group which begins to collate the emerging priorities to give some shape and coherence to them. This is a time-consuming task and the group is generally given a day off site at the Teachers' Centre to complete its work.

At one of its regular meetings before half-term, the management board itself meets to reflect on the year's work as a basis for future planning. After half-term, once the task group has finished collating responses, the management board has to meet very frequently over about a fortnight to consider the selection of priorities. It has to make judgements on which of the received suggestions seem most appropriate and pressing given the school's current context. At this stage it might also add items which have not emerged elsewhere. The board then draws up its recommendations for the coming year's SDP. This will include short- and long-term aims and objectives, ideas on a programme of implementation, the identification of lead staff and some ideas for evidence of success. The latter is a recent addition to Whitmore's SDPs and stems from the school's discussions on Monitoring and Evaluation, which was itself a priority during 1989/90. Plans for staff development form part of the SDP and the INSET coordinator attempts to cost the coming year's work. Resource implications generally are also considered by the board at this stage as the cost of some developments is sometimes a hindrance to the speed at which they can be introduced.

Before the end of the summer term, a draft of the SDP is taken to a full meeting of the governing body for its agreement or amendment; it will then be taken back to the staff.

The SDP is sent to the LEA before the end of the summer term. This is the formal bid for Local Education Authority Training Grants Scheme (LEATGS) funding for staff development activities.

Detailed planning for implementation at both small-team and whole-school level takes place at the end of the summer term and is concluded in September. So for instance, the Learning Support team met with the English Department in July to give some shape to their curriculum development work in the coming year. They discussed the courses in the English Department for the following year and agreed that their aims in working together would be:

> The introduction of new teaching and learning materials, the evaluation of the strengths and the weaknesses of these materials and further work on their development.

> The dissemination by the Learning Support Department across the school of 'processes' developed in the English Department to encourage the conditions in which effective learning can take place, e.g. the role of oral work and the drafting process.

They clarified the roles of the English Department and support teachers as reported in the minutes of the meeting:

> It was agreed that both teachers would take responsibility for the class but it was the English teacher's ultimate responsibility to see that the curriculum was being effectively taught, as they are the subject specialists.

Any discipline problems will be discussed jointly and dealt with by either member of staff as they arise.

The preparation, presentation and marking of the work will be shared jointly by both colleagues. The English teacher will induct the Learning Support teacher into the assessment process developed in the English Department. Time will be made available by each pair to discuss these issues ... a meeting at least every three weeks was agreed.

Every class will be told that they are being taught by two teachers in their English lessons because they are being taught new materials.

The Learning Support teacher will be teaching every student in the class, rather than concentrating on particular students.

More detailed planning will take place in pairs, but regular reviews will take place at joint departmental meetings in the autumn term.

At the level of the whole SDP lead staff in each priority area work with relevant teams to agree action plans which ensure each priority is broken down into manageable tasks, the methods for carrying them out and reviewing them outlined, and a timetable established. The criteria by which success will be judged will also be established at this stage.

Priorities within the Whitmore plan

Whitmore's SDP for 1990/1 highlighted nine areas and then outlined priority objectives within each. For the first time, some of these areas addressed particular needs of non-teaching staff and governors themselves. Of the nine areas, the six marked below with asterisks had featured also in the 1989/90 SDP although different priorities were identified within each:

*Policy
*National Curriculum
*Classroom practice
*Assessment
*Monitoring and evaluation
*Staff development
School office
School building
Governor support and training

Some of these areas reflected a new and discrete initiative such as that within the 'School office':

To review the work of the office in the context of LMS and establish a clear plan of how it is to function and develop.

Some priorities continued the work of previous years. The priority for assessment in 1989/90 had been 'to conclude the review of existing assessment procedures and practice and to agree a coherent school policy on reviewing, recording and reporting'. The priority for 1990/1 was 'to devise a coherent system to implement the school's assessment policy'. Some in fact reflected the ongoing work of the school, but staff wanted them included to highlight their importance, so 'Classroom practice' read:

> To continue:
>
> to develop teaching/learning strategies and the preparation of suitable resources, for the implementation of the National Curriculum;
>
> to develop effective teaching and learning materials (with particular emphasis on mixed ability), especially in the area of the pastoral programme;
>
> to relate the revised equal opportunities policy to teaching/learning strategies;
>
> the INSET begun in 1989/90 on the use of IT for both students and staff (with particular reference to computer skills/word processing);
>
> to establish cross-curricular liaison in preparation of materials (with emphasis on involving Learning Support department).

The SDP takes the priorities set out within each area and describes the general approach envisaged in tackling them. This is illustrated in Table 3.4 which shows the plan for the 'National Curriculum'.

In writing the programme of activities, staff have to consider how they will measure their effectiveness. For the National Curriculum plan they included five general and specific checks:

- Better knowledge and understanding of the National Curriculum.,
- Coherent action plan for the implementation of the National Curriculum.
  Paper presented to staff, and Upper School curriculum changes agreed. This will include some agreement on a common approach to cross-curricular issues.
- Compulsory second language for all introduced smoothly for all in Year 10.
- Plans made for Year 9 Design and Technology course.
- A system to ensure continuity in terms of content, process and record keeping between middle and high schools at Key Stage 3.

Once agreed generally, each of the elements listed in the programme of activities is turned into an action plan with specific tasks and a clear timetable. This is the job of the lead member of staff in collaboration with the members of the relevant team(s).

For the last few years, Whitmore's management board has also asked teams to specify the criteria by which success in each activity in the programme could be judged. So, to meet the 1990/1 target of preparing a Design and Technology course and system of assessment for introducing to Year 9 in 1991/2, the same team outlined the following as success criteria:

- agreement across Art, Business Studies, CDT and HE Departments to introduce the course;
- scheme of work produced;
- staff and LEA Advisers' confidence that course will fulfil both National
  Curriculum and GCSE demands.

The school has become increasingly conscious of the need to adopt a more
rigorous approach to evaluation in collaboration with the LEA advisory team.
Such evaluation often produces fresh information which can shape the base for
action in the following year.

Table 3.4 Planning for the National Curriculum

Numbers of staff involved:
- All teaching and classroom support staff

Targets
- To continue to increase whole-school knowledge and understanding of the
  National Curriculum.
- To agree and publicise an appropriate action plan for implementing the
  National Curriculum 1990–4.

This will entail:
- Concluding our review of the upper school curriculum.
- Clarifying our approach to cross-curricular themes and issues (e.g. health
  education, economic awareness, technology).
- Incorporating the external timetable for subject implementation.
- Planning for the extension of the Design and Technology course into Year 9
  in 1991.
- Preparing for the introduction of a compulsory second language for all
  students up to the age of 16 (i.e. to extend to all students in Years 10 and 11)
  in 1991.

Programme of activities
- Management board to incorporate into cycle of staff meetings (see cycle of
  meetings). Deputy head to oversee.
- Upper school curriculum group (led by deputy head) to prepare coherent
  action plan and present to staff in staff meetings.
- Upper school curriculum group to research (including visits to other schools),
  to conclude review into modular curricula and present findings to staff at staff
  meetings.
- Heads of department/heads of year to look at cross-curricular themes in
  cycle of meetings. Staff Development Day on cross-curricular themes (1 July
  1991).
- Language Department to organise second language for all students as
  compulsory part of curriculum up to 16 (head of departments, languages).
  Employment of Modern Language assistant to support introduction.
- Design and Technology team to prepare course and system of assessment
  for Year 9.
- Head to discuss with heads of cluster schools ways to facilitate Key Stage
  3 liaison in English, Mathematics and Science.

4 VAUGHAN FIRST AND MIDDLE SCHOOL

Vaughan is a co-educational first and middle (4–12) school of 360 pupils and 20 staff in the London Borough of Harrow. A new nursery has recently been established in the school. Children come from a fairly mixed catchment area reflecting a range of social and economic backgrounds. Over 30 per cent of the children have a language other than English as their home language and the school has its own Section 11 teacher. Most of the pupils in Year 11 transfer to Whitmore for their high school education. Built about four years ago, the building is an attractive one and there are many open plan areas which are used creatively by staff and pupils. The school is popular and well regarded in the local community.

The quality of its child centred work has also engendered considerable professional respect. Led by an extremely able head teacher, the school has a stable and very committed staff and an interested and energetic governing body.

Constructing the plan

When a new head teacher was appointed in the summer of 1989, the staff reviewed what they considered to be the strengths and weaknesses of the school and also Vaughan's aims statement. From this they produced lists of short-, medium- and long-term goals. This debate was conducted across the whole staff – teachers and non-teachers – in full staff meetings and in smaller groupings too. On the basis of these discussions, the head teacher produced a draft SDP which went to all staff, all governors and the attached LEA adviser. A small group was set up to make comments, criticism, additions and so on and pass them on to the head teacher. The draft SDP was also discussed by governors in sub-committees and comments passed to the head teacher and the newly appointed deputy head teacher, who then incorporated the various points made. The head presented the final draft to the governing body for agreement.

Vaughan's school development plan

The 1990/1 Plan opens with a statement of school aims and then moves on to offer a brief survey of the school's current situation in the areas of:

- Staffing
- Resources (premises, furniture and equipment, teaching resources)
- Finance
- Curriculum
- Special needs
- Governing body committees

So key changes in 'staffing' for example during 1989/90 are outlined in Table 3.5.

Table 3.5 Staffing at Vaughan School

During the last academic year 1989/90 several changes to the staffing structure have been implemented to form a senior management team and redefine staff responsibilities.

1 All staff renegotiated job descriptions.
2 New allowance holders appointed. An additional 'C' allowance for Language Development, Equal Opportunities and senior management team.
3 Two 'B' allowances for Mathematics and IT and the Arts and IT. The two existing 'B' allowances took on additional responsibility for IT.
4 One 'A' allowance for Special Needs.
5 Senior management team formed of head teacher, deputy head teacher and two 'C' allowance holders.

There has been considerable concern over the lack of bi-lingual support provided by the local authority. Vaughan is entitled to one full-time teacher from the bi-lingual service.

A similar outline on 'Special needs' in 1989/90 recorded the number of children in the school with Statements of special educational need together with the number of children whose difficulties were such that they were placed on a particular point on one of Harrow's Learning Support records. A breakdown of the support received from the LEA's peripatetic teams, such as the Learning Support Service and the Primary Project Group, was also given. It also reported that the school had appointed a Special Needs coordinator and that a review of the whole area, particularly with relevance to resources, was underway. Having given a brief review in key areas, Vaughan's SDP then moved on to describe the priorities for 1990/1 as shown in Table 3.6, together with an outline of development priorities for 1991–4.

A detailed action plan for each priority was set out along the lines of the National Curriculum plan at Whitmore. Vaughan's two other whole-school priorities for 1990/1 are set out in similar detail and the plan also contains action plans for each of the school's four curriculum teams: Arts, Humanities, Languages, Mathematics and Science.

5 CONCLUSION

By encouraging a shared and coherent approach to management and decision-making, SDPs have the potential for enabling schools to concentrate more collaboratively on the quality of learning. Comprehensive and explicit plans for development, rooted in each school's philosophy and values, provide a focus for a common understanding of what the school is about and a commitment to the direction in which the school is going. In setting out the school's intentions, these plans include decisions about priorities and thus decisions about responsibilities, activities and resources.

Table 3.6 Development plan priorities

Year 1, 1990/1
Considering that with effect from September 1990 the programmes of study for 'Technology' must be incorporated in the curriculum for Year 1, Year 2 and Year 6, staff have decided that technology should be our main concern for Year 1.

Another area that was identified as needing our consideration was that of 'English as a Second Language'. We have therefore allocated the summer term for staff development.

Testing of Year 2 will take place in May/June 1991 and we have allocated one training day for whole school development of 'assessment'.

In addition to this the four curriculum teams of Language, Humanities, Arts, Science and Mathematics are developing priorities within these areas:

Humanities
Term 1   Examine resources – consult staff – order in term 2
Term 2   Curriculum policy statement
Term 3   School development plan

Language
Term 1   Parental involvement in reading
Term 2   Curriculum policy statement
Term 3   School development plan

Arts
Term 1   Resource implications and recommendations for developing
          a multicultural approach to the arts
Term 2   Development of above
Term 3   School development plan

Science and Mathematics
Term 1   Developing investigational approaches; organisation of resources
Term 2   Curriculum policy statement
Term 3   School development plan

Although the written document has practical value as a reference point, the quality of a school development plan is based entirely on the process which has produced it. It is this which determines the real outcomes of planning, rather than the polish of the final product. This chapter has emphasised the involvement of teachers and governors in the SDP but the other partners in the school community, such as parents generally, and pupils too, could profitably be included in the planning process. Such joint ownership of the plan not only gives the school a clearer and more united sense of purpose, but also reduces the stress generated by the speed and extent of educational changes.

REFERENCE

Department of Education and Science (DES) (1989) *Planning for School Development: Advice to Governors, Headteachers and Teachers*, London: HMSO.

Chapter 4

Finding a new place
Changes in role at Ormerod Special School

Tim Southgate

Tim Southgate is the head teacher at Ormerod School, a special school for children with physical disabilities in Oxford. In this chapter he reflects on the changes that he and his staff have made to the role of his school. He describes how at the start of the 1980s they felt concern that they were unable to provide all their pupils with the breadth and quality of curricula they needed, particularly at secondary level. This led them to initiate links with mainstream schools for pupils. At first these were part-time but then a full-time arrangement was made with Marlborough School which eventually involved the transfer of the whole of the Ormerod secondary department to the Marlborough site. Integration arrangements for primary age pupils were established within a nearby primary school when they were needed and phased out as pupils were supported at their own local schools. Tim Southgate describes the way the school replaced its former purpose with a new specialist role in working intensively with young children with cerebral palsy to develop their mobility and coordination along the lines of conductive education.

1 INTRODUCTION

The integration into mainstream schools of pupils with special needs was one of the major educational issues of the early 1980s. The question of where children with disabilities and learning difficulties should be educated, both individually and in principle, became the subject of sometimes passionate debate. The integration issue, stimulated by the Warnock Report (DES 1978), encouraged by experiences in other countries and seemingly enshrined in the 1981 Act, divided teachers, administrators, advisers and psychologists from each other and from parents, some of whom felt strongly enough to take on local authorities in appeals to achieve the integration of their children.

On one side of this debate, integration was often seen as a desirable end in itself with segregation portrayed as a form of deprivation and a denial of human rights. On the other, while there were undoubtedly some who had a vested interest in the continuing existence of special schools, there were many who feared that integration would be adopted by LEAs as a cheap alternative to properly resourced special education.

This chapter will focus on the experiences of one special school for children with physical disabilities over a decade of change. At the beginning of the 1980s, the school fulfilled a conventional role. By the end of the decade, its role had grown and radically changed. While integration has been at the centre of this development, it was not viewed as an end in itself. Rather, the school has been led throughout by the needs of the children and, as these needs have changed or the perception or understanding of them has altered, so the school has responded by creating new structures and developing new approaches.

The development of opportunities for integration in order to meet the needs of the children more effectively has in turn challenged the special school to define its own role much more clearly and to refine its aims and the teaching methods it employs for those children who remain within the building.

2 RECOGNISING THE CURRICULAR LIMITATIONS

In 1980, Ormerod School had about seventy-five children on roll ranging in age from 2 to 16. Its relatively small size belied its complexity. Although generally having greater rolls, primary and secondary schools rarely accommodate the range of children present in our school. There were children of average or above average ability and, within the same age group, others who had moderate or severe learning difficulties. Add to this children with visual or hearing disabilities, those with emotional difficulties or with life-threatening medical conditions, and the scale of the curricular challenge becomes apparent.

A teaching staff of ten might appear to provide quite a favourable teacher–student ratio. However, teachers are not interchangeable components and their training, personalities and particular skills tended to confine them to limited areas of the school. Some were infant or nursery trained. Others were needed to work with individual children who had language or communication difficulties. These factors reduced the pool of teachers available to work with pupils of secondary age, and those staff who were willing and able to work in this area possessed a limited range of subject specialisms which in turn restricted the curriculum that could be provided.

As a result of trying to meet the curricular needs of those pupils of average and above-average ability of secondary age the need to look beyond the resources of the school emerged. Whichever permutation was tried, it appeared impossible to meet the needs of all the pupils in full. Either we were not providing all the subjects they needed or many were taught by generalists. If a full subject time-table was provided, then some children were unable to receive the individual attention they needed.

Part-time integration

Next door to Ormerod School is a 9–13 middle school and, although there was no notion of a campus integration arrangement when the site for the special school was chosen, this school appeared to offer opportunities for some curriculum enhancement. Arrangements were made for one boy to attend for woodwork sessions, although, because of his epilepsy, he was always accompanied by a helper. A girl with a blood disorder was placed full-time in this school, although not her local school, because her parents were anxious that she should remain near to the Ormerod facilities and nursing staff.

Although helpful for these individuals, the extent to which this middle school could be used to relieve our curricular impasse was limited. The school was full, the architecture unhelpful and the age range too young for those children who had the most pressing need. Instead, an arrangement was made with a nearby upper school for pupils to join groups for certain lessons. Two boys who had muscular dystrophy, another with spina bifida and a delicate, able-bodied girl, all aged 14, attended English and Art twice a week. The building was not easily accessible to those in wheelchairs but the staff of the host school enthusiastically rearranged the timetable and relocated lessons in order to accommodate our pupils who were transported between the two sites by school minibus.

Although a fairly inefficient use of teaching and learning time, this arrangement did enhance the learning opportunities of the pupils involved. They were provided with specialist teaching and they received it alongside other children and so gained in understanding from the many interactions between the teachers and their mainstream peers. In addition, for the first time within the special school, it challenged the notion that children should be educated together simply because they shared a physical or medical disability.

3 MARLBOROUGH SCHOOL: FULL-TIME OPPORTUNITIES

Soon, the initial part-time arrangement was developed further and the boy with spina bifida began a full-time trial period. However, the upper school occupied a large site with many steps and stairs and before long these began to cause him problems with his knees. Thinking he would need to use a wheelchair we visited another school, the Marlborough School, ten miles away in Woodstock, of which we knew only that its classrooms were largely on one level.

Fitting into a philosophy

When we arrived in his office, the headmaster, Gerry O'Hagan, immediately launched into his philosophy. As we got to know him better we came to realise how important this philosophy was to him. We had come to find out if there were any steps and stairs or anything else which might pose problems for a pupil in a wheelchair. Before we could investigate the terrain, however, we must sit and hear about the 'Marlborough philosophy'. Only later were we to realise how significant the philosophy – the hidden curriculum – of a school is in determining whether or not integration works. The speech began:

> All teaching up to 16 is in mixed-ability classes. There are no streams, no sets, no bands, nothing that identifies one child as being more or less able than another. There is no special needs department; there are no remedial classes and no withdrawal for remedial work. All children follow the same curriculum and all children are entered for public examinations.

The list went on. I had never heard a head paint such a determined picture of what lay behind the running of his school.

> This is a comprehensive school. Comprehensive means what it says. I don't believe we have a right to refuse any child from our catchment area if the parents want that child to attend.
>
> Children must be treated with trust and respect and they will respond in kind. All children can stay in at breaktimes – we aren't made to go out so why should they? When children arrive from their primary schools, we don't look at their records because these prejudice teachers' views. No one has the right to write down comments on children and parents don't receive written reports. Rather, we expect them to come to parents' evenings to talk with staff. And they do!

These seemed strange notions to us, coming from a special education tradition where almost every step a child takes is noted somewhere by someone. Eventually, however, he judged that we had grasped the Marlborough philosophy sufficiently to understand what we were about to see and we were taken on a tour of the school.

Certainly, for a secondary school, this one seemed very civilised and pleasant. It was afternoon break and pupils were milling around an entrance hall dominated by a huge plant. Our informant had been correct: almost all teaching areas were at ground level. The original building had been erected just before the Second World War and most subsequent building had been single storey. Upstairs facilities – largely science laboratories – were duplicated on the ground floor and, as children were taught in mixed ability classes, anyone in a wheelchair could simply join a group in a ground-level laboratory.

Marlborough is a country school and the approach to science naturally reflected this. There were duck ponds and gardens landscaped by the pupils, a nature reserve and even a huge greenhouse filled with beautiful houseplants, all directly accessible to someone in a wheelchair.

Not having worked in a secondary school for some years, I had forgotten the range of experiences open to pupils in larger schools. There was a music block with practice rooms, a huge sports hall, housecraft rooms and an integrated arts and crafts block. Another block housed a marvellous library and the dining hall. There were small steps into most classroom blocks but nothing that ramps couldn't handle. In the main building were a lecture theatre, a drama studio and classrooms offering a whole range of subjects. What is more, there were hundreds of pupils and dozens of teachers available to teach them. Anyone who has tried doing anything practical knows how important are the right tools for the job. Here were all the right 'tools' for teaching the range of subjects our children needed. At Ormerod, teachers had endlessly to behave like adjustable spanners, tackling a range of subjects for which they often had no training.

Returning to his office, I put the question that had been growing during our guided tour: 'You have much more to offer than we can provide at Ormerod. Would you be willing to take ten children and not just one if we send the staff to support them?'

'No problem,' was the immediate response. 'We'll take as many as you like on one condition. They must attend ordinary classes. There must be no unit or special class!'

The practice of integration

And so the relationship between the two schools began. In September 1981, six months later, nine Ormerod pupils, accompanied by two teachers who shared the support role and a classroom assistant, began the new school year at Marlborough School. (The boy who had instigated our visit was not among them, preferring to soldier on and succeed in the upper school where he had made many friends.) Most of the Marlborough staff visited Ormerod School to acquaint themselves with the pupils they were to receive. When summer exams were over, older Marlborough pupils were recruited to mix cement and install ramps around the site and make wheelchair paths through the nature reserve. The local authority agreed to install disabled toilets and a changing room, but the first year was almost over before this specialist area was completed, demonstrating how much less important are physical conditions than attitudes to successful integration.

Not that it was all easy. Of the nine pioneers, all of whom originally greeted the idea of moving with such enthusiasm, at least five found it very difficult to adjust to the pace of life and higher expectations of their new environment. One pulled out after the first day (to return several weeks later) and during the first two weeks it seemed as if the whole experiment might collapse as the resolve of others began to crumble. A great effort was made by the staff of the two schools to support, encourage and even coerce these young people until, after about half a term, they eventually settled in.

This pattern repeated itself each September for several years but now Ormerod pupils seem to make the move without anxiety perhaps because they no longer lead the sheltered lives they once did and because many have enjoyed some mainstream experience before they move to Marlborough.

In ten years, fifty pupils have made the move. Almost without exception they have gained educationally from doing so. During the first five years the pupils obtained almost fifty CSE passes between them. Although provided with some support by Ormerod staff, the success of the arrangement was largely due to the staff of the host school and to the Marlborough philosophy which guided them. Already, their stance prevented them from stratifying children either physically into groups or mentally into the more able or less able. Absorbing the Ormerod children with their range of abilities and disabilities often seemed to present hardly a hurdle at all.

Further developments

During the ten years the special relationship with Marlborough School has evolved, to some extent in directions of which Gerry O'Hagan might not have approved. He left the school at the end of 1985. By 1987, there were fewer secondary pupils at Ormerod who could be supported full-time in mainstream classes; those who could tended to be at their local schools. In any case we had to face up to the problem that the curriculum and learning environment offered to those who remained at Ormerod was depleted. Supporting the pupils at Marlborough left even fewer teachers for the residual group and these pupils had lost the stimulation of their more able peers and had a restricted choice of friends.

The new head at Marlborough was asked if a room could be provided as a base for the remaining Ormerod pupils who had more severe physical and learning difficulties. From such a room they would be able to join ordinary classes as and when it was appropriate to their needs. To his surprise, his colleagues did not discuss whether such a development should happen but only how it should be realised. As a result, a classroom – Room 7 – was made available and in September 1988 the remaining Ormerod pupils of secondary age moved in. Shortly afterwards, Ormerod was recognised as a split-site school having its secondary department on the Marlborough site.

Since that move, there have usually been about fourteen Ormerod pupils at Marlborough. Some are registered in ordinary classes and spend up to 80 per cent of their time in the mainstream, withdrawing to Room 7 to catch up on written work or for individual or small group teaching. Others are registered in Room 7, joining the mainstream curriculum only for selected subjects. They nevertheless wear the school uniform and enjoy many of the social benefits of working, eating and playing in a large, thriving school. In fact, Room 7 has become a focus at breaktimes for many Marlborough pupils; those who are based there are never short of social contact.

Development did not stop with Room 7. In 1989, the teacher responsible for organising Marlborough's own learning support system moved away and her replacement left shortly afterwards. At this point, the head of Marlborough suggested that the teacher responsible for organising support for Ormerod pupils at Marlborough might take over the coordination of learning support for the whole school. Thus, the staff and resources of the two schools have now become intertwined to provide appropriate support for all pupils who need it, both on the

Marlborough roll and on the Ormerod roll. There are many examples of this in action. Ormerod uses its TVEI (Technical and Vocational Educational Initiative) grant to buy, from Marlborough, specialist small group teaching in Science and French to help deliver the National Curriculum to pupils with severe physical and communication difficulties. Ormerod organises INSET to help Marlborough teachers to differentiate the curriculum and uses Ormerod TVEI Consortium in-service training funds to release them.

4 PRIMARY INTEGRATION

Other arrangements have been made during the past decade to meet the needs of primary pupils. In 1982, a year after the first pupils moved to Marlborough, Ormerod had a group of infants who needed access to an ordinary infant curriculum. The head teacher of a local first school for 5 to 9 year olds agreed to the Ormerod group being based in her school. Ormerod paid for a disabled toilet to be installed and had a builder knock two small rooms into one to provide a base room. However, within a few weeks this room was abandoned and the group had become fully integrated within the ordinary classes, supported there by an Ormerod teacher and classroom assistant.

This arrangement proved to be a bridge for this group. After two years the children had all moved out into their local schools. The arrangement was then closed down only to be resurrected two years later when a similar group emerged. These pupils had more complex needs and further building modifications were made. Again, they were occupied for only part of the time as the pupils were successfully integrated into the mainstream. This time, the Ormerod teacher was used to enable two large first school classes to be transmuted into three much smaller infant groups which improved the learning environment for the children from both schools. Eventually, as this group moved on to their local schools the arrangement was again closed down.

Two of the children moved on to another arrangement which had been established in the middle school next door to Ormerod School. A group of six ambulant pupils, including one who was profoundly deaf and physically handicapped, emerged in the mid-1980s, and the middle school agreed that they be integrated there with an Ormerod support teacher. A welfare assistant also acted as a signing interpreter for the deaf boy who used a portable computer as a writing aid and who also had extra teaching to encourage his language development. After two years, these pupils, too, went their separate ways, to Marlborough and to other mainstream and special schools in the country.

These arrangements flared up and faded, always in response to the children's changing needs. Because they were resourced by the special school with little if any local authority input, they were very flexible. They also provided many members of the special school staff with opportunities to teach in a variety of situations, broadening their horizons and enabling them to develop new skillls.

5 THE CHANGING ROLE OF ORMEROD SCHOOL

Given the skills of the Ormerod staff and the positive responses almost always received from mainstream schools, it might have been possible to develop integration arrangements until no children at all remained segregated within the Ormerod building. Had integration been the objective, this may well have been the end result. But integration has always been the means of meeting curricular needs and not an end in itself. It gradually became apparent that there were ways in which Ormerod School could meet the educational needs of younger physically disabled children more effectively than they could be met elsewhere.

During the 1980s, the Ormerod intake changed quite significantly. A falling birthrate, the ability of mainstream schools to accommodate a wider range of difficulties, and developing medical practice combined to mean that Ormerod School was presented with fewer children, most of whom had cerebral palsy.

Influenced by the work of the Petö Institute in Hungary where the system of Conductive Education was developed specifically for children with motor impairments, teachers and therapy staff began to explore ways to encourage children to develop their motor skills and acquire greater functional independence. This work involved working with children in groups and encouraging them to practise sitting, standing, walking and other skills without many of the aids previously taken for granted. Encouraged by the results, staff developed the work further until an all-day programme was instituted through the school. Already, children as young as 1 year old were attending weekly pre-school sessions with their parents. Now, they joined the nursery at 2 and spent all day, every day developing their independence. Using private funds, the school employed its own therapists and also Hungarian Conductors who had trained and worked at the Petö Institute. The local authority responded by establishing a programme based at Ormerod School, to encourage work with motor-impaired children at special schools for children with severe learning difficulties in the county.

The effectiveness of this programme led to parents opting for their children to attend Ormerod School from an early stage rather than joining a local playgroup or nursery.

Consequently, the school roll has increased almost to the level of a decade ago. Now, there are seven groups instead of four, with three nursery classes instead of one. Here, and in the infant and junior classes, children are toilet trained, develop balance for sitting and walking, learn to dress themselves, to eat and to communicate and acquire all those skills which will equip them to benefit when they eventually move into mainstream schools. After several years in this intensive early intervention programme, as children reach the age of 4 or 5, the school now arranges for them to begin to attend a local nursery or infant school. Gradually, and with support, they make the transition. Some make this move at the junior stage and others remain within the special school until the age of 11 when they move on to Marlborough School.

6 CONCLUDING REMARKS

In the debate about the relative merits and drawbacks of integration and segregation there has been a failure to define the purpose of special schools clearly. Special schools have traded on the general assumption that they are an appropriate (and humane) response for society to make for young people with disabilities and so fundamental questions have been avoided. Are these schools there to relieve the pressures on mainstream schools; to accommodate children they are unable or unwilling to educate? Or do they exist to benefit children with special needs; to provide a special form of education which cannot be delivered effectively within the mainstream? Should they provide their pupils with a dilute form of the mainstream curriculum throughout their school careers? Or should their purpose be to provide a specialised curriculum for a certain period of time with the objective of enabling their pupils to enter or return to the mainstream of education and society at some point?

The answers to these questions will of course vary for different children at different times in their school lives, which is why the debate about integration versus segregation is often too simplistic. Experience suggests that when children do need an ordinary curriculum this is best provided within ordinary schools. Special schools, with their limited staffing, resources and restricted peer groups, should not try to emulate what can be better delivered elsewhere. At all stages on their journey through education, however, it must be the children's immediate and future needs and not the needs of the institution or an inflexible principle which should determine their route.

Almost all children can benefit considerably from receiving their education within ordinary schools but integration should always be seen as a means of meeting pupils' curricular needs, not as an end in itself.

Integration should not take place because it is a human right or because it is more cost effective. The integration of children with special needs should take place because their needs can best be met *at that time* within an ordinary school. Special schools do have a role to play in special education and that role will continue, provided that what they offer is special.

REFERENCE

Department of Education and Science (DES) (1978) *Special Educational Needs* (The Warnock Report), London: HMSO.

Chapter 5

Moving in and moving out
The closure of Etton Pasture Special School

Roger Kidd

This chapter tells the story of the closure of Etton Pasture School after Roger Kidd was appointed as its head. In his previous school, for pupils designated as having severe learning difficulties, he had promoted the attachment of his pupils to neighbouring primary and secondary schools. At Etton Pasture, he negotiated, with parents and staff, the transfer of his pupils into resource bases in mainstream schools in accordance with a local authority policy. This involved the replacement of his school by a school catering for those pupils who had been sent out of the county to school for pupils categorised as having 'emotional and behavioural disturbance'.

1 TAKING THE JOB

Having successfully survived two days of interviews and been offered the job as head of a large, part-residential school for children with moderate learning difficulties, I felt exhausted. As I drove back to my home in the Cotswolds doubts surfaced. Yes, the higher salary would be welcome, also the cheaper housing, but did I really want to leave a school with a national reputation based on its unique integration policy? Well, I thought, I will be back with the type of children I had spent most of my teaching career with, and residential work which I had always enjoyed, and, after all, the integration of children with severe learning difficulties from Bishopswood School was almost complete.

Oxfordshire now accepted the need for all Bishopswood's pupils, including those with profound and multiple difficulties (and Bishopswood had always had a high proportion of these children) to move into mainstream. Now only the most handicapped of pupils were left behind in the purpose-built Bishopswood School. The agreed plan was for 'special care' type facilities to be built at Chiltern Edge comprehensive. Once ready, the final stage of the 'transfer of good practice' would take place. And, I thought, if children with the severest of difficulties could be transferred to mainstream then certainly those children with moderate learning difficulties at Etton Pasture School, situated in the East Riding area of Humberside, should present no major obstacle.

A new challenge! Yes, but Tim Brighouse, the then Chief Education Officer of Oxfordshire, had always been most supportive when I was battling for resources with less senior education officers whenever it was necessary to move Bishopswood from one stage to another, and he had always been keen to support local initiatives. What about this man Bower and Humberside? Time would tell! Certainly my views on integration had been discussed in detail during the last two days. Well, too late to change my mind now; being the last day of April I had telephoned my resignation to Macclesfield House, Oxford.

2 FITTING IN TO NEW POLICIES

My early attempts during the Autumn term 1986 to develop the Bishopswood model at Etton Pasture, although well received by the mainstream schools I contacted, fell on stony ground with the authority. The Principal Education Officer (Special Educational Needs), Dr Nicholas, was dismissive and indicated that my attempts had to stop. I was told that I must wait for the authority to produce its consultative document on special education. Dr Nicholas wanted a county approach not 'mavericks'! There was, I thought, a different type of bureaucracy in operation here in Humberside; so much for local initiatives. The feeling of frustration at having been slapped down vanished during the summer of 1987 when two documents were published by Humberside. The first, called *Mainstream Approaches to Special Educational Needs*, espoused the need for whole-school approaches to meeting special education needs. This was good stuff! But then in late August the much awaited consultative document, the *Special Educational Needs Development Plan* arrived. This 'green paper' brought the good news and this had been worth waiting for; its suggestions were beyond my wildest dreams. A radical five-phase approach to integration was described:

> *An outline of the possible stages for a phased restructuring of the County's special education provision*
>
> *First phase development*
> Phased contraction of special schools and units offering medium-level support: development into Area Special Schools.
> Parallel development of co-ordinated Learning Support Service with
> (i) Located Learning Support (centred on Area Special Schools) and
> (ii) Peripatetic Learning Support (centred on reorganised Remedial Service)
> Establishment of Resource Teams to co-ordinate all support services and help plan subsequent phased transition to more integrated provision.
> Development of other specialist services to meet current deficiencies in provision.
>
> *Second phase development*
> Phasing out of all special schools and units offering medium-level support.
> Consolidation of integrated Learning Support Service (incorporating both the located and peripatetic services).

Initial contraction of special schools offering high-level support.
Shift from medium-level support in special units attached to 'designated' schools towards peripatetic support in pupils' own local schools.

Third phase development
Further contraction of special schools offering high-level support.
Continued shift for high- and medium-level support from special units to peripatetic support.

Fourth phase development
Phasing out of all special schools offering high-level support.
Some 'high dependency' children still catered for in special units at 'designated' mainstream schools.

Fifth phase development
All special educational needs children supported in their own local school.

This was music to my ears! Phase 5 was a little idealistic, possibly a pipe dream. Phase 4 I knew was obtainable and akin to the Bishopswood experience which demonstrated that it was possible and desirable even for children with profound and multiple disability to receive their education in mainstream. But this was only a consultative document. Would the consultation be positive and lead to the implementation of this phased approach to integration? The authority hoped all schools and other interested bodies would discuss the document during the Autumn term and send in their responses by 31 December 1987. What about my own governing body at Etton Pasture, the staff, and – most of all – the parents?

3 NEGOTIATING WITH PARENTS AND GOVERNORS

On arriving at Etton Pasture in September 1986 I discovered that there was a commonly held belief among staff and parents that I had been appointed to close the school (oh for such power!). My views on special education had arrived before me and were well known. This rumour had to be quashed; if it persisted it could be damaging to morale. When trying to convince people that I couldn't possibly possess a mandate to close the school I reminded them that I hadn't closed Bishopswood, although the school had adopted an unusual way of working. I was, however, always keen to stress the advantages that integration could bring to children with special needs. My stance was the same as it had been at Bishopswood. If we could transfer to mainstream all that is best about a special school, i.e. its positive discrimination and its expertise (believe me, not always present) then we could create a system which had at Bishopswood been described by parents as being 'the best of both worlds'; best because to the advantages of a good special school we add the major advantages resulting from the children attending a 'normal' school. This stance was generally well received by the Etton Pasture parents and staff. However, some remained sceptical.

The anxieties of parents I could understand and sympathise with. In the past many had seen their children fail miserably in mainstream. The transfer to a special school had brought much-needed relief. In spite of many discussions with parents a few still had doubts. There was the belief that the local education authority wouldn't properly resource any integration project; they would use any attempt as an excuse to save money. Well, I had always assured them I would be no party to that! But those discussions confirmed what I already knew – that is, that any attempt to reintegrate these children would have to be carefully planned and properly resourced if the unhappiness of years ago was not to return. Parents would accept nothing less. I also knew that the correct attitude of teachers in mainstream was vital to success as was the ethos of the receiving school; it really had to believe in accepting all its pupils as being of equal importance.

In the late 1970s I had been head of special needs at Chipping Norton School, an old Oxfordshire grammar school. There I had learnt that attitudes don't change overnight just because of a head's decree or a county decree. It is a business of constant erosion, seizing opportunities where they occur and taking often small, albeit significant, steps forward at the right time. And in three years special needs provision at Chipping Norton had been transformed.

A special meeting of Etton Pasture's governors was convened for 3 November 1987. The intention was to discuss our response to the consultative document. I had been asked to pen my thoughts and I took governors through the document. We agreed that children with moderate learning difficulties could be better educated in a well-resourced mainstream situation. While we agreed with the local education authority's evolutionary approach, we felt, nevertheless, that a clear timetable needed to be determined for the East Riding area of Humberside if procrastination was not to be the name of the game. We wanted an early plan for Etton Pasture allowing it to close as a school for children with moderate learning difficulties. However, unlike Phase 2 in the consultative document, which saw a phasing out of units at this stage, we felt that the closure of a special school would require the strengthening of 'units' (resource bases) if children transferring from the special school were to experience success. We went on to suggest that, with careful thought and planning and a commitment to integration on the part of the receiving schools, in our opinion, Phase 4 was a worthwhile and obtainable aim. However we said Phase 5 was not a realistic aim because we felt some grouping of children with the most complex difficulties was desirable.

Almost as soon as our response was received at County Hall, meetings were convened and attended by Dr Nicholas, Mr Mike Wright (Senior Adviser, Special Needs), Mr Dick Elwood (County Educational Psychologist) and myself. The authority seemed particularly interested in the governors' suggestion that an empty Etton Pasture could be used for children with emotional and behavioural difficulties. The only school for these children in Humberside – Bridge View School – was full and the authority was expensively paying for over thirty children to attend special schools outside Humberside. The pressure for places was constantly increasing. Discussions continued during the Spring term 1988.

4 SETTING A TIMETABLE

A meeting of the 1981 Education Act sub-committee of the Humberside Education Committee in May 1988 considered the suggestion to close Etton Pasture School and to provide alternative provision for its pupils in mainstream. Members accepted the suggestion with formal consultations starting in autumn 1988. Formal consultation is required by the 1981 Education Act. The agreed timetable was:

1 *Monday 7 November 1988*
   (a) Consultative document distributed.
   (b) Meeting at Etton Pasture between officers of the authority and staff together with representatives of the professional associations and trades unions involved.

2 *Monday 14 November 1988*
   Meeting of the Etton Pasture School governing body.

3 *Monday 21 November 1988*
   Meeting at Etton Pasture School between members of the 1981 Act Special Sub-Committee, parents and governors.

4 *Tuesday 31 January 1989*
   Closing date for comments on the consultative document.

The consultative document and letters giving the timetable were sent to parents, governors, staff of Etton Pasture, the Director of School Services, county secretaries of professional associations, trade unions involved, and district administrators of the area health authorities.

5 CONSULTATIONS AND IMPLEMENTATION

The consultative document advocated the closure of Etton Pasture on 31 August 1990 with a new school for children with emotional and behavioural difficulties opening the next day. Alternative provision for children with moderate learning difficulties would be in the form of new designated units (resource bases) at both primary and secondary phase in five areas of the East Riding, i.e. Pocklington, Beverley, Bridlington, Hessle and Hedon. Three of these areas – Bridlington, Hessle and Hedon – were already served by units at primary phase but traditionally children had transferred from these to Etton Pasture on reaching secondary age. (All three had started off as detached segregated units but in each case during the 1980s had moved into mainstream schools.) Children leaving Etton, following a closure, would transfer to these new units and these would be staffed by teachers and aides working for a new Learning Support Service to be created in 1990.

The consultation went smoothly. At our meeting on 14 November 1988, governors gave a cautious welcome to the consultation – after all it had grown from our own response twelve months earlier. However, we stressed the new mainstream provision must be properly resourced. The Friends of Etton Pasture School Committee gave an almost identical response. Most of the parents who attended the meeting on 21 November 1988 could see the advantages integration would bring to their children. Some scepticism was nevertheless apparent; the authority would not properly resource the designated schools and was only really interested in saving money! Two parents, both with children due to leave Etton Pasture before its proposed closure date, remained unconvinced that the requirements of children with special educational needs could ever be properly met in mainstream. It was agreed that I would arrange to take some parents to visit a resource base in operation elsewhere. This helped to dispel some lingering doubts.

By the closing date 31 January 1989, only one reply criticising the plan had been received. This was from a consultant who objected to the closure because he felt closure would create difficulties when it came to providing the physiotherapy the children required! Is there, I wonder, a general lack of knowledge of what children with moderate learning difficulties do in special schools?

Why were the parents so willing to go along with the closure? I had anticipated some fairly strong opposition from a few parents because of their earlier experience with mainstream schools. Looking back I think there was a feeling of confidence in the governors and myself, a feeling that we wouldn't accept anything second rate. Also, many parents had been won over to the idea of integration in discussions with myself and other members of staff at annual reviews and other meetings from as early as 1986. Most knew that I had been involved with the successful scheme for children with severe learning difficulties at Bishopswood.

In February 1989 the parents, staff and governors received letters confirming that the County Council had endorsed the recommendations of the Education Committee to close Etton Pasture. There would therefore be further discussions regarding parental wishes and staff interests concerning suitable alternative employment.

In May 1989 the new Director of Education, Dr M. Garnett, wrote to the Department of Education and Science asking for permission to close Etton Pasture. The permission would:

greatly facilitate planning in respect of:

1 determination of alternative provision to be made for the children concerned; and
2 determination of suitable employment for the staff affected by the proposed closure.

At the same time he stated the authority's wish to use the premises to establish a co-educational special school for youngsters with emotional and behavioural difficulties.

At least twelve months must elapse between the permission from the Department of Education and Science and the closure date for a special school. It was not until the last week of August 1989 that DES permission was received. In September 1989 parents and staff were informed of the Secretary of State's approval and advised that there would be further meetings with considerations for parental concern. The staff would also have meetings to discuss protection of their interests regarding suitable alternative employment where necessary.

All parents were visited by Mr Crabtree (Assistant Education Officer, SEN) and myself during November 1989, to discuss their child's placement for September 1990. A group of nine children due to leave in 1991 would stay on in the new redesignated school to follow a specially tailored leavers' programme, four younger children with emotional and behavioural difficulties would remain in the new school but the rest, about thirty children at the time of the school closure, would transfer to the new Learning Support Service's designated 'units'.

6 THE LEARNING SUPPORT SERVICE

The Learning Support Service, of which I am now head, was formed on 1 January 1990. There are two branches to the service: located staff and peripatetic staff. Located staff work full time under the day-to-day management of the head of their school at both primary and secondary phase in the schools with designated units. Peripatetic staff support mainly non-Statemented children with learning problems attending the East Riding's 137 schools, although most of their work is at primary phase. Salaries for both located and peripatetic staff are paid from the 10 per cent of the General Schools Budget held centrally under discretionary exceptions. All schools with designated units have adopted different models varying from total functional integration to others with a mixture of functional integration and withdrawal.

All teachers at Etton Pasture were given the opportunity of having career development interviews with Mike Wright (Senior Adviser, Special Needs) during the Autumn term 1989; five are now employed with the Learning Support Service, one took early retirement, one works in a primary school, five are employed in the new emotional and behavioural difficulties school and one teacher has yet to decide on his future.

The date 4 September 1990 was the start of the Humberside new school year and one of considerable importance for the development of special education in Humberside. From this time, all children with moderate learning difficulties in the East Riding receive their education in mainstream schools. The transfer of pupils from Etton Pasture proved far easier than I had anticipated. So far there has been no major problem.

From the start of the Summer term 1991 when a new unit for infant-aged children opens in Beverley, there will be a total of 12 designated units with 22 teachers and 16 aides working with about 140 pupils. This is roughly the same as the number of pupils who were attending Etton Pasture when I arrived. Already, exciting changes are underway. Increasingly, children with moderate learning difficulties are being Statemented to remain in their local school but with extra help from the peripatetic branch of the Learning Support Service. In some of the located units there is already evidence to show that we are moving into Phase 3, with some children with more severe learning difficulties now attending. This is to be welcomed but has resource implications!

Chapter 6

Challenging patriarchal culture through equal opportunities
An action research study in a primary school

Sheila Cunnison

In this chapter Sheila Cunnison describes an action research project designed to increase the equality of opportunity of boys and girls in a Humberside primary school. She gives an account of the culture surrounding the school and the view of equalising opportunity through positive action contained in the project. She examines the attempts made to raise the teachers' awareness of both gender stereotyping and the attention given to boys and girls in the classroom, and reports on the specific mini-projects class teachers designed to work on one aspect of equalising opportunities. Her chapter provides an opportunity to reflect on the value placed on the activities of girls and boys and the way these may be related to disaffection, disruption and difficulties in learning.

1 INTRODUCTION

Implementing an equal-opportunity policy within a school involves challenging the values and culturally sanctioned patterns of behaviour not only of the children, their parents and local community, but also of the school teachers. For we are all caught in the web of the culture and values of a patriarchal society. Our identity as women and men has been constructed within such a society; we are full of hidden assumptions about the ways in which it is appropriate for women and men to behave; the differential importance of women and men in the domestic and the public sphere; the relation of women and men to authority and a host of other issues (De Lyon and Migniuolo 1989, Acker 1989).

This chapter examines the challenges to patriarchal culture made when an equal-opportunity project was implemented in a Humberside primary school in 1988–9. Those responsible for implementing the project were the head and deputy of the school, a research fellow and a lecturer from the local college. The first three were women, all feminists. The fourth was a man. Those most closely involved with the project were the deputy head, Christine Gurevitch, and the research worker, the author of this paper (see also Cunnison and Gurevitch 1990).

The school was 'new'. The authority had reorganised the system from a three-tier (primary, junior high, senior high) to a two-tier (primary, secondary) system.

A few of the thirteen teachers (nine women and four men) had worked together before, but in the main the teachers did not know one another and they did not know the children. With the exception of a male caretaker, all the support staff – secretaries, dinner ladies and playground supervisors – were women.

The building itself was refurbished Victorian, high-ceilinged and tall-windowed. A visitor was first of all impressed by the welcoming atmosphere. Orange, yellow and red paint gave an almost physical warmth. Large porthole windows in the heavy doors let the light from the big windows penetrate the whole building. Children's paintings, embroideries, murals and models livened the corridors and rooms. Green plants softened the atmosphere. The place hummed with activity but was not noisy.

Patriarchal culture in the school

The school was in an area of the city which was very much a local community, old streets with many small shops, small terrace houses, families connected by a local network of kinship ties. It was not a particularly deprived area, many men had full-time and many women part-time work. It lay on the edge of what had been a community of deep-sea trawlermen and their wives. Though the fishing had gone, the traditional culture lingered on. The women and the men tended to live different and separate lives. Most of the parents had grown up in a world where full domestic responsibility devolved on women, where men tended to be free to come and go as they pleased and where they dominated the pubs. It was very definitely a macho culture, with something of a reputation for male violence (Clarricoates 1984, Tunstall 1962). This was the culture in which the children were growing up. It impinged directly on the school. I was present when one father, whose son had just run home from school complaining about some injustice, himself rushed into school, pushed past children, teachers and other parents and threatened violence to the head. This was not the only occasion on which she was threatened. Children were also threatened by elder siblings.

In this situation it seemed to us of great importance to win the support of as many parents as possible for the equal-opportunity project. The deputy, part of whose duties included home–school liaison, put in a great deal of time talking to parents and encouraging them and grandparents to become involved. In this she was quite successful.

Before and after school mums and toddlers – and a few dads – crowded into the corridors with the smaller children and often chatted with the teachers. Parents were to be found helping in several of the classrooms. Two or three were often gathered chatting in the Parents' Room. The secretary was welcoming, the head, the deputy and the rest of the teachers were available.

This is the kind of atmosphere characteristic of many progressive primary schools. But something else which a regular visitor would have noticed, especially one who appeared during morning or afternoon break, was a small number of boys – and very occasionally a girl – standing outside the staffroom or outside the school office, their faces turned to the wall. It soon became apparent that the same boys kept reappearing. They were the school's main 'behaviour problems'. Inside the staffroom I quickly learned the names of these 'problem' boys. They were most disruptive in class, on school trips and in the playground. It was only later that I learned the names of the few girls thought of as particularly 'difficult'. The very physicality of the boys' naughtiness gave them a high profile and it proved difficult for teachers, in their attempts to exercise control, not to further reinforce this high profile. The struggle against violence was mainly, though not wholly, against boys' violence. The head had come down heavily against physical violence immediately the school opened. By the time the project started the practice of 'strangling' one another in the playground had almost been stopped.

In spite of the intentions of the head, boys also seemed to have a more prominent role than girls in a variety of class and school events. Only a few girls occupied positions of prominence, some on account of their naughtiness or cleverness, others for their ability to carry messages and organise errands because of their 'soundness and reliability'. This was one area where girls excelled; very few boys were thought of as 'sound and reliable'.

2 FITTING OUR PROJECT INTO SCHOOL POLICY

The head had introduced an equal-opportunity policy from the start. Although there was no written policy statement, all teachers were informed of the policy before appointment. Gender was used neither as an administrative nor as an organising device within the school: registers of children were listed in alphabetical order, girls and boys together; children were not segregated by sex during lessons unless there was a positive reason for doing so, nor when lining up in the playground waiting to enter the school. Moreover, the head tried to promote a school culture which encouraged and praised girls. She herself selected girls as much if not more than boys for tasks of fetching and carrying, both objects and information. In assembly she frequently changed the sex of the key character in the morning story, so girls rather than boys were the subject.

Equal opportunities also had the full support of the LEA which had, in 1984, issued guidelines to all teachers in post. But, although equal-opportunity policies can be proclaimed by local authorities and can be introduced as school policy by head teachers, they can be implemented only with the cooperation of the class teachers (Ruddock and May 1983). These are the people with whom the children spend most of their day and to whom they tend to form the strongest attachments. It is the class teachers, the people at the 'chalkface', that have to be persuaded to mount the challenge to patriarchal culture and values.

This is no easy task. Before they can challenge the patriarchal values in the culture of the children, teachers have to confront their own prejudices in this area and the way these have become an established part of their teaching practice which may have served them for many years. It was the job of those who led the project to persuade teachers to do just that and to support them through the problems and difficulties that ensued. Movement towards equal-opportunity practice is likely to be slow, incomplete and subject to revision.

Equal access or positive action?

People's ideas of what constitutes equal educational opportunity for girls and boys differ. For some it is limited to making all subjects equally available to all. The onus of making use of these opportunities remains firmly and squarely on the shoulders of the children. But we know that girls and boys do *not* make equal use of the facilities on offer. They gravitate to the skills and to the play that is conventionally thought appropriate to their gender (Clarricoates 1984). Left to themselves girls tend to play in the Home Corner, boys with construction toys. Positive action directed to boys as well as girls is needed to break down gender stereotypes (Askew and Ross 1988).

   Our interpretation of equal opportunities involved such positive action. It mounted a basic challenge to the gender-based division of labour at work and in the home which characterises our society. It involved equipping girls and boys with the same set of educational skills – in reading, number, technology, problem-solving, oral presentation. These basic skills must be acquired if the choices which children are presented with later are to be meaningful, choices about what subjects to study, what jobs to take up, what leisure pursuits to follow. Without the basic skills, the choices remain hollow and meaningless. Boys as well as girls find whole areas of experience cut off from them; their lives too, fall into conventional and stereotypical patterns. A second important aspect of our project involved broadening children's ideas about the kinds of jobs adult women and men can do and, furthermore, suggesting to them that men as well as women have responsibilities and can find fulfilment in domestic and family work.

The nature of the project

The overall project was divided into two parts, a short period for raising teachers' awareness about issues of gender and their relation to education, and a longer period during which teachers were asked to devise some strategy within their class for increasing equality of opportunity between girls and boys. Teachers were encouraged but not *required* to devise these strategies; however, all but two eventually made an attempt.

   The head asked very little of the teachers. They were expected to attend special equal-opportunity staff meetings held during the lunch-break approximately twice each term. They were expected to cooperate with the research worker in making investigations into sexual stereotypes held by children at both the beginning and the end of the project. They were asked to stand back and examine their own practice in relation to teaching girls and boys, to cooperate in the observation of their classroom practice with other teachers and with the research worker. A video camera was put at the disposal of the teachers to assist in their observations of one another. Several teachers agreed to have lessons videoed by a college technician. All teachers agreed to observations being made by the research worker at least once.

Largely because the school was new, the first term – at least – promised to be very hard work. We recognised that the equal-opportunities project might be seen by the teachers as yet another obligation. Yet the head decided to proceed. She felt the provision of equal opportunity to be fundamental to the education process. Moreover, the National Curriculum, with its implications of yet more work, was looming on the horizon: if the present opportunity was not seized there might be a long delay. The decision taken, the project got under way after the first half-term and carried on till the end of the school year.

3 RAISING AWARENESS

There were two main approaches to raising teachers' awareness. The first was uncovering the extent of gender stereotyping by children. The second was examining the extent and quality of teacher interaction with girls and boys in their class. In highlighting these areas we were making use of the findings of earlier research that gender stereotyping starts very early (Barclay 1974; Grabrucker 1988), that teachers tend to reinforce these stereotypes (Clarricoates 1984, Walkerdine 1989) and, more particularly, that they tend to pay more attention to boys than to girls (Spender 1982, Stanworth 1983) – although this does not apply to all boys or all girls (Wolpe 1988).

Gender stereotyping, jobs and domestic work

All teachers were asked to investigate gender stereotyping among their pupils. The 5 to 6 year olds were asked what they wanted to be when they grew up; the 7 to 11 year olds what their 'dream job' was and what they expected to be. They were all asked what sorts of jobs women did and what sorts of jobs men did although in phrasing this latter question we trapped ourselves in our own stereotypes. At the conclusion of the project, therefore, we changed the questions and asked the children what jobs they could think of and then whether women or men or both sexes could do those jobs. Some teachers added questions about what women and men did in their spare time and about the kinds of toys they wanted for Xmas. The young children were questioned verbally, some individually, some in small groups. The older children were asked to produce written answers.

An analysis of the jobs children thought they would do when they grew up revealed that, by 5 years old, stereotypical thinking was well entrenched. At 5 the only jobs chosen by both girls and boys were police, shop and garage work – the latter because the children were fans of the female motor mechanic in the TV serial *Neighbours*. The children described the occupations in their own words. Among those named by the girls were: 'a working girl', 'selling clothes in a shop', 'a lollipop lady', 'a nurse', 'a police lady', 'a ballet dancer' and 'a Brownie'. Those named by the boys included: 'a motorbike boy doing pizzas and chips', 'a writer at the sports centre', 'a soldier in battle – I'd kill the German that killed my grandad', 'a policeman' and 'a shoplady' [*sic*].

In the next class up the girls included the job of hairdresser, nurse and teacher, which remained the most popular throughout the school. In their dream jobs they included stardom, pop star, film star, ice skater, model and karate expert (a class was held at the school in the evenings and one or two of the children went). By 9 to 10, they dreamed also of becoming an office worker or a vet or of going to university. At 10 years some of them had become enthusiastic over the game of football, played together in the school playground. This was reflected in their aspirations. Dreams now included footballer, jockey, weightlifter and mechanic and were more popular than the more traditional nurse, teacher, secretary and office worker. Their real expectations were still quite high and included a professional footballer, model and singer as well as three nurses, a teacher, a police lady (or bank manager) and two pet-shop ladies.

Boys aimed at largely different jobs, though policeman, teacher and footballer were common to both. Among a class of 6 year olds, four wanted to become policemen, two a milkman, one a fireman, one a karate expert and one a grandad – when I suggested it might be a long way off he decided he would like to become a dad! At 7 years the boys began to include among their dreams and their expectations professional sport, the forces and the professions – though one boy was different, he was determined to become a scientist of prehistory. The dreams of 11 year olds in their last year included three professional footballers, a jet pilot, an RAF pilot, a soldier, a cartoonist, a bank manager and a teacher. Their expected occupations were two footballers, three artists (these boys had been encouraged by their teacher), an actor, a British Telecom employee and a police dog handler.

Looking at these results now what stands out is the non-traditional aspirations of the girls at the top end of the school. One explanation for this may be the support given by the head, even before the project started, to girls in general, and in particular to facilitating the efforts of those who wanted to join in school football. It was the football-playing girls who were more likely to opt for occupations which were not traditionally female. The teachers at the top end of the school, two men and one woman, were, in the early stages of the equal-opportunities project, somewhat reluctant participants. They did not support the girls' aspirations through discussion and exploration of the routes by which such jobs might be attained. The teachers of the early years, however – three women and a man – were really interested. They analysed their results; they talked to one another about them; they raised the issues in staffroom discussion. It was their concern with the high degree of early stereotyping which led them to devise strategies to encourage girls to become familiar with technical matters and boys with domestic and care tasks.

Results of the stereotype survey and a selection of class observations of other school events were made available to teachers, in a file placed in the staffroom. The verbal answers of the younger children were written down. Copies of the written work of the older children were included.

Gender and teacher–pupil interaction

Not all teachers started from the same point of awareness about the role of gender in structuring education. Only the deputy and one other woman teacher had experimented before with trying to provide greater equality of opportunity between the sexes. Not all teachers were equally eager to learn and to undertake the difficult task of assessing their own practice. With respect to observation, the deputy's time was strictly limited and there was only one researcher. However, systematic recording of the number and content of teacher–pupil interactions was carried out in all classes, in some cases for single lessons, but in two cases for longer.

Most observation, lasting over a period of six months, was carried out in a class of 5 to 6 year olds, girls and boys in roughly equal proportions. The teacher was a conscientious and highly competent woman who had always thought of herself as giving equal attention to all her children and was rather horrified when, early in the second term, observations showed that she interacted twice as often with boys as girls. In one particular question and answer session where she had responded to the greater eagerness of certain boys to answer, four had dominated the discussion – two with their enthusiasm, two with disruption. Only one of the girls was very articulate; she moved the next day to a middle-class area and a new school. More girls than boys remained silent (cf. French and French 1984).

The teacher changed her strategy. There was to be no shouting out. Though hands could be raised, she decided who to ask. Maintaining eye contact with even the most reluctant children she saw that everyone was given a turn. At this point she questioned the practice of the maths advisory teacher visiting classes throughout the school. In a demonstration lesson with her class she noticed that the girls were hanging back and avoiding eye contact. Only the boys were participating fully in the lesson. She moved the girls to the front. The maths teacher began to take more notice of them and they joined in. The predisposition of the advisory teacher to interact with boys was a point of conversation in the staffroom. It was brought to his attention. He apologised but did not change his practice.

One and a half months later, further observations with the 5 to 6 year olds showed greater equality. On one occasion, with equal numbers of the two sexes, there were fourteen interactions with girls and nineteen with boys. However the participation of girls and boys was elicited differently: only five of the girls had volunteered an answer, nine girls had to be asked; the figures for boys were seventeen and two. After another month when the teacher was involved with a strategy of positive action to interest girls in mechanics, construction and technology, records show that the teacher was carrying out her intention to interact more frequently with girls – for example, nineteen interactions with girls, thirteen with boys were recorded in one session.

Interaction and discipline

The ability of a teacher to control the degree to which she/he interacts with girls and boys depends on the ability to exert discipline or control over a class. For example, observations with a class of 8 year olds whose teacher had a reputation among the staff both for poor discipline and chauvinism showed thirty-four interactions with boys compared with twenty-seven with girls, nine of which were with one particular girl. In the same class the next day, a teacher from another class almost lost control because of disruption by the boys. The figures of interactions were forty-one for boys, including twelve with one boy, and twenty-six with girls. The head teacher came in next, read the riot act to the most offensive boys and took a lesson where the interactions were twenty-seven with boys and twenty-five with girls. She had no problems with discipline and had developed ways of getting girls to participate.

4 STRATEGIES FOR CHANGING ATTITUDES

Most teachers devised a mini-project to help break down gender stereotypes. Projects dealt first with the acquisition of skills thought more appropriate to one gender or the other, second with problems of motivating children to acquire skills conventionally thought of as gender inappropriate, and third with helping girls to gain confidence in displaying their knowledge. Motivation was addressed by using visitors in gender atypical jobs, as role models. Poster-size photographs of children with these role models were displayed on school walls. One of the most successful visitors was a firewoman. She had the children enthralled with her uniform, helmet and boots and stories of crawling through the smoke-filled rooms looking for people. But she impressed them most when she picked up the limp and supposedly unconscious figure of their large schoolmaster, slung him over her shoulder and walked off.

The problem of girls and boys gravitating to gender-based activities was particularly removed by reducing choice. All children were required to practise certain skills. In the early years this was achieved by 'structuring' play, requiring children to undertake certain acitivites, e.g. the girls to use construction toys. Confidence was addressed by using single sex groups: girls are generally more forthcoming among their own sex.

The deputy head emphasised the need to integrate work on number, reading, writing and oral work into the mini-projects.

Skills for the girls – craft, design and technology

Two groups visited a local garage. A class of 6 year olds, working in single sex groups, was given the task of designing and building a car lift. More help was given to girls than boys over the difficulties with design. Many models included wood and the children learned to use saws, hammers and nails. They also learned about a range of tools used in garage work. A young woman motor mechanic came to visit in her overalls and with her tools. After talking to the class she took small groups to the playground to examine the engine of the teacher's car. Her visit was a great success and the poster picture of her with the children peering at an engine, a favourite.

Following their visit a class of 5 year olds helped their teacher build a model garage with petrol pumps, air pump, oil, water and sand. Spare parts of cars were collected, various tools used by motor mechanics, an AA manual, a couple of old telephones. The teacher devised a scenario for role play including a driver who broke down, a mechanic, a garage attendant and a shop attendant looking after spare parts. Children took turns to carry out the role play. The class was visited by another woman motor mechanic and by a woman who worked as a paint sprayer.

Skills for the girls – football

The girls who played football wanted to join in with the boys who played in the playground. Football is often closely associated with a masculine identity and at first the man who ran the football teams thought the idea ludicrous. Then he realised the girls' performance suffered because they had been taught neither the skills nor the rules. He took them on special girls-only coaching, taught them how to kick the ball, how to pass, how to spread out. They learned the rules. The head gave them their own ball. Some of the girls joined the boys in the playground. A girl was included in one of the school teams and a girls' team played friendly matches with other girls. A young woman YTS trainee from Arsenal visited; she coached the girls on their own, then she coached girls and boys together.

The man who ran the teams and one of the women went on a course to qualify for certificates as coaches. Football skills were taught to all children from the reception class upwards.

Skills for both – critical awareness of gender roles

Boys as well as girls need to learn critical awareness, the ability to assess what they are told and to question conventional views. It is particularly important for girls/women, who comprise a subordinate group: in order to develop as in-dividuals they need to question many of the myths about the female sex.

A group of girls and boys together analysed gender pictures in a reading book used by the early years. They counted representations of males and females, assessed whether they were active or passive, and noted the roles portrayed. They found men over-represented, women practically always placed in a domestic setting. They found themselves – boys more often than girls – making assumptions that males were 'in charge' of females, that the bigger people were always males. The girls were especially unhappy about what they considered to be the misrepresentation of women and the effect this might have on young children.

Skills for boys – domesticity and care

The play of children in the reception class was closely structured. The teacher produced work cards with photographs of boys doing a variety of domestic tasks, ironing, bathing the baby, etc. Groups of boys were each given a different work card and asked to carry out the task shown. Photographs of the boys engaged in these tasks were put up on the wall outside the classroom and attracted much approval from mums.

A male college lecturer came into school, and in the school hall, in front of three classes, he bathed the 3-month-old baby brother of one of the reception class. A male nurse came in to school and talked to the two youngest classes about his job. On both occasions photographs were obtained of the children with the visitors.

Disruption, cooperative learning and reading skills

Some teachers worried, especially in the early stages of the research, that giving extra attention to the girls would mean depriving the boys of their due. Several teachers, women as well as men, worried more about slow or shy boys than slow or shy girls. Boys, after all, would have to make their way in the world of work. This concern with boys' performance is institutionalised within educational administration by a Special Needs Service which is concerned predominantly with literacy. Boys are far more likely to experience reading difficulties than girls (Blom 1971).

Concern about boys, combined with professional responsibility within the school for Special Needs, prompted a class teacher of 7 to 8 year olds to seek a mini-project within that area. She conducted her project jointly with the deputy head with advice from the college lecturer. It addressed poor reading. Both the class teacher and the deputy head had previous experience of cooperative learning through techniques of 'shared reading' (Topping 1987). Of the school's 7 to 8 year olds, twelve boys and four girls were diagnosed, using standard tests, as poor readers. All but one were judged by both class teacher and deputy head as presenting behaviour problems.

The sixteen children were taken as a separate group once a week. The children formed pairs of their choice and worked together. First they read in turn to one another, sharing a text chosen by the reader. Next, still sitting side by side, they read silently to themselves from the book of their choice. These two tasks were programmed at first for four or five minutes then for increasing lengths of time, until, at the end of thirteen weeks, they spent twenty minutes in shared reading and twenty minutes in silent reading. Books appropriate to age and reading ability were loaned to the school by the college lecturer. At the end of thirteen weeks, the reading ability of the boys had increased quite dramatically, of the girls less so. Equally noticeable, the children were far less disruptive in ordinary lessons than they had been: they had not only learned to read, they had learned to work together cooperatively.

This experiment suggests a link between reading skills, cooperative learning and disruptive behaviour, though the nature of the link is unclear. It is likely, perhaps particularly at this age, that the acquisition of reading skills decreases frustration and boredom – both of which may result in disruption – and increases confidence and the ability to join in lessons. The existence of such a link is supported by the fact that it is predominantly boys who are poor readers and boys who are disruptive.

Whatever the social processes, the consequence for the teacher was less stress and more time to spend with other pupils, mainly girls. The head of the school was sufficiently impressed with the results of this experiment that, in the next year, she instituted a once-weekly three-quarters of an hour period of shared reading throughout the school.

In the sense that it depended on the willingness of boys to engage in the same activity as their special mate, the project may be seen as depending on male bonding. But, at the same time, it gave the skilled teacher an opportunity to develop cooperation, such as turn-taking and helping one another, which is more characteristic of girls' than boys' classsroom behaviour and connected with widely acknowledged differences in the way in which women and men tend to relate to other people (Gilligan 1982). Thus developed, it could help to challenge patriarchal attitudes.

5 CONCLUSION

This, then, is the barest outline of what implementing a whole-school equal-opportunities policy was all about. To what extent can the challenge to patriarchal culture be seen as successful? At the end of the year, all but one of the teachers claimed that they had changed. They were now aware that gender did affect the provision of educational opportunity and that the process was quite complex. Girls and boys were already constituted as different kinds of people when they entered the school. Teachers had to take these differences into account when trying to equip children with specific skills. They found that teachers could make a difference, they could be fairer about the attention they gave to girls and boys. They could equip girls with skills they usually did not learn, skills closely associated with masculine identity such as carpentry and football, and they could interest girls in cars and garages (Everley 1981).

The teachers began to consider the wider implications of gender stereotyping in society at large. Some of the teachers reassessed their own careers. Some of the women began to feel more confident in their own abilities and to consider whether they might gain promotion. One of the men found himself in the pub arguing, to his surprise, the case for women fire-fighters. Most of the teachers thought about the implications for their own children.

Some of the parents, the mums, who got involved began to think about gender inequality in their own lives and the stultifying influence which stereotypical thinking had had upon them. They hoped their children would have greater opportunity. They talked about the project, they joined in activities in school and began to develop more confidence in themselves. Two started on nursery nurse courses.

Did the children change? In two classes the boys made dramatic improvements in reading, and notable improvements in behaviour: so much so that the head instituted peer-paired reading throughout the school during the next year. In the two classes involved with the craft, design and technology projects, the stereotype survey at the end of the year showed a change. The children now thought that most jobs could be done by both women and men, though one class claimed that only men could fit windows, and another that only men could build houses. In the reception class stereotypes were much more difficult to measure and probably more difficult to change. In spite of being present when the fire-woman visited, and remembering that he had been, one small boy still proclaimed with utter conviction 'women can't be fire people'. And what about a softer, more caring image for men? What was the effect of the male nurse and the man who bathed the baby? The latter was much remembered by the children; a video recording his performance was made for purposes of teaching other children. But a year is not very long; it can only be a beginning; patriarchal culture has very deep roots.

The beginning was promising. The most successful projects were those where either the deputy or the researcher put in a considerable amount of work. Whether there will be any resources from the authority to continue even minimal support to teachers is unclear. The deputy has now left the school. There is no research worker. But there is encouragement from the advisory service.

REFERENCES

Acker, S. (ed.) (1989) *Teachers, Gender and Career*, London: Falmer.
Askew, S. and Ross, C. (1988) *Boys Don't Cry: Boys and Sexism in Education*, Milton Keynes: Open University Press.
Barclay, L. (1974) 'The emergence of vocational expectations in Preschool children', *Journal of Vocational Behaviour* 4, 1–14.
Blom, G. E. (1971) 'Sex differences in reading disability', in E. Calkins (ed.), *Reading Forum*, Bethesda, Maryland: National Institute of Neurological Disease and Stroke.
Clarricoates, K. (1984) *Gender Relationships and Teacher Interaction in Four Northern Primary Schools*, University of Hull.

Cunnison, S. and Gurevitch, C. (1990) 'Implementing a whole school equal opportunities policy: a primary school in Humberside', *Gender and Education* 2 (3), 283–95.

De Lyon, H. and Migniuolo, F. (1989) *Women Teachers: Issues and Experiences*, Milton Keynes: Open University Press.

Everley, B. (1981) *We Can Do It Now*, Manchester: EDC.

French, J. and French, P. (1984) 'Gender imbalance in the primary classroom: an interactional account', *Educational Research* 26 (2), 127–36.

Gilligan, C. (1982) *In a Different Voice: Psychological Theory and Women's Development*, Cambridge, Mass.: Harvard University Press.

Grabrucker, N. (1988) *There's a Good Girl*, London: Women's Press.

Ruddock, J. and May, N. (1983) *Sex Stereotyping and the Early Years of Education*, University of East Anglia, Norwich: Centre for Applied Research in Education.

Spender, D. (1982) *Invisible Women: The Schooling Scandal*, London: Writers and Readers Co-operative.

Stanworth, M. (1983) *Gender and Schooling*, London: Hutchinson, in association with Explorations in Feminism.

Topping, K. (1987) 'Peer tutored paired reading: outcome data from ten projects', *Educational Psychology* 7 (2), 133–45.

Tunstall, J. (1962) *The Fishermen*, London: McGibbon & Kee.

Walkerdine, V. (1989) *Counting Girls Out*, London: Virago.

Wolpe, A. (1988) *Within School Walls: The Role of Discipline and Sexuality in the Curriculum*, London: Routledge.

Part 2

Integrating services for the under fives

Chapter 7

Provision for the under fives
Bringing services together

Kathryn Riley

Source: Local Government Policy Making 16 (1), June 1989, pp. 38–44.

In this chapter, Kathryn Riley describes the bureaucratic, professional and ideological divisions that have characterised the pattern of services for pre-school children in the United Kingdom. These divisions are now being challenged by a number of local authorities, though not by central government, which remains reluctant to make the links between high quality care and education for young children and the need for high quality, flexible childcare for their working parents. Kathryn Riley describes developments in Strathclyde, in Manchester and in some of the new London local education authorities which came into existence in April 1990 after the demise of the Inner London Education Authority. The aim of full unification of services is rare; greater coordination is more common.

I INTRODUCTION

Is the consumer still silent? Are the professionals still guarding their territory? If there have been changes, has central government responded? This chapter examines these key questions, and at local authority level, if not at central government level, finds a message of cautious optimism which will be welcomed by parents and by children.

The public provision of services for the under fives has largely been governed on the one hand, by local authority assessment of extreme need – largely provided within day nurseries – and on the other, by varying levels of commitment to the provision of nursery education. Levels of local authority provision of nursery education range from 8 per cent to 86 per cent of 3 and 4 year olds (DES 1987). Provision of nursery education has been linked to the political objectives of local authorities. Labour-run authorities have tended to see this as a higher priority than other authorities – the top twenty providers of nursery education are all Labour controlled (Armstrong 1989).

Public funding for other types of provision such as pre-school playgroups has been relatively small. Despite this, the Pre-School Playgroup Association estimates that 35 per cent of 3 and 4 year olds in England and Wales attend playgroups. There are no reliable figures for community nurseries, workplace nurseries or parent and toddler groups (Pugh 1988).

2 STRATHCLYDE AND MANCHESTER – TACKLING THE FIRST HURDLES

For at least a decade, discussions have taken place in innumerable local authorities about the need for effective coordination for under fives. Rigid departmentalism and professional territorialism coupled with bureaucratic inertia and a low political priority for the under fives has resulted in a few isolated examples of effective coordination but little significant change.

A new determination now seems to be emerging amongst a small band of professionals and politicians to take on that challenge again. Whether they will succeed in breaking through the barriers and obstacles to change yet remains to be seen.

Strathclyde Regional Council was one of the first local authorities to review its provision for the under fives and to set a new pattern for the future. It set up a working party of members, officers, trade unionists, health and voluntary sector representatives to examine its services. The impetus for this initiative came from a range of sources. However, an essential element in the Strathclyde initiative was a high degree of political support. Councillor Richard Stewart, at that time leader of Strathclyde, chaired the working party and gave his personal commitment to the initiative:

> The greatest future resource of Strathclyde is the young children of today, starting life with no prejudices and eager to enjoy the adventure of life. If they are to fulfil their potential, it is vital that the Council and the staff charged with helping them on their journey are fully committed to working with and for them and their parents during the child's formative years.
>
> (Strathclyde Regional Council 1985)

The working party completed a major strategy and analysis report in 1985 which pointed out the haphazard way in which provision had been developed in Strathclyde, 'Reflecting the different priorities of Education and Social Work Departments ... and the unequal strength of the playgroup movement in different localities'. The report also identified the problems facing Strathclyde – problems which are probably endemic to most local authorities:

> that the demarcation between the different types of services restricted the development of flexible services and reinforced professionalism at the expense of the client.
>
> that existing services are often not coordinated and the clear distinction between the departments and agencies that provide services are in contrast to the overlapping needs of parents and children.
>
> that Departmentalism tends to resist any change in the delivery of services and

because the pre-fives are a non-statutory service, they are given low priority for new developments.

(Strathclyde Regional Council 1985)

The Strathclyde Report also identified the need to coordinate and target services effectively and promote pre-five developments in fourteen areas of the region using urban programme funds. It recommended that all pre-five services including family and children's centres, day nurseries, registration of child-minders, and playgroups, support services such as toy libraries and home visiting, as well as nursery schools and classes should be brought together under one department – Education. The Pre-Five Unit was established in 1986 to oversee policy developments and a separate budget and committee established.

Despite the enormity of the task – Strathclyde serves a population of 2.5 million – significant developments have taken place, although in the face of substantial opposition. Administratively, 1,000 staff have been transferred from social work to the Education Department. A common system of admissions which prioritises need, has been introduced for both daycare and nursery educa-tion. The introduction of this system has been opposed by both parents and head teachers. Parents argued for the existing 'first come, first served' policy and head teachers that their professionalism was being challenged (Penn 1988).

Strong links have been established with the voluntary sector. Widespread consultation – including videos, leaflets, mobile exhibitions and displays – has taken place (Strathclyde Pre-Five Unit 1988). Training has been a key element in the Strathclyde initiative and has aimed at developing a common understanding amongst under-fives workers and reducing teachers' fears about integration. Teachers have expressed strong opposition to the Strathclyde programme arguing that the quality of nursery education would be diluted by any moves to integrate services. Training opportunities have also been offered to the voluntary and private sector.

In Manchester, the impetus for change came largely from a group of women councillors, all of whom held key positions in the authority. The city council set itself a clear definition of childcare as a right for the child – and for the parent.

The City Council is committed to a comprehensive programme of develop-ment and childcare. The ultimate goal of this programme is to provide, as a basic right, good quality childcare which meets the needs of all parents and children in Manchester. The achievement of this goal is clearly a long way off, and it will certainly require a massive shift in government policy on childcare, and considerably increased resources made available to local authorities.

(Manchester City Council 1986)

A major 'in house' survey of the workforce and a MORI survey in 1986 of one largely working-class area of Manchester, Benchill, clearly identified the demand for services. Both surveys found large reservoirs of untapped need. The MORI survey found that nine out of ten non-working mothers interested in returning to work or education could not do so because of lack of childcare provision (MORI 1986). As well as assessing local childcare needs for both working and non-working mothers, the MORI survey also assessed awareness about existing facilities and views about new council proposals for childcare.

Manchester has now committed itself in principle to developing an integrated service for the under fives. The Social Service Department has recently been restructured and under-fives provision has been brought together as a separate entity. There has also been major expansion in nursery education and in crèche provision in Colleges of Further Education.

One particular innovative development has been the creation of Children's Centres aimed at providing a wide range of services for the under fives and for young children on a neighbourhood basis. One Children's Centre has been opened, a further four have been completed and are due to open, and two more are in the pipeline. Each of the new centres will serve a small defined neighbourhood and will have day nursery provision for fifty children, parent and toddler groups and crèche facilities, before and after school and holiday use, and space for the local community (Manchester City Council 1988). As in Strathclyde, the development of such a major new initiative on under fives has been extremely difficult and the opening of the Children's Centres has been hampered by issues relating to terms and conditions of employment.

The Manchester project will provide a high quality service in areas of great need in the city. However, whilst the Children's Centres are managed by the Education Department and link closely with neighbouring schools, nursery education has been left out of the Children's Centres equation and apart from the Children's Centres, other childcare provision provided by the authority still continues to run on separate but parallel tracks.

However, the council is now considering how to move forward to achieving its objective of 'A comprehensive programme of development and childcare'. If Strathclyde is anything to go by, the biggest hurdle it will face is in persuading the nursery education lobby that integration of services for the under fives does not mean a reduction in the quality of services.

3 PLANNING FOR CHANGE

Bradley (1982) has suggested that coordination for the under fives is a continuum which goes from dissociation, through to separation, domination, liaison, cooperation, coalition, federation and finally to unification. A number of local authorities such as Sheffield, Liverpool, Haringey, are beginning to talk about greater cooperation between services for the under fives – greater clarity of purpose, communication and respect between the different providers of services for the under fives.

A number of authorities are considering federation – separate services working together and accepting each other's goals. Only one so far, Strathclyde, has made the quantum leap of moving towards unification – the budgeting and organisation of services under a single administration. Others such as Southwark have agreed this in principle, or, as Manchester or Islington, set it as an objective.

The abolition of the ILEA has resulted in a number of the new education authorities reviewing the overall provision of services for the under fives and looking at ways to develop a more coordinated or integrated service. Development plans for a number of the new education services such as Hammersmith and Fulham and Greenwich, specifically refer to this objective. Southwark has committed itself to the integration of services under the management of the Education Department to provide a more accessible and comprehensive service (London Borough of Southwark 1989).

Hammersmith and Fulham have clarified their objectives as providing a range of easily accessible local facilities to meet the needs of pre-school children and their carers:

> To achieve these objectives, a coordinated approach to planning and management is required, bringing together services currently provided by the ILEA, social services department, leisure and recreation department, the health authority and voluntary organisations.
>
> (London Borough of Hammersmith and Fulham 1989)

Greenwich proposes to set up a working group/policy unit to examine the best way to achieve its stated objective of using the transfer of education services as:

> A unique opportunity to plan, coordinate and integrate the existing fragmented pattern of education, care and leisure services to create a comprehensive network of resources, better able to meet the individual needs of children and their families.
>
> (London Borough of Greenwich 1989)

One of the many obstacles to developing an integrated service for the under fives is the confusion about whether it is possible to delegate the powers of social services to education, or vice-versa. Strathclyde has dealt with the situation by delegating most of its social work powers relating to expenditure, running and registering of playgroups, day nurseries etc., to education. However, the few remaining social work powers which it has not been able to delegate, have not proved to be problematic on a day-to-day administrative basis. The situation in Scotland has probably been helped by the Scottish Office itself which has one Minister with overall responsibility and in which the education and social work departments have a tradition of close working relationships.

Both Sheffield and Liverpool have faced some legal difficulties relating to delegation of powers in trying to establish an integrated service. However, recent advice given to the London Borough of Southwark suggests that most of these problems can be dealt with through the establishment of either an under-fives sub-committee or a joint social services and education committee (London Borough of Southwark 1989).

4 MEETING THE NEEDS OF THE CONSUMERS – PARENTS AND CHILDREN

In a meeting of local authorities, old divisions between 'care' and 'education' are beginning to break down and professionals from both camps are starting to find a common language and objectives – a process aided by increasing parental pressure to provide high quality services for the under fives.

Until recently, local authorities have not considered linking provision for the under fives to demand. The needs of parent/children consumers are still largely ignored in many parts of the country. There is no doubt however, that demand for under-fives provision is high. An OPCS survey of 2,500 mothers conducted in 1977 found for example that 90 per cent wanted some form of nursery place for their 3 and 4 year olds and 46 per cent wanted a place for their under threes (Bone 1977).

In Inner London, the breakup of the ILEA has focused attention on the needs of the under fives. In the vast majority of the boroughs, parents have registered their support for nursery education and for more after-school and holiday provision at the many consultation meetings about the future of London education. The parent–consumer lobby in London has put issues of quality and quantity of provision on the political agenda and are unlikely to let them drop.

5 CENTRAL GOVERNMENT

Central government has been slower to take up these issues. The limited attention which has been given to under fives has tended to focus only on nursery education and until recently has rarely touched on the implications of provision for the main carers of children –mainly women.

Central government has given limited support for the development of nursery education and even less for any concept of developing a coordinated and planned programme of provisions for the under fives. For example, the 1972 White Paper *Education: A Framework for Expansion* planned a nursery expansion of 700,000 places by 1981. By 1988, only 500,000 places had been created – a shortfall of 200,000. The same White Paper 'advised' but did not 'require' local authorities to take into account other provisions for the under fives when planning for the expansion of nursery education.

The only legal requirement for the local authority to coordinate is in respect of the Health Authority. Although Roger Freeman, a junior Minister in the Department of Health and Social Security stated that a House of Lords amendment to the Children's Bill to give local authorities a statutory duty to review day care provision with local education authorities, voluntary bodies and health authorities was, 'An interesting idea which we are considering sympathetically.'[1]

In January 1989 the Select Committee on Under Fives restated the importance of nursery education but had little to say about integration of services, although it argues strongly for an educational input into non-education services:

We are brought by the picture of the child's situation in the eighties, and by the evidence of parental demand to our second major conclusion that the way forward is the provision of a place in a nursery classroom for all children whose parents wish it.

There are many good playgroups and day nurseries, but in many there is scope for giving greater emphasis to educational objectives. Given the value of nursery education we would suggest that providers should make sure children in their services get something of the educational stimulation they might have received in a nursery classroom.

(House of Commons 1989)

In March 1989 Angela Rumbold, then Minister of State at the Department of Education and Science, announced the establishment of a committee of inquiry into the educational experience of under fives which was due to report by the end of 1989.[2] The terms of reference were:

To consider the quality of the educational experience which should be offered to three and four year olds, with particular reference to content, continuity and progression in learning having regard to the requirements of the national curriculum and taking account of the Government's expenditure plans.

(Bayliss 1989)

According to press reports, Mrs Rumbold hoped that the committee would bring forward recommendations about good educational practice which would influence employers who are running workplace nurseries, and areas of under-fives provision such as day nurseries, playgroups and child-minders where teachers are not traditionally employed. She also did not expect that the government's response to the committee's report would be a 'large scale investment in the public sector' (Bayliss 1989).

Although issues of educational quality are vital to services for the under fives, the narrow scope of the committee of inquiry meant that key issues about co-ordination at both central and local government level and the wide discrepancy in the level of nursery education provision throughout the country, are likely to be ignored. The scope of the committee of inquiry also failed to acknowledge that there are two consumer groups for under fives services – children and parents. The children require high quality educational experience and care and their parents – particularly mothers – flexible and accessible provision.

One major factor which could conceivably shift the government's likely response to the committee of inquiry and encourage it to consider making a 'large scale investment in the public sector', would be labour market shortages which put women's employment at a premium. The reserve army of labour will be in demand. However, a second more permanent labour market change is emerging in the long-term shift in the workforce from manufacturing to service industries. The increase in white-collar and service employment and the fall in semi-skilled and manual jobs will mean that women workers will be in higher demand.

A series of articles in the *Financial Times* has drawn attention to these issues and focused on the employment needs of Norwich to illustrate the issues. According to local surveys employment in services and high technology manufacturing could grow by 25 per cent, leaving Norwich with a shortfall of workers of 22,000. A childcare survey of two areas of the city found that 96 per cent of women said a lack of childcare facilities was a barrier to employment. It also suggested that 5,600 people in Norwich needed childcare help to take up jobs.[3]

6 TO THE FUTURE

Faced with this scenario the government may ultimately be forced at least to withdraw the hindrances to the provision of childcare, such as taxation on workplace nurseries. Given the opportunity, local authorities could play a key role in developing comprehensive services for the under fives.

If local authorities were required to work with the private sector, voluntary and community groups to draw up under fives development programmes for their area, this would greatly improve both the accessibility and the quality of provision for the under fives. Local authorities would then be in a position to provide effective links between different services for the under fives and develop a common training programme. The development of a comprehensive service for the under fives at local level would also be greatly enhanced by more effective central government coordination – and even a unitary department for the under fives.

Local authority aspirations cannot, however, be turned into effective reality merely by the provision of central government funds – even if such funds were forthcoming. The two professions involved, the 'carers' and the 'educators' have themselves to examine in detail their different perspectives to see how far they are compatible. This must be coupled with a review of the legal obligations of the two professions and a review of terms and conditions.

Even without these major changes at central government the pioneering work of the Strathclydes and the Manchesters will go on. Commitment and determination will bring about some changes. However, there are innumerable local authorities who have yet even to recognise that there is an issue. Only a major change of heart from central government will effect them and enable the committed authorities to carry out their objectives.

NOTES

1   Ministerial address: AMA/ACC/NCVCCO Conference on the Under Fives, 18 April 1989.
2   Editors' note: In the event the Committee of Inquiry failed to report and its findings were not released. The government appeared to drop even modest plans for the development of under-fives provision.
3   *Financial Times* (1989) 'Women's changing role in the workforce', series of four articles: 20–23 February 1989. Editors' note: The rapidly deepening recession in 1990 and 1991 has made the employment predictions out of date.

REFERENCES

Armstrong, H. (1989) *The Early Years: Consultation Document on Education and Child-care for the Under Fives*, London: House of Commons.

Bayliss, S. (1989) 'Short and sharp, Rumbold's way', *Times Educational Supplement*, 23 March 1989.

Bone, M. (1977) *Pre-school Children and the Need for Day Care*, London: HMSO.

Bradley, M. (1982) *The Co-ordination of Services for Children under Five*, Windsor: NFER-Nelson.

Department of Education and Science (DES) (1987) *Statistical Bulletin 9/87*, London: HMSO.

House of Commons (1989) *Education Provision for the Under Fives* (vol. 1), Education, Science and Arts Committee, London: House of Commons.

London Borough of Greenwich (1989) *Education in Greenwich: Planning a Smooth Transfer*, Greenwich Education Development Plan.

London Borough of Hammersmith and Fulham (1989) *Education in 1990: Getting it Right*, Hammersmith and Fulham Education Development Plan.

London Borough of Southwark (1989) *Future Management Arrangements of Under Fives Service*, Report to Social Services Committee, 1 January 1989.

Manchester City Council (1986) *Development of Childcare Provision*, Report to the Under-Fives Sub-Committee of Education.

—— (1988) *Children's Centre Building Programme – Phase 2*, Report to the Children's Centres Working Party and Policy Resources Committee, July.

MORI (1986) *Childcare Facilities for the Under Fives*, A survey of mothers' attitudes for Manchester City Council, Equal Opportunities and Social Services Committee, July.

Penn, H. (1988) 'Strathclyde's under fives initiatives: are there lessons for London?', Paper to ALA Discussion Forum on the Under Fives, October.

Pugh, G. (1988) *Services for Under Fives: Developing a Coordinated Approach*, London: National Children's Bureau.

Strathclyde Pre-Five Unit (1988) *Progress Report 1987–88*, Strathclyde: Strathclyde Regional Council.

Strathclyde Regional Council (1985) *Under Fives, Final Report of the Member/Officer Group*, Strathclyde: Strathclyde Regional Council.

Chapter 8

Attempting to integrate under fives
Policy in Islington, 1983–8

Margaret Boushel, Claire Debenham, Lisa Dresner and Anna Gorbach

During the 1980s Margaret Boushel, Claire Debenham, Lisa Dresner and Anna Gorbach worked in the London borough of Islington within social services for pre-school children. This chapter is an account of the way they perceived attempts to develop integrated provision for under fives and the barriers in attitudes and systems which were encountered. The first section provides an overview of provision and services in 1983. The next section describes attempts to create a clear under-fives policy. The third section looks at the faltering progress towards integrated services. The fourth section examines the formidable barriers that were posed by reorganisation of social services, local authority cuts and the demise of the Inner London Education Authority. The chapter concludes with a mixture of resignation and determination.

1 BACKGROUND: UNDER-FIVES SERVICES IN ISLINGTON, 1983

Islington is a multi-ethnic, inner city London borough with a child population of 29,000.

In 1982, 44 per cent of under fives in Islington had the use of an under-fives facility, 29 per cent on a full-time and 15 per cent on a part-time basis. Between 1982 and 1988 provision gradually increased, so that by 1988 there were 12 children's day centres, about 70 playgroups and 350 assisted child-minding places funded partially or totally through the Social Services Department, and 1,075 full-time and 824 part-time places in nursery schools funded by the Inner London Education Authority.

The Beacon Nursery, a local Mencap project, offered care five days per week to children over one year of age categorised as having severe learning difficulties. Unlike council day centres, playgroups or community nurseries, the Beacon Nursery was free. Children were collected from home by special bus and places were available on demand. The Beacon had been in existence for many years and in the past had catered for up to thirty children with a wide range of disabilities and needs. By 1983 it had half that number on roll. Since 1983 numbers at the Beacon continued to fall as it was increasingly seen as a resource for children with severe and multiple disabilities. In addition the Elfreda Rathbone organisation, a voluntary organisation helping people with learning disabilities, ran a free day nursery in the borough for a small number of children with learning difficulties.

Some integrated services emerged in the early 1980s – one playscheme was developed through a parent's initiative, and an integrated adventure playground was established by a voluntary organisation. Workers from the integrated playscheme subsequently supported a local special school in integrating under fives into a playgroup.

In addition to its mainstream schools, the borough included five special schools providing primary and secondary education to children with special needs from Islington and neighbouring boroughs – one for children with moderate learning difficulties, one for children with severe learning difficulties, one for children with emotional and behavioural difficulties, one for autistic children, and one for children with physical disabilities. In 1983 three of these offered nursery places to children from the age of 2.

The children using all of these services came from a wide range of ethnic backgrounds, though rarely was this actively and positively reflected in the type of care provided or the ethnic background of their carers.

Residential units

By 1983 residential services were designed with 'care in the community' in mind, but most were based in specialist settings. For example, Field End House had been open for three years as a specialist unit for children with learning difficulties, and was designed to offer respite 'round the clock' care. Parents had fought for this as a local resource to prevent the need for children to be placed in long-stay placements far from home. By 1988 Field End had been joined by another specialist children's respite care unit at Leigh Road.

The Social Services Department also provided thirteen short-term and long-term residential units for children in care (by 1988 their number had been reduced to eleven), none with wheelchair access and only one with any experience of caring for children with learning difficulties.

The Community Health Team

The Community Health Team had major responsibility for assessing children and recommending provision. It included physiotherapists, occupational and speech therapists, doctors, psychologists and a specialist health visitor. They were joined in the network by specialist teachers, funded by the ILEA and based in the special schools, who visited children at home before they were due to start school. This group of people met on a regular basis to coordinate services and discuss professional issues. Discussion of services to individual children also took place. This included deciding between day care or school, and parents' attitudes to different options. Often a member of the group was delegated to advise parents on a course of action.

The Community Health Team aim was to ensure a place of treatment for children from the earliest possible age, to enable them to develop to their fullest potential. They were, however, an all-White group, operating without directly involving parents and were generally committed to *specialist* care in the community. They gave support to the Beacon and Elfreda Rathbone nurseries and most members saw these settings as the best places to 'treat' children. Because of their early contact with parents they often had considerable influence in steering parents towards specialist provision.

The Special Services Team

In the early 1980s social workers were funded jointly by the ILEA and Islington Social Services Department to work with children attending two special schools and two specialist units for 'partially hearing' children. These social workers were based in the borough's Special Services Team. They all worked with some under fives attending the schools they covered. They were aware of a number of pre-school children who did not have adequate access to resources or support when parents and professionals were becoming aware of the possible extent and implications of the disability.

When a vacancy arose within this group of social workers in 1983 it was decided to appoint someone specialising in work with under fives with special needs. This might have had the effect of drawing families into the specialist system at an earlier stage. Instead, for a number of reasons, it proved to be a key step in the development of the debate about integration in Islington.

First, the post was not attached to any specialist institution. There was an expectation but not a contractual obligation that the postholder would work closely with the Beacon Nursery. Second, the worker had an alternative peer group of under-fives workers who were key figures in controlling access to all other under-fives facilities. Third, the worker was committed to the idea that treatment of a medical or disabling condition should not take precedence over the child's social, emotional and cultural needs. There was now a new worker in the network who also made an early relationship with families but who could present a broader choice of day care to parents.

2 ATTEMPTING AN INTEGRATION POLICY

The Labour Council, elected in 1982, had as a stated policy aim that every child whose parents so wished was entitled to a pre-school place of some sort. This led to the initiation of an under-fives review. The review team, set up under the auspices of the Social Services Committee, included councillors, senior departmental management and representatives of the children's day centre organisers and under-fives social workers in its membership. It proposed a network of under-fives centres throughout the borough – an idea which the under-fives workers had been anxious to promote for some time. Day care in each area would be organised and coordinated through the children's day centres which would also provide information, support and resources to parents.

The review had made no mention of children with special needs. The specialist social worker and another under-fives worker with a personal interest in the issues undertook a supplementary review to examine resources for these children. They interviewed parents, specialist professionals and mainstream daycare workers and they designed a questionnaire which was completed by workers in a large proportion of mainstream council services and voluntary organisations, as well as by some child-minders.

Broadly, the survey confirmed that parents of children with special needs had not been given a real choice of placement, and that they had to fight hard for mainstream provision if this was their choice. Parents wanted to be part of the decision-making and did not feel that they were. Many commented on lack of information about the range of facilities on offer. One Afro-Caribbean woman described how she felt that she was never given a choice of provision for her son, and objected to being told he should be in a specialist nursery for his own good. She fought hard to get him a part-time playgroup place in the group his older brother attended. Because the group had known her and her children for some time they agreed to 'have a go' and the placement went ahead. She commented:

> I had to fight every step of the way for this. No one told me about it, and no one wanted him to have it. I knew it was right for him – this is where he learnt to join in and be like other children. It doesn't matter that he's not like them. I know what is right for my child, but I'm not supposed to say.

Parents also wanted an increased availability of specialist 'therapy' time, but wanted it to be used in a more flexible way. Some parents were very worried that more integrated settings would lead to lack of attention for children with special needs.

Definitions of 'special needs' varied widely in the questionnaire responses – some defining it as children with disabilities, some including children with behavioural and emotional problems and some including children whose first language was not English. This made the survey difficult to interpret.

The findings were documented in a report *A Place For All Our Children* (CCUF 1983) and an analysis was prepared of the practical and bureaucratic problems in gaining an ordinary childcare place for a child with special needs, with suggestions for how these might be overcome. These ideas were informed by a paper which had already been produced by an active member of the local Mencap group, who had previously tried to generate the debate within the Community Health Service through the Mencap committee.

The conference: 'A place for all our children'

As a result of this work the Coordinating Committee for Under Fives (CCUF), an umbrella organisation of statutory and voluntary sector groups and individuals providing a service to under fives, decided to organise a conference to look at the issues of integration of special needs children within mainstream provision.

Prior to the conference various groups met to produce short contributions to the debate. These included parents, under-fives workers, specialist workers, children's day centre organisers and playgroups organisers. Each of these groups came up with a list of proposals which were sent to everyone attending.

About 230 people attended the conference, held in April 1985. Workshops facilitated by the speakers and the conference organising group examined integration policies, overcoming practical problems for children in integrated provision and available sources of information.

The conference made the following recommendations:

1 For a formal, universal information system, covering local and specialist resources.
2 For children's needs to be considered with parents and their wishes acknowledged and recognised.
3 For employment of extra staff where needed, and employment of peripatetic special needs workers.
4 For availability of money for equipment, toys and adaptations.
5 For enhanced payments to child-minders caring for children with special needs.
6 For priority status for children with special needs in order to facilitate access to ordinary provision.
7 For training facilities for staff in ordinary provision, specialist provision and child-minders.
8 For greater communication and sharing of resources between ordinary and specialist provision.
9 For therapeutic and professional staff to reflect the cultural backgrounds of the children, and that for all children, including those with special needs, their day-care environment and activities to express a consciousness of the multicultural society in Islington.

It was made clear that all of the above areas needed funding from health, education and social services before they could be implemented. Finally, it was felt that unless the attitudes of advisers and information-givers became more positive towards integration, none of the recommendations could be effective. The Social Services Department had responsibility for carrying out many of the recommendations of the conference. The message came loud and clear from all quarters that until council services were more welcoming to children with special needs, parents would continue to choose specialist provision out of caution.

Unfortunately, at this point neither senior management staff in the Social

Services Department nor the local councillors involved in the conference presented the Conference Report to the Social Services Committee for ratification as council policy. The core group who organised the conference were basic grade workers in the department who did not know the processes by which policy change is effected. As a result there was no informed discussion within the department or at the Social Services Committee about resource issues and the status of the recommendations remained vague.

The sub-committee

In the absence of official support we established a Special Needs Sub-committee of the Coordinating Committee for Under Fives to further the conference recommendations and the proposals of The Fish Report (ILEA 1985) on special education provision within ILEA, which favoured integration. The group eventually included representatives from health, education and social services with a small representation of parents and voluntary groups.

Battles were waged in meetings of the sub-committee and the level of organisational resistance to change became clear. Many community health workers attended and expressed their scepticism about moves to greater integration. They said children needed trained professionals to care for them and carry out their treatment programmes. They also felt that specialist workers could pass on skills and ideas to others, but it would take time. If children were integrated, workers would have to travel to many different centres and spend time training carers. Their aim was care in the community, but not anywhere in the community!

Interestingly, few of the workers at the Beacon or Elfreda Rathbone had 'specialist' training, but they had experience of specialist segregated provision and an approach which focused on the 'special needs' of a child rather than on 'total needs'.

3 THE PROGRESS OF INTEGRATION

Despite professional and organisational inertia and resistance, some things did happen! There were a number of areas where greater willingness was apparent to include children with special needs and make services more locally responsive.

Day-care provision

Successful integrated day-care placements for under fives were negotiated by the specialist social worker and the parents, or sometimes the parents alone or the parents with another committed individual. It involved hard work and long discussions, dealing with fears, anxieties and practical problems, which needed to continue long after the child had been placed. Even when day centres or playgroups were willing they were often still very nervous, and afraid of making mistakes. This could lead to over-protectiveness and care had to be taken to ensure that a child was involved in all the group's activities.

Playgroups

Following the CCUF conference playgroups responded most rapidly. To some degree they had already been catering for children with special needs. Because of their small size and their close connections with local parents, playgroups were responsive and flexible in their way of working. Despite unsuitable premises, lack of funding and a dearth of promised support from the council, many groups tried hard to accommodate children's needs. Their staff were generally willing to 'have a go', and with some information and support went a long way in challenging their own attitudes and those of other children and parents. Some children moved out of specialist provision into playgroups (full or part time) and made considerable strides in social relationships, becoming part of a community and friendship network which continued into their schooldays, whether or not they went to special school at 5 years.

Day centres

Some individual placements were being made in children's day centres. Although it was policy for all children to be welcome in council provision, in reality this was highly variable. Access was dependent on parents receiving the information and encouragement to apply, experiencing the organiser and staff of the centre as welcoming and willing to learn about and accommodate the child's needs. They had to be willing, too, to wait for a place to become available.

Some extremely successful placements have been made in council day centres. Sometimes centres were able to relieve any additional pressure on staff by allocating the equivalent of two places to one child. In some cases extra support has been unnecessary.

Child-minding

A few children were also placed with child-minders, who were awarded additional payments by the council if the child required sufficient extra attention that s/he needed to take up more than one place. This led to battles with senior management who questioned the status of the policy decision to implement the new system.

The specialist nursery

The Beacon Nursery was taken over by the council, as requested by Mencap. This could have provided opportunities for structural change and review. These never took place. Senior management failed to take a lead in clarifying the role of the Beacon in the department's services to under fives. What did happen was that the nursery staff felt themselves to be part of a wider childcare system and took advantage of formal and informal links. There was exchange of information and sometimes of staff and children. The nursery was also influenced by the council's equal opportunities policies – for example, staff took part in a conference considering anti-racist strategies with under fives. A consideration of these ideas fostered the recognition that the children had social, racial and cultural identities as well as disabilities. As a result of more able children taking up integrated placements or moving into school, the Beacon was now catering for a very small number of multiply disabled children, who were highly segregated as a result.

Residential provision

As a result of two consultation days held to examine possibilities for greater integration in residential provision for children and young people with special needs, a series of recommendations were made to and accepted by the Social Services Committee in January 1987. These included: developing a respite care service, improving mobility access in children's residential units, providing disability awareness training, developing a coordinated assessment and review system for all children and developing services for young adults. Most of these recommendations affected services for under fives.

Respite care

The Family Care Scheme, which provided care for children in their own homes, was from its inception open to children with disabilities and their families. Again, this was possible, at least in part, because the scheme coordinator was personally committed to such provision. Following the consultation days a pilot respite care scheme was begun offering twenty days respite care per year to ten families, to be planned at times and in ways to suit the families concerned. Priority is being given to children with physical disabilities for whom no other respite care service exists in the borough.

Access

At the time of the consultation exercise no children's home in the borough had mobility access. Since then plans were drawn up to make one short-term unit and one longer-term unit accessible. On completion, the use of day and residential facilities, including a family flat, were to be available to parents and children with physical disabilities or sensory impairments.

Disability awareness

A small group of specialist and non-specialist staff and a couple of parents of children with special needs together devised a two-day training course on disability awareness, directed in the first instance at staff working with young children. The course included information and discussions about discrimination, legal issues, support services, parents' views and shared care. Parents, staff with disabilities, and specialist and non-specialist staff from the department and from local voluntary organisations were involved in running the course. It was attended by workers with under fives, children's residential staff and Family Care Scheme staff and found very useful. Staff were particularly positive about the contributions from parents, the information on the support available from local specialist workers, and the practical information on such things as lifting techniques, epileptic attacks, which was provided.

4 BARRIERS IN THE SYSTEM

From 1985 onwards a number of additional formidable barriers to progress towards a coherent, integrated under-fives policy began to emerge.

Reorganising social services

After 1985 the Social Services Department underwent fundamental structural change as its ten area teams, including under-fives workers, were redistributed to twenty-four Neighbourhood Offices as part of the council's decentralisation policy. Field, day and residential services changed to an integrated line management structure, so that all day and residential services were managed through the Neighbourhood Office in which they were situated. The Department was reorganised into five geographical districts, each managed by an assistant director who also had a responsibility for particular service areas. The way these responsibilities were divided presented particular difficulties in work on integration. Three different assistant directors had responsibilities relating to children with disabilities – one for under fives, another for older children and their families, and a third for adults with physical and learning disabilities! Each Neighbourhood Office was allocated a half-time under-fives worker post, despite a large increase in workload. It was almost inevitable that this would have a negative effect on any innovative work. The issue of integration began to lose its visibility. Attitudes, especially among new senior staff, were often at variance with the council's stated philosophy towards under fives generally and towards integration in particular.

The cuts

As a result of central government policies, Islington social services suffered 8 per cent *cuts* in 1987/8 and all departments were asked to produce proposals for cuts of up to a further 25 per cent which they might have to achieve over the next two years. Cuts of that level would decimate the existing service and make it almost impossible for underdeveloped areas of the service such as facilities for children with physical disabilities, imaginative respite, and family-based care schemes and improved under-fives facilities to be developed.

Under-fives services were not identified as a priority. Instead, it proposed that the Beacon and six other children's day centres be closed over the next two years, with an increase in supported child-minding placements to compensate, in part, for this loss. The care provided by the Beacon was to transfer to special units in the remaining children's day centres. It is ironic that radical proposals for the integration of the Beacon, resisted by some specialist staff at all levels in the past, were now to be enforced by the cuts exercise. The danger was that the department would end up with the worst of both worlds – an integrated service provided in a hastily planned way, foisted on staff unprepared for the challenge and lacking the positive commitment and support that is so necessary from specialist staff and their managers.

The abolition of the ILEA

Legislation in 1988 brought with it the central government decision to abolish the Inner London Education Authority (ILEA) by 1990, despite the opposition of 93 per cent of parents in Inner London. For Islington this meant that in addition to taking over the day-to-day running and management of the pre-school, school and adult educational facilities in its area, the borough had to provide resources in areas previously funded by ILEA, London-wide. In particular these London-wide resources have been used to provide facilities for children with special needs in specialist day and boarding schools.

The borough brought in a group of consultants to produce topic papers on twelve of the major areas affected by abolition. These included issues of equality, special needs and services for under fives.

Before the decision on its abolition, the ILEA had already virtually abandoned the recommendations of The Fish Report, although some of the topic papers continued to support the idea of integration in general, unspecified ways. The paper on *Special Needs* however, written by a former director of the local ILEA division, raised the integration principle as one which was again open for discussion and decision. The document stated that the arguments for and against would be set out in some detail. The only argument stated in its favour, however, was to refer to The Fish Report ideas on equality. The author (Roy Price) then went on to state that integration may not be 'practicable'; and that 'segregation is a way to later integration'. He gave the example of a two-year Community Skills course in a local college that drew its recruits from the special schools. He also argued that the Campaign for Choice in Education advocated specialism. It so happened that a local head of a special school was very involved in this campaign. Finally, he suggested that opportunities for increased parent/governor control and 'opting-out' under the Education Reform Act might mean that schools would become more competitive and less likely to want to pursue integration. Most people in Islington, councillors included, were unlikely to have read The Fish Report or to be aware of the arguments put forward in it. In such a context Roy Price's description of the issues involved struck us as extremely lopsided.

The abolition of the ILEA also had a direct impact in the under-fives field. The under-fives topic paper suggested that all group provision for under fives should be organised through the new borough Education Department. This would lead to the transfer of children's day centres from social work to education and their possible future demise. It contained a plan to halve the number of places in children's day centres from 1989. The number of subsidised child-minding places was to be increased, but this would not provide the group experience that is such a valuable aspect of day centre provision. Neither would it allow for flexible staff allocation to meet the needs of children with particular disabilities. It was unclear where responsibility for child-minders, registration of playgroups, etc. would rest in the new organisation, but it was possible that the new provisions in the Children Bill going through Parliament would allow for those services to be provided through education departments.

Despite the difficulties in changing attitudes outlined in this chapter, there is little doubt that workers in mainstream social services provision were more prepared to accept the idea and practical implications of integration provision than those in mainstream education. In such a situation the future for integration looked bleak.

The transfer of ILEA responsibilities to the council meant that future decisions around integration and children would be mainly the brief of the new Education Committee. This committee was likely to be more responsive to lobbying and pressure from parents of children already in 'mainstream' schools and from the huge workforce in mainstream and specialist education. Such a powerbase is potentially much more difficult to change in the interests of a small discrimi-nated-against group.

The cuts and internal reorganisation in the ILEA also resulted in a total turn-about on decisions concerning the specialist social worker post. When the post-holder left in December 1987, the post was redesignated to a special school. Once again all social workers in the Special Services Team were to be attached to special schools with under fives inevitably drawn into the specialist system again. Shortly after this regressive move the post was cut completely.

5 CONCLUDING REMARKS

In 1988, integrated placements are still being achieved 'against the tide'. There was still a lack of commitment to integration from social services, health and education, even though individuals within those services were becoming increas-ingly willing to help. Parents were still placed under enormous pressure to choose specialist resources 'in the interests of the child': integrated placements were often presented as chiefly fulfilling a selfish need of the parents to deny their child's special needs.

A coordinated assessment and review system for all children had proved diffi-cult to develop. Children with disabilities and their parents tend to have most contact with specialist health, education and social services during the child's early years. Until the three agencies actively involve parents and staff from non-specialist areas in their assessment and review procedures and give equal weight to the promotion and consideration of integrated placements, such placements will remain a rarity.

Staff and parents need to be strongly motivated to seek an integrated placement in a children's day centre or nursery school. The local specialist nursery for children with learning difficulties had a much shorter waiting list and took children from the age of 2. Within social services, respite care for children with learning difficulties was provided by the local specialist units. It demanded interest and commitment on the part of the workers to try and set up respite fostering or other more integrated arrangements as an alternative.

Placements are most successful when the policy-makers and professionals involved have a positive attitude to exploring integrated care and are willing to support the care-givers and the parents. Too often, unnecessary organisational problems undermine the process. At the end of 1987, three years after the conference 'A Place For All Our Children', one council day centre offered a place to a child with a 'learning difficulty'. Some days later some staff raised objections at a staff meeting and the offer was withdrawn. Because council officers still fail to enforce council policy and because individuals involved in management are still unwilling to grasp the nettle and take up the argument the child lost the place.

Cost is not everything. It is very obvious from our experience that attitude is at least as crucial as cost, and arguments around cost sometimes act as a smoke-screen for negative attitudes.

It is now more important than ever, as we endure and try to resist the demolition of the Welfare State, that children with special needs and their families do not suffer a disproportionate reduction in services. The shift in policy, attitudes and provision begun in the moves towards integration must be continued.

REFERENCES

Coordinating Committee for Under Fives (CCUF) (1983) *A Place For All Our Children*, London: London Borough of Islington, Social Services Department.

Inner London Education Authority (ILEA) (1985) *Educational Opportunities for All?* (The Fish Report), London: ILEA.

Chapter 9

Community play

Veronica Hanson

Source: Hanson, V. (1989) 'Community play', *Special Children*, September, pp. 22–3 (see Acknowledgements).

In this article, Veronica Hanson describes a scheme that was set up by the Welsh Pre-school Playgroups Association (PPA) to encourage the integration into local playgroups of children who experience difficulties in learning. There is national funding for the scheme. Veronica Hanson describes the stages that the PPA proposal had to go through to be accepted by the Welsh Office and she goes on to describe how the county schemes are supported, managed and run now that they are in operation.

1 INTRODUCTION

Members of the Pre-School Playgroups Association (PPA) in Wales (which became an independent association in 1987) are so convinced of each family's right to choice of provision for their children that they have taken positive steps to make this possible. County 'referral schemes' have been established to ease the integration of children with special needs into the local playgroup or mother and toddler group. Once a family contacts or is referred to the referral scheme coordinator every assistance is given to that family to link into their local community group to ensure that the group is physically suitable and that any special assistance needed to enable the child to attend the group and enjoy its activities is provided.

Playgroups and mother and toddler groups offer safe and stimulating play opportunities for the children and friendship for mother and child. Playgroups are set up and managed by parent members of the group, usually through a committee and employing a playgroup leader. The groups take place in a church or chapel hall or other community building and are supported by PPA voluntary area organisers and a network of volunteers at branch, county and Wales level.

2 FINDING THEIR WAY

Children with special needs have long been welcomed into playgroups or mother and toddler groups but members have tended to worry on two counts – first, that only a minority of families with children with special needs were finding their way to playgroup, and second that the playgroup was not fully able to meet the children's needs. Two counties, Clwyd and South Glamorgan, took the lead and the nucleus of a PPA special needs referral scheme was established in each county in the early 1980s.

In 1983 the Welsh Office produced a document – *The All Wales Strategy for the Development of Services for Mentally Handicapped People/Strategaeth Cymru Gyfan Datblygiad Gwasanaethau Pobl dan Anfantais Meddyliol*. This document proclaimed to the people of Wales that members of a society with mental handicap had a right to the same services as everyone else, had the right to be treated as individuals, and might need special assistance to make this possible. The Welsh Office promised funding to initiatives developed by county social services departments in conjunction with voluntary organisations and families.

Members of Wales PPA quickly realised that these published beliefs were the same as their own, and that here was perhaps an opportunity to avail themselves of much-needed funding to establish support systems which would enable families to take their rightful place in the local playgroup or mother and toddler group. Development of an All Wales Strategy has involved long discussions at county level between social services department personnel, representatives from voluntary organisations, parents and sometimes consumers. PPA volunteers joined these discussions with a view to offering playgroups and mother and toddler groups as a resource for young children with mental handicap – an opportunity for integration right from the start. If integration at school age and afterwards is to be a real possibility a family with a handicapped child needs to be involved in the community, making friends and developing natural support systems from the beginning.

Every local authority was required to submit a county development plan for acceptance by the Welsh Office before funds were released. PPA members sought to have their 'referral schemes' adopted and given high priority within the county plan. This involved PPA volunteers and staff in the tripartite consultations at county level, the preparation of budget submissions, agonising waits while plans were considered, elation when funding was agreed, disappointment when refused, months of hard work to set up a scheme or, when necessary, to re-draft the plan to try for funding again.

3 LIAISON

In 1985 the Welsh Office agreed to fund a Special Needs Liaison Officer for Wales PPA for three years to support the referral schemes in the counties. By 1987 seven county-based PPA referral schemes had been established and a branch scheme set up in the eighth county. Funding for the schemes is varied. Every county has received some support from All Wales Strategy sources varying from core funding for a coordinator and placement costs for children with mental handicap to one-off grants or payment of incidental expenses. Every county has had to seek additional funding to support placement costs for children who do not have a mental handicap. Understandably there is reluctance within the authorities to diagnose a child under 5 as having a mental handicap, and there is a move to relax the criteria to include children with developmental delay amongst those eligible for funding.

Alternative or additional funding has been sought from social services departments (non-Strategy), health authorities, education departments, Children in Need, trusts, and by fundraising. Two schemes received grant aid from Under Fives Initiative (Wales) which came to an end in March 1988.

Each PPA county referral scheme is responsible for the finance and general administration of the scheme and employment of the coordinator. The financial requirements involve funding to employ a part-time coordinator and staff support for the scheme, expenses for coordinator and volunteers, training, publicity and placement costs for the child. Placement costs vary according to need but are likely to involve token payment for an extra helper within the playgroups and may include transport cost and playgroup fees. A toy library may be run in conjunction with the scheme.

The referral scheme works in conjunction with statutory bodies and professionals from the social services and education departments and health authorities who will be invited to referral scheme management groups. Coordinator and parent and playgroup will seek advice and support from the professionals involved with the child when this is appropriate – health visitor, social worker, physiotherapist, speech therapist, community mental handicap team. Essential equipment to enable a child to participate in a group may be provided, opportunities for training may be shared.

4 STATEMENTS

The playgroup leader may be asked if she will support the parents' contribution to the Statement of special educational needs by describing the child's participation at playgroup, his needs and capabilities, adaptation and behaviour. The playgroup leader will usually offer her observations as part of the parents' contribution to the Statement. She will not, indeed cannot, make any form of assessment but will, in discussion with the parent, describe the activities the child enjoys and his responses to playgroup life in a relaxed, familiar and friendly atmosphere.

The educational psychologist may be invited to observe a child at playgroup should this be deemed useful but will not, as a rule, carry out a formal assessment during playgroup time which would thus single the child out from his/her peers and probably deprive the other children of their leader's care.

PPA special needs referral schemes link into training courses organised generally by PPA within Wales and within the county – special needs is integrated into every foundation course and basic course. Training opportunities for helpers in the groups, for coordinators and management committees are offered. Short 'special needs' courses or informal talks may be arranged to develop confidence and awareness and understanding of integration.

Part 3

Life after school

Chapter 10

An international perspective on transition

John Fish

In this chapter John Fish draws on his experience working with the Organisation for Economic Co-operation and Development (OECD) to provide an international perspective on the opportunities in work, training and education for young people with disabilities or learning difficulties. He discusses the need for improving education and training and the way the contexts for transition to adult life have changed in the United Kingdom. He argues for the coordination of agencies involved in supporting young people and considers the major issues these agencies need to address. A number of initiatives in Europe and the United States are described. Finally he considers the part education should play.

1 INTRODUCTION

Transition from school to adult and working life has been receiving increased attention in most developed countries over the last decade. At first this was because of high levels of youth unemployment and latterly because of demographic trends. These show a growing number of older people entering active retirement and much smaller youth age groups entering employment. As a result it is important to create as many wage-earners and taxpayers as possible. A smaller labour market creates a window of employment opportunity for minority groups, including those who are disabled. It presents a chance to establish employment as a natural conclusion to education and training for these groups.

In many instances expectations have been too low. When decisions about employability are based on school performance rather than on work experience, training opportunities are often limited. Recent developments have shown that appropriate education, training and direct experience of work and living away from home, can enable a very significant proportion of those with severe disabilities to maintain themselves in employment and independent life.

For more than ten years the Centre for Educational Research and Innovation (CERI) of the Organisation for Economic Co-operation and Development (OECD) has been studying aspects of integration and transition for young people who are disabled. A number of reports on issues and innovations have been published (OECD 1986, 1987, 1988).

Although the cultural traditions and education and social systems in OECD member countries vary there has been wide agreement about the importance of transition and the nature of the process. The work has led to the development of a conceptual framework for a period which is both a phase and a process. It is a time-phase between childhood and adulthood and a process of changing from a pupil to an independent working adult.

There is also agreement about many major issues which need to be addressed. Finally, there are a number of effective innovations which have been studied in detail. If the handicapping effects of disabilities are to be minimised, appropriate education, training and support between the early teens and the middle twenties is essential.

2 THE NEED FOR EDUCATION AND TRAINING

The educational achievements of nearly half of all those completing the compulsory school period in the United Kingdom leave a lot to be desired. In addition, the academic standards of those receiving special education in secondary and special schools are not always impressive. It is one of the inequalities of the education system that the more successful you are the longer you can remain in it and thus delay independence and entry to work.

Higher and flexible skill levels are now required in the labour market – an objective endorsed by both the CBI and TUC (CBI 1989). This is a major reason for attention to transition. But, as a recent OECD publication *Labour Market Policies for the 1990s* (OECD 1990a) has shown, the United Kingdom, of all member countries, had the second lowest percentage of young people in full- or part-time education at the age of 17 in 1986–7. Although there has been some improvement, comprehensive preparation for an adult life, which includes employment, is not readily available to all who might need it.

In a European context there are many countries where a high proportion of the school population stay in school or technical education until after the age of 18. In Scandinavia and North America it is rare for young people with severe disabilities to be expected to enter employment and to live independently until after education and training up to the early twenties.

3 THE CHANGING CONTEXTS

There is new legislation affecting every aspect of transition in the United Kingdom. Those responsible for post-school education cannot ignore the changing context in which their work takes place. The Education Reform Act 1988 creates a new basis, the National Curriculum, from which to develop the further education contribution. It also creates a new framework for further and continuing education where marketing, effective performance and an appropriate response to community needs are increasingly important.

Social and Health Services have the Disabled Persons Act 1986. The parts being implemented require that a life (transition) plan be prepared with in-dividuals in collaboration with other agencies. Sections concerned with the representation of disabled persons' interests are not being implemented at present.

The Children Act 1989 also requires greater cooperation between depart-ments where the needs of children with disabilities are concerned. This will be particularly true in the final years of school and in the initial preparation of an individual transition plan.

'Care in the community', in whatever form it is introduced, will have a significant effect on transitions. The movement of individuals from institutional care to supporting arrangements in the community, the support of more people in their own homes, and the general management of disabilities by social services through individual care packages all create a new context to which a contribu-tion from further education and training will be essential. Changes are also taking place in the benefit system which it is hoped may provide more flexible support for those who are disabled, and enhance their employment possibilities.

Finally, new employment and training arrangements are being introduced through Training and Enterprise Councils. These will influence what education and training is available to support transition, how it is managed in an area, and who has access to it.

Education can only contribute one element to successful transition. To be really effective, lecturers and tutors must be sensitive to the contexts in which their institutions function and work closely with other training partners towards common ends.

4 COORDINATION AND CONTINUITY

Although an individual makes many important transitions in a lifetime, that from school through adolescence to adult life is one of the most important. For a young person with a disability or learning difficulty this transition is crucial.

Transition is a personal and confused process for the individual but for national, local and voluntary departments and agencies it is a period of divided responsibilities and fragmentation. During the compulsory school period there are usually only two centres, home and school, which coordinate services for children. After that period there are many independent contributors. The secondary school, the further education college and the adult education service, health, social and employment services, all have potential contributions to make as have voluntary agencies.

This confusion between providers is compounded by the different definitions used by departments and agencies to identify their clients. For example, Educa-tion Acts use relative definitions of performance separating disability and performance but the 1986 Disabled Persons Act uses 1948 social security defini-tions of disability. Some definitions may be administrative, others functional and some may encompass a wider group than others. After school, individuals can move into and out of departmental definitions.

There are also attempts by agencies to establish an ownership of clients. This is particularly evident where funding to agencies depends on clients served. This may involve developing life plans with the individuals for whom they are responsible in isolation from other agencies.

With so many players, in addition to the most important one – the young person – it is not surprising that there are no clear aims for the transition process. Indeed, in many countries, one government department may be paying huge sums to enable those with disabilities to become employable and to live independently while another is paying out larger sums as long as they remain dependent and unemployable.

Even if a coordinated approach to transition is difficult to achieve it should be possible for all concerned to agree a broad range of aims for transition. The OECD/CERI programme (OECD 1986) has identified four general areas in which detailed objectives should be developed:

- Employment, useful work and valued activity.
- Personal autonomy, independent living and adult status.
- Social interaction, community participation, leisure and recreation.
- Adult roles within the family including marriage.

Progress towards the achievement of these aims requires inter-agency collaboration. To pursue one aim, such as employment, in isolation from the others, such as the ability to travel to and from work and get on with other people, is ineffective.

Continuity is another significant ingredient in effective transition. OECD/CERI work has identified three stages of the process – the final school years, further education and training, and the early years of employment and independent living – between which a continuity of approach is vital.

5 MAJOR ISSUES IN TRANSITION

A number of issues are common to national and international contexts. They provide a useful agenda for discussion:

The starting point

Consideration of the process of transition needs to begin in the early years of secondary education. The place of education is also important. Attendance at a special school may automatically limit the choices subsequently offered to individuals when expectations are low and stereotyped.

The importance of further and continuing education is that valuable opportunities can be offered for individual self-appraisal and for the reassessment of potential together with the recognition of previous learning.

Inter-agency planning and collaboration

The United Kingdom is not alone in having traditional areas of responsibility and means of allocating resources which mitigate against joint planning and collaboration. Responsibility for individuals may be handed from one department or agency to another or individuals may be left to find their way through a maze of fragmented information, responsibilities and opportunities.

Empowerment

To fail to make a distinction between a disability and its handicapping effects at different times and in different situations may limit expectations. Effective education, experience and training can significantly reduce the handicaps which may arise from disabilities. Similarly, a lack of knowledge about the nature of transitions and uncertainty about relevant goals for those with disabilities may inhibit progress. Professional and agency ownership of clients is also a major barrier to empowerment.

Transitional programmes should develop self-advocacy (FEU 1990a) and should result in the individual being supported and empowered to make decisions and plan his or her life. But the shift of power from parents and professionals to individuals with disabilities, especially those who require considerable physical care, is difficult to manage.

Professionals and services have to manage the dual, and often conflicting, roles of support and empowerment. Ambivalence and uncertainty in departmental and agency policies and in the aspirations and practices of professionals, together with uncertainty about client demands, are all factors which work against empowerment.

Work with parents

Little professional work with parents is undertaken after the compulsory school period. Parents have a crucial role to play in preparing their children for an independent adult life but may in practice unwittingly inhibit that progress.

As work for the Further Education Unit (FEU 1990b) has shown, sensitive support is necessary to enable many parents to face the issues arising from their children's autonomy, empowerment and adulthood. Supporting arrangements are rarely readily available. The importance of parental support in effective transition cannot be overestimated.

Assessment

Transitional needs can only be met by assessment which both avoids categorisation and looks at *all* the future needs of the individual.

Assessment should be concerned with potential and the future education, training and support an individual might need. It is also important to recognise that, for many of those with disabilities, performance in one situation, such as school, is not always a good guide to performance in real living and working situations. Too often decisions are:

1   based on past performance;
2   confined to the requirements of one sector, e.g. education or employment; and
3   seldom based on experience and training in real situations.

New legislation lays particular stress on appropriate assessment. It is becoming increasingly clear that a transition plan, developed with the individual during the final years of schooling, to which all agencies agree to contribute is the only practical way of coordinating local services.

Continuity of support

In the United Kingdom, as elsewhere, continuity of support for disabled individuals or their families through transition is rarely available. The development of appropriate mechanisms to initiate and sustain the continuity of support and funding is a problem common to OECD member countries. There is a need to provide a single point of reference (an individual guide or facilitator or a recognised team) for young people and their families throughout transition.

Professional rivalries often prevent a single person being the means by which services to meet individual needs are facilitated. It is also necessary to understand that many people with disabilities are apprehensive of well-managed services providing continuity. Such services may be seen as diminishing personal control and choice.

6   INNOVATIONS AND INITIATIVES

There are a number of interesting initiatives in the literature including those in the United Kingdom. Those reported here are from other countries. This is not because they are immediately transferable to this country but because they illustrate particular features of transition.

The final years of school

The work of Sailor and Wehman in the United States (Sailor *et al.* 1989, Wehman *et al.* 1989) stresses the importance of an effective programme for individuals in high school. *The Comprehensive Local School* (Sailor *et al.* 1989) gives details of school programmes.

Students with severe and profound disabilities and learning difficulties are entitled to attend high school up to the early twenties in the USA. Thus, the further education element in the United Kingdom is completed in the school system although community colleges do similar work, often with an older age group, in the United States.

Sailor's book sets out a systematic training programme for young people with severe disabilities (SLD in this country) based on modified behavioural approaches. This starts in the early teens and takes students into real living and working situations. Experiences in travelling, shopping and taking part in recreational activities in the community are carefully planned with clear behavioural objectives and criteria. Vocational preparation is done in real situations in the community but use is also made of situations within schools to learn social and work skills.

An individual transition plan

The Individual Education Plan (IEP) is a central feature of special education in the United States. An Individual Transition Plan is now being introduced to follow this. The purpose of such plans is to coordinate the contributions of different agencies towards agreed transition goals which have been planned with young people and their families. The features of such plans and examples of them can be found in the books of Wehman and Sailor.

A guide or point of reference

Because of the variety and confusion of possibilities and responsibilities after the compulsory school period the need for a guide has been widely recognised by young people and their families. In a study published by OECD/CERI a number of examples are given (OECD 1990b). One which has received considerable attention is the Kurator system in Denmark. A Kurator is similar to a specialist careers teacher with additional contributions to make after school.

The Kurator is a member of the school psychologist's team who teaches children with special educational needs and is responsible for their careers education and work experience. He or she has a number of non-teaching hours for work with young people and their families after they leave school. The time available and balance of the Kurator's work may vary from one municipality to another. Support can be offered for up to four years after school. The Kurator is a facilitator who works on request with young people and their families.

Supported employment

One of the most significant developments has been the increasing open employment of young people with severe disabilities, particularly severe intellectual disabilities. Research in the United States has shown the inadequacy of the sheltered workshop model where commercial objectives limit access for those with severe disabilities and where transfer to open employment is very limited. Supported open employment is much more successful. The Genoa approach is one identified by the OECD but there are others in the United States.

The importance of the Genoa experience is that it has the backing of employers and trade union organisations. Young people are placed in open employment and trained and supported by social service teams. Salary is paid by the province or state for the first year after which the employer accepts responsibility. Support teams work with employers and fellow workers in a training programme and are also on call if there are problems.

Results are impressive. In a city with 12 per cent unemployment 300 recent placements have resulted in an over 90 per cent job retention rate after the first three years of employment.

7 THE ROLE OF POST-SCHOOL EDUCATION

It is important that those concerned with post-school education for young people with disabilities and learning difficulties are informed about the context in which they work and have a grasp of the essential features of transition. They also need to be conversant with the main developments taking place in further and continuing education.

Many of the features of effective special education, such as individual programmes and the management of a wide variety of learning rates and styles, are now expected in the mainstream of education and training – for example, work in the Teaching and Vocational Educational Initiative. The labour market will need to make effective use of the smaller groups leaving school.

To increase the labour force will require that the potential of minority groups, including those with disabilities and learning difficulties, is recognised and that appropriate training and support for them is made available. The possible introduction of individual education and training vouchers for school leavers will also provide education and training with a new challenge.

Unless the youth group has adequate guidance and counselling, individuals may find choice difficult. Vouchers may also limit the opportunities of those with special needs unless their value is enhanced to make provision of good-quality training attractive.

A recognition that education post-school is a shared responsibility is vital. Parents, social workers and other carers have an educational role as do vocational training staff, employers and employees. This means that lecturers and tutors should work with them to develop programmes and curricula. But, above all, responsibility must be shared with the young person.

The development of self-presentation, self-advocacy and of self-directed learning should all be central features of this phase of education. Supporters of those with special needs should be exemplars of such good practice. Developments of this kind have been initiated and sustained, in recent years, by the Further Education Unit. Its publications (FEU 1986, 1988, 1989, 1990c) are an important source of guidance and good practice.

8 CONCLUSIONS

Post-school education for young people with disabilities and learning difficulties has had to be fought for. In the past the case has been based on the wish to delay an unstimulated life at home or admission to a training centre. Now the grounds are more positive, namely the right to be considered for employment and as a contributor to the economy. For the individual, employment may represent the most potent symbol of adult status and integration into the community. What is being sought by many is equality of opportunity and access.

However, there are also positive grounds for governments to invest in education and training for independence and employment. Research in Scandinavia and the United States has identified the cost of lifelong dependent care for those with disabilities as something developed economies cannot sustain in the future. Only by enabling those with disabilities to contribute, if they wish, through independent living and paid employment, will the increased percentage of ageing people be able to receive the support they expect and need.

Thus, the charity image of disability must disappear. Higher expectations and effective post-school education for those who have received special education in school is not a luxury but an economic necessity. The form that post-school education should take is a matter for major discussion beyond the scope of this review.

REFERENCES

Confederation of British Industries (CBI) (1989) *Towards a Skills Revolution*, London: CBI.

Further Education Unit (FEU) (1986) *Special Needs Occasional Papers*, London: FEU/ Longman.

—— (1988) *New Directions: A Curriculum Framework for Students with Severe Learning Difficulties*, London: FEU.

—— (1989) *Working Together?* London: FEU.

—— (1990a) *Developing Self-Advocacy Skills*, London: FEU.

—— (1990b) *Transition to Adult Life*, Bulletin no. 3, London: FEU.

—— (1990c) *Perceptions of Special Needs in Further Education*, London: FEU.

Organisation for Economic Co-operation and Development (OECD) (1986) *Young People with Handicaps: The Road to Adulthood*, Paris: OECD.

—— (1987) *Active Life for Young People with Disabilities*, Paris: OECD.

—— (1988) *Disabled Youth: The Right to Adult Status*, Paris: OECD.

—— (1990a) *Labour Market Policies for the 1990s*, Paris: OECD.

—— (1990b) *Bridging School to Work*, Paris: OECD.

Sailor, W., Anderson, P. L., Halvorsen, A. T., Doering, K., Filler, J. and Goetz, L. (1989) *The Comprehensive Local School: Regular Education for All Students with Disabilities*, New York: Paul H. Brookes.

Wehman, P., Moon, M. S., Everson, J. M., Wood, W. and Barcus, J. M. (1989) *Transition from School to Work: New Challenges for Youth with Severe Disabilities*, New York: Paul H. Brookes.

Chapter 11

The rhetoric and reality of transition to adult life

Jenny Corbett and Len Barton

In this chapter Jenny Corbett and Len Barton take a critical look at the concept of 'transition into adult life' for young people with disabilities and those categorised as having learning difficulties. They argue that the barriers to participation which exist in society should be given greater recognition. They discuss the approaches and difficulties encountered in further education and youth training. They describe a reality in which pressures to exclude and marginalise young people with disabilities or those categorised as having learning difficulties, are still very strong.

1 INTRODUCTION

This chapter examines the currently popular notion of 'transition to adulthood' in order to illustrate the complex and contentious nature of integration into adult life. It is a process of transition which all young people have to pass through but which is experienced differently as a result of such key factors as class, race, gender and disability (Cross and Smith 1987, Griffin 1985, Willis 1977). Integration into adult life is constricted within social and economic boundaries. 'Transition to adulthood' involves a wide diversity of progressions beyond school into further education, training programmes, employment and community living. The extent to which individuals are able to participate in employment, leisure and social interaction, for example, will be an indicator of the reality of their 'adulthood'.

This broad view offers a wider concept of 'integration' than the narrow educational framework which predominantly confines debate in this area. It also places 'transition' in a political arena in which the tensions between rhetoric and reality are highlighted. We are concerned to challenge the extent to which those involved in this restricted form of transition are offered any real choices in decision-making.

2 CONCEPTIONS OF 'TRANSITION'

A failure to address the nature of the society into which integration is being advocated reveals the fundamental weakness and inadequacy of much of the literature dealing with this issue. If integration is seen merely as a response to individual needs, then the unequal, offensive and divisive nature of society remains unchallenged. Given the degree and stubbornness of such inequalities, the topics that concern us are those of power, choice, entitlement and social justice: issues of rights, not needs.

The question of how to empower those people marginalised through disabilities and learning difficulties is, thus, a central one. Government documents and official statements concerning integration are replete with romantic and ill-defined language. The Warnock Report, for example, contends that there is a

> widely held and still growing conviction that, so far as is humanly possible, handicapped people should share the opportunities for self-fulfilment enjoyed by other people.
>
> (DES 1978: 99)

and the Council of Europe's Report on *Measures to Promote the Social Integration of Mentally Disabled People* states that:

> The integration of mentally disabled people into society means that persons with mental handicaps of any degree should be able to live as normal a life as possible.
>
> (Council of Europe 1986: 9)

Just as with these statements about integration, an unchallenged view of 'normality' is subsumed within the rhetoric of 'adulthood'. Adulthood is, thus, largely perceived in consensual terms with the emphasis being upon enabling the individual to be 'as normal as possible'. 'Normality' is a nebulous concept unless we ask whose normality is to be valued and emulated? As it is professionals who generally define what they regard as 'normality', this allows limited scope to negotiate flexible boundaries to accommodate a range of perspectives.

Abberley (1989) argues that the specific form of normality being advocated becomes disabling in itself as it inhibits expressions of difference. He claims, moreover, that such a view is

> not only profoundly mistaken as to the source and nature of the multiple disadvantages experienced by disabled people, but that its propagation, in the context of modern Britain, serves not to combat but to perpetuate the oppression of disabled people.
>
> (Abberley 1989: 56)

The argument of achieving 'self-fulfilment' and of 'living as normal a life as possible' is seriously flawed when set against the context of an environment that is essentially oppressive and unadaptive and in which professional power establishes and perpetuates patterns of dependency.

Opportunities for meaningful decision-making on the part of marginalised groups are largely cosmetic. Barnes (1990) made a recent study of the role of day centres for disabled young people, in which few opportunities were offered for significant decision-making despite the operation of ostensibly progressive policies. This research illuminated the contradictions of a transition from passive schooling to day centre provision. Where young people were not used to making independent decisions and had become conditioned by special education, they found this move into a more adult environment difficult to adjust to. Staff encouraged debate but these users

> apppeared to have little interest in the sort of discussion groups generally seen as furthering mutual support and understanding ... The more able in the group felt they 'couldn't tell us anything we don't already know' or they were 'depressing', while the remainder said that they did not like them because they made them feel inadequate.
>
> (Barnes 1990: 136)

It is not only the limitations of the day centre model of care but also the legacy of segregated schooling which makes taking over control so difficult.

'Transition to adulthood' suggests a journey to a substantive destination to which we all travel. However, the real passage which most of us experience is unpredictable and irregular. Griffiths argues that

> Adulthood is not recognised as a single event evident to everyone. Instead, a number of small changes in status and recognitions of the progress towards adult status takes place over a number of years.
>
> (Griffiths 1989: 5)

There is not one form of adult status but a hierarchy which reflects the way in which society values different groups. For those at the lowest levels, the quality of this transition places them in a severely restricted form of 'adulthood'.

For an increasing number of young people, 'transition' is into vagrancy. Recent research has illustrated that the raising of the minimum age of entitlement for Income Support in 1988 has forced young people to be dependent on their families and has inhibited their transition to adulthood (Harris 1988, Whynes and Ferris 1990). The majority of those young people who leave home to live rough are found not to have chosen this course but, rather, to have had it thrust upon them by circumstances. Hostels which offer short-term care for the young homeless find their clients are usually the most vulnerable and difficult (Hutton and Liddiard 1990).

This form of 'transition' from residential care or the family into homelessness can instil a sense of despair and dependency which becomes habitual. Wallace and Cross (1990) suggest that young people in the 1990s are no longer setters of trends but 'have become to some objects of pity and concern' (Wallace and Cross 1990: 7), more vulnerable and dependent than in the recent past.

3 TRANSITION THROUGH FURTHER EDUCATION

The whole concept of 'transition to adulthood' is problematic. The period affects all young people and involves a series of stages over a number of years, which are influenced by social and economic status. Yet for some it appears to form the focus of their curriculum. The curriculum for most young people who have left school involves academic or vocational courses which prepare them for specific adult roles. By contrast, a curriculum for young people with disabilities or learning difficulties often centres around a 'preparation for adulthood' as if this constitutes a recognisable area of study.

In the curriculum framework for students with severe disabilities called *Transition to Adulthood*, Hutchinson and Tennyson (1986) acknowledge that, despite the title of their curriculum and their aim of extending choice, their actual capacity to change current opportunities for students on completion of the programme is negligible. Thus, the rhetoric of choice and entitlement is met by the reality of devalued citizenship. The language of such curricula denies the real economic and cultural oppression experienced by disabled people. Yet Hutchinson and Tennyson are well aware of the frustrations facing their students and seek to combat them:

> Jealousy and resentment between the different agencies involved with disabled people are often deeply entrenched and extremely difficult to break down. 'Who pays for what' often results in essential facilities or care being postponed or withheld indefinitely whilst the 'professionals' argue the case amongst themselves.
>
> Alternatively, in the present economic climate, the power relationships between the different agencies may result in professionals vying to serve the needs of prospective clients since they have vested interests in defining the needs of their clients and expanding the numbers they serve in order to safeguard their own jobs. It is all too easy for this system to lead to a 'disabling' rather than an 'enabling' context for students' adult lives, thus negating the benefits of a college-based 'Transition to Adulthood' course.
>
> (Hutchinson and Tennyson 1986: 68–9)

The authors go on to offer examples of students whose transition from college has been one of experiencing limited choice and often unsuitable placements. They even suggest that

> Such problems lead us to question the purpose of a 'Transition to Adulthood' course. It is felt that much of the progress students make whilst in college will be lost if they are not able to go on to meet fresh demands in new situations.
>
> (Hutchinson and Tennyson 1986: 72)

If this form of 'transition' becomes simply a retrograde return to passivity, it can be seen as a complete negation of all that the college course sought to encourage:

Indeed, it has been said by some professionals in the field that we are doing the students a disservice by attempting to break through their apathy since their main chance of happiness lies in their passive acceptance of traditional 'care' facilities. Naturally, we as a staff find this attitude totally unacceptable. If nothing else we hope that by attending college the students will have gained the confidence and determination to go out into the community and demand that changes be made.

(Hutchinson and Tennyson 1986: 72)

Within this framework, 'transition' becomes a new form of responsibility and awareness, a way of viewing the situation.

A common practice of 'transition' is that from special school to college of further education. Despite a commitment to curriculum entitlement (FEU 1989), institutions have commonly narrowed opportunities by the provision of separate courses or by restricting the participation of disabled students in a full range of general education classes. Social and life skills classes have often been created with the overt intention of facilitating the integration of students with disabilities (Dee 1988), yet they may lack certification and have low academic status. Although notions of autonomy and self-advocacy are central to many courses, there is evident tension between the aims of course tutors and the constraints imposed by parents and post-college opportunities (Dee 1988, Wertheimer 1989). Such 'ghettoisation' is supported by the familiar practice of transferring special school staff and a skills-based curriculum into special needs departments in colleges.

A move towards student autonomy might be seen in an increasing emphasis upon the value of students entering into negotiation about their individual programmes, including the assessment process. However, Major (1990) argues that inequalities of power between student and teacher mitigate against any real negotiation. Fay (1988) also argues that 'negotiating' with students can be personally intrusive and involve a hidden assessment of 'qualities such as "willingness", "drive", "reliability" and even "self-awareness"' (Fay 1988: 27). Fay contends that such activities 'colonise private space' (Fay 1988: 27). An invasion of privacy into the lives of vulnerable individuals is masked by the rhetoric of empowerment with the implication that it is being 'done with rather than to trainees' (Fay 1988: 26).

4 TRANSITION TO YOUTH TRAINING

Another aspect of transition is that from school to youth training. This offers programmes in vocational areas such as carpentry, office skills, catering, hairdressing, building, word processing, banking, sport and the arts. These programmes are of two main kinds: the one based with employers offering the most favourable route to jobs; the other, workshop-based, simulating employment and with implications of unemployability. Hollands (1990) illustrates the way in which young people themselves challenge aspects of the training programmes:

> Some young people refuse to accept that they are deficient in the skills and cultures necessary for many working-class jobs. As such, they often see through life and social skills training and develop common-sense critiques of the curriculum.
>
> (Hollands 1990: 73)

In supporting a transition to adulthood, how does youth training differentiate between groups of young people? For some young Black trainees, disproportionately represented in workshop-based schemes, the programmes serve to shape them into acceptable employees within a market which discriminates against them and to ease them gently out of their aspirations into the reality of restricted choice (Corbett 1990). As this liaison officer recognised, the basic level of skills training equipped them only for unskilled work and they had to learn to cope with compromise:

> so that even if we get a young person coming out of the workshops that may not be the best electrician going, we can find them something in a related area – an electrical warehouse, where their knowledge of the bits that they know will be put to good use and they'll still be in that environment they want to work in.
>
> (Liaison Officer 1988, in Corbett 1990: 97)

This 'transition' is one of learning where you fit into society rather than one of practising choice.

'Life skills' training supports this delicate process:

> Perhaps, not surprisingly, in a short space of time life skills training has become detached from the wider objectives associated with liberal humanist education: the point being that teaching young people *about* society has been replaced by criteria designed to alter their *relationship* with it.
>
> (Gleeson 1990: 188)

Youth training can act as a form of 'moral rescue' from the penalty of unemployment, in which trainees perceive their transition into training itself as a form of moral superiority:

> George, a former school truant and now a construction trainee, said: 'At least I did something ... but the others, you saw them at school, just lazy.' Others spoke of their gratitude to YTS and how it 'worked for me'.
>
> It was in this way that YTS helped to sustain an individualistic and divisive work ethic.
>
> (Lee *et al.* 1990: 133)

Within this work ethic, girls are encouraged to accept tasks in Youth Training Scheme (YTS) institutional care programmes which prepare them for often distasteful and uncomfortable future roles as unskilled care staff (Bates 1991).

In exploring the ways in which young people are guided into employment, Bates recognises that:

> Young people do not 'go gently' into employment. The work required to bring them there is not a bloodless operation.
>
> (Bates 1991: 1)

For some young people, especially those in areas of high youth unemployment who are attending special youth training programmes for trainees with learning difficulties, this operation may never succeed in bringing them into employment (Wilkinson 1990). Transition through training is shown to be a process in which vulnerable young people are stratified into the slots allotted to them rather than being engaged in real decision-making about future choices.

5 CONCLUDING REMARKS

Transition is shaped by different opportunities and experiences and is a development which highlights inequalities. For some young people with disabilities which require a high level of care, this stage can be one of experiencing frustration in the limits of housing provision and support services (Fiedler 1989). Their 'transition' may be no more than being found a placement in residential care after the completion of an independence training college course (Corbett 1991). The reality of their adulthood may include exclusion from the labour market (Oliver 1989). If they are fortunate enough to become involved in an initiative which supports their progress into employment, this can lead them into another level of experience. Newman (1990) described a young man with cerebral palsy employed as a council clerical officer on a Sheltered Placement Scheme. He was assessed as only able to work at 50 per cent of the rate for the job and only half his wages were paid under the scheme. As it turned out, his skills on the job have led to the department trying to regrade him into a more demanding post. Without initial support, this transition would have been impractical.

Class, race and gender differences can determine the quality of transition in terms of what training is provided and where it leads. The level of support which young people receive from parents and mentors will also have a significant effect upon the process of transition, for it is a stage in which their dependency is visibly apparent. The rise in youth homelessness is a testimony to the need for consistent support during this vulnerable period.

Much of the rhetoric of 'transition' fails to recognise the complexity of the social world. It is only within this complexity that 'transition to adulthood' can be understood.

REFERENCES

Abberley, P. (1989) 'Disabled people, normality and social work', in L. Barton (ed.), *Disability and Dependency*, Lewes: Falmer Press.

Barnes, C. (1990) *'Cabbage Syndrome': The Social Construction of Dependence*, Lewes: Falmer Press.

Bates, I. (1991) 'Closely observed training: an exploration of links between social structures, training and identity', Paper presented at the International Sociology of Education Conference, Westhill College, Birmingham, January.

Corbett, J. (1990) 'It's almost like work: a study of a YTS workshop', in J. Corbett (ed.), *Uneasy Transitions: Disaffection in Post-compulsory Education and Training*, Lewes: Falmer Press.

—— (1991) 'Moving on: training for community living', *Educare* 39, 16–18.

Council of Europe (1986) *Measures to Promote the Social Integration of Mentally Disabled People*, Strasbourg: Council of Europe.

Cross, M. and Smith, D. (1987) *Black Youth Futures: Ethnic Minorities and the Youth Training Scheme*, London: National Youth Bureau.

Dee, L. (1988) 'Young people with severe learning difficulties in colleges of further education: some current issues', *The Journal of Further and Higher Education* 12 (2), 12–22.

Department of Education and Science (DES) (1978) *Report of the Committee of Enquiry into the Education of Handicapped Children and Young People* (The Warnock Report), London: HMSO.

Fay, P. (1988) 'Stalling between fools: contradictions in the structure and process of YTS', *The Journal of Further and Higher Education* 12 (2), 23–50.

Fiedler, B. (1989) *Living Options Lottery: Housing and Support Services for People with Severe Physical Disabilities*, London: The Prince of Wales' Advisory Group on Disability.

Further Education Unit (FEU) (1989) *Towards a Framework for Curriculum Entitlement*, London: Further Education Unit.

Gleeson, D. (1990) 'Skills training and its alternatives', in D. Gleeson (ed.), *Training and Its Alternatives*, Milton Keynes: Open University Press.

Griffin, C. (1985) *Typical Girls? Young Women from School to the Job Market*, London: Routledge & Kegan Paul.

Griffiths, M. (1989) *Enabled to Work: Support into Employment for Young People with Disabilities*, London: Further Education Unit.

Harris, M. (1988) 'Social security and the transition to adulthood', *Journal of Social Policy* 17, 501–25.

Hollands, R. (1990) *The Long Transition: Class, Culture and Youth Training*, Basingstoke: Macmillan.

Hutchinson, D. and Tennyson, C. (1986) *Transition to Adulthood*, London: Further Education Unit.

Hutton, S. and Liddiard, M. (1990) 'Homeless young people in hostels – some practical considerations', *Youth and Policy*, no. 31, 40–2.

Lee, D., Marsden, D., Rickman, P. and Duncombe, J. (1990) *Scheming for Youth*, Milton Keynes: Open University Press.

Major, B. (1990) 'The changing FE structure: a basis for conscription?', in J. Corbett (ed.), *Uneasy Transitions: Disaffection in Post-compulsory Education and Training*, Lewes: Falmer Press.

Newman, S. (ed.) (1990) *Workmates: A Study of Employment Opportunities for Disabled People*, London: Mainstream.

Oliver, M. (1989) 'Disability and dependency: the role of education', in C. Struiksma and F. Meijer (eds), *Integration at Work*, Rotterdam: Pedologisch Instituut Rotterdam.

Wallace, C. and Cross, M. (eds) (1990) *Youth in Transition*, Lewes: Falmer Press.

Wertheimer, A. (1989) *Self-Advocacy and Parents: The Impact of Self-advocacy on the Parents of Young People with Disabilities*, London: Further Education Unit.

Whynes, D. and Ferris J. (1990) 'Why do the young homeless leave home?', *Youth and Policy*, no. 31, November, 36–9.

Wilkinson, A. (1990) 'Complicated lives: students with special educational needs in the inner city', in J. Corbett (ed.), *Uneasy Transitions: Disaffection in Post-compulsory Education and Training*, Lewes: Falmer Press.

Willis, P. (1977) *Learning to Labour: How Working Class Kids Get Working Class Jobs*, London: Saxon House.

Chapter 12

Supporting special needs in further education

Maureen Turnham

Since 1983 Maureen Turnham has been a lecturer in a college of further education with responsibility for a group of students categorised as having severe learning difficulties who are on a 'life-preparation' course at her college. In this chapter she discusses her preconceptions and first impressions of further education, then describes her own and her students' experience of their course and their attempts to participate with other students in the life of the college. She questions the selection procedures for students with difficulties and disabilities and discusses the barriers to participation posed by the arrangement of the buildings and people's attitudes. She reviews her own changing perceptions in the light of a commitment to equality of opportunity for all learners.

1 IMPRESSIONS OF FURTHER EDUCATION

My mother saw it. My colleague saw it and cut it out for me. I didn't see it but when I was presented with the job advert from a local newspaper the words leapt out at me: 'Lecturer: Special needs' in the college in the borough where I used to teach before becoming a peripatetic home teacher for pre-school children. Lecturer! I remember, several weeks after my successful interview, discussing my impending change of job at a party with a neighbour who works at the local university. My quizzing about the intellectual world which I was about to enter with some trepidation left him with a wry smile, which puzzled me for some time after, as my naïvety about the world of further education lasted well into my early days in college.

My initial perceptions of a college of further education might have begun on a lofty plane, but I was soon brought down to earth with a bump. Upon being introduced by the special needs coordinator as the new tutor to a group of students with severe learning difficulties, I heard several groans of 'Oh no, we thought we'd got rid of you ...'. Several of my ex-pupils, some of whom I'd first taught when they were 7 years old, grimaced at me as they carried on preparing their lunch. They had made the transition to college 'inhabitants' in the two years since I had left the borough. It was to take me some time longer to undergo the metamorphosis from a 'teacher' to a 'lecturer'. Some of that initial group of students and myself already had known each other for several years and knew each other's families. They all knew my younger sister, for example. She went to a special school, and continued to be a voluntary helper at the school where I taught when I left.

Some first impressions and early experiences of college life remain clearly in my mind – what was this new world where the academic staff all taught, but many of them were not 'teachers' like me but engineers or nurses or painters and decorators? My knowledge of the history of further education, and of how my college had evolved from a county technical college, was scant. I was thrown into a jungle of new jargon. The language of special education had long been tucked under my belt, but now I was faced with filling in timetables with terms such as 'DD' time – departmental duties, to the uninitiated – in other words, time when I was not actually in direct teaching contact with students. College induction programmes for staff new to FE were in their infancy at that time and I probably felt content in the knowledge of my own 'expertise'. After all, I had nine years' experience in special education. Surely, further education could not be so different?

2 THE DEVELOPING 'SPECIAL NEEDS' PROVISION

Seven years later, my experience of further education has grown and my perceptions of it have inevitably changed. Our college's initial provision for 'students with special needs' was established in 1978 – a 'discrete' course for students with moderate learning difficulties or, in some instances, school leavers from high schools who needed extra support before joining training schemes.

The lecturer appointed to teach the students, who was later to become the college's special needs coordinator, once told me about those early beginnings as 'part of the Engineering Department, based in a hut on the field'. For a long time I assumed she was joking, but not only was I wrong, I was also ignorant of the hard facts of life about the value of students with special needs and the staff who work with them. Talking to colleagues from other establishments at a conference some years later, I was struck by the similarities in their early beginnings – often in a portacabin or separate annexe from the main college building, or in accommodation previously occupied by a school. Stories of inferior accommodation, equipment and materials, effectively deemed to be 'good enough' for students with special needs, seemed to far outweigh reports of a stated commitment for those students being backed up by provision that was dignified and appropriate.

The life preparation course

In 1983 we began to provide a course for students with severe learning difficulties. This provision was established as a result of several pressures, not least of all parental lobbying for an alternative option to adult training centres. For many young adults with severe learning difficulties this was not much more than a decade after they became 'entitled' to full-time education.

A former school for children with severe learning difficulties, a single-storey building three miles from the main site, therefore became a college annexe. It began as, and has remained, the base for nursery nurse students and for 'life preparation' students (referred to not as 'special needs' students but prefixed by the title of the course they are following – the same as other students!). The building also houses the relevant staff, including the senior lecturer who is the college's special needs coordinator.

Opportunities for the integration of students were present from the beginning. For instance, there is a shared student common room, shared toilet facilities for all students (there is one adapted toilet/bathroom), and equal access to facilities such as the juke box (donated by the Students' Union, but removed when it failed to show a profit!) and the vending machines. The annexe has few refectory facilities, and on some days it seems that the queue for the coffee machine snakes endlessly around the corridors.

During queuing periods, there have been occasions when I have witnessed nursery nurse students, with the best of intentions, 'helping' life preparation students, for example by operating the machine for them or by 'allowing' them to jump the queue. I have to admit that, in the early days, it was with mixed feelings that I intervened – suggesting, for example, that life preparation students really ought to take their turn the same as anyone else. The mixed feelings were, perhaps, a little cowardly on my part. While I saw no justification for positive discrimination in the coffee queue, I was aware that prejudice can stem from the most unexpected beginnings. Something as innocuous as suggesting to another student that a life preparation student should be allowed to take the coins out of her purse unaided may, inadvertently, upset the nursery nurse student in the short term. However, in the long term, I feel sure that continuing input (both formal and informal) into initial nursery nurse training can only serve to extend students' knowledge about the nature and implications of severe learning difficulties. How nursery nurses and other students choose to use this knowledge is another matter entirely.

Joint craft

Conscious of our lack of truly integrated teaching sessions, and freshly inspired by a successful 'joint' activity weekend at a local Outward Bound Centre, we made plans to change the structure of one particular curriculum area. It was decided that a double staffed session of craft, with one group of life preparation students and one group of nursery nurse students would be on the timetable once a week. The nursery nurses were initially given a talk on the nature of what was, in essence, a pilot scheme for functional integration. It was explained that it was hoped that they would 'befriend' a life preparation student for craft sessions, working alongside each other on a variety of projects. The projects were pitched at different levels, so that in the strictest sense the students were working in a parallel fashion. Although this pilot was not monitored formally, it was hailed by participating students and staff as an unreserved success, generating a substantial commitment to equality for students with severe learning difficulties, and a sound knowledge, on a practical level, of many of their needs. One unexpected spin-off was the growth of a few genuine friendships. The increase in confidence in many of the life preparation students was another benefit.

Flushed with success we repeated this timetabled session, with the original members of staff, the following year with different students. The results were disappointing. With hindsight, there *were* 'rumblings' from some nursery nurses during the early stages of the course, but the matter only came to a head when a small group of nursery nurses made a formal complaint to a course tutor. They felt that they were 'not getting on' with their craft work or were 'held back by the students with severe learning difficulties'. The outcome was that a second room was negotiated and the students returned to the pattern of separate and segregated groups.

During a further meeting about the problems, some of the nursery nurse staff expressed their concern over the attitude of this group of students. They felt that their students are in the caring field and 'ought naturally to empathise with students with severe learning difficulties'. I would question this, as I feel we are treading on dangerous ground if we even contemplate trying to impose our values in this way, however strongly we feel personally. It seems obvious to me now that several factors involved could have been given more thought. There could have been greater consultation with both nursery nurse and life preparation students and due consideration given to the fact that completed craft projects are an important part of a nursery nurse's final assessment. We now have an opportunity to benefit from lessons learned, as, during the past year, we have undertaken a pilot scheme to integrate life preparation students with Sports and Leisure students who are following a City and Guilds course.

Feeling established

Our life preparation student numbers have grown continually and encompassed students from outside the district as happens on other such courses. This was partly because our college's provision for students with severe learning difficulties was being recommended by careers officers from other authorities. A pat on the back! It felt like confirmation that we had got it right. This seemed to be further corroborated when we were invited to join the second phase of a research project being undertaken by the National Foundation for Educational Research and the Further Education Unit. Other colleagues working in schools or adult training centres from our authority were also asked to participate, as together we had previously set up a voluntary curriculum development group to look at authority-wide provision for young people and adults with severe learning difficulties. This group had met almost every week for nearly two years. The national research project resulted in the publication of *New Directions: A Curriculum Framework for Students with Severe Learning Difficulties* in early 1988 (Dee 1988).

Curriculum principles

From the very beginnings of the 'life preparation' course, we tried to write an independence curriculum, and to follow the principles of 'normalisation'. Every opportunity to maximise the differences between school and college life was seized. For instance, the college day for life preparation students is the same length as for other students. The possibilities for integration, that do not exist in a segregated, all-age special school, are many – as students begin to mix, sometimes for the first time, in a community setting with other adult learners. The college environment may offer less 'protection' than their school, but it offers the chance to broaden horizons. One example of this is in the chance to meet and work with non 'special needs' staff.

Students have the opportunity to join the college library and are encouraged to join the Students' Union. They are given a copy of their own group's timetable, whether or not they can read, and they are timetabled in a variety of rooms, with different tutors on two different sites. Travelling is done on public transport – we have a college minibus which tutors can book for residentials, visits and regular timetabled activities, such as the Leisure Centre. Supervisory duties at break and lunch-time are carried out by non-teaching assistants. In general, the staff/student ratio is rarely as good as in a school for children and young people with severe learning difficulties. However, as our special needs coordinator rightly emphasises 'we are a college – not an extended special school'. The whole ethos of a college of further education is different to that of a special school – from the funding and the staffing to the size and complexity of the sites. We share the annexe base with nursery nurse students and staff. An early rule of thumb became 'if the nursery nurses don't do it, neither do we'. We talked with our students about the freedoms of college life, and suggested that they might judge whether or not certain behaviour was 'age appropriate' by looking at the nursery nurses (incorrectly and naïvely assuming the latter would unfailingly provide the models we sought!). This mechanism ended in total failure when, after lengthy and various attempts to persuade several female life preparation students to give up wearing white ankle socks in favour of tights, short socks, mostly white, suddenly became very fashionable and seemed to adorn every other pair of ankles in the building.

With hindsight, I question some of my early motives and certainly now see different ways of exploring choices with students. One route for beginning to make informed choices is through self-advocacy, where students are encouraged either to speak up for themselves or to use an advocate who speaks on their behalf. Self-advocacy complements 'normalisation' and it is an issue which, recently, staff have actively begun to promote. The Open University's *Patterns for*

Living: Working Together has generated much interest in this area (Open University 1989).

Selection procedures

At present, we select students for the life preparation course, following a baseline assessment devised by myself and colleagues which is carried out during a links week when potential students attend college full time. We didn't have interviews, but a young person had to 'gain' a place none the less, as we had criteria for entry onto the course. I suppose I felt that this fitted in neatly with the selection process for other students. Also, we had no 'medical' back-up, as is often the case in special schools, therefore we felt unable to meet the needs of students with profound multiple disabilities.

I can recall talking to Lesley Dee, 'New Directions' project leader, about her teaching experience in South Thames college and her approach to 'FE for all'. When she spoke about learning difficulties or special needs she included everyone, even young people with severe 'challenging behaviour'. This represented a very different target group to the one with which I was familiar, and it seemed an alien approach to me. I was worried that it could dilute or blunt our provision. I thought that it undermined the satisfaction of 'getting a place in college' for students with severe learning difficulties. However, I now realise that perhaps the only person who felt intimidated by 'FE for all' was me. Our selection procedure has resulted in no places being offered to students with profound or multiple disabilities or severe challenging behaviour.

Our selection procedure still exists, but I want to see it changed to one which is more equitable. National reflections currently focus upon the need for college to be 'responsive' in order to ensure that individuals can gain access to the curriculum 'regardless of any disability or special learning need they may have' (FEU 1990: 11). In considering the issue of entitlement to access, my college would be required to look at two groups of learners hitherto excluded – students with profound or multiple disabilities and students with challenging behaviour. The life preparation course, in its present form, is unlikely to meet their specific needs, but the curricular content could serve as a starting point for designing new provision which would. The possible stumbling blocks would be financial and attitudinal barriers to these learners. It is my belief that our life preparation students are not 'valued' by many colleagues, so how would they react to learners seen to be 'less able' or more difficult to cope with?

3 COUNTERING OBSTACLES TO INCLUSION

There are a number of issues which still concern me about continuing education for students with disabilities, just as they did when I entered college life – for example, the fear and ignorance that often surrounds this seemingly homogeneous condition known as 'disability', and the unmitigated prejudice and stereotyping of people who do not 'fit' into a mythical category commonly known as 'normal'. However, I hope I am not so complacent that I am unable to acknowledge the difficulties of trying to bring about change. It is a lengthy and wearing process.

Attempting to challenge and change the attitudes of individuals who feel discomfort or exhibit prejudice when faced with the possibility, or reality, of encountering people with disabilities is both a responsibility in my job and intrinsic to my personality. I believe in the precept of 'person first, disability second'. I believe that students with disabilities need to be valued as people, and any establishment that implies this on paper needs to put policy into practice. Our college, and authority, now has an equal opportunities policy document. I am departmental representative on the Equal Opportunities Sub-committee. When the college policy and the sub-committee was first constituted, I was enthusiastic – teeth at last! Unfortunately, two years later, we are trying to rectify an original omission – the word 'disability' does not appear in the policy document. Unfortunately, it is not possible to just insert the word 'disability' into the document, as there are several procedures which must be adhered to, not least of all submission to the governors appointed since financial delegation some months ago.

I failed to realise for some considerable time the importance of commitment from the top down. Once again it was during some exchanges with colleagues from other establishments that I began to realise the significance of 'who is on your side'. Senior management who truly support the right to continuing education for all learners are worth their weight in gold to lecturers who may be struggling to persuade colleagues, in their own department/school/division or otherwise, that students with special needs are entitled to be included in the further education system.

Negative statements such as 'I don't know how you can work with them' or 'they don't belong here – this is a college', which were once like a red rag to a bull to me, no longer insult or injure as they did. I have grown used to the fact that I will never 'convert' some colleagues however enthusiastic, persuasive or reasoned I am. I no longer vociferously challenge those who insult; instead, I may casually invite them to come for a coffee and see/meet some students. Alternatively, if faced with a determined 'It's not on ... I/we are not trained/paid/supposed to teach these students', I do not launch into a tirade on equal opportunities but try to draw breath instead and substitute a concerned ear about the anxieties of dealing with students seen to be different. It's not always easy or straightforward, and I still have difficulty in dealing with such sweeping generalisations as: 'he's a Down's Syndrome – they can be very stubborn, can't they?'; 'mentally handicapped ... they can be quite violent if they don't get their own way'. Apart from the danger in such misconceptions, the terminology used by some colleagues when referring to anyone with a disability can be disturbing. I refer to my students by name and would never refer to any of them as 'a Down's Syndrome', just as I would never refer to any of my friends who wear contact lenses as 'a myopic'.

Students with learning difficulties do encounter prejudice, and confronting prejudice is rarely an easy task. As a group, they are marginalised in a society that places a high value on being clever and articulate. Within a large establishment such as a college it is unlikely that they will avoid some name-calling or jokes at their expense. We do have strategies that can be used – from advising the students with learning difficulties to ignore insults, to implementing the equal opportunities policy which finds such discrimination to be indefensible.

Questions of physical access

The physical barriers to integration for students who have special needs will undoubtedly continue to pose problems in my own establishment, and those of colleagues, and are due, not least of all, to the ever-increasing constraints of finances. At the time of writing, plans to join two buildings with a walkway to improve access to the second building, which has no lift, have been scrapped. In the current financial climate, which sees us wrestling with colleges managing their own budgets and, in our own authority, reeling from the outcome of poll-capping, the expenses involved in improving physical access are likely to be competing with numerous other worthy but expensive causes.

Physical barriers to integration often receive much publicity. However, it is not good enough to assume that physical restrictions to access to college buildings can be removed, in one fell swoop, by the construction of a ramp or the fitting of a handrail. The ramp, for instance, needs to be of the correct gradient, something which, in my experience of discussing such matters with colleagues, appears to be overlooked with alarming frequency! I discovered that, for instance, one of our students was unable to propel her wheelchair up the ramped entrance to our annexe, a former special school building, without the dangerous likelihood of tipping backwards. A subsequent ramp built on to a fire exit out of one of the rooms was better, though the aforementioned student had long since left.

Any 'make do and mend' philosophy which applies to facilities and provision for any group of learners, including students with disabilities, is regrettable and short-sighted. Regrettable because it compounds a belief that there is a group of learners with lower status that the rest because they have been labelled as having 'special needs'. Short-sighted because no amount of patchwork planning can be a substitute for a blueprint for services that has commitment, consultation and collaboration ingrained, like a name through candy rock.

4 THE FUTURE

There are new developments ahead in FE, such as new funding arrangements, which I hope will not add to the difficulties of access for any student who may require specific support for learning. There are also planned changes within community living which are likely to have significant implications as 'different' client groups such as ex-patients from long-stay hospitals move into the community. The need for a student-centred approach, perhaps not always present in some sectors of FE, is likely to become increasingly vital to tailoring programmes to meet the individual needs of those learners not traditionally seen as 'student material'.

Very recently, some of 'our' students have, like many of their peers, 'voted with their feet'. They did not turn up for sessions they considered boring and did not meet their needs. They are speaking up for themselves and expecting, rightly, that they will be listened to by staff and that their opinions will have the same validity as those of the next person. The current emphasis upon 'empowerment', and the belief that 'the more self-empowered a person becomes, the more able he or she will be to enable others to be the same' (Fenton and Hughes 1989: 19), is effecting a shift in approach generally, and in my own personal practice, from a passive model of students. My earlier justifications of an elitist selection procedure for our target group of students are incompatible with my commitment to equality of opportunity. I obviously cannot swear allegiance to the principles of equal opportunities then justify the exclusion of some students purely because of the severity of their disability.

However, the access route to our college for these students with additional difficulties seems likely to be long and winding, requiring commitment not only from staff such as myself, but also from those senior staff who are the policy-makers and who control the purse strings. Many changes would need to be made to meet the needs of those learners. These are likely to range from an amendment to our current equal opportunities policy document (correcting the omission of 'disability') to a need to employ more staff, possibly from another discipline such as health. In a climate of radical spending cuts, the latter seems highly unlikely.

Putting theory into practice is far from simple. Nevertheless, my beliefs have changed over the last years and the message is clear: I no longer think in terms of 'further education for not quite all' but of providing access to learning for everyone.

REFERENCES

Dee, L. (1988) *New Directions: A Curriculum Framework for Students with Severe Learning Difficulties*, London: Further Education Unit.

Fenton, M. and Hughes, P. (1989) *Passivity to Empowerment*, London: Royal Association for Disability and Rehabilitation.

Further Education Unit (FEU) (1990) *Planning FE: Equal Opportunities for People with Disabilities or Special Educational Needs*, London: Further Education Unit.

Open University (1989) *Patterns for Living: Working Together* (P555M), Milton Keynes: Open University Press.

Chapter 13

A hard journey in the right direction
Experiencing life beyond an institution

Linda Shaw

In this chapter, Linda Shaw describes her experiences of supporting Elizabeth and Helen in their South London flat – initially as a member of their team of workers and later as a friend. Her knowledge of and friendship with the two women also enable her to describe what life was like from their point of view. Elizabeth and Helen were living in the community after many years in an institution for people classified as 'mentally handicapped'. Linda describes the details of their daily lives, the problems that arose in trying to set up a network of support that was sufficient, stable and yet not undermining of the women's growing independence, and the different reactions of Elizabeth and Helen to their new life. Despite the difficulties and the continuing insecurity of support, Linda concludes that life for Elizabeth and Helen has been improved by their time in the community and that the hard journey is worth it.

1 INTRODUCTION

Elizabeth and Helen moved into their own basement flat in an inner-city suburb in 1987. They are middle-aged and spent nearly thirty years together at the same mental handicap hospital but lived separately for the two years before the move into the community because Helen was transferred to a smaller institution. The move was part of the 'community care' initiative adopted by health authorities to provide housing and support services in ordinary settings for people with learning difficulties.

I was a member of the health service team supporting Elizabeth and Helen at the time of the move and I have stayed in touch with them since, as a friend and advocate. I have written this account on their behalf, based on my knowledge of the women, observations of their lifestyle, and discussions with them and their support workers. The women's real names and some details about their lives have been disguised to protect their privacy.

2 STARTING AN ORDINARY LIFE

More than two years after the move from institution to ordinary housing, Elizabeth and Helen are still learning about community living and adjusting to its demands and possibilities. The women's days are beginning to include the mix of activities, experiences and relationships which make up ordinary life for most people. Their daily routines are starting to reflect their preferences and abilities and to include a level of personal responsibility.

As well as having to adapt to major changes in their status, environment, lifestyle and relationships, Elizabeth and Helen have to cope with the adjustments made by the people on whom they depend. Health service staff and managers are still developing the new skills and the framework necessary to offer a quality community care service. Neighbours and business people, many of whom are confronting disability for the first time, have yet to work out ways of behaving with respect towards them and ways of making links which are welcome and helpful. The women's long separation from the mainstream means that increasing their participation in ordinary life is an inevitable learning process for everybody involved. The realisation that the transition from exclusion to inclusion is a slow manoeuvre and that community care evolves rather than happens became clear soon after Elizabeth and Helen arrived at their new home.

The first few months of life in the community were dominated by support workers' sense of heavy responsibility about the twin tasks of meeting the women's physical and medical needs and, at the same time, enabling them to be as independent as possible. One member of the staff team of nine had nursing training; two had been teachers and the rest were from a variety of other backgrounds. The balance between doing too much and doing too little for Elizabeth and Helen, who both use wheelchairs, had to be continuously readjusted. Staff received basic instructions, but the appropriate ways to help each woman with personal care, diet and medication (for epilepsy) had to be worked out through discussion with the helpers.

From the beginning of her tenancy Helen took pride in having a home of her own. She coped well with the change-over and immediately welcomed any opportunity to take part in household activities. 'It's my job', is her prompt response to any attempt to take over tasks she wants to do herself. Helen's ability to enjoy herself and express her objections effectively make her an easy person to help, although she is sometimes criticised for being demanding.

Elizabeth found the move to community living much more difficult. On many occasions during those first few months, she was moody, tearful and uncommunicative. At the worst times she refused to leave her armchair in the lounge all day and occasionally overnight, saying she was too frightened to go to bed or to the bathroom. She cut herself off from comfort by clenching her fists, screaming and occasionally kicking when people approached. She was also frightened of doing housework and passed on jobs to a support worker, announcing: 'She can do it.' Professional advice about Elizabeth's unhappiness was that she was in a state of 'mourning' and that time would improve matters.

In those early stages, support workers, who were highly motivated to give Elizabeth and Helen a 'better life', felt that the demands of the women's physical needs, together with Elizabeth's state of mind, undermined hopes for their social progress. The basic business of looking after them felt so demanding and emotionally wearing that there seemed little time left to introduce them to 'real living'.

3 WIDENING HORIZONS

Looking back, there's no doubt that we were too impatient and were unprepared for the major impact of the change from institution to community care on all concerned. As the third anniversary of the women's arrival in the community approaches, there is a marked improvement in Elizabeth's sense of well-being and greater participation by both women in activities beyond domestic and care routines.

The women may spend large parts of the day on personal care, preparing and clearing up after meals and doing their laundry. They have to overcome difficulties to accomplish these tasks so the amount of time involved increases the more the women participate and the less support workers take over. Although lengthy domestic and care routines are to some extent a reality of disability, it is necessary to work out a level of sharing between the women and their staff which allows a varied day and does not make a drudge out of anybody.

A typical day for Elizabeth and Helen includes the usual range of personal and domestic tasks involved in looking after themselves and their flat with support, together with popular leisure activities such as watching television and listening to music. Helen may do some painting and Elizabeth likes to work at drawing shapes and picking out words as first steps in reading and writing. Some form of keep fit exercises or dancing in the flat is a feature on most days as are trips out to pursue activities in connection with their developing social programme.

Such social activities as going to adult education classes, taking trips out in their car, going to church, visiting friends and being visited, now happen on a more regular basis. Around the time I was compiling this report the women attended three adult education classes a week – for music, keep-fit and self-advocacy.

They had recently been on separate holidays, met support workers' families at their homes, danced at a party and had their photographs taken cuddling the few weeks' old daughter of a woman Elizabeth met at church. A trip to London was planned and they were expecting two visits – one from an elderly relative who'd been in touch after receiving a holiday postcard and another from two people who used to live in the flat upstairs and had telephoned asking if they could call by.

Elizabeth compiled the following list, with support, of what she likes about living in her own home.

- Because of Helen.
- Going out.
- Likes seeing Linda.
- Likes the workers.
- Because of my car.
- Going to church.
- Having visitors.
- Having a fish tank.

Elizabeth was also asked if she would like to make a list of what she does not like about community living but could not think of anything for the moment. She says that in the future, in addition to her current activities, she wants to learn to read and write and to plant flowers in the garden. She does not want to do housework.

Helen is not interested in making lists about her life, preferring to talk about the more immediate experiences of her recent holiday and birthday. Her speech is not easy to understand but she effectively communicates her complete approval and enjoyment of the busy week when she went away. She'd been 'everywhere', she says, raising her arms and pointing in many different directions. She is an outgoing, cheerful person with an ability to communicate her feelings, to get along, and find enjoyment in most situations. She often opens conversations by telling people brightly: 'I got up this morning', which seems to reflect her talent for being delighted by what is deeply ordinary.

Helen's main problems since she moved into her own home have been a period of illness, which caused her much discomfort, and a spate of difficulties in accepting personal care from temporary staff.

Helen's personality does not seem to have altered significantly since her move into the community, although she has become more tolerant. In general, she has simply become more herself; opportunities to participate have increased and she has responded to most of them enthusiastically.

Elizabeth, on the other hand, has changed significantly. For a start she looks different. She is slimmer and looks more of a woman, in clothes which are appropriate for her age. She slouches less in her wheelchair, raises her head more and looks at people in a more direct manner. She says she does not like housework but she can manage some tasks. She can count out and administer her own drugs and explain her own needs during visits to the doctor. She is exceptionally good company when she is happy. She is curious and asks many questions about people and situations around her, including her own disabilities and difficulties. She works hard to understand issues which confuse her and is learning to be patient with herself when, as she puts it, her brain 'gets stuck'. She expresses much appreciation for what she considers beautiful and is beginning to show and receive affection. How to tell when a person has become a friend is the latest of many difficult questions to which Elizabeth struggles to find answers.

Elizabeth is learning to speak up for herself. She says 'no' more often, rather than suffering or withdrawing, and she is able to remind people of her difficulty in concentrating on more than one thing at a time. I received a straightforward message recently when I telephoned her flat for a chat: 'Elizabeth says she's busy.' She is sorting out the conundrum of being a 'high grade' in hospital and a 'person with a disability' in the community. At times it surely is very difficult for her. She still has periods of withdrawal and sadness but they are decreasing.

4 A SHAKY SUPPORT NETWORK

Community care for Elizabeth and Helen involves an extraordinary network of services which has yet to operate to full capacity and efficiency. Elizabeth and Helen have made progress despite the weakness and unpredictability of this shaky, official safety net. It is a constant concern that they might have achieved much more if services had been better and that they may regress if services don't improve.

The women's direct support comes from a staff team working in twos at their flat during the day with one person sleeping overnight. Behind this front line is a complicated structure of health, social, housing and financial services, management and monitoring systems. During the first years of the women's life in the community, the full-time team of health authority support workers has been regularly understaffed, with temporary cover being provided by a private nursing agency. None of the original team who were with the women at the time of the move still work at their flat.

I left the team because the low pay would not cover the cost of my share in a mortgage to buy my own flat, and because I found it difficult to reconcile the separate roles of paid worker and friend, when Helen and Elizabeth recognised no such distinction. I was sad to leave but felt that a turnover of paid staff was unavoidable with the present pay and conditions. I reassured myself that nothing could stop me keeping in touch with the women on a voluntary basis, provided they wished to remain friends.

The period during which I have been writing this chapter has seen one of the worst staffing levels ever at the women's flat. At one stage half the permanent health service posts were unfilled and agency staff worked in the flat on a daily basis. The consortium responsible for looking after the women's housing and financial affairs, as well as providing some monitoring of the quality of service, had temporarily to reduce its operations because of staff shortages. Members of the health authority team set up to give advice on the 'physical, psychological, communication and mental health needs' of people with learning difficulties are often difficult to contact when support workers want to discuss problems relating to the women.

It is only recently that Elizabeth and Helen have had the benefit of a full-time manager whose job is to provide support, supervision and leadership to staff working in their home.

The effective operation of an Individual Programme Plan (IPP) for each woman is a major casualty of the haphazard delivery of services. The IPP is a system for mapping out individual goals, specifying means of achievement and assigning responsibility for progress. It is the most reliable method available for trying to ensure that the principles of community care policy agreed by the health authority – community presence, community participation, competence, respect and choice – are actually made available to the users of a service. The system aims to involve service users, and their friends and relatives, in planning individual lifestyles in the community, working out strategy and reviewing progress. The written document produced in the process belongs to service users and provides them with necessary information to challenge service providers if they don't fulfil their contributions to the plan. The Individual Programme Plans of Elizabeth and Helen, which took two attempts to get off the ground because of staff changes and inadequate training, have been virtually suspended – even before the first reviews – because of the latest staffing upheaval.

Support staff who remain with the women worry increasingly about the lack of continuity. They are concerned that agency staff and new staff who don't know what the women have achieved will undermine progress, or even reverse it, by underestimating their capabilities. The lack of fully operational IPPs, which could have provided a safeguard against inconsistency, adds to workers' anxiety that Elizabeth and Helen are being let down.

While the community care service sorts out its shortfalls, Elizabeth's enthusiasm to learn to read and write could be overtaken by boredom and depression. Helen's frustration with people who don't appreciate her could result in a marked reduction in her tolerance level. According to one worker there had already been an occasion when she found Helen being 'fed, wiped and pushed round the house'.

Support workers also worry about the effect of setbacks on the generally negative attitudes of many people in the community to people with learning difficulties. 'It's a vicious circle', explained one worker. 'People with learning difficulties are not respected to begin with and because the women's Individual Programmes, including skills training, are not in place, they are not progressing as well as they could and they are not getting respect.' A senior manager agreed that because of staff shortages in the flat, planning and development for the women had taken second place to 'keeping people afloat'. When new staff were appointed development could move ahead again. Regarding community care in general in the authority the manager insisted, 'We haven't got there yet, but we are certainly going in the right direction.'

Elizabeth and Helen express rather similar sentiments about their new way of life. 'It's all right', 'I feel all right', they say. 'I'm happy', 'I'm settled', 'Now I know what it feels like', 'I got out on the right side'. They have not expressed any wish to return to living in an institution full time, although Helen occasionally likes to visit the hospital where she was a resident immediately before the move into the community. And while support staff are adamant about the need for improvements in services and organisation, nobody believes the women would be better off returning to institutional care.

5 CONCLUSION

Elizabeth and Helen's initial experience of life in the community has brought them unhappiness and difficulties. There has also been much learning, laughter and warmth which has extended the enjoyment and understanding of everybody involved. The new community care service has enabled the women to claim their places as citizens in their neighbourhood and take a tentative hold of a share in the goodness of ordinary life. Opportunities have become available to them which would have been impossible in hospital. From the women's point of view, the need in the future is for a more reliable and responsive support network and a wider circle of friends and acquaintances to help them strengthen their hold on, and increase their share of, life in the community.

Part 4

The experience of families

Chapter 14

Fools and heretics
Parents' views of professionals

Chris Goodey

In this chapter Chris Goodey reflects on the diagnosis, assessment and categorisation procedures employed by 'professionals': doctors, psychologists, teachers and administrators. He argues that such procedures and the decisions about a child's acceptability within mainstream education which may follow from them, are underpinned by competing philosophies about a child's acceptability as a human being. It is this philosophy, he argues, rather than a body of technical knowledge, which drives the behaviour of professionals in their interactions with parents. He supports these contentions with the words of parents of children with trisomy 21 whose reactions to, and following, the birth of their children belie the simplified professional stereotypes which he sets beside them. He concludes by suggesting that membership of the group that accepts children with disabilities as full members of the human tribe, is open to all.

1 A HUMAN FAILING

What is it to be human? The segregation of school pupils who have disabilities or learning difficulties poses this question immediately. Professionals segregate according to expert criteria, but 'what is it to be human?' sounds like a philosophical question – in which case it is also a political one – rather than something for experts to decide. We as a group, defining ourselves as human, decide whom to include and whom to exclude as members of this group. We do it when we decide what it is acceptable for people to be able or unable to do. We do it when we decide that someone is unable to attend a school we have already described as 'comprehensive'. We do it when we decide that the sibling rule – that a child can attend the same school as a brother or sister – does not apply (the assumption here must surely be that siblings can belong to different species). Alongside the ideal common sense of the saying, 'Nothing human is alien to me', we operate the opposite principle too: nothing alien is human to me. In our own society we leave it to certain specialised people to decide, in practice, who is alien to the species and where the alien should be put.

Expert classifications of disability and difficulty, and the apparatus of assessment that goes with them, appear to be scientifically objective. But in fact this appearance is only the distorted mirror-image of the reality I have described. We have already *chosen*, more or less deliberately, whom we want to belong and whom not. We then *invent* criteria to back up the choice, delegating our responsibility to professional specialists. The appearance of scientific objectivity is painted on afterwards. It gives credibility to the particular choice we as a self-defining 'human' group have made, and reinforces the validity of that choice by obscuring the fact that we make it voluntarily, rather than have it imposed on us by scientific laws which are unquestionable and necessary.

If it is all just a matter of philosophy, then anyone can voice an opinion on it, and there may be differing views of what 'humanity' consists of behind it all. Philosophies clash and compete. As far as those who experience difficulties in learning or have disabilities are concerned there are 'excluders' and 'includers'. The excluders, since theirs is the prevailing view in our educational and other institutions, want to keep convincing the world at large that their choice as to who belongs is the only possible one. This necessitates them saying something about the rival philosophy of the includers in addition to conveying the appearance of expertise. History has shown that the favourite way of dealing with any fundamental philosophy opposed to your own is to abuse its advocates as being fools and heretics – that is, to exclude the people along with their philosophy. The Catholic Church and the Soviet state under Stalin, for example, found ways of doing this to people who advocated different theological positions from the established one. In our case, the excluders want to keep out *both* kinds of fool: people with learning difficulties themselves and their fool advocates, those people who represent the rival philosophy and advocate their inclusion.

Natural experts?

The includers are not always merely disinterested advocates of a philosophy, but people who have become so through experience, through the sheer amount of time they spend with members of the excluded social group. 'Parents' are the best example, though not the only possible one. I put the word in inverted commas to highlight a mystique about parenthood. There is no reason why having some coincidental sperm-and-egg relationship with a child should entitle someone for that reason to be seen as a 'natural expert', as distinct from a very clever, highly qualified one. But if criteria for inclusion and exclusion are not technical and professional but based on a philosophy about what human beings are, then parental expertise cannot be different in kind from that of professional (un-natural?) experts. As one of the parents in the interviews described later says, 'When they say, you're the experts, parents are experts, what they really mean is – you get on with that little bit over there, and we'll get on with the really important stuff over here.' Conversely, of course, not all parents of children with disabilities see their children as members of the human species.

Most parents, though, have a world-view which as you may expect does include 'their' children as fully paid-up members of the species. This observation has occasionally even found its way into the specialist literature, but it is easy to miss its full significance. For parents, this world-view may not be 'philosophical' in the sense of something that is calculated, worked out and argued, though it can be and often is. It is a way of life. Deny or threaten it, and you deny and threaten someone's existence. They will strive to validate it, and even prescribe it for you and everyone else: not just 'this is how we live', but 'this is how one *ought* to live'.

In the prevailing exclusionist literature, which is controlled by the professionally intelligent, the attitude that what professionals define as 'intelligence' does not matter, and that their child's humanity does, may be seen as a symptom of pathology as severe as (and similar to) a child's intellectual disabilities. It is a lack, a disqualification, an inability to face the reality of their child's disability.

Because it is pathological it must not be allowed to appear in public in its own form. To borrow from the classic language of the history of slavery, parents in this sense are 'physically alive but socially dead': we do not see them. They contain endlessly frustrated plantation slaves who are rebellious at assessments and in encounters with professionals, but whose views only reach daylight in fragmented and unvalidated form; and they contain house slaves who agree with everything that goes on and use 'massa's' language and concepts, but who believe something else all the time and are waiting for the day. In short, they are a colonised people. But in common with other colonised people such as the Algerians under French rule described by Frantz Fanon or the Black Americans by Stokely Carmichael in the 1960s, they believe that they and their children should themselves be the civilising force to overcome the 'civilisation', the predominant philosophy and way of life, that has colonised them. The stakes are high: it is not just a question of particular social groups ('What is it to be Black?', 'What is it to be a woman?'), but of the very qualifications for inclusion in the human species. They believe they have a different and better answer to the question, 'What is it to be human?'

2 WORDS OF EXPERIENCE: A RESEARCH PROJECT

My opening observations are not random reflections, but arise directly from a piece of research. Between 1987 and 1989 I conducted in-depth interviews with nearly forty parents of children with trisomy 21 (so-called Down's Syndrome) who were between the ages of 2 and 7. I had several interviews with each parent individually, speaking to nearly 90 per cent of the total population group in a borough with a wide class distribution and a large ethnic minority population (see Goodey 1991). Before I began the formal research I had been aware from the few parents of children with trisomy 21 I knew that there was more disquiet about their negotiations with professionals and the treatment of their children than had made its way into the academic and professional literature on parents and families. Second, I also knew that this disquiet existed alongside other more conventional attitudes which perfectly fitted the portrayal of parents usually found in that literature. After beginning to interview people in depth, I realised that, to explain this juxtaposition of apparently contradictory values within individuals, I needed to go beyond the conceptual framework set by clinicians and sociologists alike. A shared language between parents and professionals did not necessarily mean shared attitudes. It may be that when we express our opinions, we only have available to us ready-made sets of ideas, 'discourses', other people's words which we choose from, string together in different ways and think (mistakenly) to be our own; these include 'expert' ideas and the colloquial, common-sense versions of them absorbed by ordinary people in one way or another. But we have something else too which is genuinely our own, even though we don't choose it, and that is experience. It became clear from talking to parents that I had to see *how* what they said actually hooked up with their experience, the fine detail of it, and not to assume that I knew exactly what kind of lived experience lay behind a familiar form of words.

Parents as truth tellers

Even in order to get this far, I had to believe that what I was being told by people about their experiences and feelings was the truth, or essentially the truth. I may have been wrong proportionately as many times as the result of an amniocentesis turns out to have been wrong: that is, being wrong in both cases amounts to a hypothetical possibility, but is not normal. I decided, for example, that if a parent told me they had dreamt about having a 'Down's baby' before the birth – in the medical literature, this is a classic after-the-event self-deception – they had in fact had such a dream. If they said they had not been upset on being told the diagnosis, this actually was the case; they were not suffering from amnesia. If they became angry at things said to them by professionals, as a majority of them did at some point, the horrifying causes of their anger were true, and were not projections of their own distress on to the professional concerned. To accept the truth of these accounts is a simple but giant step, and one which the academic and professional community is by its own self-definition incapable of taking: a social group which bases its very existence on its own claims to cleverness would risk its life if it opened even one ear to the voices of fools and heretics, especially when the topic itself is about foolishness in the form of 'learning difficulties'.

In what follows I have used my interviews with parents as a counterpoint to a professional judgement.

3 SHOCK, HORROR AND DEMYSTIFICATION

'When parents are first told that the baby has Down's Syndrome they are *all* deeply shocked' (Cunningham 1982: 28).

Bernadette: With my other babies they've mostly left them quite close to me, but she was put over to the side, the doctor was slow in coming, and she went over and checked her over, instead of coming to speak to me as they usually do – she went out again and didn't even look at me [laughs] ... I had an instant bond with Marie – I thought she was beautiful the moment she was born – I can really say that. I thought she was beautiful, and I didn't mind about her being Down's Syndrome. Mentally I was prepared to cope with it you see, I'd made my mind up right through my marriage that I would.

Every one of these parents can recount stories of being not believed, not looked at, not spoken to: that is what dead people experience, if the dead have experiences. For Bernadette, it's amusing. From this paediatrician's reaction, it seems as if the clinical notion of deep shock as a natural reaction is itself a projection of that professional's anxiety on to the parent.

Pat: He was six months old and I'd gone down for his second immunisation and I mean the doctor I went to see was a family doctor – I've known him since I was a baby – and he just, he was looking at him and he just said, 'Is your husband Chinese?' And I said, 'No.' And he just stuck the needle in his arm, and he said, 'Well, I think the baby's a mongol', and he showed me the door and that was it. He wasn't looking at me. He was kind of looking down and twiddling his pen, you know ... and I mean I know it sounds stupid, but I didn't mind, I think I knew anyway. I mean when he was born they laid him on me, he'd had the cord round his neck three times and he looked like a tortoise with his long neck and this little tiny head [laughs]. And I thought blimey, he's a mongol, you know, when you're looking at them, and then I was looking at the nurses and waiting for everyone to say something, and nobody said nothing. And then I thought, I couldn't say 'Here, is this baby a mongol?' in front of Stan, I think he would have fell over.

Pat has reasons not to mind. The baby is already six months old, and she has already made the diagnosis herself, at birth. In addition, both her own parents had considerable physical disabilities. Both she and Bernadette have realised beforehand that the boundaries of human experience are wider than those indicated in the Mothercare catalogue. What about those who haven't?

Rita: Well the doctor was crying, she had tears in her eyes, and she said, 'We've got some news.' And then the stupid thing, the doctor said to me, 'Does she look like anybody in your family?' I said, 'Well you don't have to tell me, I know she's a mongol.' She said, 'Oh – you a nurse?' I said, 'No, I can just tell by her face' ... So I went back and see the baby in the incubator and then I went back to the ward. None of the nurses spoke to me, nothing, till 2 o'clock that afternoon, which I'd had her at 7.30 in the morning ... Yeah, yeah, well I completely rejected her. As soon as I knew she wasn't a hundred per cent, I just didn't want to know her ... The exact feelings ... I wanted her to die ... And I'll tell you the only reason I took the baby home was because Martin wanted her.

Now this looks more like it: a normal, natural reaction, even if I do have to search through several of the transcripts on my desk to find one. 'Natural': does this mean that we all have a gene that determines we will be shocked? In the clinical literature, the word 'natural' is left undefined (the medical description of this kind of shock goes back to the nineteenth-century discovery of 'hysteria' and its symptoms in women). Rita, however, takes care to define it, and is aware of the surrounding social circumstances. The baby had been taken away immediately and wired up in an incubator for three days. Since Rita has been sent to Coventry, she has not told that it is physically possible for her to open up the incubator herself and put her hands in. Eventually a nurse does show her, and then 'Once I'd touched her, she was mine.' She is further handicapped by having a sister-in-law (a nurse herself) who visits immediately after the diagnosis has been made and starts discussing fostering and adoption procedures. Most importantly, Rita, just as she makes her own diagnosis, knows – unlike the professionals – exactly what the 'shock' is and that it comes from somewhere:

Rita: You know, the old story, my first thoughts when I had her, well one of my first thoughts, was Oh, I've got one of them kids that have silly haircuts, silly anoraks, spend all day on buses or all day in a home, weaving baskets, and that was my first thought ... I don't know, I always said I'd never took the piss out of these children, but I'm sure I must have done at school, but I must admit I *was* embarrassed. I was embarrassed giving birth to a mongol. If we was educated with handicapped, you know, if we'd mixed with them ... but we never saw them. I'd never spoken to one till we had Louise, you know, which is not fair on us normal people ... They're anti-social, handicapped people, and they're kept that way. They're all at a different school all day, and they shop at different times ... but you never see them in restaurants and why shouldn't they be? They're just *there*, you know.

Like many of the parents, Rita readily agrees with the professional maxim that 'It's natural to feel shocked', but she clearly does not take this to be some scientific and objective concomitant of the situation, something in her genes. Such parents know that it is something they have been socialised into by a segregated society, and that things could have been otherwise: that they *ought* to be otherwise (It's not fair ...').

Between the apparent extremes of these examples lie all sorts of individual circumstances. Some parents' reaction to the diagnosis is nullified by the additional diagnosis of some life-threatening physical condition such as meningitis or a heart defect, which to them is more distressing. Some may have previously had a miscarriage or an infant who died. For others who went through distress, over and over again the *concrete* feelings behind the abstraction of 'shock' have to do, not with newly existent beings whom one doesn't know, but with existing people in one's life – partners, family, etc. And none of them fails to recognise where these negative feelings come from, that such feelings have been *taught* by a particular upbringing and environment. 'Shock' and 'trauma' must be seen as an example of what psychologists call reification: sets of concrete interpersonal and societal relationships are turned into an abstract 'thing' which dominates our language and hence our way of thinking. This self-perpetuating process of mystification that denies real feelings and experiences is a necessary prop to the status, power and basic philosophical values of a way of life; the teaching of negative feelings must go on. What needs to be emphasised, though, is that direct experience – becoming part of a way of life that includes the alien in a wider definition of what it is to be human – seems to be almost the only way of achieving demystification.

Brian: The only problem I had was people thinking I had problems.

4 'COMING TO TERMS': WHOSE AND WHAT TERMS?

> For many parents it is as though the child they were expecting is dead. Many doctors think that it is important for parents to recognize these feelings and to go through a period of mourning for their lost imaginary baby ... These feelings ... may diminish in time so that the parent can come to terms with the fact that the baby has Down's Syndrome.
>
> (Cunningham 1982: 31, 39)

A couple of hours after drafting this, I receive a call from a local health visitor asking advice about a child who has just been diagnosed. She tells me that 'the mother is just going through the process of grieving for the child she hasn't had' (the child is already eight months old): the health visitor's instruction in the art of creating unpersons has been exemplary, and no doubt she is keen to pass this on to the mother.

Sharon: At school when you have these, you have lessons about childbirth and babies and things, nobody ever says like not all children are born, you know, normal. Antenatal classes should talk about it. Although I said to my husband when I was pregnant, what if I have a handicapped baby? And he said he wouldn't be able to cope, but it was in the pretext that it would never happen to us. But you've got to think about it if it *does* happen to you. I mean if it does, you, I think you find a way of coping with it. There's no connection between the thought beforehand, and when it happens to you something different happens.

Dave: I'd always tended to shy away from them, like, because like I say I think it's the fear of the unknown, what you've been told. If you don't understand something you normally tend to be a bit aggressive towards it, don't you? ... Looking at what Micky's like and everything, when I thought before what it would be like and what the situation actually is, I think basically you're in another world, you know what I mean? Because it *is* another world. Because what you're thinking it's going to be like is completely the opposite of what is happening.

For both ways of life and for both sets of values, excluders and includers, the language of 'coping' and 'coming to terms' describes the transition between one world and another world; this much they agree on, even if the values they attach to these worlds are totally opposite. Many parents can put their finger on a moment or incident when they experienced this transition, which they often mark as rebellion.

Phil: When the paediatrician come in next morning, I mean he only was in there two seconds, he looked her up and said 'Typical mongol', either 'Typical mongol features' or 'Typical mongol face', it was one of the two he said, and I could have killed him ... They put Jenny [Phil's wife] in a grotty old side ward so that she didn't upset any other of the patients, no one come in and tell us anything. I grabbed one of the midwives, the senior one there, and I said to her, what happens now? And they reiterated that they would like Becky to stay in for tests but Jenny could come home, and Becky was a bit jaundiced you see. I said what happens if she hadn't had Down's Syndrome, they said she could have gone home, so I said: 'That's it, wrap her up, we're going home. Start life as we mean to go on, we'll go home.' That afternoon a friend came round, Ruth and Jim, and they come round with a bottle of champagne, the best you could buy, and it was just like we'd had a baby ... I mean I'd had a sort of cry I suppose, but at the actual time I was glad I had a daughter [after two sons]. And after he said typical mongol, I think, I don't know, it's awkward to explain: everything seemed to fall into place.

Just as the clinical professions can provide parents with the language and the concepts with which to take a negative view of the child, so they can provide the unwitting stimulus for the parent to enter a new, positive world in which things 'fall into place'.

Helen: For some reason I thought of it that they've given me this monster of a baby that I wasn't going to be able to love, and some woman came round – she may have been the hospital social worker or an almoner – and spent about an hour telling me how this was going to completely change the course of my life, I was going to be saddled with this child that would need twenty-four hour care and attention, and I had to think carefully about whether I wanted that for the rest of my life, i.e. was I going to keep him – virtually talking me into not keeping him, and I think the turning-point was that I felt there was something coming from the outside that was, sort of, really trying to urge me to reject him, and that I rebelled against it. So that I can't say I had any positive feelings in the first place, but the realisation that everybody else had negative feelings made me love him.

The majority of parents reported being presented covertly or overtly with an opt-out clause when the diagnosis was first made, often couched in terms of: 'Leave the baby here for a couple of days, go home and think about it' ('it' being unspecified). Cunningham (1982) reports that if parents decide to give up the baby permanently, it is 'for the parents who make it, the right decision'.

It is important to note here than even if a parent is gripped by those negative fantasies that the textbooks claim to be real and universal, she is also immediately capable of embracing a critique of the values she is confronted with. Perhaps we are now in a position to give, from a parental perspective, an alternative interpretation of what exactly it means to 'come to terms with' a child's disability. For the clinical and educational professions (and the lay notions which derive their values from them), their very practice makes it clear what fact it is that you 'come to terms' with: you have not given birth to a member of the human species as we define it, and to which we allocate certain rights and social roles, but to an object of pathology – a 'monster', to use a technical term employed in medical anatomy. For the parent, the same phrase means the inverse: I have not given birth to the monster which my upbringing and socialisation led me to believe I'd had, but to a normal member of the human species as I now define it.

This widening definition of what it is to be human, couched in sociologically aware terms, runs throughout the responses, and is further expressed in attitudes to amniocentesis and abortion in subsequent pregnancies. In medical practice, and especially in medical economics, it is assumed that the identification of a foetus with a disability by amniocentesis (CVS) will inevitably lead to an abortion. Yet, only a small proportion of the parents interviewed would even contemplate termination of a subsequent pregnancy should a test turn out to be positive. Some who had subsequent pregnancies had refused any kind of test, despite in some cases being aggressively pressurised by the hospital. Others had undergone a test because they 'needed to know', not because they had any intention of terminating. Even where doubts are expressed about 'having another one', they are stated in terms which imply a criticism of social arrangements rather than in terms of personal coping.

Jeanette: They're such lovely babies you'd have twenty of them. I'm not sure, though. I'm not sure I could stand shlapping up and down to that bloody clinic time and time again.

Similarly, cosmetic surgery is seen in the professional literature as an option (some parents choose it, some don't), or even as a kind of cure, especially by the surgeons contracted to perform it, whose understanding of the issues extends as far as the principle that if people see a physically normal child they will react to it 'normally' and will elicit normal behaviour. No doubt cosmetic surgery is performed, even encouraged. In this sample, however, not one parent wanted it for their own child, and in general they were more prescriptive about what was morally correct for other parents here than on any other issue.

Pat: The surgeons are God, anyway, aren't they? I mean it was like years ago I heard things about Down's children with holes in the heart and why bother to do it, but now everything's changing – let's make them more normal. But why do that? I mean they're normal to us but they're not normal to other people, so why should we make them normal to them, just to please society? I mean the world's made up of all different coloured people – why shouldn't we have different faces and all? If we all walked round with the same face and same coloured skin it would be pretty boring, wouldn't it?

The world of normality is redefined. No longer a matter of distribution across a norm, of statistics and probability, 'normality' itself is simply a common-sense, inclusive definition of what it is to be human, with wider boundaries redefined from experience.

5 LUCKY LEPERS

'I am fortunate. I do not truly know what it is like to have a child with Down's Syndrome' (Cunningham 1982: 16).

Kathy: Scott is the best thing that ever happened to us. I think it was more, I thought if people would feel sorry for me, then I wouldn't be able to cope with this thing, like. I didn't want any pity, that was the thing I was worried about: that people were going to pity me. I didn't want people to think I couldn't cope with it, like, 'cos I knew I could. I'm *never, ever* going to be frightened of anything again. Before I had Scott I would never say boo to a goose. But I think all the time where you have to keep on fighting all the time, so now like you get so mouthy in the end you can't shut up, you know [laughs], you end up winning the argument 'cos you can't shut up, like. You've had to be like that all the time, otherwise you feel like you ain't getting there, they're getting the better of you, like ... 'Cos you listen, don't you, when you've had the baby they are supposed to help you and advise you, so you take all their ... but then you can only take so much, and you think *these* must be the mad ones, like.

Beverley: In actual fact me having Devon, I've never met so many real people ... He's made us really meet real people, you know what I mean, people with handicapped children, and to me I find them more real than some of my friends that live in another world, fantasising about the future, you know, 'What's the kids going to be when they grow up?' I wouldn't plan a life out for my child, I couldn't possibly do it, you know ... My priorities in my mind's eye is better. Their priorities to me is out the window, if you understand my meaning. My priorities in life is smaller, more compact, but their priorities is for about ten, fifteen years from now. God forbid anything should happen to their children, never mind their house, or their car. It stand out like a sore thumb sometimes when I'm with them, I find people with handicapped children are real people, are people who are people with their children being, talking to them, instead of things that they can give them, you know. Maybe I've swapped lenses ...

Phil: Well I would say that if I had my life over again I wish and hope that everything happens the same, and I think at the end of the day Becky had been the cream on top of the cake ... Perhaps my opinion on morality's changed, you know, that there is right and wrong and all this and that you've got to accept people. I mean I know what it's like to be Black. I feel now that I've got an epitaph at the end of my life that I *did* something, I wasn't a taker ... I mean we still live, which is a sad fact, but we still live in a society where we were like lepers, we still live in a society where you can still reject, and it shouldn't be that; you shouldn't have the option to reject, you should have the support there.

Bravery, contact with social reality and a sense of justice are the themes of these three extracts. If they are symptoms of leprosy, then we are indeed 'fortunate' to know what the experience is like.

6 LAST WORDS

I have quite intentionally cited only one example of the available professional and academic literature. Apart from being one of the most widely read and influential books, it is also more enlightened than most of the published work getting through to teachers, health visitors, therapists and parents too. It does not appear to take a lofty clinical viewpoint, but partakes of the language of partnership and equality between experts and parents.

I have ignored such central and prestigious characters in the drama as Professor Wold of St Bartholomew's Hospital, who is seeking to perfect a cheap, early diagnostic test for trisomy 21 during pregnancy on the interesting grounds that it costs £500,000 (not accounting for inflation) to look after a person with trisomy 21 for life. Let us skirt round Professor Joan Bicknell, a major authority in child psychiatry. In a bang-up-to-date textbook (see Bicknell 1988), she lectures future generations of health and social service professionals on imparting what they are to perceive as 'sad, bad news' to parents. Following a time-honoured tradition of psychiatric categories, she elaborates the 'bereavement response' to diagnosis into a farrago of stages (none of whose terms, as far as I can make out, has ever been defined): (1) 'Shock', (2) 'Panic', (3) 'Denial', (4) 'Grief', (5) 'Guilt', (6) 'Anger' (in general), (7) 'Anger Against Professionals', (8) 'Bargaining' and finally (9) 'Acceptance'. Anyone who wants to explain away the material I have offered in the interview extracts will merely have to look up item (7).

Let us return to the measured tones of Cliff Cunningham. Earlier I mentioned Stokely Carmichael; and here is the White liberalism of mental disability issues. Why am I using his work to set alongside the interview extracts? I am saying that we are confronted, beneath a language which is often common to both parties, with two competing moral philosophies, and that the language of partnership is a mirage, a deliberate and partisan disguise for the fact that one of those philosophies holds power while the other comes from beneath the underdog. There are not 'professionals' and 'parents'. There is a strange tribe that believes in spells, psychometric assessments and incantations, and there is a tribe of what Beverley, Devon's mother, calls real people. The beauty of it is that while not everyone can become Black or become a woman, anyone can join the 'real people'. They may be parents or they may only have letters after their name, but what they have in common is this: they know that intellectual perfection and the criteria for measuring it are chimeras. In our society this knowledge is dangerous, subversive, and – make no mistake – will be dealt with as such. The best way of dealing with it, perhaps, is to draw parents into a prevailing set of values about intelligence and humanity on the grounds of an 'equal partnership' that is spurious and reinforces the attitudes underlying segregation.

REFERENCES

Bicknell, J. (1988) 'The psychopathology of handicap', in G. Horobin and D. May (eds), *Living with Mental Handicap*, London: Jessica Kingsley Publishers.

Cunningham, C. (1982) *Down's Syndrome: An Introduction For Parents*, London: Souvenir Press.

Goodey, C. (1991) (ed.) *Living in the Real World: Families Speak about Down's Syndrome*, London: The Twenty-One Press (available from Newham Parents' Centre Education Shop, 745 Barking Road, London E.13).

Chapter 15

Ruled out or rescued?

A Statement for Balbinder

Elizabeth Grugeon

Source: Grugeon, E. and Woods, P. (1990) *Educating All*, Chapter 3, London: Routledge.

Elizabeth Grugeon provides a detailed account of her association with Balbinder Singh and his family. She was a friend and adviser for the family as they tried to negotiate a path through an education system which was not always easy to understand. Balbinder was the subject of a Statement and Elizabeth Grugeon charts the process from an initial expression of concern about Balbinder's lack of progress by the primary school to his transfer to a special school for pupils categorised as having 'moderate learning difficulties'.

1 MY INVOLVEMENT WITH THE FAMILY

A long-standing friendship with an Asian family who were neighbours of mine led to my being involved in the process of Statementing their youngest child, Balbinder Singh. He was 6 years old and had been at the school for three terms when the head, knowing that I was a neighbour and friend of Balbinder's mother, invited me to go with Mrs Singh to a meeting with the educational psychologist. The head explained that he and the class teacher felt that Balbinder was making little progress and they were worried about his lack of concentration and poor language. They were considering the possibility of a place in a special school for children with moderate learning difficulties which could offer 'smaller classes and more individual attention'. His transfer would involve a lengthy and complicated assessment procedure, and they wanted me to help to explain this to Balbinder's parents and to reassure them. This chapter is an account of the process and is an attempt to see it from the family's perspective.

I had known the family for some years as I had been Mrs Singh's English tutor on a local authority adult literacy programme. Balbinder was 3 years old when I first started visiting the house, a very sociable child who eagerly awaited my arrival and the chance to play with the bag of toys I always brought with me. Over the years, in my role as home tutor to his mother, I had had a privileged relationship with Balbinder and his family. By the time he started school I had already been an intermediary between the family and the town hall, the DHSS, the local social services, the medical profession and school. Mr and Mrs Singh kept most of their official correspondence between the pages of their telephone directory and on my weekly visits we sorted out the milk tokens, rates demands, post office giros, all of which made linguistic demands which were beyond the level of their competence. Mr Singh, a Kenyan Asian, confessed to me, after I had been a friend of the family for several years, that he was neither fluent in Swahili, the language of his education up to 13, nor in Punjabi, his mother tongue. However, the family spoke Punjabi exclusively at home and had very strong views on the need to do this. They were concerned that the boys should not lose touch with their language and culture.

The two older boys, aged 5 and 7, were competent in both languages. Balbinder seemed slower to talk and his mother was worried about his reluctance to speak English. As both parents spoke to him in Punjabi for most of the time this did not seem surprising. I reassured Mrs Singh that once he started play-group there would be an improvement. In fact the health visitor diagnosed a problem with speech at his screening at age 3, and he began attending the local health clinic for speech therapy. Mrs Singh mentioned this once or twice but did not seem to set much store by it. She continued to express concern at what she felt to be his backwardness at speaking English. I wondered how many people he had the opportunity to speak to outside his family.

However, the playgroup run by local parents had not been the success for Balbinder that we had hoped. There were complaints about his behaviour. He did not seem to know how to play, would not settle down, ran about too much and fought with the other children. At home, whenever I visited, he always seemed the same docile, attractive child sitting silently watching TV in the impeccably tidy and attractive furnished living room of the very small, terraced house. In the house, the lives of the three young boys seemed quiet, calm and disciplined. But the large hall at playgroup, the number of activities, different experiences and other children seemed to produce excitable and often aggressive behaviour in Balbinder. The staff were also worried about his speech, not seeming to take into account the fact that this was the first time he had come out of a Punjabi-speaking environment and was having to cope with new experiences in a foreign language. His mother's fluent, though inaccurate, English and confident manner may have led them to expect more of him. Mrs Singh worried about him a great deal, and was often very angry at his apparent lack of progress. She wanted him to learn to count, begin to write, and above all to speak English.

She and the children visited my house regularly at this period, so that I could hear the oldest boy, Ravi, read. He had already overtaken his mother and she did not know how to cope with the graded readers he brought home from school or his teacher's request that she should hear him read. Whenever they visited me I listened to him reading. He was quite fluent but seemed to read without comprehension. I felt that the texts he was reading did not speak of familiar experiences or vocabulary. I remember him struggling with a story where understanding of the narrative depended on the reader knowing about canals. He could read the words – *canal, lock, barge* – but the illustrations of an urban canal with tall, industrial buildings and long painted boats portrayed an unknown landscape. At 8 he was rapidly becoming a non-reader. The idea that reading might be for pleasure had not occurred to him. Balbinder was always pleased to come along for these sessions, to play with my children's toys and run in the garden. Mrs Singh brought her letters and forms for me to elucidate.

I was constantly surprised at the extent to which she needed explanations for even the most taken-for-granted aspects of junior school life. The list of clothing for a school trip included 'night-dress' and 'sponge-bag'. The Singh children slept in their underpants, and she wondered whether I could lend her a 'night-dress' for Ravi and also a sponge. Almost all documents sent home from school were incomprehensible. Letters inviting parents to join the parent–teacher association, visit the 'Spring Fayre', to volunteer for 'parent-governor elections', or attend a 'Maths Workshop' were put in the bin after my attempts to explain them. Schools unwittingly erect a language barrier which must exclude great numbers of parents. End of term reports contained phrases like 'his development of spatial awareness' or 'his confidence on the apparatus'. However phrases like 'is working hard', 'always tries his best', 'is beginning to show some improvement' did not fool her. She interpreted them quite accurately to mean that her children were under-achieving and the message she took from them was almost always a negative one.

On one occasion Mrs Singh had asked me to go with her to visit one of the boy's teachers. The teacher was brusque and busy. She brushed aside Mrs Singh's assertions that her son was not making progress by telling her repeatedly that it was unreasonable to expect anything more; she used phrases like 'He is well below average', 'He is slow', 'He is in the bottom set, you must accept that. You can't put it there if it's not there.' Mrs Singh was not satisfied. She wanted to know why he never brought anything home, why he had no reading book. His teacher explained that homework for 8 year olds was not school policy and Jeetinder was called in to show his mother that he could read. He produced his reading book, one of the 'Pirate series' by Sheila McCullagh, and read quite fluently. The teacher suggested that Mrs Singh could help by reading with him, Mrs Singh to read one line, Jeetinder the next; she was evidently unaware of the possibility that Jeetinder's reading could be more competent than his mother's.

Looking at a piece of work on the board Mrs Singh said she wanted her son to write like that. The teacher, by now worn down by Mrs Singh's refusal to accept Jeetinder's limitations, told her that it had been written by 'a highly intelligent girl'. She continued to try to convince Mrs Singh that although Jeetinder was in the bottom set he was doing well and was not 'the bottom of the bottom set'. None of this convinced Mrs Singh who left the classroom saying in an unusually dictatorial tone to the class teacher, 'I want you to sort him out and bring home-work home.' Later, I tried to mollify her by pointing out that the teacher had said what a nice boy he was. Looking me straight in the eye she replied, 'Nice is in every child.'

The school's educational psychologist had made contact with the family when he had been involved in an assessment of Jeetinder, the second son, now in the fourth year at the school. There had been concern about his progress at the same stage as there now was for Balbinder's. Mrs Singh had been visited at home and the head had arranged for me to be present so that I could explain and reinforce any suggestions. In the event, I found this difficult as they seemed inappropriate. The psychologist had suggested among other things that Mrs Singh could help to improve Jeetinder's spoken and written language by reading to him at bedtime and could help to improve his numeracy by encouraging him to spend and account for his pocket money. Both ideas were culturally alien to Mrs Singh. There were no English children's books in the house, and the boys did not shop on their own nor have regular pocket money. Neither parent was fully literate in English or their mother tongue. Mrs Singh had seemed mystified by the advice, as she believed the school should be responsible for progress in English and mathematics and shrugged helplessly when I suggested that parents also had an important role.

2 THE STATEMENTING PROCESS FOR BALBINDER

My contact with the family had lapsed for a while when the head asked to see me to request help in explaining the Statementing procedures to Mrs Singh. The head told me that Mrs Singh had been coming to school regularly to express concern about Balbinder's lack of progress. The class teacher and the head were also worried; they felt that, 'after four terms at school, he is the slowest in the class'. Their concern was that in September, when he should be moving into the second year infants with his age cohort, he would be far behind. The head had asked the educational psychologist to come and assess him with a view to producing a formal Statement of Special Educational Needs. Standardised tests had shown that 'whereas his two older brothers had scored better on verbal ability than on visual motor ability, Balbinder had performed equally poorly on both'. As a result the educational psychologist had been investigating the possibility of a place at a local special school for Balbinder. They now wanted to explain all this to Mrs Singh and hoped that I would be able to explain the implications of what they were going to say.

The same morning Mrs Singh had approached me in the school foyer, handed me a bag full of letters, and burst into tears. I realised that I hadn't visited her for some weeks and agreed to go to her house after school.

As an outside observer drawn into the Statementing process by the professionals involved, I had a neutral but not disinterested role. I kept a diary of events and attempted to chart the process by which 6-year-old Balbinder was removed from mainstream education.

March 3: The initial meeting

Meeting with the head, the school's educational psychologist, Mrs Singh and myself at school.

The head explained to Mrs Singh that Balbinder was not making much progress and that because of class sizes he would be unlikely to receive the kind of attention he needed. He explained that at Cedars (the local authority's school for children 'with learning difficulties') where classes are small and the teachers are specialists at coping with Balbinder's sort of problems, he might do better. He stressed that it was essential for Balbinder to start at Cedars as soon as possible, if he was going to catch up. He seemed to be suggesting that once Balbinder had been at Cedars for a while, he might be capable of re-entering mainstream education at middle school transfer. This was an idea she was to hold on to throughout the process.

Both the head and the educational psychologist stressed the positive value of Cedars and the likely problems for Balbinder if he stayed on at his present school, which they told her did not have the expertise to cope with his needs. By suggesting this they began quite unwittingly to undermine her confidence in the school and in herself. She became very upset and confused, clearly feeling that Balbinder's failure was her fault. She cried a lot repeatedly saying 'He always wants to play . . . he just wants toys.' When she was calmer, she also made it clear that she felt that a stricter approach that forced Balbinder to concentrate and work harder was all that was needed. She felt that he was not doing well because he was not trying hard enough, and that his teachers were not making him try hard enough. She listened intently as they explained the Statementing procedure. They stressed that the decision to send Balbinder to Cedars would be made by Mrs Singh and her husband. The first stage would be to visit the school and then return to discuss the matter again. A date was arranged for the following week for both events and I agreed to go with them.

What I did not realise at the time, but discovered later, was that Mrs Singh had no idea that transfer next September had been suggested – she expected that it would happen straight away.

After she had left, the head and educational psychologist explained the Statementing procedure in more detail. In the past they had waited until after the school screening tests at 7-plus but felt that this was leaving it too late. In Balbinder's case it was not simply that he was a slow learner. There were what the head called 'social concerns' behind his transfer. He was developing self-control in the classroom, but found it harder on the playground where it seemed that he was easily influenced by other children to behave badly. As he put it, 'He reverts when he is with naughty children.' They had not given these reasons for transfer to his parents. Yet they were clearly important considerations as far as the school was concerned.

It was not a foregone conclusion that there would be a place available at Cedars since there is a lot of pressure on special school places in the county. As the head of Cedars was making his entry list for September already, and would have to submit it by the end of the week, the educational psychologist was going to request a place for Balbinder before Statementing him. Thus it was essential to get Mr and Mrs Singh's agreement as soon as possible. Later on the same day, I visited Mr and Mrs Singh at home. Over tea and food we talked about the school's suggestion. Mrs Singh was upset; she felt rejected by the school her children had been attending for five years. She was depressed and angry with Balbinder. She had been crying and said that she had been 'feeling awful' all day. She clearly found it hard to sort out the implications of what was being suggested. However we agreed to visit Cedars together in a few days' time.

The difficulty she was having in making sense of the boys' education was illustrated by the packet of letters she had brought to school in the morning. One from the LEA was about her 8-year-old son's transfer to middle school, an event generating a great deal of paper including a list of the available schools; another letter from the LEA explained parents' rights of choice and appeal, also dates of open evenings; yet another letter from the school to which he had been allocated required the parents to sign the tear-off slip and return it to their present school. Fortunately, I noticed that he had been given a place at a different school from his older brother and that it was actually a matter of filling in the appeal form requesting a place at another school. I suggested that they should also accept the invitation to take him to visit his new school's Open Evening. Mrs Singh said she would go if I came too but not otherwise. Another letter from the middle school was about a visiting theatre group and asked for money as well as a tear-off slip. We discussed with her 10-year-old son whether he wanted to see the play and we put the money for a ticket in an envelope. To his chagrin we threw away the letter about a skiing holiday. At nearly £400 for a week in Austria his parents were not interested.

In the evening I consulted a friend who is also a local head teacher. Her school has a high proportion of ethnic minority children where I felt Balbinder might not have seemed such a problem. In her opinion, it was unlikely that he would get a place at Cedars at such a late stage in the year. She also felt that age 6 was too early to make what she saw as a drastic decision – once out of mainstream education she felt he would be unlikely to get back.

At this stage in the proceedings, my own feelings were mixed. If the school felt it could not cope with Balbinder then maybe he would be better in a more sympathetic environment. On the other hand Mrs Singh would lose all her social contacts in the local community once she did not have to take him to school every day. The school gave her a point of reference and contact with other mothers. The middle school which both her older boys attended was a long walk from her home and made little or no attempt to involve parents. If Balbinder was bussed to Cedars every day she would be effectively cut off from any real involvement in her children's schooling, and from an important part of her own role within the community as the mother of a young child at the local school.

On the other hand I knew that her confidence in Balbinder's school had been profoundly shaken by the interview with the head and educational psychologist. If Balbinder didn't get a place at Cedars this year she would become even more anxious about his progress.

March 9: Visiting Cedars School

The head made us very welcome. He began by talking to Mr and Mrs Singh about the school. He stressed the normality of the children who attended it. He explained that children came to Cedars when their own school could not give them the individual help with basic skills which they needed. He explained that when a child becomes anxious he or she may stop learning. Cedars, he told them, was a special school because it had special teachers with special skills and training. All of the sixteen teachers in the school were experienced in teaching children with learning difficulties. Another special feature was the size of the groups, ten in the first year, twelve in the second and fifteen thereafter. Balbinder would be in a group with ten children.

Mrs Singh seemed to be listening intently but I guess that a lot of what was being said went over her head. I am not sure that she even knows the word 'special'; and phrases like 'learning difficulties', 'becomes anxious', 'experienced' are not necessarily familiar. After a while she asked, 'These children, do they learn it at the end?' The head replied that the school offered ideal circumstances and that most children responded positively. There is an annual review in which a report is made on the child's progress. All parents, he told them, have the right to say, 'I want my child to leave', and he said, 'Our job is to help the child go back.' They review this possibility annually and he explained that when they have identified children who will go back they let them go into mainstream school for at first a morning and then one day a week. At the moment six children would be going back into middle school in September. At this point Mrs Singh said comfortably, 'They have learnt, that's nice.'

The head went on to explain that the school's job was to understand each child's problem. He told them that many children learned more slowly. He illustrated different ways in which reading, for example, could be taught, and how some children may not be 'mature' enough to cope with a 'look and say' approach, or may not develop that way. He explained how 'look and say' uses eyes, while phonics uses ears. Mr and Mrs Singh listened politely but, possibly, were confused by all this specialist terminology.

He went on to tell them about the school. The children started at 5 and could stay until 16. They could also leave at any time. Each part of the school – lower/middle/upper – resembled mainstream school, the difference lying in the size of the teaching group. At 16-plus they go on to college for up to two years and follow courses which will lead to work. Several of the 15 year olds were on work experience at the moment.

He then took us round the school. The lower school had its own grassed and paved play area with plentiful equipment. The rooms were small, purpose built, had carpeted floors, and each teacher had a non-teaching assistant. It was an intimate small-scale non-threatening environment. I was particularly impressed by the art room. The workshop and home economics area were also impressive, and the school had three computers. Outside was very pleasant with views over open fields and a local park. Part of the senior side had been landscaped to make an attractive outdoor work area with wooden table and benches made in the workshop. There was a swimming pool and a distant view of the donkey field. There seemed to be few ethnic minority children, one in each class perhaps, certainly none in the youngest group.

After the visit the head talked about the importance of parental involvement. He explained that regular contact and discussion of ways in which parents can help at home was vital: 'Together, we can achieve more.' The school had an open-door policy. He then put it to Mr and Mrs Singh that they would have to think about whether they would like Balbinder to come to the school. He explained that there were a limited number of places, with sixteen or seventeen taken up for September already (I wondered whether this meant Balbinder might be unlucky, but did not like to ask).

He explained the procedure by which Balbinder would be given a place. The educational psychologist would prepare notes on Balbinder. He himself would visit Balbinder at his present school. He stressed, 'We only want him to come if it's right. Nothing happens until you say yes.' Then Mr and Mrs Singh would come again with Balbinder, and finally they would receive a letter from County Hall. Again, he stressed that the final decision lay with them: 'He will not come until you sign it ... in the end you decide.' Mr Singh asked his first question: 'Would it be next September?' The head said that that would be the case and that Balbinder would stay for as long as he needed their help. However they could make the decision to take him away 'at any time'.

Mrs Singh asked 'Do you have the same holiday?' and then spoke for the first time about Balbinder. She seemed distressed, 'I mean Balbinder, he used to just sit by the telly, even now he still ... he wants toys ... he doesn't want to do the things, he wants to do all the time what he wants to do ...' The head nodded reassuringly, seeming to listen, but he did not encourage her to talk about Balbinder any more. Instead he went on to tell them that the shortest time they kept pupils was for two years but that usually they tried to move people back into mainstream at the time for transfer to middle/upper school.

He told them that the educational psychologist was very good and really knew the children. Mrs Singh, still pursuing her own thoughts, said, 'I wish he was just like other children, like my other children.' The head said it was important to think about 'whatever is best' for Balbinder, and went back to what the school catered for – 'people think it's for mentally handicapped'. 'It doesn't look like one', said Mrs Singh very positively. The head told them that there were many different special schools in the county and explained where and what each one was for, reassuring them that Cedars is 'a school for children who have difficulty getting started with basic skills'. Its job is to help children 'who are struggling'. He gave Mr and Mrs Singh a school booklet and saw us out. We rang for a taxi and while we waited, looked at books of photographs of school plays, trips, art work and sports days. Both Mr and Mrs Singh seemed surprised and relieved by the normality of the school. Mr Singh told me that one of his brothers-in-law had told them it was a school for mentally handicapped. This had clearly been worrying them both.

When we got home I could see that they were ready to agree to the move. It was also evident that they had not weighed up the consequences. It all seemed easy – they sign on the dotted line and Balbinder would be virtually taken out of their hands. Despite the school's stated intention to involve parents as far as possible, I seriously doubted whether Mr or Mrs Singh would be capable or prepared to enter into the kind of partnership the school envisaged. Looking through the booklet the head had given them, I guessed that they would have some difficulty making sense of it. They would probably need help with sentences like, 'Class teachers, together with the help of the remedial specialist, ensure that there is a detailed understanding of the learning difficulties of each individual child.' Terms like, 'environmental work', 'a full curriculum', 'special programmes of work for language development' would need to be explained to them. The school's expressed intention is that 'Parents are helped to understand the nature of the learning difficulties of their child and are encouraged to visit the school frequently to develop that understanding and to continue that approach at home.' Neither Mr nor Mrs Singh have the confidence to take on such a role.

March 12: Coping with the procedure

I met with Mrs Singh and the educational psychologist in the head's room. Mrs Singh was very certain – she and her husband had decided that they both want Balbinder to go to Cedars. I tried to explore the problems Mrs Singh would have in attempting to be a fully participating parent but the educational psychologist seemed to feel that this was a problem common to many Cedars parents.

The educational psychologist spent some time explaining the legal side of Statementing, which is complex. He told us that it would take many weeks to sort out and would involve a variety of procedures, such as a medical, reports from the school and visits. There would be twenty-nine days between the initial letter from County Hall and any action. The sheer amount of information seemed daunting. I arranged to visit that afternoon and to go through it with Mr and Mrs Singh.

When I arrived they showed me the letter they had received from the Chief Education Officer that morning which explained the proposed Statementing procedure:

The learning difficulties being experienced by your child were discussed and you agreed that your child probably has a special educational need which requires further investigation. Therefore it is proposed to carry out an assessment of your child's needs under the Education Act 1981 with your agreement.

The letter was at pains to stress the parents' involvement and their rights: 'If it is agreed that the Authority should determine the special educational provision for your child ... your further rights under the Education Act 1981 will be explained to you.' An enclosed booklet gave further general information about the provision of special education with an addendum summarising the legal rights of parents in relation to the assessment process. In this, the mysterious twenty-nine days was explained: 'Parents will have a period of 29 days in which to seek further information from the Chief Education Officer and to make representations and submit written evidence.'

Since they had evidently made up their minds, none of this seemed important to them. Going through the Cedars' brochure with them, however, they were pleased to find a statement which they could relate to, namely that the school sets out to help children, 'who are having problems in learning to read, find spelling and writing difficult, are unable to express themselves well, are unable to settle and concentrate ...' All these seemed to relate to Balbinder's needs as his parents saw them and Mr and Mrs Singh were beginning to seem happier. As they understood it, after a short while Balbinder might be sorted out and returned to mainstream. I did not feel so optimistic. The brochure stated clearly that while some children transferred back to mainstream schools, 'the majority remain until they are 16 years of age'.

June 5: Testing

Visited Mrs Singh at home. She told me that she had been present when Balbinder was tested by the educational psychologist. Balbinder had had to do a lot of puzzles. The psychologist had said he was good with his hands. Mrs Singh said he would not sit down and kept walking about. She said he was the same at home, only wanted to play with toys and watch TV, he wouldn't do any 'work'. I was not sure what she meant by 'work'. She went on to her worries about Jeetinder who still wasn't bringing anything home from school. She was being racially harassed and was afraid to go out into her garden. Her husband was away in India for three weeks. People were throwing things over her garden wall and someone had painted on the front door. We spent a lot of time discussing this. In some ways Balbinder seemed the least of her problems at the time. Perhaps it was a relief that matters were being taken out of her hands. We agreed to meet at school the following week.

June 10: The information for the Statement

First, the head went through the school report, details of birth, address, etc. There was a brief account of professional intervention to date. Before starting school he had attended the child development centre, received speech therapy and since had been seen on several occasions by the educational psychologist.

Then, there was a description of the child's functioning: he had taken a long time to settle into school, e.g. routine and order of the class. He had communication problems – speech and English language were not good. He had difficulty 'sounding' because of this, and it was thought to be affecting his progress in learning to read. The head attempted to explain to Mrs Singh how children have to learn the initial sounds of words and how having two languages can impede this. I think Mrs Singh understood. Balbinder has also had difficulty learning colours, numbers and sounds. His progress was slow because his retention was poor.

At this point Mrs Singh looking concerned said, 'You think there's something wrong with him inside of him?' The head said, 'No, he's not ill.' Mrs Singh agreed that it must be the way he forgot things. The head said 'Yes, he does have difficulty remembering – particularly sounding', and felt that this could be because he was perhaps more fluent in Punjabi.

There were discrepancies in the report. On the one hand Mrs Singh was told that his drawing and writing were immature, that he was still drawing and writing like a very young child; yet later she was told that he was very good with a pencil and talented at art! Having said that he was very immature the report added that there had been considerable improvement, but it had taken a long time (he had only been at school for four terms and had had a change of teacher). The head stressed that what Balbinder needed was to be in a small group, not in a class of twenty-three. In order for him to maintain interest he needed to work in short spurts. In his present situation, his difficulty in concentrating took up a lot of the teacher's time. The head then commented on his social development. Here they felt there had been much progress. Balbinder used to be 'wild', but he had learned to share and to take part in group work, despite still being a very lively child.

The head then went on to describe the aims and provision of special education. Since Balbinder clearly made more progress in a small group where he could have a lot of attention, and where all worked at the same pace, this could be an answer. The head felt that the boy needed somebody permanently watching him. Also he needed a lot of talking in English, as he was still not sounding words clearly. Further he was a very active child, and needed specialist apparatus. They had all the necessary facilities and resources at Cedars. The head was very persuasive, showing concern for the way Balbinder would react when (or if) he fell behind. As he was already behind in mastering the basic skills which lay the foundation for all further work, he felt that Balbinder needed a lot of help if he was to do justice to his abilities. And he said very kindly, 'That's our view of Balbinder.'

The educational psychologist gave his report. He reiterated that Balbinder's problems with language had needed attention before school. He stressed that he was a very likeable little boy. However, observing him in the classroom he had noticed his immature behaviour. He ran about a lot, and found concentration difficult. Despite much improvement in pencil and art work there had been none in reading and other school work. He was fidgety and in a dream world when being given instruction in a group. Often he watched other children and then followed and copied them.

The psychologist commented that Balbinder had liked having a reading book and clearly wanted to read but when it came to reading he did not understand what he was doing but relied on guessing. He clearly wanted to do well, wanted to read but needed a lot of extra help. When asked questions he gave one word answers, though he used two words on occasion, as in 'boys swimming', 'wet play'. On the tests he gave him he was better on puzzles and patterns, poor on those involving speaking and understanding.

He felt that Balbinder needed to work slowly and not be pushed – he needed more time and specific help to speak in sentences. At this point Mrs Singh said, 'They are not allowed to speak English at home.' She felt that he spoke better in Punjabi and that he remembered better in Punjabi. She referred to her own family: parents, brother and sisters who all spoke English at home. She found this very odd. At the weekend when she had taken Balbinder to stay with his grand-parents in Coventry, her brother had been trying to teach Balbinder to say 'Can I', or 'May I' instead of 'I want to'.

The educational psychologist listened tolerantly to Mrs Singh's comments, did not respond to them but simply repeated that Balbinder needed to be with teachers who were experienced in working with small groups. Mrs Singh said that she felt that Balbinder would always do what was wanted if it suited him. The educational psychologist told her that one of the teachers from Cedars had visited Balbinder in school and made very positive comments. It seemed that a place was available but that all the complex procedures had to be completed before it could be offered to them. He still had to have a medical. The head would speak to the school doctor that same day. Social Services would write to Mrs Singh. The procedure was necessarily long-winded but it could be completed by the end of term. Mrs Singh expressed a worry about Balbinder refusing to dress himself and ordering her to get him ready for school when he could do this perfectly well if he wanted to. The educational psychologist said this was under-standable while he was feeling rather unsettled. The head said he would chase up the documents.

Mrs Singh seemed bewildered by the amount of information she had been given. I promised to go and see her again on Friday morning. Throughout this interview Mrs Singh, who was still struggling to grasp the implications of what the head and educational psychologist were telling her, attempted to contribute. Her anecdotes were treated courteously but no real response was made. It seemed that now the process was under way her contribution was not required.

June 12

I visited Mr and Mrs Singh. Mrs Singh and I talked Mr Singh through the meeting, point by point. He agreed with the head's account of Balbinder's lack of concentration, which obviously worried them both a great deal. He listened to what I had to say about the procedure still to be gone through and hoped that they would soon hear whether Balbinder had a place. I said that this was almost certain but the process was rather slow. Mrs Singh agreed to tell me when she heard from the doctor. They both understood that this was a formality and that he was not thought to be 'ill'.

What particularly concerned me was their feeling that Balbinder seemed to understand and respond better in Punjabi. Mrs Singh expressed her feelings that it was very important for all her children to speak Punjabi and she was afraid that they might not do this if she and Mr Singh spoke English. Both parents were very concerned that he should get more appropriate help and were now convinced that this would be provided at Cedars.

June 22: Acceptance

Mrs and Mrs Singh had received a letter offering Balbinder a place at Cedars. They had understood the gist but needed help. We filled in the acceptance form and phoned the school about a visit. The school secretary said all the September intake would be invited for a morning before the end of term. Balbinder, who had been excluded from all deliberations about his future, had not seen his new school yet.

July 15: Balbinder visits his new school

Mrs Singh, Balbinder and I set off to visit Cedars School. Balbinder was very subdued. His mother said he was not happy about the new school, and wanted to stay where he was. He had, after all, had five terms there, he would be 7 in December. He did not speak all the way. Mrs Singh remarked what a long way it seemed. We were early and stood in the playground. Balbinder looked around but clung to Mrs Singh. We went in and were ushered into the hall where a number of other new children were looking at books of photos of school trips and events. We were asked to sit in the third and fourth rows and the lower school children filed in. The head explained that the school had a lower/middle/upper division and the lower school head briefly explained that the children were going to show the parents and new children what they had been doing. Each year group described a recent trip and showed photos and work they had done. The classes were small, as was the number of ethnic minority children. There were one, or possibly two, Afro-Caribbean children overall and one or two Asian children in each group. Mrs Singh and Balbinder noticed each one and commented. It was hot and the demonstration went on much too long, but it gave us all some idea of how caring the teachers were and it was a practical illustration of what the school was trying to do.

The children were then asked to go out to play. Balbinder was very reluctant and clung to his mother. He had lost interest in the activities. There had been too much 'talk and show' early on and he had been wriggling about, scraping his chair back and causing Mrs Singh to reprimand him constantly. It looked as if we would have to take him out but an older Asian boy came and took him away, and he went quite confidently. The head then told the parents about travel, uniform, swimming (once a week all the year round), the PTA, illnesses, notes for absence or non-swimming and, above all, contacting the school whenever in doubt. We were then taken to have coffee and the school secretary handed out official forms for the parents to fill in. Mrs Singh filled them in although she had already expressed alarm at the number of notes she was going to have to write to the school.

Classes were allocated and Balbinder was to be in class 1 with a Mrs Allinson and a nursery assistant. It was small, with its own toilets and washbasins and an entirely private playground. Balbinder ran outside straight away, gesturing to me to come and look at it. In the playground they had a sturdy wooden house with door and windows, climbing and swinging equipment and lots of small bicycles and tricycles. In the classroom, photos of the trip to the seaside were on display and there were small circular tables. It was all on a scale much more appropriate for children than the high vaulting of his previous school and there was much more play equipment. This filled Mrs Singh with horror. She was worried by the way he roamed about touching everything, and during a long chat to Mrs Allinson expressed her concern that he could not get on with anything, and could not write or read. Mrs Allinson was very reassuring. However, Mrs Singh clearly saw Cedars as a temporary phase. Earlier on, in the playground, as Balbinder had gradually gained confidence and begun to explore and use things Mrs Singh had said, wistfully, 'I do hope Balbinder learn so quickly he will soon go back to his school.'

On the way out the head knelt down to say goodbye to Balbinder, who was still looking rather mystified but was much less clinging and was smiling more. In the car on the way home he sat alone, opened the window and put his head out. It was very hard to imagine what he made of what was going on. No one had consulted him and he didn't seem to want to talk about it. In all these transactions Balbinder seemed a shadowy figure. Decisions were being taken about his future which no one could explain to him. Over the last few months he had become rather withdrawn and mistrustful; a subdued version of his former self.

At Cedars Mrs Singh had instantly made friends with a young Asian woman (wearing trousers and a shirt) with a little girl who was evidently a year older than Balbinder. She and Mrs Singh spoke in Punjabi but her English sounded local and I suspected that she preferred to speak English. However, Mrs Singh was pleased to meet her and generally liked all the teachers and what she saw. I wondered whether she had any misgivings. The distance will certainly be a problem. What she was making of this experience was also hard to imagine. Choice seemed to have been taken away from her, but some of her anxieties had also been allayed.

3 PROGRESS REPORT

In September Balbinder started at Cedars. My contact with the family became much less frequent. Their circumstances had changed: Mr Singh had a full-time job, they had taken a big step and purchased their council house and Mrs Singh now felt that she needed permanent work herself. The job she finally acquired during the summer holidays meant leaving home before the children and returning after them. The coach which picked up the Cedars' children stopped about five minutes' walk away from their home. Balbinder had to be seen onto it, and met at the end of the day. For the first few weeks of term this was a problem. Mr Singh could take him to the bus when he was on late shifts and collect him on early shifts. His brothers aged 8 and 10, whose school was a long walk in the opposite direction, had to be relied on to take this responsibility when their father could not. The whole operation caused Mrs Singh a great deal of anxiety. By half-term, a local parent with a child at Cedars had offered to put Balbinder on the coach in the morning and let him stay at her house until he could be picked up in the evening. Mrs Singh had now effectively become cut off from her children's education just as Balbinder had been cut off from local peer group relationships. She occasionally contacted me, and for a Christmas present gave me a photograph of Balbinder taken at school and made into a calendar. This showed him sitting at a desk, pencil in hand: his mother's vision of what school should be about. She and Mr Singh had visited the school for a Christmas event and had been pleased to hear that Balbinder was being moved into the second class. She had been worried that he was still playing too much and not learning anything.

From January to July my contacts with the family were infrequent and concerned the progress of the two older boys. My advice was sought on several occasions when the family did not know how to cope with quite serious problems concerning the behaviour of one of them. Balbinder was no longer a worry. However, in July Mrs Singh phoned to ask whether I could go with her to Cedars' open evening. She wanted my opinion on Balbinder's progress. I was not able to go with her, but, as I was in contact with the school's section XI[1] teacher at the time, I arranged to visit on my own. The section XI teacher, who had particular responsibility for Balbinder, said that he was the least of her worries. He had been moved to a higher class, seemed well adjusted and chatted a lot when she worked with him. His class teacher also felt that he was making progress. Both parents had come to the open evening and she had been able to talk to them. They had also come to school earlier in the year for the annual assessment meeting, a statutory requirement for children who are the subject of Statements.

Looking back to her first encounter with Balbinder a year ago, when she had visited him at his previous school, she said that she had been shocked. He had been on the periphery of a large class and little attempt was being made to involve him in what was going on. She had felt at the time that he was 'pretty borderline for special school'. It seemed that in a school where he was in such a minority, his language and ethnicity had been defined as particular problems requiring the rather Draconian solution of Statementing. His present class teacher and the section XI teacher both agreed that he was a slow learner, but felt that he did not exhibit the behavioural problems nor degrees of learning difficulty that characterised many of the children in the school. This was borne out by observing him in the classroom, where he was sitting quietly working, in contrast with the much less controlled behaviour of other children in this small group. In this environment he appeared to have become a model pupil.

However, despite the small class and the specialist attention he was still considered far behind for a 7 year old. He could not read or write independently. His written work, like both his brothers', was neat and controlled, consisting of short accounts of daily events which the teacher had transcribed and he had carefully illustrated and copied. The question of return to mainstream schooling was not being considered.

Later, talking to his teacher after a year and two terms at Cedars, it seemed that Balbinder's conversational language was developing well; he could hold his own in a small group often initiating topics of interest, describing, explaining and enquiring. However, his teacher warned that proficiency in conversational language should not be assumed to equate with proficiency in cognitive or 'academic' language. She reported on his 'good imagination, something which shows up particularly in his drawings which always contain fine detail'.

Out of mainstream education perhaps for the rest of his school career, Balbinder is no longer defined as a problem. His re-entry, however, either to mainstream or to the start of adult working life, may not be achieved so smoothly. The process of Statementing has disrupted his normal development. It has not taken into account the evident disjuncture between the cultural norms of his home and community and those of the school. In a more recent conversation with his mother she was still worried about him despite good reports from the school and the fact that 'he now speaks both languages all right'. Her lack of contact with the school, the distance and her work made her feel helpless: 'I can't rely on myself – I don't know – working all the time – how could I know.' Balbinder would be 8 at Christmas and she saw no evidence of the improvement in learning to read and write that she was hoping for.

NOTE

1   Section XI teachers are provided through central government funds to support the education of ethnic minority pupils.

Chapter 16

On being a client
Conflicting perspectives on assessment

Derrick Armstrong and David Galloway

This chapter looks at the perceptions of parents of their role in the assessment of their child's special educational needs as part of the Statementing process carried out under the 1981 Education Act. The analysis is based on observations of professional–parent and professional–child interactions during the assessments of thirty children referred to the Schools Psychological Service in three LEAs because they were thought to have emotional and behavioural difficulties. In each case these observations were complemented by interviews held with the participants.

1 INTRODUCTION: PERCEPTIONS DIFFER

Perhaps it is not surprising that, without exception, the professionals to whom we talked stated emphatically that their overriding concern was to act in the interests of their child clients. Likewise, they expressed a desire to involve parents at the centre of decision-making. The former is consistent with the ethical codes of their professional associations (e.g. Association of Educational Psychologists (1984) Members Handbook). The latter, recommended by The Warnock Report (DES 1978), was established in law by the 1981 Education Act and supported by subsequent advice to professionals issued by the DES (1983, 1989).

Does the 1981 Act assist or inhibit cooperation between professionals and parents? On face value the Act formalises a cooperative framework. In practice, however, the bureaucratisation of the professional–parent relationship and the assessment process may lead to a situation in which the primary function of parental involvement is to legitimise professional decisions.

Many parents felt that their own contribution to the assessment was only taken seriously when it supported what the professionals were saying. On many occasions in our study we found a sharp contrast between the professionals' perception that a high degree of consensus had been reached and the parents' perception that they had agreed to a course of action because they saw no other real choice, particularly if the urgent needs of the child and other family members were to be quickly met.

In the following section we use case history data to identify ways in which the professional–parent relationship operates within the context of the 1981 Act.

This is followed by a discussion of the impact the 1981 Act has had on the notion of partnership.

2 CONFLICTS OF INTEREST: THREE CASE STUDIES

Each of the examples in this section illustrate the complexities which lie behind the definition of problem and special need by professionals in what they believe to be a collaborative relationship with parents.

John: defining parents as part of 'the problem'

Cooperation with parents may be made particularly difficult where the professional identifies a conflict of interests between parents and child. For example, the home situation may be seen as the single most important factor 'causing' the child's behaviour problems. Rather than being seen as partners in the search for a solution parents may be seen as part of the problem (Moses and Croll 1987, Wood 1988). Because they are viewed in this light parents may respond with diffidence to those carrying out the assessment of their child and simply reflect back and reinforce professional perceptions.

In John's case the stated reason for referral for formal assessment was his behaviour in school. However, underlying this was his teachers' deeper concern that he might be a victim of physical and sexual abuse. The evidence in support of these allegations was vague and in the event unsubstantiated despite an extensive Social Services investigation which ran parallel to the Statementing procedures.

In drawing her conclusions about the family situation the head teacher pointed to the 'fact' that John's parents were only cooperative on the surface. 'Mum was initially cooperative ... and Mr Peel was likewise "quite cooperative" until the decision was made to Statement ... after that he opted out and didn't contact me.'

Mrs Peel, however, saw things differently, saying of the head, 'She seemed to be assessing me rather than John ... it's like she's shifting the blame on to me ... she used to speak to me like I was a really bad mother. I used to come home in tears.'

The school found some support for their interpretation of Mrs Peel's behaviour from a community nurse who tried to work with the family: 'She thinks there's evidence of sexual abuse; soiling, language and sexually overt behaviour.' In addition the nurse, too, thought that the parents were uncooperative and that they were hiding something. She stated in her report: 'On the occasions of visiting home I have felt most unwelcome and am therefore limited in the intervention I can provide.' She recommended that a meeting with Social Services would be helpful to alert them to the 'dynamics' of this family and to advise them that 'as professionals we were anxious that we had not managed to engage and intervene within the family and explore deficits in the parenting role'.

Following the nurse's report a meeting was held with Social Services. According to Mrs Peel who was invited to attend:

> All different people went in the meeting – the health visitor, the doctor, teachers – but I couldn't go in. When I was allowed in the child abuse officer was in the chair and he told me that his behaviour was the behaviour of a child who was being sexually abused. They said they were not saying it was, but it was the behaviour. I went home in tears. They asked me to take the children for a full medical. I didn't want to but I was frightened they would think it was true, so I let them do it. I felt because they couldn't come up with anything else they brought this up to show it was something at home ... it's all been dropped now I think.

From the perspectives of both professionals and parents the attempt to build a cooperative framework directed towards meeting John's needs had broken down. According to the professionals the breakdown happened because the parents were the cause of the child's special needs. Consequently, cooperation was defined by the professionals in terms that allowed them, in the words of the community nurse, to 'intervene within the family and explore deficits in the parenting role'. The parents were expected to accept the authority of the professionals even though there is little evidence to support their judgement.

The parents' sense of disempowerment was at this stage complete. Cooperation with the professionals required acceptance of the framework within which John's needs had been professionally cast: that it was their deficits as parents which had created John's needs. On the other hand, refusal to cooperate would have been perceived by the professionals as reinforcing the latter's initial perceptions. The definition of a problem, its source and the 'needs' that arise from it are frequently established by professionals at an early stage and as we see here the parents, because they lack information and power, may find it very difficult to challenge such assumptions.

John's case also suggests how the perceptions of those professionals involved at an early stage of an assessment and the actions that follow may influence, direct or constrain the later perceptions and actions of other professionals. The educational psychologist (EP) expressed surprise that on every occasion he had met John the latter had always been attentive and cooperative but felt that 'We have to accept what we are told about his behaviour by his teachers.' For this reason when the head teacher eventually excluded John permanently from school because of his behaviour the EP accepted that the school were acting reasonably in the circumstances and that they had made every effort with John. The EP observed that 'John's language is so adult and behaviour so violent to other people that the school could not put up with it any longer.' On the other hand, the psychologist also recognised how the scope for his own intervention was restricted by the school's actions. 'The exclusion shuts doors in terms of possible recommendation.' Likewise, the EP, after visiting the family on a number of occasions, said that the community nurse's impressions 'don't ring true with my own experience'. He also felt that the evidence of abuse was unconvincing but given the involvement of other agencies in this area it was beyond his remit to challenge it in compiling his advice for the Statement.

Mrs Peel thought the EP to be more sympathetic than the other professionals she had encountered and that made it easier for her to convey her views to him. None the less her experiences with those other professionals led her to believe that she could not affect the result of their deliberations. She felt she had no power to determine or influence the decisions taken by the LEA and its professional advisers. To her the prospect of a Statement is 'a load of rubbish. It's a legal document ... but they've been telling me that all along. I get a bit of paper and it's more official but I still don't get anywhere.' However strongly she felt about the rights and wrongs of her situation she had no sense of power over its outcome.

George: who needs support?, what support is needed?

In this section, by looking at the case of George, we examine the interactive process and power relationships underlying the development of an apparent consensus. We show how this consensus was identified as strong from the perspective of a professional, yet fragile and disempowering from the perspective of George's parents.

George is a 9 year old attending a primary school in a working-class part of town. According to the head teacher 'It may look very nice but we have a lot of difficult families and children.' George comes from a large family and the home situation is acknowledged by his parents to be stressful because of overcrowding and financial difficulties. One of George's brothers was recently placed in a residential school for children with moderate learning difficulties as a weekly boarder. The family have experienced a lot of conflict with George's school and since moving home some twelve months ago have made efforts, unsuccessfully, to transfer their children to a different primary school.

George was referred to the LEA for formal assessment under the Act on the grounds of emotional and behavioural difficulties as an 'urgent case'. His teachers reported that the problem was 'behaviour in class and at home'. In school, George was described as 'aggressive ... he wanders about instead of getting on with his work ... he won't conform ... he's like his brother ... generally he disturbs other children. He disturbs their work.' Those behaviours were identified by his teachers as arising directly from the problems George faced in the home.

At the outset the willingness of George's parents to cooperate with the school staff in discussing the home situation and how this might affect George's behaviour in school was used by the teaching staff as evidence in support of their case that George's needs could not be met within a mainstream school. As the assessment progressed those two factors were at the forefront of the school's case to the educational psychologist:

(a) Disruptive behaviour in school.
(b) Management problems at home identified by the parents themselves.

We can see here how, at an early stage, the discourse of needs was established. The main feature of this discourse was that George's needs were conceptualised within the framework of the teachers' perceptions of their own needs: in particular the threat George was seen as presenting to order and discipline within the school. The EP's role was seen by the teaching staff as being to advise the school. The EP was 'brought in' in response to the teachers' perception that they lacked the skills to manage George's behaviour.

However, despite the way teachers represented their views Mr and Mrs Short doubted the severity of the problem: 'I don't think he's any worse than other kids – he's picked on by the school.' Their stated wish was for him to be moved to another mainstream school. As regards the home situation their perspective was subtly and significantly different from that of the school. They acknowledged the stressfulness of the family situation but wanted help toward removing the stresses rather than to have George removed from the home. It is important to recognise their willingness to consider residential school in this context. When it was suggested to them as a possibility it was understood by them as an opportunity for a breathing space *in the absence of any other alternative*. It was a *misperception* of the parental perspective that was used by the professionals to legitimise the latter's recommendations. This is illustrated in the following exchange:

Mr Short: There used to be a place in Scotland where kids could go to give parents a break. I don't know if there's anything like that round here. You've got to think of the kids as well. They've never had any holiday.

EP: I'll try to make some enquiries about holidays. I do feel that George will need some special schooling – he's not getting what he needs. Not because of anything to do with the school but he needs special help – I think we should think about your feelings. Let's try and get some help for you and the family.

Thus the EP links parental desire for respite from family stress with the notion of special schooling. Once this link is established Mrs Short is asked to consider a residential placement and the parents' own anxieties about their family situation and needs are used to justify the proposal being put forward.

The different perspectives of EP and parents were reflected in the confusion over what had been decided at that meeting. The EP wrote in a memorandum to the LEA: 'I feel that George would benefit from placement in a residential school for pupils with emotional and behavioural problems. Mr and Mrs Short would be happy with a weekly boarding place.'

When questioned by a researcher Mr and Mrs Short restated their preference for a placement in an alternative mainstream school. They also reaffirmed their opposition to a residential school placement.

Mrs Short: I couldn't handle George at weekends if he was away all week.
Elder daughter: [referring to John, George's brother, who boards at an MLD school]. It makes him worse. John says 'You've sent me away and don't love me.'

Yet Mrs Short, despite her strongly held views, expressed resignation in playing little part in the decision-making process, a resignation based in part upon experience. 'We didn't get much to do with John's assessment. I didn't want him to go to residential school at all.' The professionals were seen by Mrs Short as decision-makers and therefore when asked about the outcome of the meeting with the EP she was unclear because 'I haven't been told.' The parents believed, however, that the outcome of the assessment would be a placement in a special school whatever their own views.

In a later meeting between parents and psychologist the former, in response to the psychologist's efforts to identify/impose a consensus, again attempted to articulate their own understanding of George's needs.

EP: Last time I saw you we felt that we should be looking at some kind of school with weekly boarding.

Mrs Short said she would prefer George to attend a mainstream school.

EP: That's where you would like him to go?
Mr and Mrs Short: Yes.
EP: One possible school would be weekly boarding – if you visited there would be no guarantee.
Mr Short: To be honest with you we have one child already at one of those schools and when he comes home he's a lot worse.

The psychologist in a separate interview with the researcher expressed the belief that this 'fact' was evidence of the unsuitability of the home situation. This contrasted sharply with the parents' belief that the child's poor behaviour at home was a consequence of the latter perceiving himself to have been rejected by the family because he had been sent to a boarding school. The psychologist suggested that the parents themselves really wanted George to be placed in a residential school but did not wish to appear that they were rejecting him. 'They see residential school as an alternative to "care" but it has less stigma for them. I think that's what they've really wanted all the way along.' The psychologist justified his own persuasive efforts with this belief that he was actually helping the parents to come to terms with a decision '*they really want to make*'.

EP: What I suggest we do – nothing's going to be decided today – I can arrange for you to have a look at one of these weekly residential schools – at this stage we're saying let's look.
Mr and Mrs Short: That's OK.

The validity of the psychologist's interpretation of parental motives in this case is difficult to assess. In the end it depends upon 'professional judgement'. Whether or not it is correct, it quite clearly differs from the parents' explicit account of their perception of how the decision has been reached and the implications it will have for George.

Mr Short: As far as I'm concerned they give up too soon.
Mrs Short: The way they were talking at that meeting George is going to residential school. It's going to make him worse.

Tom: refusing to play the game

Our third example focuses upon conflicting perceptions of the purpose of assessment under the 1981 Act and the relationship between information and control. It raises questions about how the Act itself can become a controlling force to limit parental action.

Twelve months ago Tom had been placed two half-days each week in an off-site unit for disruptive children. This placement followed the breakup of his parents' marriage which was acknowledged by his mother, not his father, as having a serious effect upon Tom's behaviour. After the breakup the parents were awarded joint custody and Tom resided for part of the week with each. Mrs Jones felt that this arrangement was itself disruptive and should be changed. Mr Jones did not agree. He felt that Tom caused him no problems and it was Tom's relationship with his mother that was at the root of the difficulties he had.

Tom had recently been referred by his mainstream school to the Psychological Service for assessment under the 1981 Act because teachers felt they should receive additional support for Tom's periods in mainstream school. The EP in this case felt that even more drastic measures might be required. In his view Tom was being used as a pawn in the relationship between his parents and unless his parents did come to an arrangement whereby 'a more stable home situation' was provided, Tom would benefit from a residential school placement.

Tom's mother was highly critical of the way the mainstream school was handling him but agreed to the assessment because she felt it might help him. Initially she welcomed the professionals' involvement because she believed this might result in help and advice in identifying the reasons for Tom's deteriorating behaviour.

Once the assessment had begun Mrs Jones soon became disillusioned. She complained bitterly about the lack of information she was receiving. Perhaps this reflected a lack of clarity about the purpose of the assessment and the conflicting expectations participants held of its outcome. Mrs Jones expected feedback and dialogue about the development of an intervention strategy. When she later challenged the EP she was told she should have contacted the Education Welfare Officer (EWO) designated by the LEA as being the 'named person'. She couldn't recollect having been informed of this. In any case she had not expected that her role in the assessment would be limited to receiving information back from an

EWO: 'We didn't ask for it [the assessment] – it was the education system who said it should be done – if I accept them into my home I don't expect them to disappear for twelve months, if they invited themselves in.'

Mrs Jones felt that the slow progress of the assessment and the limited information she received created new problems instead of resolving existing ones: 'It introduces so much trauma – you're getting all the criticism all the time but you're not getting any information because it takes so long.'

Access to information, however, was not the only problem Mrs Jones faced. A lack of common agreement over the objectives of the assessment was something Mrs Jones had not anticipated. Whereas she had seen the assessment as a way of addressing Tom's unsettled home situation, establishing an objective base line from which she and her ex-husband could identify how their differences were affecting Tom, the EP refused to become involved in this area. 'It's difficult if I'm to remain neutral.'

Yet the EP was willing to use this dispute as a justification for his recommendation for residential schooling. In addition, Mrs Jones was dissatisfied that little attention appeared to have been given to Tom's problems in school. She had been told on one occasion by the EP that Tom's behaviour problems might have been the result of frustration over reading difficulties. She had found this information to be very positive 'because they can focus on dealing with it now, it spells out a lot of hope'. Yet she felt little had been done to address this problem in school and if in these circumstances she now accepted residential school she would be giving up on Tom. None the less the EP continued to recommend residential schooling. Mrs Jones's response was 'No way am I going to agree with that.' On the other hand, on a different occasion she expressed feelings of depression and powerlessness in the face of professional opinion, conceding that she might allow him to go to residential school if it could be shown that it was in his best interests.

Once the EP had recommended residential schooling in his report Mrs Jones expressed little confidence in her 'rights' under the law. But she remained determined to play an equal part in defining the nature of her child's needs. She had seen the initial stage of the assessment process as an opportunity to enhance her role in the decision-making but saw it as restricting her power. She therefore decided to abandon reliance on official procedures. She moved house and with the cooperation of the new local head teacher changed Tom's mainstream school, and withdrew him from the off-site unit. The EP and LEA were now presented with a *fait accompli*. According to Mrs Jones they had little option in the circumstances but to allow her decision a 'chance to fail'.

3 DISCUSSION: DISEMPOWERMENT BY PARTNERSHIP?

The 1981 Education Act clearly states the procedures that must be followed to maximise parental involvement in the decision-making process. It identifies the range of information that must be made available to parents and the right of parents to contribute their own advice and evidence to the assessment. Moreover, procedures are established for parents to seek clarification, state objections and appeal against recommendations. A strong case can be put forward to demonstrate that no decision can be taken without full consultation with parents and due deference to their views.

In practice there is increasing evidence that the rights of parents under the Act are not always given prominence. A number of commentators have suggested that once the assessment procedures have been initiated parents become increasingly marginalised in the process. Dyson (1986), for example, drew attention to the ways in which professionals' confidential files often contain materials contributing to the social stereotyping of children and their families. This information might be circulated informally amongst professionals but parents remain ignorant of its existence. Chaudhury (1986) and Rehal (1989) identified how parents of ethnic minority children may be disadvantaged during special needs assessments by the failure of LEAs and professionals to take account of language and cultural factors. Goacher et al. (1988) found marked differences between LEAs in the role parents are allowed to play. 'It seems certain that even the small change in the balance of power between professionals and parents brought about by the Act have yet to be realized in a number of Authorities' (Goacher et al. 1988: 59).

It might be suggested that the disempowerment of parents arises from a combination of LEAs seeking to maintain control over the distribution of resources and professionals seeking to secure the autonomy of their professional role. Yet we can find evidence of LEAs taking their responsibilities under the Act for involving parents very seriously, presenting information and reports in ways designed to make the assessment meaningful and accessible to parents. None the less, even in these cases parents may find the concepts of 'disclosure' and 'involvement' to operate implicitly as disempowering forces. Mittler and Mittler (1982) make a similar point when they argue that a clear distinction should be drawn between the concepts of 'partnership' and 'involvement'. Whilst the former emphasises the sharing of power as well as expertise, the latter contains an implicit assumption of professional expertise and control.

Swann (1987) has argued that as long as segregated provision exists, a means to select and allocate children will be needed. This, he suggests, is the main purpose of Statementing. Because Statementing is concerned with the allocation of resources rather than with the identification of needs strict limits are placed on the power of parents to affect the Statementing process. If Swann is correct the identification of needs will be resource-led. The 1981 Act itself may be read as implicitly setting out this principle, and Galloway and Goodwin (1987) have demonstrated its operation in practice. As Swann (1987) argues, without the power to make decisions about resources, parent involvement within the 1981 Act is concerned 'with recruiting parents as resources in the education of their children, pursuing goals defined by professionals' (Swann 1987: 193).

The way in which the concept of 'need' is defined by the 1981 Act may also serve to reinforce the limits on parental power. The Act abolished the ten categories of handicap identified under the 1945 Handicapped Pupils and School Health Regulations (DES 1945) and replaced them with the concept of 'special educational need'. 'Need' was redefined in terms of learning difficulties significantly greater than those of the majority of children. This shifted the conceptual focus away from needs as defined in relation to the child's handicap towards educational needs arising from learning difficulties. None the less, there remains a focus upon the child as having needs rather than upon the situation as creating needs (Oliver 1988). An important implication of this is that while a particular situation may give rise to various differing, and sometimes conflicting needs (the needs of teachers, parents, other pupils, the LEA and indeed the LEA's professional advisers), the conceptual focus upon the child encouraged by the Act inhibits the development of a theoretical framework within which the interplay of needs can be examined. On the other hand, psychologists frequently have the task of mediating between the needs and interests of the different participants involved with the child and their key role in the decision-making process. Despite the 'rights' parents are given under the Act this is a form of power that parents are rarely able to exercise.

Parental involvement in decision-making is often restricted to identifying those aspects of the child's behaviour that fit or do not fit with the views of the professionals. Parents are marginalised, not because professionals deliberately exclude them but because they are denied the opportunity to influence how need is conceptualised. Moreover, in practice, they may lack the power to negotiate on equal terms with professionals about the interrelationship between the needs of different participants in the assessment. By conceptualising the child's needs in a way that fails to acknowledge the significance of this wider context the Act reinforces and legitimises the disempowerment of parents.

We can see how this occurred in our first two case studies. In both cases the parents' resignation to the inevitability of the assessment outcome arose from their having no opportunity to determine or seriously influence the objectives of the assessment nor to contribute to the conceptual framework within which their children's needs were being assessed.

In the third case Mrs Jones refused to accept the proposals put forward by the professionals for meeting Tom's needs. Whereas at first she had welcomed the assessment she later came to the view that she was being given no say in the objectives of the assessment. She, too, felt that she was denied the opportunity to make a genuine contribution, in cooperation with the professionals, to the understanding of Tom's needs and the circumstances in which they were being created. Ultimately, this led her to challenge the way the professionals conceived Tom's needs. In her eyes, she could only do so by stepping outside the framework imposed by the Act. Her direct challenge to the authority of the professionals forced them to acknowledge an alternative conceptualisation of Tom's needs which carried with it quite different implications for the outcome of the formal assessment of those needs. In addition her action outside the assessment

Chapter 17

Supportive parents for special children
Working towards partnership in Avon

Ronnie Broomhead and Philip Darley

Ronnie Broomhead and Philip Darley are founder members of Supportive Parents for Special Children, a group established in Avon to work cooperatively with professionals to provide support and information to parents of children who experience difficulties in schools or who have disabilities. They describe the origins of the group, the training of parent volunteers to work with other parents, and their involvement in local authority policy developments.

1 GETTING STARTED

Despite our children's different handicaps or problems parents like me often find that we have many experiences and feelings in common. Most of us get confused by the education scene which always seems to be changing. Few of us really understand the 1981 Education Act. We don't know what all the professionals actually do. Everyone feels muddled by the National Curriculum and local management of schools. It's very worrying if we're trying to get our child into the local school; and I've been told it's just as worrying if you're trying to get your child out of the local school into some specialist place. Parents and professionals don't seem to talk the same language and misunderstandings can sometimes have disastrous effects. We're always being told that there's not enough money to go around; so we feel as if our children may never get what they really need.

(A parent of a child with special education needs)

Supportive Parents for Special Children (SPSC) grew out of the needs of parents for support and information and the desire of the local education authority (LEA) and other professionals in Avon to help them. There was already a long-standing history of mutual cooperation between different professionals and agencies in the county. This sense of mutual trust between professionals gave them the confidence to look for ways in which they could work more constructively with parents. At the same time there were parents who wanted to improve services for their children and who realised that this could be achieved by getting into closer dialogue with professionals. What was needed was a catalyst to bring the two together.

procedures also gave Mrs Jones the power to negotiate with other participants. By securing the support of the head teacher and staff of a different mainstream school she was able to place her opposition to a recommendation for residential schooling on a firm footing and insist that her understanding of Tom's needs be tested in practice. Thus Mrs Jones's power inside the assessment process was increased by her having identified and pursued sources of strength outside that process.

ACKNOWLEDGEMENTS

This article arises out of a research project on the 'Identification of Emotional and Behavioural Difficulties: Participant Perspectives', funded by the Economic and Social Research Council, Research Grant No. R 000 23 1393. In addition we are grateful to the necessarily anonymous educational psychologists, and to their clients, who agreed to take part in this research.

REFERENCES

Association of Educational Psychologists (1984) *Members Handbook*, London: AEP.
Chaudhury, A. (1986) *Annual Report*, London: ACE.
Department of Education and Science (DES) (1945) *The Handicapped Pupils and School Health Regulations*, London: HMSO.
—— (1978) *Special Educational Needs* (The Warnock Report), London: HMSO.
—— (1983) *Assessment and Statements of Special Educational Needs*, Circular 1/83, London: DES.
—— (1989) *Assessments and Statements of Special Educational Needs: Procedures within Education, Health and Social Services*, Circular 22/89, London: DES.
Dyson, S. (1986) 'Professionals, mentally handicapped children and confidential files', *Disability, Handicap and Society*, 1, 165–71.
Galloway, D. and Goodwin, C. (1987) *The Education of Disturbing Children: Pupils with Adjustment Difficulties*, London: Longman.
Goacher, B., Evans, J., Welton, J. and Wedell, K. (1988) *Policy and Provision for Special Educational Needs: Implementing the 1981 Education Act*, London: Cassell.
Mittler, P. and Mittler, H. (1982) *Partnership With Parents*, Stratford on Avon: National Council for Special Education.
Moses, D. and Croll, P. (1987) 'Parents as partners or problems?', *Disability, Handicap and Society* 2, 75–84.
Oliver, M. (1988) 'The social and political context of educational policy: the case of special needs', in L. Barton (ed.), *The Politics of Special Educational Needs*, London: Falmer.
Rehal, A. (1989) 'Involving Asian parents in the Statementing procedure – the way forward', *Educational Psychology in Practice* 4, 189–97.
Swann, W. (1987) 'Statements of interest: an assessment of reality', in T. Booth and W. Swann (eds), *Including Children with Disabilities*, Milton Keynes: Open University Press.
Wood, S. (1988) 'Parents: whose partners?', in L. Barton (ed.), *The Politics of Special Educational Needs*, London: Falmer.

In 1987 the University of London Institute for Education (ULIE) was commissioned by the DES and the DHSS to research the extent to which the 1981 Education Act was being implemented across the country, and second to design training materials to enable local authorities and health authorities to improve their performance in this respect. In response to an invitation from ULIE, Avon Education and Social Services and Southmead Health Authority agreed to work together as part of a pilot project. At this stage the research was only directed at officers of these statutory authorities. In Avon, officers argued that this approach was lopsided. The 1981 Education Act actively promoted partnership between parents and professionals. After some discussions with ULIE it was agreed to involve some parents in the project. A number of special task groups were set up and one of these was concerned specifically with the role of parents in the assessment and Statementing process.

As the research project neared its end and the ULIE staff packed their briefcases, the parent task group made up their minds to stay in business. By this stage they believed that if parents of children with special needs were brought together with thoughtful professionals, this could result in a long-lasting cooperative venture which would have a profound effect on local educational practice. Now was the time to put their belief into practice.

Philippa Russell from the National Children's Bureau was asked to come and speak on parents' rights at a public meeting. Many parents were invited through their local schools but only a handful came. But what became apparent in the course of that meeting was that this was a singular group of people – already busy, without time to spare – and yet already sharing a common vision of what parents and professionals might achieve together. We agreed to continue to meet in order to form an independent organisation, which was to become SPSC.

Why was there a need for yet another organisation? Professionals already had several associations where they could meet to discuss their concerns about providing services for children with special needs. Parents for their part had a range of societies set up to promote the interests of different disability groups. What was to be special about SPSC was the fact that parents and professionals were meeting together and that the parents who formed the central core had children with a variety of different disabilities and special needs from emotional and behavioural problems and specific learning difficulties to more severe physical and sensory disabilities and learning difficulties.

2 TRAINING PARENT VOLUNTEERS

It was the principal aim of the group to support parents and encourage them to take their rightful role in the procedures of the 1981 Education Act. Some parents were unaware of just how vital their unique perspective was in the assessment of their children's special needs. Even if they were aware they were unsure of what they should be commenting on or how to do it.

How could we help them? We started to look around the country at other parents' organisations and we became interest in SNAP (Special Needs Advisory Project) in South Wales who train parents to give advice and support to other parents. We felt that this was a good way to help empower parents and we decided to have another open meeting to publicise the group and to promote the idea of developing our own parent volunteer service.

This time a school hall was packed with parents, professionals and members of voluntary organisations. At this meeting some of our parents gave moving accounts of their personal struggles to obtain the right education for their child. You could feel a buzz of excitement mixed with anticipation. The parents' stories had given us a glimpse of the real stress carried by families with children with special needs. It was being acknowledged here that, sadly, professionals' attempts to help sometimes added to that sense of strain. The fact that such honest accounts could be shared demonstrated the potential of this organisation. But there was also anxiety. Would parents go over the top? How would the many professionals who were present react? Might this become a forum of unrelieved blood-letting? It didn't. There was a willingness on the part of both parents and professionals to acknowledge that these problems exist. Professionals now understood the feelings that parents carry. Parents too knew that by and large professionals have the children's best interests at heart. There was a commitment that night to work together to make things better. We knew that this would not be easy. There would be other times of tension and indeed there have been.

At the meeting more than thirty people expressed an interest in being trained as a parent volunteer. The training itself has been led by two educational psychologists and a social worker. Recently they have been joined on the training panel by one of the trained volunteers. The training has three goals:

- *To enable people to come to terms better with their own situations.* This lessens the possibility that their own experiences will cloud their ability to understand fully what it feels like to be another parent with a different perception of their predicament.
- *To give participants a basic knowledge of the spirit and letter of the 1981 and 1988 Education Acts together with local policies and resources.* It is also possible to help them realise that they don't need to be all-knowing. It is perhaps more important to know where to turn for more information when required.
- *To equip participants with certain basic listening skills to enable them to look for the 'theme behind the words' as they talk with other parents.* They also need help to deal with strong feelings and face potentially daunting situations like child abuse.

We held a day workshop to introduce the topic of volunteering. This resulted in twenty-eight people signing up for Phase One, a four-session evening course which focused on basic information and an exploration of their own experiences. Many parents found this quite a demanding process, particularly when reliving painful memories. They were helped to work through these feelings and have later reported that this was a useful and essential aspect of the training.

The second phase, though less emotionally draining was more demanding on time as it was set up as a full ten-session evening course. A total of fourteen people enrolled for this and a further five of the original group were to enrol in a repeat of the course a year later. Phase Two deepened their knowledge and introduced them to basic listening skills and assertiveness. We used role play to enable them to practise working as volunteers and included consideration of powerful feelings and practical aspects of the work.

At the end of this thirty hours of training it was left to the participants to decide whether or not to offer themselves as volunteers. In fact all fourteen did so. In a repeat of the course a year later another twelve volunteers were added to that number.

3 ESTABLISHING A BASE

While the training was under way we became more aware of parents' wider needs that could not be met by the volunteer service. Parents needed information, so we set up termly open meetings and workshops. Talks were given on such topics as 'The Role of the Psychology Service', 'The Parental Contribution to the Statement' and 'The Law and Special Educational Needs'. Workshops were arranged in practical matters such as 'Help Your Child to Read', 'Helping Children Think and Learn' and 'Making Big Books'.

Most of these meetings were held in a warm, comfortable and well-equipped church which was, thankfully, free of charge. Finance has been, and still is, a nagging problem. Societies like Mencap, The Down's Association and The Spastics Society have helped us and we have received some money from charitable trusts and through our own fund-raising activities. So far grant applications to the statutory authorities have been unsuccessful. We have however received some indirect funding from the LEA through professional time freely given, help with photocopying in the early days, and through the provision of a base at low rent.

It had become increasingly necessary for us to have an office from which we could run our parent volunteer service. As we became better known the founding members were getting a stream of phone calls at their homes with requests for help, support and information. There was a need for a centre, some secretarial help and for a coordinator to relieve the pressure on individuals and help us to work more efficiently.

Our base has been open for telephone help three mornings a week during term-time over the past year. We managed to raise funds to employ a part-time secretary and a volunteers coordinator. This coordinator has become a key person in our group now, working many more hours than she is paid for. Volunteers come into the base to deal with telephone enquiries and with calls left on the answerphone. With experience all our volunteers have grown in confidence and parents who have rung up or met our volunteers have said how much they welcomed the practical information and support which they have received. They have been particularly appreciative of the volunteers' understanding and professional skills.

4 CONTRIBUTING TO POLICY

At an early stage we felt it would be helpful to meet regularly with the LEA to discuss issues surrounding the 1981 and subsequent Education Acts where they affected children with special needs. The LEA understandably did not want to appear to be treating one voluntary group differently from the others and so we took on a coordinating role with other voluntary groups, arranging a termly meeting with special education staff to discuss issues of common concern. Initially only a few groups joined us, but this has slowly grown so that now our voluntary bodies' group has members with a wide range of concerns and interests.

Our principal aim when we started was to help and support parents. From the start we resisted suggestions that we should become a pressure group as we felt we were only a few parents who had no mandate to speak on behalf of others. Over a period of two years and with the support of the Education Committee, SPSC has developed relationships with several people in key positions in the LEA through mutual goodwill and understanding. We were concerned too, not to lose the increasing level of partnership that was being developed. However, as time went by we found more and more parents were becoming upset and anxious. We heard increasingly that support teaching was being reduced; some children were being refused Statements. At this time some of the officers who were most committed to working with SPSC left the LEA and we were faced again with building relationships with a new management team. At the same time budget proposals, influenced by fears of poll tax capping, threatened services for children with special needs. Our growing concern was heightened by news of a Special Education Review which would lead to reorganisation of special education in Avon. This we feared might lead to serious cuts in services.

We found various ways to voice our concerns. Our first step was to call a public meeting inviting local councillors to listen as parent after parent spoke about the needs of children with a whole range of disabilities. Eventually the budget was passed with no cuts to the services we were concerned over. There were obviously many reasons for this but we believe we played a significant part in that decision.

Since that meeting some of our members have been invited to serve on working groups in the Special Education Review where they have been able to advocate better assessment procedures, clearer acknowledged rights for parents and children and, above all, well-resourced provision which offers parents a choice. We have held open meetings enabling the LEA to explain their plans to parents and more importantly making it possible for parents to express their views publicly. We are now asking the LEA to approach us at an early stage when they start to develop plans, so that we can be more truly in partnership with them.

5 CONCLUDING REMARKS

Most of our meetings are very busy with between 100 to 400 people attending. There is always so much work to do that there rarely seems to be enough time to support each other. This has led us to set up four local support groups across the county which meet on a monthly basis. On these occasions parents and professionals meet together informally and much help and support is exchanged in this way. Sometimes only two or three people come. We believe that numbers do not matter; what is important is that there is always a friendly face and a listening ear for those who need us. Sometimes support groups organise their own open meetings mainly to raise the profile of their group in the area. For the most part these meetings serve as occasions when the carers can get cared for themselves.

In less than three years SPSC has come a long way. Many parents now feel less isolated and more able to participate at a realistic level in planning for their child's education. Professionals, too, have deepened their understanding of parents' concerns and have begun to adapt their working practice to encourage greater participation with parents. As one educational psychologist put it:

> Parents need to be informed. They need to be able to lobby for their child. They need the information and the skills. For the group at large it's helping individuals to fight their corner, to become more confident and to negotiate on equal terms.

Part 5

Integration and disability

Chapter 18

My story

Judy Watson

Source: Rieser, R. and Mason, M. (eds) (1990) *Disability Equality in the Classroom: A Human Rights Issue*, London, Inner London Education Authority, pp. 53–6.

Judy Watson is Head of English at a girls' secondary school in Kent and is a member of the National Union of Teachers' Working Party on Disability.

In this chapter she describes her own education and her working life as a blind teacher. She had glaucoma as a baby and her sight deteriorated, despite surgery. She describes her experience of special schools, her university course, and her efforts to train as a teacher and lead an ordinary working life.

I was born in London in 1951. When I was four months old, my parents took me to the doctor because my eyes were very red and I had been crying a lot as if I was in pain. The doctor immediately referred me to the Royal Eye Hospital where I was found to have glaucoma.

This is an eye condition which can usually be controlled with pills, drops and surgery, but after thirteen operations it was clear that my sight was deteriorating quickly and I was sent to a school for blind children when I was 7 years old. I wore glasses at this time and could see well enough to walk round on my own and was able to read print if I held the book close to my face.

My school was called Linden Lodge and was a mixed boarding school. I was allowed home at weekends which was quite easy because I lived about half-an-hour away by tube. However, when I was 11 I was transferred to Chorleywood College for Girls with Little or No Sight. This was the equivalent to a grammar school to which girls were sent from all over Britain.

Consequently, we were only allowed home four Sundays each term: it was felt that those from Scotland, Ireland and the North would not be able to go home at weekends so no one should. I hated that and felt that I really lost touch with my family.

I was never very happy at school but gained my O-levels and A-levels and left at the age of 18 to go to Kent University where I did an English degree. By this time my sight was very poor: glasses did not help any more but I could still read newspaper headlines if I had my nose touching the paper. I had a sound academic education and had learnt Braille but was not at all prepared for the 'sighted' world. We had not mixed very much with sighted people of our own age and we all left school feeling a certain hatred and fear of them. Perhaps I was luckier than most because I have a sister who is two years younger and she had taken me to discos and introduced me to her friends. Many girls at school had never been to a disco or had a boyfriend or even been shopping with someone of their own age. I think this experience has led me to believe passionately that children with disabilities should be taught in mainstream schools.

I enjoyed university life although it seemed to take me a long time to settle. It was very hard work because reading Braille books is much slower than reading print and, in any case, much of the material I had to read wasn't in Braille. This meant I had to ask for volunteers from the other students to read to me. I typed my essays for my tutors and did my exams in Braille. After my exams had finished, I read my answers on to tape and one of the audio-typists transcribed them ready for marking.

While I was at university, I had my fourteenth and final eye operation. This was unsuccessful and I lost my sight completely when I was 21 and in my third year. It was also at this time that I was married. We were far too young and I was under a lot of pressure. As a result, the marriage was never very successful either. My sight didn't disappear overnight: it went very slowly so that one week I could see a bus-stop in the distance but the next week I couldn't. By the time I got my degree, I was finding mobility a real problem just with a white stick so decided to apply for a guide dog.

I trained in Scotland with my first dog, a golden retriever called Randa, and I was delighted with the amount of freedom this gave me. For the first time in ages, I could go shopping on my own or visit friends. Guide dogs aren't magical, so I have to know where I'm going in order to give instructions. She follows simple commands like 'Forward', 'Sit', 'Left', 'Right' and 'Find the stairs' or 'Find the door'. When I start work at a new school or move house, I ask someone who can see to teach me my routes and then I can get from A to B with my guide dog. It would be pointless to put me in the middle of London and expect me to find my way round with my dog – we would quickly become lost!

Shortly before I left university, I decided I wanted to be an English teacher and started applying to do a PGCE (Post Graduate Certificate of Education) course. My friends and acquaintances thought I was crazy: they couldn't understand how I would manage with classroom control, preparing lessons and marking. I knew that I would be able to overcome these obstacles if I thought about it hard enough. Clearly, teacher-training colleges shared the view of my friends and I was rejected by nine institutions before being accepted by Christchurch College, Canterbury. September 1973 saw me embarking on my new career with my new guide dog and tons of determination.

While on teaching practice, I quickly realised that I could control pupils with my personality and that I could use my hearing to detect any chewing gum in their mouths and that crisps make a tremendous noise. In my lessons, I always ask that everyone sits in the same place and it is easy to identify who is tapping a pen or talking when they shouldn't be.

I use Braille books in the classroom and plan lessons, mark work and complete various administrative tasks with the help of readers. While at college and in the early years of my career, my readers were volunteers but now the Training Agency gives me money to pay someone. It's much better this way. My present reader is called Ruth and she comes to my home in the evenings at seven o'clock so that she can read to me. When we are doing marking, she reads out the work and corrects spelling and punctuation, then she tells me what it was she had to correct and I tell her what mark and comment to write at the bottom.

Having successfully passed my teaching course, I started work in September 1974 at the Sheppey School in Kent, a mixed comprehensive school of 1,800 pupils. I was very happy there even though I found it hard work. Teaching requires a great deal of energy and everyone finds it exhausting, particularly when they are new to it. I used to get fed up with working all day and then coming home to readers and having to work every evening as well. I still have to do that and still get fed up with it at times, but most teachers work in the evenings so it isn't that unusual.

I find that everything takes me such a long time: other teachers seem to be able to mark a set of work in an hour or an hour and a half; it will take me double that. Some GCSE assignments can be very long and it is not unusual for me to take five hours to mark a set of those! Reading aloud is just such a long process. It is absolutely essential that I am organised. I can't go into school and think, 'What shall I do with my third years today?' I have to plan ahead come what may. I have a filing cabinet at home where I keep my resources and I ask my partner, Matthew, to find a particular worksheet or activity sheet and then I can take it into school ready for photocopying for a class. In fact, Matthew helps me a lot. When I'm getting behind with my marking or I've got a tremendous amount of admin to do for the department, he helps out at weekends. I think he knows more about English teaching than any other non-teacher in the country!

I am now Head of Department in my fourth school and still love teaching. With Matthew's and Ruth's assistance, I think I do a pretty good job of teaching and running the department but it has not always been that easy.

Having worked at the Sheppey School for several years, I was promoted and given a scale two with responsibility for the third year curriculum and administration in the English department. I still wanted more challenges though and applied for so many jobs – I didn't count but it must have been getting on for a hundred. Head teachers did not even request to see my references; they obviously had many applicants, saw 'blind' written on the form and decided that there was no point in interviewing me. My lucky break came when I applied to do an exchange with an American teacher and was accepted.

In August 1984, Matthew and I – with daughter Hazel aged 8 – flew to Portland, Oregon, and I taught at Beaverton High School for a year. Hazel loved her school and I certainly loved mine. American teachers do not have the same stressful timetable as we do here, the maximum number of classes being five and only two courses being taught. This meant only two lots of preparation, at least one free period guaranteed every day and school finishing at 2.30 p.m. The staff were expected to stay until 3.30 p.m. so that they did an eight-hour day. (School started at 7.30 a.m.) This meant my readers came to school in the afternoon, I finished marking and preparing by 5 p.m., and then I walked home for a free evening. I really missed that when I returned to England.

Shortly after starting back at Sheppey I applied for, and was given, a job as Second in Department at a mixed secondary modern school in Whitstable. I had experienced blatant discrimination at Sheppey where a young teacher in my department was promoted over me to a scale three so I was very pleased to leave. I loved my new job and almost two years later I applied for a Head of Department post at a girls' secondary modern in Ashford. I have been doing it for a year now and enjoy it very much. The kids are great! I have always found that though; kids don't have the same prejudices and inhibitions as adults and I always feel very 'normal' and accepted in a way which doesn't happen with most adults.

My classes are incredibly helpful; someone does the class register, they take it in turns to be 'hands person' so that they don't all shout at once and I have no end of volunteers to do things when I need them. Two fifth year girls clear my pigeon hole, read me anything urgent and do photocopying, etc. They are brilliant!

I don't want anyone to think that I am 'Superwoman' or anything like that. I am just a very ordinary person who gets cross and is moody and I certainly annoy Hazel a lot of the time now that she is a teenager. I still get angry and depressed about being blind. I don't like it and wouldn't wish it on my worst enemy. I do feel that society should meet my needs more than it does. I don't see why I should always have to compete on equal terms. I know my life would be so much easier if I could see and I particularly regret that I can't drive or see my own daughter. I saw a television programme a couple of years ago where a woman had an operation and regained her sight. It really made me cry and Hazel was very surprised. Just because I usually seem so accepting of my disability doesn't mean to say that I have come to terms with it. I'm not sure that I ever will. I do know, though, that I am going to try to fight for my rights and the rights of other people with disabilities in the future. It's about time that we said what we wanted and that we were listened to.

Chapter 19

Internalised oppression
How it seems to me

Richard Rieser

Source: Rieser, R. and Mason, M. (eds) (1990) *Disability Equality in the Classroom: A Human Rights Issue*, London, Inner London Education Authority, pp. 29–32.

Richard Rieser is a geography and humanities teacher and vice-chair of the National Union of Teachers' Working Party on Disability. He had polio as a baby.

In this chapter, Richard describes the painful and enduring effects of the treatment he received and the social isolation he experienced in hospital. He describes how his parents fought to secure physiotherapy and an education for him within the mainstream. Richard describes his anger and frustration and the way in which he tried to be tough to compensate for his disability. He was eventually able to develop a positive self-image as he drove himself through secondary school and university. He describes the support of his wife, Susie, and his experiences of being a disabled parent. Richard became active in the Disability Movement in 1987 when his head teacher put his name forward for redeployment on the grounds that he could not adequately supervise games.

I only know what my life was like without a disability from what my mother told me I was like before I was nine months old, when I got polio. Apparently, I was already walking around, and would have been very 'athletic' if I hadn't caught polio in the hot summer of 1949.

I can't remember the next six months when I was in hospital alone. Parents were not allowed to stay in those days. I can feel the scars on the back of my head where I endlessly turned my head while the rest of my body was incarcerated in plaster of paris. It was the theory then to keep the body completely still to prevent 'deformity'. The Royal National Orthopaedic Hospital at Stanmore did not agree with these 'feudal' methods, and smashed the cast with a hammer when I arrived from Great Ormond Street after my parents had objected to my treatment. Unfortunately the effect on my mind of enforced separation and incarceration before my first birthday cannot be got rid of in such a manner.

My memories of my younger childhood were of pain from my treatment and forcing myself to do all sorts of things. My parents were both of the view that I should learn to walk without a calliper or surgery. I underwent manipulative treatment by the Nurse Kenney method. Mrs Estrid Dane of Notting Hill Gate was to be my mentor. Looking back I shall always be grateful to my parents for this.

Daily we took the 31 bus after nursery or school had finished. For years my limbs were stretched and twisted until they felt like they were being pulled off. I remember frequently lying in the road, screaming at my mum that I didn't want to go, but she always enticed and encouraged me. This treatment, together with my parents' and my own attitude, seems to have been very successful as I grew up to walk without a stick for a number of years. In fact I found a letter from Sir Denis Browne, my Harley Street specialist who saw me when I was 18. He could not believe the progress I had made as he did not think I would walk at all. Physically I could do a great many things, but my personality was less resilient to growing up disabled.

With my parents' 'strong' encouragement I attempted things like walking, swimming, climbing trees, riding my tricycle and later my bike. If I could do all these things with only one arm and one leg working properly, surely I was 'better' than all those around me who seemed to have everything in working order? Of course sometimes there were things I could not do, like running or balancing on a scooter. Reading and spelling seemed to allude me in the same way, and my messy writing and drawings were much ridiculed in my kindergarten (as my dad called it) and at my schools, and indeed still are by my colleagues. Then I felt depressed and sad. Still I was 'tough' and was forever out leading adventures on local bomb-sites and around the streets.

These early pendulum swings of mood have stayed with me most of my life. I recollect when I was occasionally to glimpse my lopsided gait in shop windows, not believing it was me, but at the same time knowing it was and being shocked and depressed. I felt these changes of mood most acutely in my teenage years when I thought I was ugly and unattractive. Because I thought I was unattractive I think I made myself so. I was also very unsociable and impolite.

Prior to my 14th birthday I had been a semi-literate bully, not getting on well at school, and referred to child therapy by Freud's daughter who helped run the school where I ended up for seven years, Town and Country. The head teacher of our local LCC primary school, George Elliot, had refused to have me at the school. My parents would not send me to the local special school. They kept me out of school in protest until an 'ordinary' school was found which the LCC paid for. I was also very much against being put with 'those' children. I remember visiting Essendine Special School and feeling sick at seeing all the children with false legs, callipers and wheelchairs. My parents had over-compensated so much that I could not find any connection between 'those' children and myself.

Town and Country could not really be described as an ordinary school. It was a private, co-ed 'progressive school' located in two large Victorian villas in Eton Avenue. It specialised in taking sons and daughters of diplomats and various 'creative' people's children. The teachers were largely eccentric, traditional and ineffective. I was disruptive, preferring to mess about than learn. There was a big emphasis on foreign languages which I found most difficult, probably because I could not understand the rules of my own language. I was able to act the 'hard' man in the playground and get away with it. This was because I spent most of my leisure time out with my street gang and Town and Country children were a lot softer and more middle-class.

I remember wishing my dad worked in a factory or on the buses like my Scout/street mates and was not an artist and erstwhile teacher. I once told him to get a proper job much to his annoyance. I rejected his artistic side and my own. I think it was also for this reason I blocked foreign languages as my dad could speak at least three fluently. The need to be tough, to cope, to be what is now called a 'super-cripple' left no space for sensitive feelings and 'soft' creativity. These feelings of mind were much reinforced by my avid attendance at Cubs and Boy Scout activities. The competitive, physical, cruel, jingoistic attitude that prevailed in the scouts was just what I needed to forget who I was. I threw myself into scouting, gaining all sorts of proficiency badges and eventually becoming the youngest Queen's Scout at 15. I put a brave face on things I found incredibly difficult or impossible. In one way they treated me as if I was just the same as all the others and I suppose that was why I liked it. The problem was I wasn't just the same!

At other times the cruelty of the boys was just too much with their calling me names and jeering at me. On one occasion I was pegged to the ground with wet grass and slops smeared all over me and left in the hot sun for several hours. This was because I could not peel the potatoes well with a knife, a task I found too difficult due to my polio arm. This ritual was supposed to make a man of you, but it just made me and the others hard, uncaring and insensitive. This was not good for me as I got rid of my emotions beneath a veneer of bravado. I was unable to feel the strength of character I later found from being open to my feelings and so being conscious of my disability and my limitations, which also led me to try to be more sensitive and empathetic to others.

This contradiction was to make me most unhappy and a fair amount of my time was spent in doing damage to myself, either by excessive drinking or various 'accidents' which led to my damaging various parts of myself. From the age of 15 to 19 I used to arrive home two or three nights a week in a completely drunken state, quite often being sick all over the place. I broke or damaged my left arm and right leg which I relied upon. I stuck a garden fork through my right foot and messed about with my toe nails which were in-growing so they got septic and required surgery about eight times, and there were many other injuries. This pattern of self-injury continued into my 20s and early 30s and was likely to occur whenever I was depressed. I didn't like myself and I was pretty sure no one else did either. I had a string of psychotherapists at the Tavistock Clinic, but they did not help me as their method was to strip away my defences without putting anything positive in their place. In fact it was not till I was in my 30s that I found a humanistic therapist who used bio-energy. She was really the first person to make me feel good about myself.

But I am jumping ahead. To go back to when I was 13. I was becoming aware that Town and Country was not doing me any good. A lot of my mates in scouts were at the local secondary modern, Kynaston, and their stories of events at the school told round the camp fire made me want to go to a 'proper' school with workshops, laboratories, gyms, caning and prefects. I decided with some trepidation to leave the soft cocoon of Town and Country and immerse myself in an all-male, secondary modern. The head teacher himself was disabled and that was probably why he accepted me, although I was put a year below my age because of being so 'backward' – I could hardly read and write.

Kynaston was altogether different to anything I had experienced so far. The kids and teachers were tough and there was really no mileage in a crippled bully so I quickly switched into competing with my mind and became more embarrassed by my body. I was also made fun of for my German name and for being Jewish. Anti-semitism was rife as it still is in most schools. I denied my paternal Jewish lineage. Anyway I justified this because my parents had brought me up outside the Jewish culture and as an agnostic. If goaded too far I would still lash out at the perpetrator. But it was the indirect avoidance of me, the whispering, the staring looks that I couldn't hit out at that were far more damaging. I was not often allowed to forget my body, being the butt of jokes and jostled and pushed in corridors or on the stairs. Most harmful was being told almost daily that I was an 'ugly cripple' and I would 'never have a girlfriend'. (One of my therapists told me that if I worked hard everything would be all right at university where I would have girlfriends! I was so worried this would not come to fruition that when I thought I had failed my A-levels I seriously contemplated suicide.)

In PE and the playground I felt oppressed and belittled by the way I was expected to do things I couldn't do. I skived and joined clubs so I needn't go to games or the playground and eventually I decided to get a note from my mum to exempt me from games and PE. For nearly three years I was not asked by any teacher if I wanted to use the lift in the six-storey building. This when I was obviously having problems with the stairs during lesson changes.

Later, although still suffering huge gaps in my formal education, I was able to get five O-levels, then another three and three A-levels. I was now competing intellectually. In this my middle-class background became more of an advantage. My verbal arguing abilities that had really been my main defence against what I viewed as the stupidities of teachers, adults and other children, came to the fore. I became more concerned with the wider good, equality and justice, and by intellectualising these arguments moved into wider political activity. For the next twenty years I was really concerned with socialist politics, at university, in geography, in trade unions and teaching. I had blocked off those parts of me I found it difficult to deal with. Intellect rather than emotion ruled my life, I did eventually marry and have a child but I could only cope with life by thinking I could do everything.

In the last ten years sexual and personal politics, including discrimination of various sorts, have become much more important to me. This is also the time I have had a relationship with Susie. When she first met me I projected a strong image of being 'able-bodied'. I remember us going to a pub together in the early days where the seats were all taken. I stood up all evening and was grumpy. On the way home Susie asked me what had been wrong. I had to think hard and then I realised I had been in pain all evening. She said she would have asked someone for their chair if she'd known. I was horrified at the idea of admitting it or letting people know I needed help and said they would use it against me or think me weak. She was the first person to question my view of myself!

Over many years I have been indebted to her for supporting me in looking at my own disability afresh which has made it possible for me to join the fight for the rights of disabled people. She has helped me to admit to the things I cannot do, to the physical discomfort and pain I am in most of the time so that I can ask for help with dignity. This is still incredibly difficult for me but is very necessary. I feel I am much more open now. I have also come to terms with many of the spectres of my earlier years.

But also during this period my disability has worsened considerably. I now cannot walk at all without a stick. My old injuries to my left arm and right ankle cause me considerable pain and sometimes prevent me walking at all. I now sometimes use a wheelchair and my fear is that one day this will be a permanent necessity. When my second child was born I found it much harder than with the first, eleven years previously, to carry him around and do all the things one has to with a baby. Now he is nearly 2, there have been times when I have feared for his life as I have been unable to reach him before he falls. Our local community nursery had never thought that the children of disabled parents should be a priority and despite much argument by us they still don't.

It wasn't until summer 1987 when, against my wishes, my head teacher identified me for redeployment because my disability restricted my ability to supervise games, that I saw the need to fight the discrimination against us as disabled people collectively and move towards the Disability Movement. Now I know that I need to join with other disabled people who are campaigning and organising against society's attitudes and discrimination towards us. But I also know that each disabled person has to work through the layers of oppression we have accumulated inside ourselves. Our personal experiences as disabled people become internalised. Our perceptions of ourself mirror the attitudes and actions towards us. Dealing with this requires more than projecting the blame onto society.

Whatever social changes take place, and most certainly these must be worked for, we will still have to deal with the discomfort and pain we may have or the things we want to do and can't. Living with our disabilities will raise questions of valuing ourselves, of self-image, of self-criticism, and of confidence that disabled people will need to work through. Even in a society where real equality has been achieved, and we seem to be retreating a long way from such a possibility at present, we still need to gain collective strength from other disabled people as we work through our situation and feelings anew. By sharing this we will continue to have the fortitude for the struggle for life that will always be ours.

Chapter 20

The Integration Alliance
Background and manifesto

Micheline Mason

The Integration Alliance is a broad-based group of people and organisations who are campaigning for the introduction of new legislation which will ensure the right of all young people with any kind of disability or learning difficulty to a fully supported mainstream education. In this chapter, Micheline Mason, a co-founder of the Integration Alliance, outlines the obstructions encountered by various groups who were fighting separately for the same goal: ex-students with disabilities, teachers with disabilities, parents with disabilities, and parents of children with disabilities. She ends by talking of the need for allies to work with the Integration Alliance.

1 INTRODUCTION

The Integration Alliance has been formed by creating bridges between a number of groups of disabled people and parents of children with disabilities. Disabled people, active in the Disability Movement, became parents of children who also had disabilities. This formed links with the parents' support organisations. A collaborative project between a disabled parent and a disabled teacher in the writing of *Disability Equality in the Classroom: A Human Rights Issue* (Rieser and Mason 1990) connected the two strands together in a powerful alliance. In 1989 we set up a conference called 'Integration Now' which brought many individuals together. The conference requested that its steering group should set up an organisation to build on the connections being made, and the steering group set up the Integration Alliance officially in November 1990. Our manifesto is included in the appendix (see p. 229).

2 DISABLED EX-STUDENTS

As disabled people we have been struggling for a long time to liberate ourselves from the chains of an able-bodied culture which does not value us, and which tries to teach us to accept an unequal status in our societies. In the last few years we have begun to achieve a level of unity and organisation beyond that ever achieved by disabled people before. We have formed self-representative organisations in many countries of the world, with an international 'umbrella' organisation called Disabled People's International (DPI), recognised as the voice of disabled people by the United Nations. Recently we have been joined by the parallel development of a self-advocacy movement of people with learning difficulties, under the 'umbrella' of People First.

Those of us who live in countries which still support the practice of segregating young disabled people from our non-disabled peers and educating us separately, have long recognised the crucial role this plays in perpetuating our inequality. This practice is a *prerequisite* of segregation later in life, in special colleges, 'training centres', sheltered workshops, residential homes and hostels, separate transport, segregated social activities and holidays, and the under-representation of disabled people in positions of authority or power.

For historical reasons many populations have been heavily conditioned by what people have called the medical model of disability. This is a view of disability which defines it as a medical problem, belonging to the individual concerned, which needs treating, curing or at least ameliorating. It is fundamental to the philosophy of segregation which separates young children from each other on the basis of their medical diagnoses, and then designs a curriculum which is aimed at 'normalising' the child as far as possible. This curriculum often includes physical therapies, life-skills such as shopping and bed-making, and individually drawn up programmes of work on numeracy and literacy and other academic or vocational subjects.

Disabled people have rejected this model as one which misrepresents the problem of disability completely. Although we do, of course, have medical conditions which may hamper us, the major disability we face is that caused by the social and environmental barriers placed upon us by the structures of our societies. As these are all created by human beings, they can be removed by human beings, and replaced by structures which facilitate our participation in life instead of our exclusion from life.

The removal of barriers to participation in education is a key issue because, first, it is where as young people we develop our basic attitudes towards ourselves and each other and, second, because our inequality of education leaves us disabled people at a great disadvantage in comparison with the non-disabled adult population who currently control most of our lives.

Those of us who have been educated within the special school sector seem to have a very different viewpoint on it to those who provide it. The biggest point of difference is over the importance placed on our so-called 'special needs' over and above our ordinary needs. In fact the provision is more often focused on our conditions instead of us as human beings. As very young children we are still separated from our non-disabled friends and neighbours, from their non-disabled brothers and sisters, and sometimes even from their parents in order to have our 'special needs' attended to. The normal need for closeness, security, unconditional love, play, familiarity which everyone accepts is necessary for a non-disabled child to develop well, is somehow forgotten when it comes to a disabled child. We are sent away to 'improve'.

It is quite commonly assumed by professionals that nearly all children with disabilities have some degree of learning difficulty, as well as some degree of emotional and behavioural difficulties. The mistake they make, however, is believing that this is caused by their having a disability, whereas we know that they are mostly caused by the way we are treated because of the disability. Apart from the break-up of relationships through segregation, disabled children suffer from an enormous loss of control over their lives.

It is true that many children have little control over their lives because of the way that adults view children. But disabled children may be subjected to therapies which they have never asked for and programmes of development which have goals not of their choosing. They may be sent to places without their consent, and may depend to enormous degrees on adults to enable them to express ideas of their own. They may not be able to make their protests understood, and any protests may be seen as symptoms of their disabilities which require more 'treatment'.

Glebe School, for example, which is 'A day special school catering for second-ary aged pupils who have experienced some learning difficulties' states that it aims to 'Encourage independent thought as far as it is practical and generally acceptable to society.' Compare this to the view of disabled children described by Irene Feika (1990), DPI's information officer:

Children are a non-renewable resource. They are the citizens and decision-makers of the future. Their perceptions of today will affect all of us tomorrow ... Children with disabilities are all too often perceived as having less value, which then negatively affects their self-esteem. We can no longer allow this to go on ... The degradation and humiliation many children with disabilities experience when they are warehoused in institutions must not be allowed to continue ... DPI needs to take a leadership role in facilitating the full equality and development of children with disabilities. They will one day lead our movement and need to be well informed about the issues, as well as the solutions.

(Feika 1990: 2)

The model of disability which is of our choosing, is, therefore, a social model, and the philosophy implied by integration is at its very heart. Disability is an equal opportunities issue, in the same way as race, class and gender are equal opportunities issues. Equal opportunities means the removal of barriers to parti-cipation, and for disabled children and children with learning difficulties these are many. The very first being the assumption by the able-bodied world that our education is their affair, not ours. This is why it is crucial that as disabled people and people with learning difficulties we create our own platform from which powerfully to challenge this misconception. From there we – disabled and non-disabled people – can go on to work out together what kind of an education system we need in order to learn how to live together well.

3 DISABLED TEACHERS

While the 1981 Education Act went a little way at least in attempting to assist the integration of disabled children into mainstream schools by the provision of extra resources through the Statementing process, there has been no concurrent awareness of the needs of adults with disabilities who are employed by the education service. Richard Rieser (1988), a disabled teacher, representing the NUT Working Party on Disability wrote in *The Teacher* magazine:

> For those wishing to be teachers, LEAs and Colleges must be satisfied '*as to the health and physical capacity*' of all teachers and trainee teachers. Medical Advisers are given the powers to classify as unfit to teach anyone with physical or psychiatric disorders likely to interfere seriously with regular and efficient teaching ... The threat of physical unfitness to teach hangs over many teachers who therefore keep quiet about their disabilities. For many who become disabled during the course of their career, early retirement or the sack are very real threats. This is a huge waste of training and talent which could be overcome if there was less prejudice from colleagues and a more positive and flexible approach from LEAs and the DES ... Team teaching, job-sharing, the providing of ancillary helpers, adaptations of buildings and alternative teaching methods would make it possible for many who at present cannot gain entry, or are squeezed out of teaching, to make a worthwhile career.
>
> (Rieser 1988: 13)

In 1985, Dr Lane Jones of Lord Mayor Treloar College noted that fewer of her (physically disabled) students were getting accepted at teacher training colleges. In reply to her consequent research into the matter, forty colleges refused applicants on the grounds of physical inaccessibility which had been made worse by recent amalgamations, with only ten colleges saying they would welcome applications. However, even of these ten, only two said they were completely accessible, and only one of those had addressed the issue of accessible teaching practice.

Given that a good number of disabled teachers have no option but to work within the segregated sector, if at all, we are leaving mainstream schools with almost no positive adult role models for disabled children amongst the adults working in their schools. This in turn helps to reproduce the false view society holds of the capabilities of disabled people.

4 DISABLED PARENTS

Part of the false view society holds of disabled people is that we are 'cared for' rather than carers. Most people do not recognise that we are often parents playing active, caring roles for our children. Unfortunately the pressures of being a disabled parent have made it very difficult for us to organise ourselves in any united way to look at the barriers which face us in our role as parents. However, whenever we meet in twos or threes, our exclusion from the school life of our children looms high on our list of concerns. All the same things which exclude or make difficulties in participation for disabled children and teachers, also affect disabled parents. Lois Keith writes of her struggle to gain access as a wheelchair user to her daughter's school:

> It took us two years, a lot of hassles and many 'phone calls and letters to Divisional Office to make the dustbin ramp which was steep and treacherous, safe for independent wheelchair users and to get the door widened. At this stage we still hoped to get a lift installed which would give us access to the whole school ... On the day I deputised my husband to discuss this with the head teacher, it became clear that the Authority was not going to provide a lift and that the Head, in these difficult times, did not consider this issue anywhere near the top of her list of priorities. It was in this conversation that she mentioned that she had in fact had complaints from other parents about wheelchairs 'clogging up the corridors' at the beginning and end of school ... I doubted that the Head would have repeated a racist remark to a Black parent who had come to discuss an issue of equal opportunities with her ... It was yet another example of both the prejudices and the lack of awareness of the issues around disability.
>
> (Keith 1990: 123)

People with learning difficulties also become parents with very specific needs to enable them to participate actively as 'partners' in their children's education. In a chapter on 'The parent's perspective' in The Fish Report (ILEA 1985) it was argued that:

> Parents who have themselves experienced educational failure are more likely to be found amongst the parents of children with moderate learning difficulties and with emotional and behavioural difficulties ... We met a number of parents whose literacy skills were limited, including several participating in adult literacy classes. Written communications and home–school diaries would be inadequate for these families, but staff awareness of parents' reading difficulties would be unlikely unless the parents had actually met the teaching staff. Difficulty in reading should be considered as a factor in poor parent/ school contacts.
>
> (ILEA 1985: 141, 142)

With the progress of the overall Disability Movement and the consequent contact between parents, the possibility of organising disabled parents as a specific group is now becoming a reality.

5 PARENTS OF DISABLED CHILDREN

Parallel to the development of a Civil Rights Movement of disabled people has been the development of organisations of parents of children with disabilities.

Not all these could be said to be complementary to our movement, but with the advent of the 1981 Education Act there was a coming together of parents who understood the basic philosophy underpinning integration, and recognised that it was a right for their children.

The Act required that when a child was made a subject of a Statement local authorities assessed in detail the extra needs a child may have 'over and above those usually provided' within the education system, and that they made these extra provisions available. Parents were expected to participate in this assessment, and their expressed desire for a mainstream or segregated placement would be taken into account. Two major organisations formed, 81 Action, later called Network '81, and The Parents' Campaign for Integrated Education. Their aim was primarily to advise and support parents to use this new legislation effectively.

Members of both organisations became increasingly aware that the conditions surrounding integration were a flaw in the Act. The Act states that after parents' views are taken into account three further conditions may exempt a local authority from providing a mainstream place for a child. It can argue that education in the mainstream is incompatible with the needs of the child, or with the needs of other children in the school, or is an inefficient use of resources. Furthermore the processes of assessment, Statementing and reviews outlined in the Act were causing great distress to many parents and children. There was an assumption that the problem lay in some deficit in the child (the medical model of disability again) and not in the education system. The child is described, usually, in very negative terms. The parents are advised not to approach potential schools until the Assessment procedure has been carried out, which may take a year or more. This is so that the local authority can recommend its own choice of school in which they feel the child's needs can best be met – usually one of their own special schools. Once this school has been named on the Statement, parents have to appeal or fight for another school if they do not agree with the decision. Because in reality one can only assess a child's needs in relation to the environment in which the child must function, the discussion of provision on a Statement can be inadequate or inappropriate for any other school than that named. For example, a child who uses a wheelchair may be completely independent within a properly accessible environment, but may need a full-time primary helper in a school full of stairs. Or partially sighted children may have no extra needs in a school which already has equipment such as closed circuit TV installed, but may need these pieces of equipment written into a Statement if they are to attend a school which has no such facilities. The 'lack of resources' is often used as the reason for designating the 'specialist' school as the most appropriate placement for any child. And a mainstream school will not be encouraged to take a child who has a Statement if that Statement does not make a commitment to provide the *relevant* resources. This has turned into a trap for parents.

Most parents who have been successful in obtaining a mainstream placement for their child have done so by pre-empting the whole process, finding a school with a positive, cooperative head teacher and staff, working out with them what resources would be needed, and then writing the reports for the Assessment accordingly. Many parents, however, are not confident enough to do this, relying instead on the advice from the local authority.

Even when a mainstream place has been obtained, it is never guaranteed to continue. Legally the Statement must be reviewed annually at least, because children 'develop'. One of the questions to be addressed every time is 'Does the school placement continue to be appropriate?' For parents with a child in a mainstream school the worry is always, of course, that the answer will be 'no'. Parents do not have the same right over reviews as they had over the original Statement, particularly the right to appeal to an independent panel if they disagree with the provision. Given that segregation is, therefore, still compulsory in some cases, and that this segregation can mean boarding school, parents of disabled children cannot yet be said to have achieved equal rights with parents of non-Statemented children.

Because so many parents failed to secure the mainstream provision promised by the Act, the parents' organisations found themselves in a dilemma. It seemed that parents still needed support to get the best education possible for their children, wherever they were placed. The fact that some parents were forced into accepting segregated placements for their children did not mean that they no longer needed the support of other parents. This pressure, along with the financial pressure to obtain charitable status, led both groups to drop their explicit campaigning aims, becoming more general educational support groups for parents. Working in isolation it was impossible for parents to achieve their original goal, but for those for whom integration is still the burning desire, working in cooperation with other affected groups, especially the Disability Movement, seems to offer new hope.

6 ALLIES

To achieve change of the magnitude which we wish, it is vital that we have allies who will make themselves known and will join forces with us. The allies are already there in great numbers. There are the obvious ones to whom we are married, or whose brothers and sisters, parents or grandparents have disabilities; our children's friends; our friends; the professionals who support our children within their schools and colleges; the organisations which have been formed explicitly to support integration. But there are also large numbers of 'allies-in-waiting', particularly parents, teachers and young people who do not wish to be separated from their disabled fellow citizens but who would rather learn how to be good friends.

The legacy of the 'medical model of disability' has installed such fear and apprehension within all of us, which is reinforced by segregation. Many adults today express their wish that they had grown up with disabled people so they would have 'known what to do'. They genuinely desire an education system which will not deprive their children of the chance to learn about disability, and to be at ease and confident with disabled friends. The practice in integration shows that everyone benefits, and that it must be contributing towards us building a better world. While we feel that it is important that the Integration Alliance is an organisation controlled by disabled people, the support and contribution of large numbers of allies is essential to our success and will be actively sought.

APPENDIX

THE MANIFESTO

The aims adopted at the inaugural meeting of the Alliance are:

- New legislation to uphold the right to mainstream education for all, thus ending compulsory segregation.
- Physically accessible mainstream nurseries, schools and colleges in every area.
- Facilitators in every such establishment, to assist pupils who need non-teaching support to make full use of the facilities.
- Individual programming and extra teaching support, for all pupils and students, including those who have any degree of learning difficulty.
- Specialist skills (e.g. speech therapy), and appropriate equipment and training in its use, available to all educational establishments.
- A governor in every school with specific responsibility to support the interests of pupils with disabilities and learning difficulties.
- The employment of, and support for, disabled teachers within mainstream nurseries, schools and colleges.
- Realistic limits to class size.
- Sign-language to be taught as a Modern Language in all schools and colleges.
- Appropriate training for teachers within, and transport to, adult education classes, especially adult literacy classes for those people currently suffering from educational deprivation.
- The recognition of disabled parents as having an equal right to full involvement in the school-life of their children, including serving as parent-governors.

REFERENCES

Feika, I. (1990) 'Children: our most precious non-renewable resource', *Vox Nostra*, no. 2, p. 2.

Inner London Education Authority (ILEA) (1985) *Educational Opportunities for All?* (The Fish Report), London: ILEA.

Keith, L. (1990) 'On being a parent with a disability', in R. Rieser and M. Mason (eds), *Disability Equality in the Classroom: A Human Rights Issue*, London: ILEA.

Rieser, R. (1988) 'Struggling to overcome discrimination', *The Teacher*, 14 March 1988, p. 13.
—— and Mason, M. (eds) (1990) *Disability Equality in the Classroom: A Human Rights Issue*, London: ILEA.

Chapter 21

The concept of oppression and the development of a social theory of disability

Paul Abberley

Source: Abberley, P. (1987) 'The concept of oppression and the development of a social theory of disability', *Disability, Handicap and Society* 2 (1), pp. 5–19.

In this chapter, Paul Abberley argues for the importance of the concept of oppression in gaining an understanding of the way disability is produced and people with disabilities are treated in society. The chapter is concerned with outlining the development of this 'social theory of disability'. He examines the meaning of the concept of 'oppression', the way social conditions affect the nature and origin of impairments, and how the disadvantages experienced by people with disabilities share common features with other oppressed groups in society. He concludes by summarising the way the oppression of people with disabilities can be related to economic and social conditions.

1 PREFACE

I would like to preface this article with some short autobiographical notes, not because I think these are ultimately relevant to the adequacy or otherwise of the ideas put forward, but rather because an understanding of the context in which the material was produced may make clearer the reasons behind certain concerns and emphases.

At the age of 5 I contracted poliomyelitis in the last major epidemic of the disease to occur in this country. I spent six weeks in an iron lung, eight months in a hospital bed, and by the age of 7 had regained sufficient mobility to attend a state primary school. Some twenty-five years later, working as a lecturer in sociology, I began to receive requests from some of my colleagues to talk to their students about 'disability'. My first response was one of annoyance and resentment, since I had spent most of my life, as many 'successful' disabled people do, attempting as far as possible to deny and ignore what is in fact a very obvious collection of impairments. But beyond this, I felt that, as a sociologist, I had nothing to say about disability, since the small amount of academic material I was familiar with struck me as both inadequate as an explanation of my own experiences and quite foreign to what I considered 'good sociology'.

Further investigation, during a year's study leave at the University of

Warwick, convinced me that, with a few notable exceptions, the sociology of disability is both theoretically backward and a hindrance rather than a help to disabled people. In particular it has ignored the implications of significant advances made in the last fifteen years in the study of sexual and racial inequality, and reproduces in the study of disability parallel deficiencies to those found in what is now seen by many as racist and sexist sociology. Another aspect of 'good sociology' that I feel is generally absent is any significant recognition of the historical specificity of the experience of disability. In my own case, had I been born a few years earlier, before the development of respiratory support systems, I would have died; a few years later and the advent of effective vaccination techniques would have made my contraction of the disease improbable. In view of this, and similar related considerations, I came to understand my own disabilities in terms of a unique conjunction of factors, a view which I now try to apply to disabled people in general. It is on the basis of such ideas about myself as a disabled person that the following work has been produced.

2 INTRODUCTION

A number of writers, most recently Mike Oliver (1986) have employed the term 'oppression' in the analysis of disability. However, the meaning attached to this term is ill-specified. Oliver, for example, in an earlier draft of his paper, though not in the published version, where any attempt to give precise meaning is absent, uses it interchangeably with exploitation, and it is not defined but rather seen as an 'obvious' but difficult-to-substantiate characteristic of 'social relations under capitalism'. While this is clearly an advance on the 'personal tragedy theory of disability' criticised in the same article, for the notion of oppression to be a useful one the term must be more clearly specified, both in general and in relation to disability in particular.

To draw an analogy between disabled people and groups to whom the term oppression has been applied is by no means a new occurrence. In the literature of disability a number of studies comment, but no more than comment, on the similarity between disabled/normal interactions and those encountered in studies of race relations. Barker for example remarked as long ago as 1948: 'the physically disabled person is in a position not unlike the Negro, the Jew and other under-privileged racial and religious minorities' (Barker 1948: 31), while Handel in 1960 observed that his report 'sounded as though we were considering a problem of race relations instead of disability' (Handel 1960: 363). Again Chesler in 1965 claims to have found that individuals manifesting high ethnocentrism, or high rejection of outgroups, also expressed rejection of the physically disabled (Chesler 1965: 877–82).

A recent study in the *Journal of Maxillo-facial Surgery*, reported in *New Society* in June 1985, claims that on the basis of a photograph study 'children don't start reacting badly to abnormal looks until they are at least 11 years old' and that consequently 'discrimination against funny-looking people is not some innate result of evolutionary forces, it is socially learned' (*New Society* 1985). There is a striking parallel here to Davey's book length study of racism and its acquisition (Davey 1983). Interestingly, amongst the studies reported in this volume is one (Richardson and Green 1971) where it was found in a sample of White children in London schools that visible physical handicap was a greater deterrent to friendship than blackness. In Davey's discussion this is regarded as an 'encouraging' finding! (Davey 1983: 113). But despite observations and insights of this kind, the sociological literature of disability has carried such ideas no further. [. . .]

It is clear then that if the notion of oppression is to be of use in the analysis of disability in society, and most importantly of use to disabled people in understanding and transforming their own situation, we must clarify and develop what is meant by the term.

3 THE CONCEPT OF OPPRESSION

Given the complexity of theoretical issues surrounding theories of oppression (Barrett 1981, Brittan and Maynard 1984) at this stage it is possible to say only in broad outline how a theory of oppression could inform our understanding of the situation of disabled people in Britain today. To argue that we need to analyse the position of disabled people as a form of oppression is not to make the claim that we can arrive at a monolithic theory of oppression into which we can fit women, Black people, disabled people or gay people depending on which particular oppressed group is under discussion at the time. A crucial feature of oppression and the way it operates is its specificity, of form, content and location; so to analyse the oppression of disabled people in part involves pointing to the essential differences between their lives and those of other sections of society, including those who are, in other ways, oppressed. It is also important to note that probably more than half of the disabled people in Britain today suffer the additional burden of racial and/or sexual oppression (Campling 1981, Confederation of Indian Organisations (UK) 1986).

To claim that disabled people are oppressed involves, however, arguing a number of other points. At an empirical level, it is to argue that on significant dimensions disabled people can be regarded as a group whose members are in an inferior position to other members of society because they are disabled people. It is also to argue that these disadvantages are dialectically related to an ideology or group of ideologies which justify and perpetuate this situation. Beyond this it is to make the claim that such disadvantages and their supporting ideologies are neither natural nor inevitable. Finally it involves the identification of some beneficiary of this state of affairs.

The term oppression, while regularly encountered in discussion of racial and sexual disadvantage and of the 'national question', does not appear in encyclopediae of social science, nor in the generally useful *A Dictionary of Marxist Thought* (Bottomore 1983). *Collins English Dictionary* gives four meanings for the word oppress:

- to subjugate by cruelty, force, etc.;
- to lie heavy on (the mind, imagination, etc.);
- to afflict or torment;
- an obsolete word for overwhelm.

In talking of racial or sexual oppression we are clearly not employing any one of these definitions, although aspects of all four meanings are contained within the term [...]. Class analysis *per se* has emerged as an unsatisfactory tool for the analysis of racial and sexual disadvantage, which is experienced in addition to, or perhaps more accurately through, people's class experiences. It is to such sets of experiences that the concept of oppression is addressed.

> Oppression and exploitation are not equivalent concepts.... Exploitation speaks to the economic reality of capitalist class relations for men and women, whereas oppression refers to women and minorities defined within patriarchal, racist and capitalist relations. Exploitation is what happens to men and women workers in the labour force; woman's oppression occurs from the relations that define her existence in the patriarchal sexual hierarchy – as mother, domestic labourer and consumer. Racial oppression locates her within the racist division of society alongside her exploitation and sexual oppression. Oppression is inclusive of exploitation but reflects a more complex reality. Power – or the converse, oppression – derives from sex, race and class, and this is manifested through both the material and ideological dimensions of patriarchy, racism and capitalism. Oppression reflects the hierarchical relations of the sexual and racial division of society.
>
> (Eisenstein 1979: 22–3)

For this author oppression is not an alternative explanatory device to exploitation, rather it is addressed to a different order of phenomena, those connected with a person's gender or race experiences rather than their class experiences. Oppression is complementary to exploitation, extending the range of Marxist analysis to cover areas the latter concept cannot reach.

In developing theories of sexual and racial oppression it has been necessary for theoreticians of the women's and anti-racist movements to settle accounts with biology, which in both cases has been employed to explain and to justify social disadvantage. For a theory of disability as oppression however an important difference arises when we consider the issue of impairment. While in the cases of sexual and racial oppression, biological difference serves only as a qualificatory condition of a wholly ideological oppression, for disabled people the biological difference, albeit as I shall argue itself a consequence of social practices, is itself a part of the oppression. It is crucial that a theory of disability as oppression comes to grips with this 'real' inferiority, since it forms a bedrock upon which justificatory oppressive theories are based and, psychologically, an immense impediment to the development of political consciousness amongst disabled people. Such a development is systematically blocked through the naturalisation of impairment.

Further, the evaluative connotations are cognitively as well as effectively contained in terms which themselves imply deficiency, in contrast to 'woman' and 'Black'. This is not to suggest that perceptions can be changed by changing words but to point to the deeply entrenched rejection of 'impairment' as a viable form of life and to the 'common-sense', 'natural' and 'unconscious' nature of ideologies of impairment, disability and handicap. This rejection of the authenticity of impaired life forms is exhibited both in the obvious form of what Dartington *et al.* (1981) call the 'less than whole person' view, and its inverse, the 'really normal' ideology, which finds its expression in everyday life in the exceptionalism of 'but I don't think of you as disabled', denying a key aspect of a disabled person's identity in what is intended as a compliment. Compare this phrase to 'played like a White man' and 'she thinks like a man'.

What is required is essentially an attitude of ambivalence towards impairment, that is 'co-existence in one person of love and hate towards the same object' *Concise Oxford Dictionary* (1964). Impairment must be identified as a bad thing, in so far as it is an undesirable consequence of a distorted social development, at the same time as it is held to be a positive attribute of the individual who is impaired. An analogy may be drawn here with the feminist treatment of so-called 'women's troubles'. The key distinction that must be made is between the prevention of impairment, on the one hand, and attitudes to and treatment of people who are already impaired on the other.

A pertinent recent example of the necessity for such a distinction is displayed in the boycotting of the 1985 Manchester International Conference on Education of the Deaf by the British Deaf Association and the National Union of the Deaf. 'The objection is that the main discussion will be the development of electrode implants, which have the potential to restore "hearing" even to the totally deaf, provided that they once could hear' (*Guardian*, 5 August 1985). The education chairman of the National Deaf Children's Society said that deaf children could lead a full life using other forms of communication such as sign-language. 'They shouldn't get the idea that the thing is to be more like a hearing person at any cost' he said (*Guardian*, 5 August 1985). While the boycotters' attitude to impairment is one of ambivalence, as defined above, and thus of respect for disabled people, the members of the medical profession who determined the agenda clearly expressed their own rejection of the disabled state by determining that a dubious 'rectification' procedure, to which they raised only *technical* objections, should be the main business of a conference which occurs once every five years.

Yet if the inferiority embodied in impairment is understood as purely or primarily biological in origin, the suggested analogy with racial and sexual oppression appears to be an inherently dubious one, since the core of such theories is that disadvantage is ultimately a social and not a biological product. A theory of disability as oppression then must offer what is essentially a social theory of impairment.

4 IMPAIRMENT AS A SOCIAL PRODUCT

The general tendency within medicine has been to attribute most impairments which are not identified as the consequence of acute illness and infection to 'normal' wear and tear on the human body. Causation, on this view, is ascribed either to 'germs' or to 'life'. Any 'social' involvement is presented as secondary or peripheral to the major identified patterns of 'natural' causation. But an alternative account of the origin of impairments is at least as viable.

To take the major cause of impairment in Britain, some 5 million people are thought to suffer from osteo-arthritis, and some 1 million from rheumatoid arthritis (British League Against Rheumatism 1977). While often regarded as 'simply' a degenerative process,

> a number of rheumatic problems are known to arise in connection with various occupations. Unfortunately economic factors have usually not allowed this knowledge to be fully exploited. Primary prevention would call for changes in methods of working and in the job environment, and these are often costly.
>
> (Arthritis and Rheumatism Council n.d.: 11)

Thus an alternative view of this major cause of impairment would locate explanation not at the 'natural' or 'individual' level, but in the socio-economic context of its occurrence, of which 'physical degeneration' is by no means an independent variable. To extend this argument further, the pace and direction of the development of preventative and ameliorative techniques are themselves the product of socio-economic factors, which are in turn effected by what are fundamentally political decisions. Thus at both these levels social aspects of impairment causation may be discerned.

Whilst most incapacity resulting from injury sustained at work is categorised as of relatively short duration, about a third results in permanent or possibly permanent damage (Pearson Commission Report 1978). In addition to accidents, some 16,000 people a year contract an industrial disease as prescribed under the 1975 Social Security Act, the main categories being infective dermatitis (10,000), traumatic inflammation of the tendon (3,400) and beat knee (1,000). However, the comparison of such statistics, based on DHSS records which exclude certain diseases known to be caused or exacerbated by industrial injury, to a personal injury survey, led Pearson to conclude:

> There were substantial numbers of illnesses where there appeared to the sufferer to be a probable link between the illness and conditions of work, possibly amounting to five times the number of prescribed diseases recorded by the DHSS.
>
> (Pearson Commission Report 1978: vol. 2, 66)

Nichols (1986) echoes this sentiment, as have other writers who argue that official figures on work-based impairments constitute merely the tip of the iceberg

(Kinnersley 1973, Thunhurst 1982, Navarro 1982), and argues further that since 1978 the rate of disabling injuries and deaths in manufacturing industry has increased.

Mirroring impairment caused by the process of production is that attributable to the willing or unwilling consumption of its products. While perhaps the most notorious recent example in Britain is the drug Thalidomide, other products of the pharmaceutical industry are, or should be, similarly implicated. Of the 70,000 personal injuries attributed by Pearson to defective products or services (about 2.5 per cent of all injuries) around half involved prescribed drugs.

At the World Mental Health Congress in Brighton in July 1985, Dr David Hill, Senior Psychologist at Walton Hospital, Chesterfield argued that 25 million patients throughout the world had suffered irreversible brain damage as the result of the administration of powerful tranquillisers such as Largactil (*The Guardian*). His critics made no attempt to rebut this contention, but simply averred that there was no alternative.

At a world level, the deleterious health effects of prescribed drugs is chillingly documented (Muller 1982). While, in the 'developed' world at least, vaccination has reduced to a trickle the number of cases of many diseases, vaccine-related damage has itself caused impairment in those who have paid the individual cost of general health improvement. The development of effective vaccination techniques has also had the paradoxical effect in some cases of disadvantaging those who have already been impaired by a disease. For example:

> The end of the recurrent epidemics of polio meant that the disease, and therefore its victims, lost their high profile. There was a reduction in new research on the disease, its process, and its management. This meant that knowledge about the epidemiology and pathology of polio has been essentially stalled at the level of medical knowledge in the mid-1950s. . . . Part of the context of any particular disability is its topicality in the medical or in the public eye. Like cancer today, polio once attracted attention beyond its actual level of threat to the population; however, once immunization removed that threat, polio became a 'non-issue'.
>
> (Kaufert and Kaufert 1984: 616)

It should be noted that any removal of the threat of polio is only a local one. Contrary to general medical belief in the 1940s and 1950s, polio is by no means a 'disease of civilisation'; recurrent outbreaks are still endemic in much of the world, where vaccination has been seen as unnecessary or where methods of administration have been ineffective.

It is estimated that the world population of disabled people is around 500 million, over two-thirds of whom live in developing countries, and that one in ten of the world's children is physically or mentally disabled. Some authorities argue that up to 50 per cent of world disablement is either preventable or can be ameliorated significantly at a cost of a few pounds per head (Shirley 1983). For example, around 6,000 children go blind each year in Tamil Nadu due to easily remediable vitamin A deficiency. Yet Dr Michael Irwin, UNICEF coordinator for the International Year of Disabled People said, 'only 1 or 2% of the disabled children in the Third World are reached by any rehabilitation' (*The Guardian*, 1981). Another major contributory factor in the aetiology of impairment is nutrition; yet it is universally recognised that world food supplies exceed world need, and that malnutrition today is a consequence of political decisions, not 'acts of God'. As far as the majority of the world's disabled people are concerned, impairment is very clearly primarily the consequence of social and political factors, not an unavoidable 'fact of nature'.

Returning to the developed world, advances in medicine have had the effect of increasing the survival rate of previously 'non-viable' individuals, producing an increased proportion of severely and multiply impaired young people – the improved survival rates of people suffering from Down's Syndrome and spina bifida are cases in point. The generally unquantified effects of environmental pollution, and the impairing effects of the consumption of foodstuffs, tobacco and alcohol on individuals and their future offspring must also be noted, although here I will deal with these aspects no further.

Impairment may result from so-called hereditary factors or injury incurred at or soon after birth. Data from the National Child Development Study showed an incidence of serious defects which were congenital or had arisen shortly after birth as 30.8 per thousand live births. By 7 years old the incidence was 19.6 per thousand, about half resulting in disablement. A further nine per thousand had very poor sight, and three per thousand poor hearing (Davie *et al.* 1972). The example of Phenylketonuria (PKU) reveals the complex interconnection between congenital and social factors in the production of impairment. This hereditary inability to metabolise the amino-acid phenylalanine may today be detected and, through dietary control, mental retardation be prevented. Prior to the development of methods of detection and treatment, it may have appeared eminently reasonable to characterise the disorder as a congenital one; it would now appear equally correct to characterise it as socially determined, in that only individuals born in environments in which tests for the presence of the PKU phenotype are not conducted, and where there is no available treatment, will suffer the subsequent impairment. It would thus seem impossible adequately to draw a dividing line between genetic and environmental, and thus ultimately social, factors. Rather, the designation of genetic factors as primarily causative is itself a judgement determined by knowledge, interest and intention, in other words, a political judgement.

It is possible at this point to clarify the nature of the claim that *impairment* is to be understood as social in origin, and to distinguish it from the more usual sociological generalisations about the social origins of *handicap*. The latter position, at least in its more worked out forms, presents handicap as totally the product of social meanings, in other words as reducible to 'attitudes'. It implies that a change in attitudes could abolish disability. Claims about the social origin of impairment, however, are directed at the explication of the social origin of what are material and biological phenomena. [...]

Thus such a view does not deny the significance of germs, genes and trauma, but rather points out that their effects are only ever apparent in a real social and historical context, whose nature is determined by a complex interaction of material and non-material factors. For example, while the link between tobacco consumption and lung cancer, bronchitis and ischaemic heart disease is demonstrably a material one, the occurrence and incidence of tobacco consumption is to be understood primarily in terms of social factors, as is the level and kind of ameliorative provision available.

At a political level, focusing upon kinds and rates of impairment, posing as they do, in an explicit and graphic form, the contradictions between the potentially beneficial nature of medical science and its restrictions and deformations in the capitalist mode of production, can be seen as forming a materialist basis for a theory of disability as oppression. [...]

5 COMMON FEATURES OF DISADVANTAGE

A characteristic of the literature of racial and sexual oppression is that it identifies certain generally common features of economic, social and psychological disadvantage suffered by members of the oppressed group. The nature and extent of these disadvantages is by no means uniform or constant between groups or within groups over time, and can only be adequately described after detailed empirical investigation. Considerable literature exists to indicate the material disadvantages suffered by disabled people. To take only one example, Townsend (1979) produces a picture of low pay, longer hours, worse working conditions and housing, coupled with a higher likelihood of unemployment. For the purposes of this chapter I shall assume this study's findings as typical, reliable and valid, and explore this dimension no further. In addition to material and economic disadvantage, another extensive body of work, of which perhaps the most famous example is still Goffman's *Stigma* (Goffman 1963), documents social and psychological disadvantage from what is explicitly or implicitly an Interactionist perspective. From the point of view of a theory of disability as oppression such studies are important in that they can be viewed as identifying and describing the social mechanisms by which the conditions described by social accountants such as Townsend are produced and reproduced. Care must be taken in 'translation', since a common feature of such studies is the assumed inevitability or 'rightness' of what is described. However, taken together and adequately reinterpreted such studies can form an important element in the development of a theory of disability as oppression. For example, Katz *et al.* (1978) found that

Identical behaviours have different social meanings when produced by a normal and by a disabled person. The pleasant competent 'wheelchair bound' group leader aroused anger and got less help because she appeared to violate the stereotyped stigma role requirement which seems to require the disabled person to suffer and be inadequate. When the confederate in the wheelchair was caustic and hostile, this seemed to confirm social expectations and subjects were willing to offer more help.

(Katz *et al.* 1978: 506)

In commenting on such examples we should endeavour to map out key features of the stereotype of the disabled person which a particular social formation produces and acts towards real disabled people in terms of. Our objective should be the explication of the material conditions which generate such stereotypes, not the mere description found in Interactionist approaches and empiricist psychology.

One key aspect of this stereotype in modern Britain is that whilst his/her 'primary identity' (Shearer 1981: 23) resides in disability, the legitimacy and value of this identity is simultaneously denied. Whether perceived as 'tragic' or 'brave' a total identity of the person and the disability is assumed – but at the same time the disabled state is taken for granted as necessarily illegitimate to the extent that:

A crude and obtrusive imitation of a 'normal' body is held to be preferable to an elegant and efficient tool that makes no pretence of being anything other than what it is.

(Sutherland 1981: 75)

and

There's a tremendous emphasis on a child who's had polio or whatever to walk.... It's like standing up is considered infinitely better than sitting down, even if you're standing by standing in a total frame that weighs a ton, that you can't move in, which hurts and takes hours to get on and off and looks ugly. It's assumed that that is what you want and that that's what is best for you.

(Sutherland 1981: 73)

The importance of the body in modern Western society has been noted, for example in feminist literature and in considerations of youth culture, although any systematic sociological study has until recently been absent (Turner 1984). For disabled people the body is the site of oppression, both in form and in what is done with it. The prohibitions upon deaf children signing to each other as 'something evil, like wanking; things you do with your hands that you're not supposed to' (Sutherland 1981: 56) are the mirror image of the unrealisable ideals of physical perfection and competence constantly presented in the media and in conventional sporting and recreational material. But perhaps more significant than the requirements and prohibitions on what you do with your body as a disabled person are the things that are done to it. These 'rapes' and 'carryings off into slavery' correspond for disabled people to the more publicised features of sexual and racial oppression, and are often perpetuated in everyday life by the actions and the gaze of 'normal' people. [...]

The stereotype of disabled people (as implied and in turn produced by the disability logo appearing on lavatory doors and motor cars) is of young people in wheelchairs as a result of MS, amputation, etc. This is far from the reality of the vast majority of disabled people. The mean age of the 'young chronic sick' on Wood's (Wood 1978) calculation was 50.3 years in 1978, only 9.8 per cent of disabled people being less than 45, a fact which has prompted a minor terminological amendment in the most recent literature, with 'young' renamed 'younger' (Royal College of Physicians 1986b: 4).

Causes of impairment were also found to be at odds with the stereotype.

Table 21.1 Causes of severe disability

	%		%		%
Arthritis	31	MS	2.8	Paraplegia	1.3
Stroke or Parkinson	15	Amputation	1.5	Polio	0.7
Cardio-respiratory	13				

Source: Derived from Bury 1979. Similar calculations can be made on the basis of data in Royal College of Physicians 1986a.

There are a number of implications significant for a theory of disability as oppression which arise from this misidentification. Given the prevalent causes of impairment, the significance of the activities or inactivity of the medical agencies should not be underestimated, as it frequently is in certain sociological studies, and by those members of the general public who claim to view disabled people as 'just like everyone else'. Were the majority of disabled people subject to relatively stable conditions for which no medical interventions were appropriate such positions would be more tenable, but the predominant biological causes of impairment are conditions for which modern medicine at least lays claim to some ameliorative competence.

The stereotype addresses itself to people who, were they not disabled, would be expected to work – thus the Poor Law concerns with legitimacy described by Stone (1984) surface again, in public perception and concern if not in statistical reality (on Bury's calculation 57.9 per cent of impaired adults were over 65 years of age). This group is also that identified in the Royal College of Physicians' report (1986a) as the one for whom provision is least adequate, and who are also identified in more anecdotal sources as subject to the most demeaning of 'tests' in seeking mobility allowances (*The Guardian*: letters, Aug. 1986).

This misidentification, while merely puzzling to Bury, can be seen as performing a number of important functions for the present social system. First, by directing attention away from impairment associated with ageing, it naturalises this aspect of the situation, and reduces the amount of perceived disability in society, so that disability appears as 'exceptional'. In reality about 5.5 million, or one in ten people in Britain today are disabled, approximately the same as the proportion of the workforce who are currently suffering from unemployment.

Second, it focuses on that aspect of disability, namely its ability to effect potential workers, which is the primary concern of capitalism, for which the 'problem' of disability is why these people aren't productive, how to return them to productivity, and, if this is not seen as economically viable, how to handle their non-productivity in a manner which causes as little disruption as possible to the overriding imperative of capital accumulation and the maximisation of profits. Yet if the primary object of such theories is the 'young' disabled people, their effects reverberate far beyond their immediate subjects. One effect of the downgrading of the disabled state is to lead all people, including the 'young' disabled themselves, to deny their own suffering and to normalise their situation, thus maintaining the existing structures of social organisation and of work. Beyond this, society as a whole is affected, via the propagation of the work ethic and notions of normalcy implicitly contained in such theories. At this level there is a parallel with the argument (Brittan and Maynard 1984) that racial and sexual oppression are integrally connected to masculine power in the notion of masculinity as mastery over nature. The points raised by Hunt (1966: 146), who argues that disabled people challenge the prevailing norms of society in five main ways, 'as unfortunate, useless, different, oppressed and sick', indicate how the mode of being of disabled people can be seen as constituting a paradigmatic negation of masculinity as thus conceived.

As in the cases of women and Black people, oppressive theories of disability systematically distort and stereotype the identities of their putative subjects, restricting their full humanity by constituting them only in their 'problem' aspects. The more fashionable but equally unacceptable liberal reaction to this view is to deny all differences – similar to the assimilationist perspective in race relations, and thus similarly devaluing and denying the authenticity of an impaired person's experience, dissolving real problems in the soup of 'attitude change'. Both these viewpoints contain the explicit or tacit assumption that 'impairment' is a universally acceptable and primary explanatory factor. This can be seen particularly in the 'mourning' theories criticised by Oliver (1983), and reaches its most refined and nonsensical expression in such pronouncements as 'he had the required toughness of mind – despite, or perhaps because of, legs crippled by polio' (Heren 1984).

As with racism and sexism, a theory of disability as oppression must at some point face the question of who benefits from oppression. While certain individuals and groups can be seen to accrue short-term advantage (a consideration of the manufacture, supply and fitting of artificial limbs in Britain today provides graphic examples of this) the main and consistent beneficiary must be identified as the present social order, or, more accurately, capitalism in a particular historical and national form. These latter distinctions are important ones if we are to understand variations in policy and attitudes between nations and over time (Mitchell 1985).

6 CONCLUDING REMARKS

I have largely argued from analogy and through criticism of extant theoretical perspectives on disability. But this analogy has, I hope, been a sustained one, and the criticisms have not been random. Taken together they imply a number of things about what an alternative theory, a theory of disability as oppression, will be concerned with and what it will look like, in contrast to oppressive theories. In conclusion I will try to make these points more explicit.

Some of the general effects of the oppression of disabled people are as follows:

- It discourages individuals from trying to take up the 'privileges', to use Stone's (Stone 1984) somewhat curious term of disability and thus exempt themselves from the work process.
- Because of negative stereotypes and material disadvantages connected to disability it encourages people, where possible, to normalise suffering and disease so as not to include themselves in a despised and disadvantaged sub-group.
- It helps to constitute part of a passive 'sub-class' of welfare recipients (Leonard 1984) which serves as a powerful warning against falling off the achievement ladder.
- By presenting disadvantage as the consequence of a naturalised 'impairment' it legitimises the failure of welfare facilities and the distribution system in general to provide for social need, that is, it interprets the effects of social mal-distribution as the consequence of individual deficiency.

In contrast to this, a theory of disability as oppression will attempt to flesh out the claim that historically specific categories of 'disabled people' were constituted as a product of the development of capitalism, and its concern with the compulsion to work. This remained until the late nineteenth century largely the task of legal agencies, but the rise of scientific medicine resulted in the transfer of policing from legal to medical authorities. While this clearly led to certain transformations in the situation of disabled people, medical ideology too devalues the impaired modes of being, at the same time as it naturalises the causes of impairment.

A theory of disability as oppression, then,

- recognises and, in the present context, emphasises the social origins of impairment;
- recognises and opposes the social, financial, environmental and psychological disadvantages inflicted on impaired people;
- sees both 1 and 2 as historical products, not as the results of nature, human or otherwise;
- asserts the value of disabled modes of living at the same time as it condemns the social production of impairment;
- is inevitably a political perspective, in that it involves the defence and trans-

formation, both material and ideological, of state health and welfare provision as an essential condition of transforming the lives of the vast majority. of disabled people.

While the political implications of such an analysis are apparent, the conceptual consequences are also profound, since such a notion of disability as oppression allows us to organise together into a coherent conceptual whole heretofore isolated and disparate areas of social research, and potentially to correct the results of such theoretical myopia.

In summary, to apply the notion of oppression usefully to the complex of impairment, disability and handicap involves the development of a theory which connects together the common features of economic, social and psychological disadvantage with an understanding of the material basis of these disadvantages and the ideologies which propagate and reproduce them. Only such an account, specific and systematic, can move discussion beyond the level that it has reached so far, by bringing to bear the tools of today's social science, rather than those of the day before yesterday.

ACKNOWLEDGEMENTS

I would like to thank Sue Abberley, Caroline Freeman, Dee Northover and Christine Webb for their various contributions to the genesis of this chapter.

REFERENCES

Arthritis and Rheumatism Council (n.d.) *Arthritis Research: The Way Ahead*, London: ARC.

Barker, R. G. (1948) 'The social psychology of physical disability', *Journal of Social Issues* 4(4), 28–42.

Barrett, M. (1981) *Women's Oppression Today*, London: Verso.

Bottomore, T. (ed.) (1983) *A Dictionary of Marxist Thought*, Oxford: Basil Blackwell.

British League Against Rheumatism (1977) *Rheumatism: The Price We Pay*, London: BLAR.

Brittan, A. and Maynard, M. (1984) *Sexism, Racism and Oppression*, Oxford: Basil Blackwell.

Bury, M. R. (1979) 'Disablement in society', *International Journal of Rehabilitative Research* 2, 33–40.

Campling, J. (ed.) (1981) *Images of Ourselves*, London: Routledge & Kegan Paul.

Chesler, M. A. (1965) 'Ethnocentrism and attitudes towards the physically disabled', *Journal of Personality and Social Psychology* 2, 877–82.

Confederation of Indian Organisations (UK) (1986) *Double Bind – To be Disabled and Asian*, London: CIO.

Dartington, T., Miller, E. and Gwynne, G. (1981) *A Life Together*, London: Tavistock.

Davey, A. (1983) *Learning to be Prejudiced*, London: Edward Arnold.

Davie, R., Butler, N. and Goldstein, H. (1972) *From Birth to Seven*, London: Longman.

Eisenstein, Z. (1979) 'Developing a theory of capitalist patriarchy and socialist feminism', in Z. Eisenstein (ed.), *Capitalist Patriarchy and the Case for Socialist Feminism*, New York: Monthly Review Press.

Goffman, E. (1963) *Stigma*, New Jersey: Prentice-Hall.

Handel, A. F. (1960) 'Community attitudes and adjustment to disability', *Outlook for the Blind*, no. 54, 363.

Heren, L. (1984) *The Observer*, London, 30 December.

Hunt, P. (1966) 'A critical condition' in P. Hunt (ed.), *Stigma*, London: Chapman.

Katz, I., Farber, J., Glass, D. and Lucido, D. (1978) 'When courtesy offends: effects of positive and negative behavior by the physically disabled on altruism and anger in normals', *Journal of Personality* 46 (3), 506–18.

Kaufert, J. and Kaufert, P. (1984) 'Methodological and conceptual issues in measuring the impact of longterm disability', *Social Science and Medicine* 19, 609–19.

Kinnersley, P. (1973) *The Hazards of Work*, London: Pluto Press.

Leonard, P. (1984) *Personality and Ideology*, Ch. 8, Basingstoke: Macmillan.

Mitchell, P. (1985) *A Comparison of Social Provision For People with Disabilities in the Netherlands and the U.K.*, London: RADAR.

Muller, M. (1982) *The Health of Nations*, London: Faber.

Navarro, V. (1982) 'The labour process and health international', *Journal of Health Services* 12, 5–29.

New Society (1985) 'Findings', 7 June.

Nichols, T. (1986) 'Industrial injuries in British manufacturing in the 1980s', *Sociological Review* 34, 290–306.

Oliver, M. (1983) *Social Work with Disabled People*, Basingstoke: Macmillan.

—— (1986) 'Social policy and disability: some theoretical issues', *Disability, Handicap and Society* 1, 5–18.

Pearson Commission Report (1978) Vols 1 and 2, London: HMSO.

Richardson, S. W. and Green, A. (1971) 'When is black beautiful? Coloured and white children's reaction to skin colour', *British Journal of Educational Psychology* 41, 62–9.

Royal College of Physicians of London (1986a) *Physical Disability in 1986 and Beyond*, London: RCP.

—— (1986b) *The Young Disabled Adult*, London: RCP.

Shearer, A. (1981) *Disability: Whose Handicap?*, Oxford: Basil Blackwell.

Shirley, O. (ed.) (1983) *A Cry for Health – Poverty and Disability in the Third World*, Frome: Third World Group and AHRTAG.

Stone, D. (1984) *The Disabled State*, Basingstoke: Macmillan.

Sutherland, A. (1981) *Disabled We Stand*, London: Souvenir Press.

Thunhurst, C. (1982) *It Makes You Sick – The Politics of the NHS*, London: Pluto Press.

Townsend, P. (1979) *Poverty in the United Kingdom*, London: Penguin.

Turner, B. S. (1984) *The Body & Society*, Oxford: Basil Blackwell.

Wood, P. H. N. (1978) 'Size of the problem and causes of chronic sickness in the young', *Journal of the Royal Society of Medicine* 71, 437–41.

Chapter 22

Disability as a social construct
The labelling approach revisited

Mårten Söder

Source: Söder, M. (1989) 'Disability as a social construct: the labelling approach revisited', *European Journal of Special Needs Education* 4 (2), 117–29.

In this chapter Mårten Söder discusses the ways in which social factors affect the nature of disability and our understanding of it. He concentrates on a discussion of labelling theory and argues that proponents of integration have systematically misunderstood it. He suggests that they believe that integration avoids labelling and that integrationists deny the significance and experience of disability.

1 INTRODUCTION

Over the past decade developments in the field of special education have been in the direction of integration and normalisation. The ideology motivating these changes has emphasised the importance of social factors upon the development of disabled children and youngsters. More specifically, theories of labelling have become common, emphasising how categorisation through diagnoses and labels underlines the handicap and diminishes opportunities for personal development. The labelling approach has had some impact on research, but even more so on policy-making.

The basic assumptions of the labelling approach and its application as an ideology for change in services for persons with disabilities are discussed in this chapter. First, the meaning and basic assumptions of this approach are clarified by distinguishing them from those of other theories of social factor influence, and then the ideological application of these assumptions is critically examined. It is suggested that policies intended to be 'non-labelling' are actually attaching a new meaning to disability, a meaning that tends to render disability invisible. In a final paragraph the need for research that analyses this kind of development and its consequences is discussed.

2 SOCIAL FACTORS AND DISABILITY

Rejecting simplistic reliance on the medical/clinical perspective that has traditionally dominated disability research, many researchers have stressed the importance of taking social factors into account. But taking social factors into account can be done in different ways. In the field of disability, at least three different approaches to the social dimension of the phenomenon under study can be identified.

The epidemiological approach

The first approach is what I will call the 'epidemiological approach'. In this approach the relation between disability and environment is seen in causal terms. The basic assumption is that disability is an abnormality, situated within the person. Such a disability can have many causes. Social factors are among possible causes contributing to the deficiency of the individual.

Epidemiological studies traditionally build upon this perspective. The main goal is to describe the distribution of disabilities within different substratas of a population, locating it in a geographical and social structure. But usually the ambition is not limited to description. Information thus gathered is interpreted in causal terms.

Take a simple example. Suppose we do a study of the distribution of severe mental retardation in a society and find that it is overrepresented in areas with a particular type of industry and among workers in that industry. Our immediate reaction is to ask questions about causality. Is there anything in the work environment that can explain our finding? Do they work with dangerous substances? Is there pollution from industrial waste? The descriptive data are interpreted as a memento to search for the causal link. Basically we view disability as a disease, caused by an agent that our data can help us to identify. The information about social distribution of disability is interpreted as the first factor in a causal chain.

The adaptability approach

A second way of viewing the relation between disability and environment is to see the disability as the outcome of interaction between individual and environment. Consequently, disability is not, as in the epidemiological approach, viewed as an intrinsic personal characteristic. It is seen as a result of the interaction between a specific individual and his/her environment. Natural human variation provides endless variety in many characteristics. Whether certain characteristics turn out to be disabilities depends on the demands and expectations of the environment. If the individual, due to some characteristic weakness or shortcoming, is unable to respond to the demands in a proper way, disability is a fact. Disability can thus be said to be a relation between the individual and the environment, rather than an abnormality within the individual.

This relational assumption about disability has led to a focus on the capability of the individual to adapt to different demands and expectations in the environment.

The adaptability approach has a long history in mental retardation research (Doll 1948). But its main focus has been on the individual, emphasising his ability to adjust to environment. It was more or less given official status by the American Association of Mental Deficiency (AAMD) definition in the beginning of the 1960s, that conceptualised mental retardation as two-dimensional, defined both by the level of intelligence and the adaptive ability. The work of Mercer (1973), however, has shown that the adaptability approach can be used to ask questions about environment as well. Being the outcome of a process between individual and society, the adaptive process can be studied from the environmental as well as from the individual side. This is what I understand to be 'the social system perspective' presented by Mercer.

The social constructionist approach

There is a third way of viewing the relation between disability and social environment. In this approach the link between the individual and environment is that of social meaning. The world is seen as socially constructed. We live in a world which becomes meaningful to us through the use of shared symbols. Getting to know the world is to learn the meanings, through language, that we attach to different phenomena in our environment. Our relation to the world is conditioned by our interaction with others. Through that interaction we learn to take the perspective of others towards ourselves and the environment.

Following this approach, disability is defined by the meaning we attach to different kinds of physical and mental deviations. Disability is, so to speak, 'in the eye of the beholder'. We literally construct disabilities by interpreting such deviances according to socially anchored values and beliefs.

The implications of symbolic interactionism for the study of deviance have been worked out by several theorists such as Goffman (1963), Becker (1963) and Scheff (1984). They all point out the dramatic effects of categorisation and labelling. The label might, from the perspective of the labeller, be seen as a neutral, descriptive or scientific diagnosis, but in fact it is something much more. It puts the person in a category that is loaded with social meanings and preconceptions. As a result, diagnosing disability is far more than simply describing some peculiarities in that person's behaviour. It is putting him in a special category, making him a special person. The characteristic of being disabled is ascribed to the whole person and all his other characteristics become interpreted in light of his disability. The personality freezes, so to speak, in the format of disability, the format being set by the preconceptions that constitute the culturally determined meaning of that particular disability.

Labelling is a process. By being labelled, the person enters a deviant career. His self-image is affected by the meanings he meets in his environment. Particularly if these meanings are shared by and communicated to him through those significant others with whom he has close relations, he will internalise the image inherent in the label.

This interactionist mechanism is often strengthened by actions that typically accompany the labelling, especially segregative measures. Most clearly such mechanisms have been demonstrated in connection with institutionalisation. The standardisation of stereotyped meaning becomes stronger in an environment where several persons labelled the same way are objects of special treatment. The effects of such treatment for the moral career of patients in total institutions has been dramatically described by Goffman (1961). He calls the career 'the process of mortification', which signifies that the self-image acquired outside the institution is systematically destroyed and, finally, leads inmates to behave like and see themselves as inmates.

The end-product of the process is a person who conforms to the expectations inherent in the social label. To stress that this is an adjustment to social expectations, and thus a socially created state of affairs, it is often called secondary deviation. Secondary deviation is thus to be distinguished from the primary deviance, the deviance that by being labelled started the whole process.

This short summary of the basic reasoning in interactionist labelling theories gives some insight into the meaning of disability as being socially constructed. The social meaning attached to certain persons creates – in the form of a self-fulfilling prophecy – the condition that is then treated as caused by nature and objectively given.

This approach differs from the two other approaches described above. The epidemiological approach has as a basic assumption that disability is a disturbance within the person with environment treated as a potential cause of such disturbances. The adaptability approach realises the relativity of disability and sees environment as posing thresholds for varying capabilities. But the social constructionist approach is much more radical in its relativistic ambitions. Environment is seen as the creator of (the social meaning of) disability.

3 THE LABELLING APPROACH AS IDEOLOGY

The constructionist/labelling perspective has influenced some research in the field of disability. One type of study that is in accordance with the assumptions of this approach captures the social meaning that persons with disability themselves attach to the world they live in (Edgerton 1967, 1984, Evans 1983, Lea 1988). Another type that sometimes refers to labelling theory is evaluative studies of mainstreaming and integration (e.g. Johnson and Johnson 1984).

But the greatest impact of labelling theory, I would suggest, is not in research, but in criticism of traditional services and the formation of a new ideology for services to disabled people. The important insights and postulates of the social constructivist approach have fired actions against segregative services and professional power.

Labelling theory and social criticism

Sharp criticism of services based on labelling theory has been formulated. The general theme of the criticism is that traditional services in several ways create and confirm a status of incompetence and dependency for persons with disabilities.

The role of professionals has been targeted (Croxen-John 1988, Finkelstein 1980, Kelley 1988, McKnight 1981). Professionals are paid officers, with their own ethical rules and scientific perspective worked out by their own community and legitimated by official authorities. Professionals are the active agents in the labelling process, defining the presence of disability in other persons. They are the ones who trigger the whole process of social creation of deviance. Critics have particularly noticed the imbalance of power inherent in this process. By having the prerogative of definition, professionals exert control over other human beings. It has also been pointed out that the self-interest of professions not only makes them defend that prerogative, but makes them work to preserve a state of affairs in which disabled people are kept in their dependent and powerless state. Professionals' continuing existence depends on keeping others in a dependent position.

Another target of the criticism is, of course, segregation. As noted above, segregative measures, such as institutionalisation, are extreme examples of how secondary deviation is created through labelling. Segregation has been attacked basically on two different grounds. First, segregation, the separation of persons with a common characteristic from the mainstream of society, is seen as something morally bad in itself. We have no right, the argument goes, to treat certain persons that way. Segregation is seen as opposed to values of equality and equal opportunity. Second, segregation is bad because it creates negative effects for the individual. Secondary deviations – in extreme forms, institutional neurosis and other consequences – are harmful for the labelled person.

A third target of criticism – closely related to but more general than the criticism of segregation – is the standardised routine treatment that follows from treating a group of persons according to the label they have in common. This makes us insensitive to individual differences. By 'freezing' the whole person in the form of a label we reproduce and legitimise such routine treatment. A more flexible or 'subject oriented approach' (Kelley 1988) is suggested, based not on collective labels, but on the individuality of the person.

The policy reforms that should follow this criticism are implicit in the criticism: institutions should be abolished; integration instead of segregation; more flexible services and less power to professionals.

This criticism is based on social constructionist and, more specifically, labelling theories. But on the way from scientific theory to a tool for normative criticism some of the basic elements of the theories seem to get lost. In using the theory for criticising traditional services and arguing for 'non-labelling' ones, simplifications are made that are contrary to the original theories. These mistakes are important as they lead to an over-optimistic and omnipotent attitude towards what can be accomplished by 'non-labelling' approaches. I will, in the rest of this chapter, try to identify those errors and discuss their implications both for professional ideology and research.

The fallacies of the 'anti-labelling' critique

Many critics have applied the labelling theory in a superficial and normative way. In so doing some of the bases of the constructionist approach are forgotten. I will point out three mistakes that often accompany such a superficial application.

The first mistake is an epistemological one. When applying the social constructivist approach in areas like disability, such a mistake is close at hand. The mistake can perhaps be called 'voluntarism'. The world is seen as constructed by the social meaning we ascribe to it. If we are dissatisfied with something in that world, the way to change should be to change the meaning that is ascribed to it. If we find the consequences of disability to be unsatisfactory, so the argument goes, let's change the meaning that creates these negative consequences.

This is voluntarism in the sense that the meanings laid down are supposed to be alterable by individual actors. It disregards the fact that such meanings are anchored in a total world of experience that is given to us, through socialisation, and stands out as an objective reality in itself (Berger and Luckmann 1967). We are constantly reproducing and changing that reality. But in so doing only part of the changes are consciously and rationally planned. The meanings are embedded in a structure. We can change the meaning of single objects, but we have great difficulties in forecasting all the consequences of such a change. The rational actor is only deliberately manipulating the top of an iceberg, treating 'the nine-tenths that lies below as an unquestioned and, perhaps, even more interestingly, unquestionable background of matters that are demonstrably relevant to his calculation, but which appear without being noticed' (Garfinkel 1967: 173).

The meaning attached to a label such as 'disability' is interrelated with a structure. That structure cannot be changed solely as a result of good-will on the part of the reforming subject (Oliver 1987). Moreover, the reformist is taking part in the constant interaction that gives meaning to the world. His attempt to change the meaning of labels presupposes that there is a phenomenon that has been 'mis-labelled'. He is not able to define the phenomenon away (of course, it would be possible to deny that there exists any such phenomenon as disability in the first place, but that would be a much more radical view that would call for quite another type of social criticism than the one usually attempted on grounds of labelling theory). So, by arguing against labelling, what he is doing is taking part in a reshaping of the meaning attached to the label, not necessarily getting rid of labelling.

Social criticism based on the labelling approach is thus caught in a paradox. Wanting to avoid creating negative labelling effects, but unable to step out of the world of meanings, they are merely attaching an alternative meaning to the phenomenon (disability).

Aside from the epistemological error, at least two more points are disregarded in this type of application of labelling theories. The first is that labelling is defined as what might be called 'formal' or 'administrative labelling', that is labelling by authorities/professionals. But labelling goes on also in informal ways. In school, peer groups and families – all the time social meaning is reproduced in daily life. The fact that formal labelling by professionals and experts has been the subject of such focus is, of course, because their labelling, given their status and the segregation consequent upon labelling, has had such obvious and severe effects. But removing formal labelling does not mean that labelling – i.e. the ascription of meaning according to a pre-defined label – does not take place. Such labels are (as pointed out by Richardson 1975) used in informal social settings as well.

The criticism of professionalism and segregation often seems to disregard this basic fact. This is one of the reasons why discussions about integration and mainstreaming have been caught in a rather strange debate of whether such policies in and of themselves create spontaneous contacts, foster better attitudes and more positive self-images. To most persons it would seem obvious that physical proximity in itself cannot do that automatically. But somehow proponents of this policy seem to have overlooked that the ascription of meaning is something that goes on in all ordinary social life.

To the extent that informal labelling is acknowledged, it is attributed to prejudice and negative attitudes. But this interpretation tends also to be a voluntaristic one. The analyst places himself outside the world of social meaning, diagnosing misconceptions in others and aiming at changing these misconceptions through strategies of 'attitude change'. Of course, it is necessary to combat and change misconceptions and negative attitudes. But attitudes are not just misbeliefs held by ignorant people. They are, just like labels and social meanings, embedded in a structure in which the analyst also takes part. They can therefore only be fully understood from the 'inside', not by superficial categorisation as 'bad' or 'good' from the 'outside'. That type of 'inner' understanding seems to me to be a characteristic of most successful attempts at changing attitudes (Donaldson 1980, McConkey and McCormack 1983, Sandler and Robinson 1981). (For a further discussion of attitude research and 'prejudice-interpretations', see below.)

The second mistake is to disregard the process nature of the labelling process. For a child identified as disabled at birth, labelling starts at that very moment. It has even been suggested that the first seconds and the way the mother makes or does not make eye-contact with the baby is the starting-point of the ascription of social meaning to the child (Kelley 1988). The process of interaction with others and the development of his self-image starts here. The effects of labelling by experts later in life is superimposed on the self-image created through primary socialisation. Although socially created, the personality by this time is an objective manifestation of earlier experiences. Thus it cannot be changed by any sudden and optimistic new way of treatment. The fact that identity and self-image are socially created does not necessarily mean that they are easily changeable. You don't change identity like you change clothes.

The voluntarism implicit in the application of labelling theory can thus be summarised as a belief in the possibilities of rationally changing social structure (or part of it) by avoiding formal labelling. It disregards the fact that social reality is embedded in a structure, that ascription of social meaning goes on in all social life, and the earlier experiences of a labelled person.

Researchers basically sceptical of the social constructionist approach have put a lot of effort into showing that 'non-labelling' policy does not in and of itself lead to radical changes in the social situation of persons with disabilities. Research on integration and mainstreaming in schools shows that merely physical placement of a disabled child among non-disabled peers does not lead to positive social contacts (MacMillan and Morrison 1984). The self-images of disabled children are not automatically improved by being placed in an integrated setting (Johnson and Johnson 1984), nor are the attitudes of non-disabled peers (Gottlieb *et al.* 1984).

But rejecting the hypothesis that avoiding formal labelling and physically integrating disabled people would lead to social contact, positive attitudes and self-image does not show that the social constructivist approach is wrong. According to that approach social definitions of disability are an integral part of the informal social interactions of everyday life. But it does show that the oversimplified ideological application – with its assumption that disability would not have any impact on the lives of disabled persons in an integrated setting – is wrong.

The rather paradoxical consequence of the 'anti-labelling' critique is that it creates a new social meaning for disability. In spite of the ambition to avoid attaching meaning to the disability, what critics are actually doing is to suggest an alternative meaning: disability is unproblematic, just like any other characteristic and should not be dealt with in any special way.

The bearers of this 'new' meaning of disability are very much new groups of specialists sometimes designated as semi-professions. The criticism of traditional professions thus forms the basis for the creation of new professional ideologies, which in its ambition to avoid labelling is just creating an alternative social meaning to the fact of disability.

New professionalism

The medical profession is perhaps both the most analysed and most criticised profession in this area. It stands out as the ideal type of a strong profession, with its own scientifically based perspectives and ethical rules, power to perform its tasks according to those rules, and legitimated by society (Friedson 1970, Greenwood 1957).

The medical profession also stands out as typical of the kind of profession that is criticised by anti-labelling activists. Medical diagnoses derived from specialised knowledge carry all the hallmarks of what formal labelling is about. It is also undoubtable that medical doctors performed a key function as formal labellers for traditional segregated structures.

Today new services structures are developing. These are integrated, decentralised structures, in which the disabled person will come into contact with many different professions, not specialised in working only with disabled clients.

These professions are sometimes characterised as semi-professions (Berglind and Pettersson 1980). They do not have the same power position and status as traditional professions. Nor do they have any established position in a hierarchical structure. The power they do have is based on the fact that they are working in close contact with the client, thereby deciding the ultimate quality of the services given. They are 'front-line workers' or 'street-level bureaucrats' (Lipsky 1980). I am thinking of groups such as teachers, special teachers, social workers, occupational therapists, vocational counsellors, and so on.

The recent structural changes within the public sector tend, however, to give increased power to these groups. Changes towards decentralisation, as well as the managerial ideologies adopted by the public sector, giving more discretion to front-line workers and steering by goals rather than by rules, strengthen their position. They are given more freedom to allocate resources and to assign priority to different kinds of problems and clients.

Unlike traditional professions (such as medical doctors and psychologists), these groups have no scientifically established body of knowledge of their own on which to build their methods and their own status. But many of them are striving to reach this characteristic of a strong profession. In promoting their professionalism, they are developing their own frame of reference sometimes in the format of scientific theories and sometimes formulated as ethical principles. Whether put forward as theories or ethical guidelines, they are anxious to formulate the 'right' kind of principles and attitudes in dealing with clients (one example is the so-called 'nursing theories', see Lundh *et al.* 1988).

The perspective on disability that these professions tend to adopt, and which is emphasised in their training, is very much the ideology based on the superficial, voluntaristic interpretation of labelling theories. The perspective stresses that by not labelling disabled persons we can limit the handicapping effects of disability. Instead of focusing on the disability, making it the basic characteristic through which all the personality is interpreted, it is looked upon as just one of many personal characteristics. Persons with disabilities should, according to the argument, be treated as if they didn't have any disability.

The 'solution' is, of course, no solution at all. It is rather a way of suggesting a new type of social meaning to a human condition. Just realising that disability is in a sense socially created does not allow us to step out of the social constructivist game. Non-labelling approaches suggest a new meaning: disability is no problem, it should be disregarded and not seen.

The new social meaning is basically telling us not to see the handicap, to make disability invisible. In their well-meaning intentions the new professions want to apply a holistic view, not to focus on disabilities and the weaknesses but rather on the strong side of the personality of the client. Its proponents are so busy de-dramatising the disability that they forget what a dramatic influence such a characteristic can have in a person's life. This leads to a normalising strategy, where the typical 'existential stance' of the disabled is that 'he is superficially different but basically the same as everyone else', denying the experience of problems relating to his disability (Anspach 1979: 769).

Instead of traditional professionalism which led to labelling and segregation, we are thus facing a new professionalism urging denial of the experiences and problems of people with disabilities. Or, as Abberley (1987) has put it,

> As in the cases of women and Black people, oppressive theories of disability systematically distort and stereotype the identities of their putative subjects, restricting their full humanity by constituting them only in their 'problem' aspects. The more fashionable but equally unacceptable liberal reaction to this view is to deny all differences – similar to the assimilationist perspective in race relations, and thus similarly devaluing and denying the authenticity of an impaired person's experience, dissolving real problems in the soup of 'attitude change'.
>
> (Abberley 1987: 16)

This well-meaning denial of the problems of disabled people is developing as a professional ideology in a time when service structures are undergoing changes that in themselves tend to make the needs of disabled persons invisible.

Segregation is abolished and integration, deinstitutionalisation and decentralisation is being implemented. The driving forces behind this development are twofold. First, there is the well-intentioned ideological commitment: not to label and treat separately, but to integrate. Second, the financial crisis of the state that motivates the search for less expensive alternatives.

Obviously, there is a risk that the humanistic ideology is being 'used' for more pragmatic purposes. The well-meaning ideologies of new professions can be used for reductions in quantity and quality of services.

The social meaning inherent in those ideologies – that disability is nothing dramatic and disabled persons should be treated 'as if' they did not have any disability – neatly fits the ambitions of forces that want to reduce public spending. If there is no problem with having a disability, then not only can we get rid of traditional forms of services, but we can avoid all special kinds of support as being potentially labelling and segregative (Söder 1984).

4 IMPLICATIONS FOR RESEARCH

It is my firm belief that in order to understand the social dimension of disability we need much more research on the social meaning of disability, and how it is created, maintained and changed.

There is a problem, however, that studies of social meaning tend to be so moralistic. The development of labelling theories that I have described – from an interpretative scientific tool to an ideology for social criticism; from an insight into basic mechanisms of social life to a voluntaristic theory of action – has also affected the direction of research. Research tends to get caught in disputes about whether different kinds of policies are 'bad' or 'good', 'right' or 'wrong'. Instead of asking questions about the processes that give meaning to disability, research poses normative questions about what the 'right' attitude towards disabled persons should be, whether integration is 'right' or 'wrong', and so on.

This tendency, I think, is due to the voluntaristic mistake. Knowing the mechanisms of labelling does not mean that we can step out of the social world of meaning and proclaim that we know what the right attitude and right form of treatment should be. This attitude presupposes that we know a lot about the basic social processes involved; but, in my opinion, we know very little about the social mechanisms which are at play here. We need to know much more about how social meaning is created, how disabled and non-disabled interact in concrete situations and how social meanings are maintained, reproduced and changed.

Researchers in this area need a more humble attitude towards social reality; not pretending that we know all about how the situation of disabled persons is affected by their environment, but that we need to study it more carefully.

I think there are three areas that stand out in need of more research, and where the omnipotent moralistic attitude can lead to distortions if not balanced with a more genuine scientific stance.

Attitudes towards persons with disabilities

The first area is research on attitudes towards disabled people. Much of this research is built upon an assumption that such attitudes are prejudiced and negative. Underlying this assumption is the idea that there is a 'right', 'positive' and 'good' attitude. Much research effort has been devoted to changes in the presumed 'positive' direction.

But looking more closely at the research underlying this assumption reveals that the conclusion of prejudice is rather dubious. The studies most often referred to are quantitative ones that simply measure the extent to which respondents are able to differentiate between persons with and without disabilities (Richardson 1976, Yuker and Block 1986). They have (as pointed out by Altman 1981) documented that persons usually have a negative evaluation of disabilities, not necessarily of disabled persons. There is, as demonstrated for example by Whiteman and Lukoff (1965), quite a difference between evaluating the characteristic of disability in a negative way and extending that evaluation to persons with disabilities.

There are also studies that reveal positive attitudes towards persons with disabilities. Some studies have shown altruistic responses built on sympathy to disabled persons (Samerotte and Harris 1976, Carver *et al.* 1978). Others, using surveys of the opinion poll type show great willingness of the public to give political priority to reforms in favour of persons with disabilities (Kamieniecki 1985, McConkey and McCormack 1983).

An interpretation that seems to fit far better than the one in terms of prejudice is one of ambivalence. This ambivalence has also been demonstrated in several studies (Langer *et al.* 1976, Lewis 1973, Siller and Chipman 1964). The ambivalence interpretation reconciles the different types of results from other studies. We have a tendency to evaluate negatively the disability as such. On the other hand, we have a tendency towards altruistic behaviour towards disabled persons. These two basic value dimensions create the ambivalence shown to be a typical response in encounters with disabled persons. But how this ambivalence is handled we know very little about, partly because research indicating ambivalence has been focused on initial encounters in experimental situations.

I think we need to know much more about how this ambivalence is handled in concrete daily life situations. Social research needs to dig deeper into this question, instead of over and over again trying to confirm the assumption that the public is prejudiced and negative. To do that I also think that attitudes need to be analysed in other dimensions than positive/negative or prejudiced/non-prejudiced. We need to know what's going on before we can evaluate it in terms of consequences for the disabled person.

The adaptive process

The second area where more research is needed is in the crossing-point between what I initially called the 'adaptive' approach and the 'constructivist' one. As I stated, much of this research has taken a direction limiting the adaptive process to the adaptive behaviour of disabled persons. A lot of energy has been put into finding individual criteria to predict social adaptation. According to several reviewers, these attempts have not been very successful. One of the reasons might be that the question of adaptation has been tackled from a traditional positivistic methodological perspective.

But the process of adaptation is a complex one that involves many variables and, above all, is a process of how the disabled person and those with whom he interacts are engaged in a social constructivist game. To study that process, we need a more qualitative approach that highlights the subjective definitions of situations and the meaning structures in which it takes place (Edgerton 1984, Söder 1987). The complex and variable nature of social processes calls for a more anthropological approach rather than simple counting and predicting by simplistic variables.

The role of 'new' professionals

How disabled persons are treated by professionals and what kind of social meanings are communicated by different service structures and the actions of professionals is the third area where more research is needed. This has been the traditional area for research based on the labelling approach. But much of that research has analysed and condemned the labelling practices of traditional professionals and the existence of segregative environments. Investigators plead for a normative non-labelling approach, to the extent that they do not see the changes that are going on and the new social meanings that they themselves have helped to create.

We need to study the new professions and their role in the changing service structures. How are disabled persons affected by meeting professionals who constantly tell them (explicit or implicit) that their disability is nothing but one characteristic among others? What is the role of this new professionalism in decentralised service structure? How is the de-dramatising ideology maintained by different professional groups, and how does it affect the attitudes of other significant persons to the disabled?

In order to answer questions like this, I think we have to restate the basic questions of the social constructionist approach. The assumptions of that approach can help us in searching for the true implications of changes going on right now. But in order to do that, we need to realise how little we know about the social reality of disabled persons and persons important to them in different ways. Maybe researchers also need to step down from the arena of reformers and change-agents, stop competing in that arena with politicians and professionals and do what we are supposed to be good at: analysing social reality.

REFERENCES

Abberley, P. (1987) 'The concept of oppression and the development of a social theory of disability', *Disability, Handicap and Society* 2 (1), 5–19.

Altman, B. M. (1981) 'Studies of attitudes towards the handicapped: the need for a new direction', *Social Problems* 28 (3), 321–37.

Anspach, R. R. (1979) 'From stigma to identity politics: political activism among physically disabled and former mental patients', *Social Science and Medicine* 13A, 765–73.

Becker, H. S. (1963) *Outsiders*, New York: Free Press.

Berger, P. L. and Luckmann, T. (1967) *The Social Construction of Reality: A Treatise in the Sociology of Knowledge*, New York: Anchor Books, Doubleday.

Berglind, H. and Pettersson, U. (1980) *Omsorg, som yrke eller omsorg om yrket* [*Care as a profession or care about the profession*], Sekretariatet för framtidsstudier, Stockholm.

Carver, C. S., Glass, D. C. and Katz, I. (1978) 'Favourable evaluations of Blacks and the handicapped: positive prejudice, unconscious denial, or social desirability?', *Journal of Applied Social Psychology* 8 (2), 97–106.

Croxen-John, M. (1988) 'Disabled people's terms', in M. Söder (ed.), *Impairment, Disability and Handicaps*, Report 88: 1 Swedish Council for Planning and Coordination of Research, pp. 35–43.

Doll, E. A. (1948) 'The relation of social competence to social adjustment', Reprinted in M. Rosen, G. R. Clark and M. S. Kivitz (eds), *The History of Mental Retardation: Collected Papers*, Baltimore, Md.: University Park Press, vol. 2, 267–75.

Donaldson, J. (1980) 'Changing attitudes toward handicapped persons: a review and analysis of research', *Exceptional Children* 46 (7), 504–14.

Edgerton, R. B. (1967) *The Cloak of Competence: Stigma in the Lives of the Mentally Retarded*, Berkeley, Calif.: University of California Press.

—— (1984) *Lives in Process, Mildly Retarded Adults in a Large City*, Monographs of the American Association on Mental Deficiency no. 6, Washington, DC.

Evans, D. P. (1983) *The Lives of Mentally Retarded People*, Boulder, Colo.: Westview Press.

Finkelstein, V. (1980) *Attitudes and Disabled People*, New York: World Rehabilitation Fund.

Friedson, E. (1970) *Profession of Medicine: A Study in the Sociology of Applied Knowledge*, New York: Dodd, Mead.

Garfinkel, H. (1967) *Studies in Ethnomethodology*, Cambridge: Polity Press.

Goffman, E. (1961) *Asylums: Essays on the Social Situation of Mental Patients and Other Inmates*, New York: Anchor Books.

—— (1963) *Stigma: Notes on the Management of Spoiled Identity*, Englewood Cliffs, NJ: Prentice-Hall.

Gottlieb, J., Corman, L. and Curci, R. (1984) 'Attitudes toward mentally retarded children', in R. L. Jones (ed.), *Attitudes and Attitude Change in Special Education: Theory and Practice*, Reston, Va.: Eric, The Council of Exceptional Children, 143–5.

Greenwood, E. (1957) 'Attributes of a profession', *Social Work*, July.

Johnson, D. W. and Johnson, R. T. (1984) 'Classroom learning structure and attitudes toward handicapped students in mainstream settings: a theoretical model and research evidence', in R. L. Jones (ed.), *Attitudes and Attitude Change in Special Education: Theory and Practice*, Reston, Va.: Eric, The Council of Exceptional Children, 118–42.

Kamieniecki, S. (1985) 'The dimensions underlying public attitudes toward Blacks and disabled people in America', *American Behavioural Scientist* 28 (3), January–February, 367–85.

Kelley, K. (1988) *Disability and Adult Status. Concepts, Policy Issues and Practical Dilemmas*, OECD Educational Monographs no. 4.

Langer, E. J., Fiske, S., Taylor, S. E. and Chanowitz, B. (1976) 'Stigma, staring and discomfort: a Novel-stimulus hypothesis', *Journal of Experimental Social Psychology* 12, 451–63.

Lea, S. J. (1988) 'Mental retardation: social construction or clinical reality', *Disability, Handicap and Society* 3 (1), 63–9.

Lewis, J. F. (1973) 'The community and the retarded: a study in social ambivalence', in R. K. Eyman, E. C. Meyers and G. Tarjan (eds), *Sociobehavioral Studies in Mental Retardation*, Monographs of the American Association on Mental Deficiency no. 1, 164–74.

Lipsky, M. (1980) 'Street-level bureaucracy. Dilemmas of the individual in public services', New York: Russel Sage.

Lundh, U., Söder, M. and Waerness, K. (1988) 'Nursing theories: a critical view', *IMAGE: Journal of Nursing Scholarship* 20 (1), 36–40.

MacMillan, D. L. and Morrison, G. M. (1984) 'Sociometric research in special education', in R.L. Jones (ed.), *Attitudes and Attitude Change in Special Education: Theory and Practice*, Reston, Va.: Eric, The Council of Exceptional Children, 93–117.

McConkey, R. and McCormack, B. (1983) *Breaking Barriers: Educating People about Disability*, Human Horizons series, London: Souvenir Press.

McKnight, J. (1981) 'Professionalized service and disabling help?', in A. Brechin, P. Liddiard and J. Swain (eds), *Handicap in a Social World*, London: Hodder & Stoughton, 24–33.

Mercer, J. R. (1973) *Labelling the Mentally Retarded*, Los Angeles, Calif.: University of California Press.

Oliver, M. (1987) 'Re-defining disability: a challenge to research', *Research Policy and Planning*, Spring, 9–13.

Richardson, S. A. (1975) 'Reaction to mental subnormality', in M. J. Begab and S. A. Richardson (eds), *The Mentally Retarded in Society: A Social Science Perspective*, Baltimore, Md.: University Park Press.

—— (1976) 'Attitudes and behaviour toward the physically handicapped', *Birth Defects: Original Article Series* XII (4), 15–34.

Samerotte, G. C. and Harris, M. B. (1976) 'Some factors influencing helping: the effects of a handicap, responsibility, and requesting help', *Journal of Social Psychology* 98, 39–45.

Sandler, A. and Robinson, R. (1981) 'Public attitudes and community acceptance of mentally retarded persons: a review', *Education and Training of the Mentally Retarded*, April, 97–103.

Scheff, T. J. (1984) *Being Mentally Ill: A Sociological Theory*, 2nd edn, New York: Aldine.

Siller, J. and Chipman, A. (1964) 'Factorial structure and correlates of the attitudes toward disabled persons scale', *Educational and Psychological Measurement* XXIV (4), 831–40.

Söder, M. (1984) 'The mentally retarded: ideologies of care and surplus population', in L. Barton and S. Tomlinson (eds), *Special Education and Social Interests*, London: Croom Helm/Nichols, 15–34.

—— (1987) 'Relative definition of handicap: implications for research', *Uppsala Journal of Medical Sciences*, supplementum 44, 24–9.

Whiteman, M. and Lukoff, I. F. (1965) 'Attitudes toward blindness and other physical handicaps', *Journal of Social Psychology* 66, 135–45.

Yuker, H. E. and Block J. R. (1986) *Research with the Attitudes Towards Disabled Persons Scale (ATDP)*, New York: Center for the Study of Attitudes toward Disabilities, Hofstra University, Hempstead.

Chapter 23

Integration, disability and commitment
A response to Mårten Söder

Tony Booth

Source: Booth, T. A. 'Integration, disability and commitment: a response to Mårten Söder', *European Journal of Special Needs Education* 6 (1), pp. 1–15.

In this chapter Tony Booth attempts to clarify and provide a response to some of the issues raised by Mårten Söder in the previous chapter. He examines ideas about labelling and argues that Mårten Söder misrepresents labelling theory and is mistaken in viewing all proponents of integration as non-labellers who deny the significance of the experience of disability. He analyses the assumptions underlying Söder's chapter and suggests that they involve a false view of science which systematically distorts Söder's judgement and obscures his commitment. The chapter is both a critique and a positive contribution to a discussion of integration, disability and commitment.

1 INTRODUCTION

I am prompted to write this article by my reaction to the issues raised by Mårten Söder in Chapter 22: 'Disability as a social construct: the labelling approach revisited'. In his chapter he discusses the relationship between 'labelling theory' and the theory and practice of 'integration' and 'normalisation'. He argues that the theory has had a considerable influence on 'integration' and 'normalisation' policies and practice but that such policies have misapplied its insights. He sees 'integration' and 'normalisation' as 'non-labelling' policies which involve a denial of the significance of disability and an over-optimism about the way such policies might affect the position of people with disabilities. He calls for this 'omnipotent moralistic attitude' to be tempered with 'a more genuine scientific stance'.

In part my reaction is defensive. As a proponent of integration policies myself, I do not enjoy the portrait which Mårten Söder presents of people like me. I do not agree with the way he characterises integration theory and practice and wish to explain why. But I hope my response is also constructive. I believe it is important to attempt a close analysis of the work of others and to enter into dialogue with them.

Mårten Söder's chapter raises important issues. It is possible for the significance of disability to be misunderstood and for people to have unreasonable expectations about what can be achieved by educational reforms. However, I will argue that he fails to define his terms or to substantiate his particular claims. For example, he assumes that 'integration' and 'normalisation' have simple agreed definitions though their meanings are hotly contested. He does not offer evidence to support either the degree of influence of labelling theory or his identification of 'integrationists' with those who propose 'non-labelling policies'. He makes no reference at all to the experiences of people or to the examples of practice which might support or refute his contentions. It may be that he could put forward impressive evidence in support of his assertions but as his paper stands, in assuming what he is trying to prove his argument becomes circular.

Whilst claiming to examine the underpinnings of 'integration' and 'normalisation', he fails to scrutinise his own assumptions and I will argue that this leads him into contradiction. He appears to make the error which he attributes to the integrationists: he fails to recognise the significance of the experience of disability. He believes that he is conducting a neutral scientific enquiry which is obscured when people are committed to a particular direction of practical change. However, I will argue that it is his commitment to a particular view of social science which provides the ideological basisfor his mistakes and an ambivalence about the relationship between theory and practice. It is a view which leads him to write as if his audience, the readers of a European Journal, share a common experience wherever they live and can pool their research findings. This is a further way in which he fails to acknowledge the significance of difference.

Now, we do not always give such close attention to the writing of others. Often we use their ideas as a prompt for the development of our own. We skim and reflect without going back for a closer reading. This chapter is also a plea that on occasion we take the time to engage in a more detailed analysis and challenge of each other's work.

In framing my response I have not limited myself to criticising Mårten Söder's ideas. I have also interpreted them and tied them down to examples from my own experience and reading. Providing both a critique and a contribution to the debate has raised problems of structure for this chapter which I have puzzled over and tried to resolve. First I review Söder's ideas about the social nature of disability and the contribution of labelling theory to such understanding. In the following section I explore the relationship between labelling theory and the practice of normalisation and integration. I ask who the supporters of the non-labelling ideology might be, define the nature of integration and normalisation policies and ask how far they conform to Söder's caricature of them. I then draw together what I believe to be the source of Söder's mistaken analysis in a particular ideology of science. Finally I argue that all exercises in social science reflect overt or covert commitments and attempt to reveal those contained in Söder's chapter.

2 LABELLING THEORY AND THE SOCIAL NATURE OF DISABILITY

Mårten Söder describes the ways in which disability is to be seen, not as a physical, bodily state but as the way a bodily impairment affects an individual in a particular social context. In examining the social nature of disability Söder includes the epidemiological approach which uncovers the relationship between the occurrence of disability and environmental factors such as pollution or poverty, themselves arising through social priorities. However, Paul Abberley (1987) points out that physical factors such as pollution cause impairment rather than disability though it is apparent that poverty may be involved in raising the likelihood of impairment in babies, in increasing the incidence of childhood accidents, as well as in increasing the disabling effects of any particular impairment.

Söder calls his second 'social' way of viewing disability the 'adaptability approach' in which disability is seen to be relative to the demands of particular settings. Disabilities are reduced, for example, when the physical environment is adapted for, or responsive to the needs of, people with disabilities. They are also affected by psychological and social demands. Here an adaptability approach overlaps with a *social constructionist* view which is concerned with drawing attention to the significance of the personal and cultural understandings of disability for the lives of and interactions between people with and without disabilities. The meanings that are given to disability, the 'social constructions', are as real, constraining and enabling in their effects as bricks and mortar and the physical state of an individual's body.

Söder sees labelling theory as an aspect of the social constructionist approach. When applied to disability labelling theory is concerned with giving an account of the way people come to be defined as having disabilities, the nature of these definitions and the effects these have on the way they are viewed and treated. It is about the formal and informal processes of assessment and categorisation. Söder describes the way a 'label' may be attached to an individual during the diagnosis of his or her difficulties:

> The label might, from the perspective of the labeller, be seen as a neutral, descriptive or scientific diagnosis ... in fact it is something much more. It puts the person in a category that is loaded with social meanings and preconceptions. As a result, diagnosing disability is far more than simply describing some peculiarities in that person's behaviour. It is putting him in a special category, making him a special person. The characteristic of being disabled is ascribed to the whole person and all his other characteristics become interpreted in the light of his disability. The personality freezes, so to speak, in the format of disability.

> (Chapter 22: 248)

While, here, Söder appears to be describing formal classification of people with disabilities by professionals, he later argues that a failure to keep informal categorisation in mind is one of the mistakes made by those that apply the theory.

As a result of categorisation people may be treated uniformly, they may be negatively stereotyped, and a particular view of them may be reinforced, for example, by segregation or institutionalisation. Eventually they may conform to the expectations others have for their development. This carefully structured social process may come to be seen as a natural and inevitable consequence of a particular impairment.

What are labels?

What does Söder include as 'labels'? He tells us that labelling is 'the ascription of meaning according to a pre-defined label' (Chapter 22: 252), though this does not take us very far. The closest we get to a definition and an example occurs halfway through the paper when he refers to 'a label such as "disability"' (p. 251). He uses that term a further sixty-one times in singular or plural. He also writes of 'disabled children' (pp. 246, 253), 'persons with disabilities' (pp. 250, 253, 257), 'disabled people' (pp. 253), 'disabled persons' (pp. 253–8, six times on p. 257), 'the disabled' (pp. 255, 256, 258). From this context of disability it is likely that he would include, as labels, other terms such as 'abnormality' (p. 247), 'mental retardation' (p. 247), 'severe mental retardation' (p. 247), 'mental deficiency' (p. 249), 'deficiency' (p. 247), 'physical and mental deviations' (p. 248), 'handicap' (p. 254). This list can be extended from the references, where in addition to the above terms, 'mental patients' and 'blindness' occur. Should 'inmates' or 'patients' (p. 249) also be included?

Of the above list the terms that seem most questionable are 'patient' which I have offered and 'disability' which is Söder's central case. Both these terms are recognisable as part of ordinary language in a way that others are not. I included 'patient' as a label because I am aware of the way it expresses a power-relationship between people and medical professionals, connotes a passive state, and may be a contested status conferred on, for example, an elderly person who moves between his or her home and a hospital, or on a person with physical disabilities who becomes a resident in a group home. To the extent that children and adults with disabilities see themselves as 'under the doctor' it can come to characterise a persistent, chronic, state of being. I would suggest that whether or not we regard 'patient' as a label depends on whether we wish to draw attention to the process by which it is conferred. Similarly, I would argue, 'disability' becomes a 'label' when it is seen to be conferred as part of a labelling process involving relationships and contests of power.

Formal and informal labels

Söder is clear that labelling is not to be confined to official settings; labelling occurs both when professionals conduct formal assessments, diagnose problems and recommend medical, educational or residential consequences and also when individuals are treated and categorised informally by those around them or by themselves. Presumably he intends words like 'stupid', 'thick' or, in my part of the world 'divvy', as well as 'cripple', 'spas' or 'spastic' to be included here. He would include the experience of Richard Rieser, a London comprehensive school teacher, and co-author and compiler of a pack on *Disability Equality in the Classroom* (Rieser and Mason 1990). He had polio when he was nine months old:

> It has left me with an impairment in my left leg, chest, back and right arm. As I grew the bones and muscle development were affected so my legs and arms are of different sizes with a restriction of motor ability ... My experiences as a teenager in a mainstream secondary modern of continual name calling, bullying and the uncaring attitude from the majority of teachers led me to adopt a super cripple stance and attitude to myself which meant a tendency to overreach my capabilities with the subsequent impact on personality. When 12 years later I returned as a teacher to a boys' comprehensive I still experienced name calling from the kids and other teachers' ignoring my needs.
>
> (Rieser and Mason 1990: 85)

Richard Rieser describes the way he and his parents fought off the categorisation of others: 'the doctors' reactions to my impairment was that I would not be able to walk or use my right arm, but my parents brought me up to use them very effectively' (Rieser and Mason 1990: 85).

Rieser thus helps us to avoid a simplistic view of labelling as a one way uncontested process; a view which has been prevalent enough for labelling theory to be thought to involve a 'crude sociological determinism' in the words of Lemert (1972).

3 LABELLING THEORY, INTEGRATION AND NORMALISATION

Söder writes of the way 'The important insights and postulates of the social constructivist approach have fired actions against segregative services and professional power' (Chapter 22: 249). He believes 'the greatest impact of labelling theory ... is not in research, but in the criticism of traditional services and the formation of a new ideology for services to disabled people' (p. 120). Reading these statements it might seem that he approves of the possibility that theory should be about and have an influence on practice. He writes of a 'social critique' of segregation and professional power. Yet he goes on to describe a 'new ideology' derived from labelling theory in wholly negative terms.

I believe he misrepresents the impact of labelling theory. He underestimates its effect on research whereas there is a large body of research literature describing the 'deviant careers' of categorised groups (see Higgins 1986, Scott 1969).

However, he exaggerates the role of academic ideas in setting agendas for policy-makers. He might equally have rooted challenges to segregation and professional power within a history of political and moral struggles concerning human and democratic rights. Elsewhere he has argued for the dominant influence on policy of the forces of social control. A wish for economic 'efficiency', he suggests, can be the real, hidden, driving force behind humanitarian rhetoric (Söder 1984). However, neither the humanistic nor the monetarist agenda owe a great deal to labelling theory.

In fact, a strong case can be made for the reverse direction of influence: that a concern with the oppression of powerless minorities and their physical and economic segregation is at the root of the development of labelling theory. This commitment has led to criticisms from those who see labelling theory as impure science, entangled with a particular political interest:

> The labelling theorists side with the underdog, and they apparently equate the underdog with those on the margin of society, who because of their societal attributes, are ill-equipped to prevent the imposition of a deviant label. Those on the margin – for example, the poor and the black – are particularly likely to be labelled deviant.
>
> (Gove 1980: 14–15)

Far from being a corruption of the theory, a concern with integration and normalisation are seen to be at its foundation:

> The societal reaction theorists have assumed that when members of society label a person as deviant and/or funnel him or her into the societal mechanism set up to deal with deviant behaviour, these members are manifesting an exclusionary reaction.
>
> (Gove 1980: 21)

In focusing on the mistakes of those who, he claims, have used labelling theory as a basis for policy change Söder misrepresents the debate which has taken place about labelling theory itself.

The 'non-labelling ideology'

According to Söder, then, the principles of labelling theory are corrupted by practitioners to form a 'non-labelling ideology' which appears to involve a simplistic sentiment of the sort: 'labelling or categorisation is wrong and should stop'.

> In using the theory for criticising traditional services and arguing for 'non-labelling' ones, simplifications are made that are contrary to the original theories. These mistakes are important as they lead to an over-optimistic and omnipotent attitude towards what can be accomplished by 'non-labelling' approaches.
>
> (Chapter 22: 250)

Söder uses the word 'ideology' to mean a systematic set of mistaken ideas which guide practice. The principal misconception among the set of beliefs which comprise this 'non-labelling ideology' is said to be 'voluntarism' which involves: 'a belief in the possibilities of rationally changing social structure (or part of it) by avoiding formal labelling' (p. 252). This is in turn founded on a failure to understand that 'social reality is embedded in a structure, that ascription of social meaning goes on in all social life' and it ignores 'the earlier experiences of a labelled person' (p. 253). This is the over-optimism of practitioners who are said to advocate the abolition of a formal set of procedures for diagnosing and categorising disability and to believe that ending formal categorisation by psychologists and doctors would revolutionise the lives of people with disabilities. He goes on to characterise this non-labelling ideology as denying the facts and experience of disability: 'disability is no problem, it should be disregarded and not seen' (p. 254). Söder identifies these proponents of the 'non-labelling' ideology with supporters of integration and normalisation, who believe that 'disability would not have any impact on the lives of disabled persons in an integrated setting' (p. 253).

To support his notion of a 'non-labelling ideology' Söder draws on the view of Paul Abberley that there is a 'fashionable ... liberal reaction' to the negative stereotyping of people with disabilities, which is to 'deny all differences – similar to the assimilationist perspective in race relations, and thus similarly devaluing and denying the authenticity of an impaired person's experience' (Abberley 1987: 16).

Are there supporters of a 'non-labelling ideology'?

The charge that there is a large group of people who deny or obscure the significance of disability by adhering to a set of false beliefs is an important one and requires close attention. I believe that some supporting evidence could be marshalled but unfortunately, from Mårten Söder as from Paul Abberley, apart from a repetition of the charge, we do not get specific examples of it in practice.

According to Söder this view is pushed by a wide range of new professionals, 'teachers, special teachers, social workers, occupational therapists, vocational counsellors and so on', who 'unlike traditional professions (such as medical doctors and psychologists) ... have no scientifically established body of knowledge of their own on which to build their methods and their own status' (Chapter 22: 254). Now, leaving aside the issue of who should be regarded as the 'oldest profession' in this group are we really to believe that all the so-called new-professionals speak with one voice and deny 'the experiences and problems of people with disabilities'? Do they all believe that 'persons with disabilities should ... be treated as if they didn't have any disability'? (Chapter 22: 254).

Since 'disability' is the one example of a label Söder provides, we might find a reluctance to use the word 'disability' as the pre-eminent feature of those purveying a 'non-labelling ideology'. In the United Kingdom the official cultivation of the terms 'special educational needs' and 'learning difficulty' to refer to some pupils who experience difficulties in schools and all pupils who have disabilities, might be the kind of view Söder has in mind (DES 1978, 1981). Has there been a similar terminological imperialism in Sweden? Certainly the changes in the UK mirror changes in the USA where 'individuals with exceptional needs' became accepted currency in some states.

The use of these terms has created considerable confusion. My impression of their use is that in practice they often convey the same meaning as Cyril Burt's (1937) phrase 'the backward child'. There is an ambivalence about whether there is a virtue in avoiding all mention of 'deaf' or 'blind' pupils or pupils with 'cerebral palsy' and at times this makes it difficult to know what writers or speakers have in mind. For example, in a book entitled *Humanities for All*, in a series on Special Needs in Ordinary Schools, the authors reveal their dilemmas with terms:

> We shall avoid the use of labels as far as possible and resist the temptation to enter the debate over definitions in the belief that this is unhelpful and often counter-productive. As teachers, we are not interested in whether a child is classified as having learning difficulties which are described as 'mild', 'moderate' or 'severe'.
>
> (Clarke and Wrigley 1988: 5)

Later on the same page these authors tell us: 'Our chief interest is with those who, under a different classification, used to be called "slow learners".' There was certainly an ambivalence in The Warnock Report (DES 1978) in the UK which appeared to abhor categorisation whilst advocating an expansion of categories for the collection of official statistics.

Do the non-labellers believe in integration?

Whilst The Warnock Report might contain an example for Söder of the adoption of some aspects of a non-labelling ideology it is not at all clear that it was committed to integration in any straightforward way, as I have argued *ad nauseam* elsewhere (see Booth 1981). In fact Söder's claim that 'Over the past decade developments in the field of special education have been in the direction of integration and normalisation' (Chapter 22: 246) is untrue as a blanket statement of change in the United Kingdom (see also Swann 1985). Söder fails to indicate the limits of this or any of the generalisations in his paper. Perhaps if he had been aware of the limited moves towards integration in some countries Söder might have reflected on the way the rhetoric of integration can hide the fact that the *status quo* is being maintained. I would suggest not only that many of those who espouse some aspects of a non-labelling ideology do not support integration but also that many of those who espouse integration in theory show no commitment to it in practice.

Integration and normalisation policies

In trying to understand the range of positions that are involved in policies of integration or normalisation it is as well to examine how the terms are used. Although he never defines them, Söder assumes that the definitions of normalisation and integration are obvious, identical and uncontested. He seems unaware of the attempts by the Scandinavian originators of the concept of normalisation to distance themselves from its Americanisation (Perrin and Nirje 1989) or of Wolfensberger's (1980) attempt to defend his interpretation.

Perrin and Nirje reject the priority given by Wolfensberger to conforming behaviour and emphasises the *acceptance* of 'persons with their handicap' (Perrin and Nirje 1989: 221) who are to be allowed the same opportunities, including opportunities for diversity, as others. They draw attention to Nirje's definition of a normalisation principle as making available 'patterns of life and conditions of everyday living which are as close as possible to the regular circumstances and ways of life of society' (Nirje 1976: 231). These authors would accord to people the right to live in retreat if they chose to do so.

'Normalisation' is rarely used in an educational context in the United Kingdom though there are significant exceptions (see Lynas 1986). 'Integration' is commonly used to describe a variety of non-segregated settings and also as a *process of increasing participation* in the mainstream. Like others, I have linked a notion of integration to both a comprehensive principle and a principle of the equality of value of the participants in schools. Pupils with disabilities and those that experience difficulties are part of the diversity of pupils whose difference is to be recognised and celebrated. Integration can be seen to be about the enchancing of the power of some pupils within education or as a response to the 'needs' of pupils determined by 'assessment' (see Booth 1988). I am not attempting here to explain the complexities and conflicts within policies of integration but to indicate that they are there, are ignored by Mårten Söder and have a bearing on the nature of these policies.

Do the integrationists believe in non-labelling?

I have come across advocates of integration who do conform to some aspects of Söder's caricature; these are Paul Abberley's assimilationists who use the notion of normalisation as involving the attempt to fit all people within a single 'normal' template. I have analysed Wendy Lynas's (1986) book about the integration of deaf and partially deaf pupils (Booth 1988), and she might well correspond to Abberley's 'liberal reaction'. I pointed out how she denied prejudice about the deaf and advocated a system of education which led pupils to attempt to deny the significance of their deafness in the service of a narrow definition of normalisation. She saw this as:

> Making the hearing-impaired as like or as similar as possible to his hearing peers ... attempting to eliminate as far as possible those differences that

distinguish him from 'normals' such as poor speech, lack of comprehension, limited language and consequent low academic attainments.

(Lynas 1986: 63)

She saw the educational salvation of deaf students as being achieved through the acquisition of spoken English which was to be the height of 'their personal aspiration' (Lynas 1986: 251). While I would argue that Wendy Lynas denies the significance of deafness, in part, I am not sure that I would call her approach 'non-labelling'. At some level she may be only too aware of the impact of deafness on pupils. The way it can take deaf pupils out of the control of hearing educators may lie at the heart of her position (Lane 1984). At one point in her book she does recognise that 'a severe and profound hearing loss represents a serious barrier to the educational development and normalization of a deaf pupil' (Lynas 1986: 113). But her oralist convictions prevent her from seeing sign-language as a potentially liberating force.

From my own experience, when I worked as an educational psychologist, I can remember seizing on some of the ideas of 'labelling theory' as lending support to my view of the arbitrary features of the referral and categorisation process that went on in some schools, particularly in relation to pupils who were thought to be difficult in their behaviour. I remember a school where I thought of the deputy head as the member of staff with special responsibility for 'enhancing deviance'. One pupil, of Italian descent, was regarded early in his school career as being at the centre of a 'Mafia' of misdemeanours by pupils and although I could detect no difference in his troublesomeness from many other pupils there was a constant battle by the deputy head to have him removed from the school. I resisted the attempted 'labelling of Luigi', the adding of a value to his behaviour which marked him out for special consideration and disposal.

Earlier in my career, before I had encountered ideas of labelling theory, I had come to criticise the way some of the pupils who passed assessment criteria came to be categorised as 'educationally subnormal' and sent to special schools. There were the biases in the labelling process identified by Jane Mercer (1973), whereby some pupils, those who were Black for example, were more likely than others to complete the full categorisation course. But I felt there was a more fundamental fault in the process which represented the segregation of some pupils as natural and inevitable. There were other ways in which the education system might respond to the diversity of pupils in schools. It is difficult to predict whether Söder would diagnose from these examples a tendency in me to adopt a 'non-labelling ideology', or see them as an appropriate response to segregative processes. Neither of my examples involved pupils with disabilities but both sets of experiences reinforced the development of educational principles which included integration. It is the application of the official categorisation process to children without an identifiable disability which may have provoked the most frequent criticisms. However I, and others, have extended the critique to the way pupils with disabilities are said to be 'in need of special schooling' as if this were a natural consequence of their disability and a natural solution to the difficulties pupils face.

While some advocates of integration may adopt some of the characteristics of Söder's non-labelling theorists, others do not. He has an image of these people as uniformly foolish dupes of a shared ideology. He cites their ignorance that labels are used in informal settings as leading them to especially dubious assertions:

> This is one of the reasons why discussions about integration and main-streaming have been caught in a rather strange debate of whether such policies in and of themselves create spontaneous contacts, foster better attitudes and more positive self-images. To most persons it would seem obvious that physical proximity in itself cannot do that automatically. But somehow proponents of this policy seem to have overlooked that the ascription of meaning is something that goes on in all ordinary social life.
>
> (Chapter 22: 252)

Who are these people who believe that placing two people together will guarantee that they express positive feelings for each other? Do they also tell us that placing men and women together guarantees heterosexual contact or that Black and White people always live in racial harmony?

I suspect there are rather more people who would speak of contact between people as a precondition for a re-evaluation of their relationship. Paul, who has spina bifida, had been used to being the only child with a disability in his school and, in a new mainstream school, he found it hard to accept that children, who had more severe physical disabilities than himself, had a worthwhile contribution to make to the activities and community of his classroom. But Paul has begun to rethink his view of others with disability and his relationship to them. Being with them was a necessary part of this process.

At some points the contradictions produced by the overstatement of Söder's position are glaring. We are told that according to a non-labelling, integrationist, philosophy: 'Instead of focusing on the disability, making it the basic character-istic through which all the personality is interpreted, it is looked upon as just one of many personal characteristics. Persons with disabilities should . . . be treated as if they didn't have any disability' (Chapter 22: 254).

Is Söder suggesting here that a disability *should* be 'the basic characteristic through which all the personality is interpreted'?

But what does Söder believe happens in a non-labelling, integrationist approach? Is he suggesting that a child with cerebral palsy is re-categorised as being without a disability, or is never diagnosed as having cerebral palsy or the fact that he or she has cerebal palsy is ignored in the school setting? If the child has severely restricted mobility, what happens when he or she wants to use the toilet? Is a child with severe visual disabilities denied the use of low vision aids or the option of using Braille? Is it the specialist teaching for a bilingual deaf child that is denied? Now I recognise that some pupils with disabilities and many who experience difficulties in learning fail to get the support they require in mainstream schools. But equally, in my experience as well as in the literature there are many examples of appropriate support.

I have recently completed a study in a mainstream, primary school which includes pupils with physical and visual disabilities. As well as being ordinary members of mainstream classes these pupils have access to a very high level of support.

The support and special equipment is continually evident in the classrooms as is the disability of some of the pupils. Liam has cystic fibrosis and has twice daily physiotherapy but otherwise his disability is not visibly evident though it certainly makes a difference to his life, the way he thinks of himself and the feelings of his family and others about him. Madeleine is in the same classroom. She has athetosis and cannot voluntarily leave her electric wheelchair. She has no speech and communicates using a computer and a 'light-talker' operated by a knee switch. An assistant is present to support her most of the time and she can also call on the support of a specialist teacher of children with physical disabilities who transferred, like Madeleine, from a nearby special school when it closed.

Despite the evident recognition of the implications which the particular disabilities of these children have for their class teacher, for most of the time – as for many others in the school – the category 'child with disability' is submerged:

> It isn't something that's uppermost in my mind unless it affects the way they think ... for instance Manni, when we were doing poetry on darkness, asked me why people are frightened of the dark. He lives in a dark world ... so I was brought up short against his disability, but normally I never think about it.

What would Mårten Söder make of this statement? Is it disability-denying, 'de-dramatising' so that the significance of the disability is lost? Or is it a consequence of getting to know anyone well that characteristics which seem salient on first meeting may later take on a different importance?

Will Swann (1987: 307) has reported a conversation with four classmates of a pupil in a mainstream school, who has severe brain damage as a result of an illness as a baby. It has left her with multiple disabilities:

Swann: Do you think of Sam as someone very different from you?
All: No ... not really.
Chris: Well, first time you think so, but once you get to know her it's OK.
You just think of her as a normal person.
David: She was when she started coming into our class at first.
Chris: It was hard, it was hard to get used to it, but once you got used to it, I liked it myself. I think it gave more ... it would be boring if there wasn't anyone, you know ... like I think it's more adventurous with people like that.

I would argue that these pupils, as well as the schoolworkers and pupils in the earlier school, operate a sophisticated model of disability in which the differences related to the disabilities of some of the pupils are recognised without them becoming 'the frame in which the whole personality of a pupil is frozen'.

Söder is in danger of adopting a position like that of some professionals who may seem to accuse parents of failing to face up to the disability of their child because they regard him or her as an ordinary family member (for example, see Bicknell 1988).

Söder's error is to overstate his case without proffering evidence to support it. After all, changing (rather than abolishing) formal categorisation procedures might have some effect in reducing (rather than removing) negative consequences of labelling for some (rather than all) people with disabilities.

Do those who do believe in integration have a greater tendency than others to indulge in non-labelling fantasies or the underplaying of disability? After all, isn't it a criticism of some of those who urge segregation that they deny the impact of separate development on the lives of people with disabilities? In fact, under some circumstances disability can have little significance. Groce's description of the community where 'everyone ... spoke sign language' is a case in point (Groce 1985). And to think of a characteristic as significant does not mean that it retains its significance at all times for all people with disabilities.

4 THE MISUSE OF SCIENCE

Söder argues that those who advocate integration or normalisation misguidedly adopt 'an omnipotent moralistic attitude'. The cure for this disorder is the adoption of 'a more scientific stance'. This may seem odd coming from someone who provides so little evidence for his assertions. Where evidence *is* offered, for example, to counter the unsubstantiated assertion that 'merely physical place-ment of a disabled child among non-disabled peers' automatically leads to 'positive social contacts' (Chapter 22: 253), he collates evidence from a variety of studies to support or refute contentions about practice in any culture or sub-culture. The view of science which underlies such a belief has led Söder into over-generalisation and contradiction.

In his use of evidence Söder assumes that the experience of children and young people with disabilities is identical everywhere, a view diametrically opposed to a social constructionist view relying as it does on shared meaning to determine the nature of disability. Although, I presume, he is most familiar with development in Sweden, his paper implies he lives in a uniform world where national and cultural boundaries mean little in terms of differences in social structures, institutions or personal experience. The findings of research studies and the pronouncements of academic papers are pooled from a number of countries. For example, drawing on a group of American studies, themselves derived from working with diverse populations, he concludes that:

> We have a tendency to evaluate negatively the disability as such. On the other hand, we have a tendency towards altruistic behaviour towards disabled persons.

(Chapter 22: 257)

But who is the 'we' here? Are these statements meant to be true, equally of Hartlepool Football Supporters Club,[1] members of the British National Front Party[2] and the Swedish Academy of Dance and Drama?

In assuming that research findings have a wider application than the populations from which they are drawn Mårten Söder is not doing anything particularly unusual, though the fact that a practice is common does not confer it with sense. In his terms, it may imply that it has ideological as much as scientific backing. Of course, it can be legitimate to extend the scope of findings from one group to another if the two groups live under similar social and physical constraints. Some of the countries of Europe have displayed a common development. The countries of the 'Capitalist West' display a considerable unity in the development of their social institutions. However, as the events of 1989 have brought home to some of us, national identities can be concealed by a common characterisation of a country as a member of 'the Eastern Bloc'. How far east or west, north or south, is the 'we' of Mårten Söder's assertion meant to extend?

This issue may appear more prominent because his article appears in an international journal. However the temptation to generalise is part of a particular approach to social science research which has a long history. Mårten Söder believes the proponents of integration and normalisation deny or 'de-dramatise' differences related to disability. Yet in the interests of maintaining a particular ideology of science he appears to underplay differences in culture and social structure.

Susan Lea (1988), whom Söder mentions, might share his view of research. She reports on a study with six people categorised as 'mentally retarded'. She tells us that 'they are aware of the stigma associated with being labelled as mentally retarded, and feel this acutely' (Lea 1988: 68). She concludes that:

> It is important for mental and medical health professionals amongst others to relinquish their protective and paternalistic attitude and cede to the mentally retarded person the right to make his or her own decisions.
>
> (Lea 1988: 69)

Susan Lea's study was undertaken in South Africa. Should we assume that studies of 'stigma' and 'paternalism' have the same meaning there as elsewhere?

In fact Söder's commitment to the findings of 'research' wherever it is conducted, leads him to override the accumulated knowledge of experience. For much of the paper he asserts and reasserts the fallacy of a non-labelling anti-segregation position which urges the 'denial of the experiences and problems of people with disabilities' (Chapter 22: 255). Yet on page 256 he is able to assert that research 'reveals that the conclusion of prejudice [towards people with disabilities] is rather dubious'; just as he tells us that 'we have a tendency towards altruistic behaviour towards disabled persons' (Chapter 22: 257).

He places himself in clear opposition to many people with disabilities including Paul Abberley (1987), whom he quotes elsewhere as being in support of his stance. Paul Abberley sees the oppression of people with disabilities as so central to their experience that 'oppression' becomes an essential meaning of 'disability'. It is a failure to recognise this oppression and its social origins, rather than any deficiencies in an integration philosophy, which leads to the dangers of advocating a position towards people with and without disabilities, as towards Black people or women, that 'treating them all the same' is all that is required.

For Söder when there is a conflict between science and sense, science triumphs. When viewed through neutral, scientific spectacles, oppression and prejudice disappear.

The neutrality of labels?

Söder attempts to extend his position of 'scientific neutrality' to the labelling process itself and again engages in contradiction. On the one hand he tells us:

> The label might, from the perspective of the labeller, be seen as a neutral, descriptive or scientific diagnosis ... in fact it is something much more. It puts the person in a category that is loaded with social meanings and preconceptions.
>
> (Chapter 22: 248)

Yet he shrinks from advocating the use or avoidance of particular labels and hence is apparently happy to see current practice, including his own, unchallenged. He asserts that labels just like 'social meanings' and 'attitudes' can 'only be fully understood from the "inside", not by superficial categorisation as "bad" or "good" from the "outside"' (Chapter 22: 252). He is caught here in an existential paradox. For as a language user he has to make choices about his own use of words and he has to take responsibility for these choices. Is he denying that there can be such a thing as disablist language which uses discriminatory terms? This is an issue which has received increasing attention (see Editorial, *Disability, Handicap and Society*, 1987, vol. 2 (1); Deloach and Greer 1981). Richard Rieser tells us 'certain language which is offensive to disabled people or dehumanises or objectifies us should be avoided' (Rieser and Mason 1990: 87).

In a group of people moving into community housing from mental handicap hospitals, Tim Booth and Ken Simmons (1989) report on how people express their view of the terms used to describe them: 'one woman was overheard bitterly complaining to a friend that someone at her day centre had referred to her as mentally handicapped' (Booth and Simmons 1989: 19).

These authors reported a letter from a 'people first group' in which they had argued: 'we want to be treated like ordinary people, "mental" makes people think we are stupid, silly and dumb' (Booth and Simmons 1989: 22).

As Söder points out the meanings which attach to words are not under voluntary control in any straightforward way. Yet the meaning of words may change in part as a result of the struggles of people to define themselves. The meaning of words is constituted through their use. Anyone struggling to change and make reference to a concept at the same time will be aware of the contradictions that can result. Thus Bogdan and Taylor (1982), 'dispute the efficacy and validity of the concept "retarded" for any person, including those with the most profound organic neurological impairments'. They do this in a book subtitled 'the social meaning of mental retardation'.

While contests over meaning may result in new stigma attaching to previously neutral or even positive labels this messiness of language use has to be tolerated if the experience of people with disabilities is to be taken seriously. What of sexist or racist language? When on page 248 paragraph 5 Söder writes as if it is only males that can have deviant careers is this exclusionary language?

Avoiding commitment

It appears that Söder believes it is possible for researchers in education or social science to prepare their neutral reports and leave it for others to draw conclusions for practice.

> Maybe researchers also need to step down from the arena of reformers and change-agents, stop competing in that arena with politicians and professionals and do what we are supposed to be good at: analysing social reality.
>
> (Chapter 22: 258)

He distances himself from the traditions of action research or participatory or empowerment research in which commitments may be openly stated (see Lather 1986). But if researchers are to stop soiling their hands with the dilemmas of practitioners they may well end up by constructing, describing and analysing a social reality which has no relationship with the world of practice and hence nothing to say about it. The divisions between theory and practice, researchers and practitioners cannot be maintained, in reality. He may wish to advise against the engagement of research in practice but how can he disqualify practitioners from doing research? And what happens when we close our research files and go home? Must we avoid any commitment to causes, then?

5 CONCLUSION – WHAT ARE SÖDER'S COMMITMENTS?

Whether we make them explicit or not, our commitments are revealed in what we choose to write about and how we write about it; in the research questions we ask and the methods we choose to answer them. Just as 'labelling theory' itself may be based on a set of values about the unequal power distribution in society, Söder's paper reveals his own.

What do I know of Mårten Söder's commitments from reading his paper? Take the issues of segregation and integration. I believe Mårten Söder would say that he wishes to display no preference. He would like to remain as a neutral observer on the sidelines of social change. Would a neutral observer reading his article conclude that policies towards people with disabilities should have been left as they were with provision confined to segregated settings? His criticisms are primarily directed at the advocates of desegregation. Does this amount to a commitment to a return to a previous *status quo*?

In avoiding questioning of disablist terms he is committed to their use. However, perhaps Söder's greatest commitment is to a particular view of science and sociology. On this view pooled and accumulated wisdom acquired by disinterested researchers using particular methods provides general knowledge and theoretical understanding across barriers of culture and language.

Lemert drew attention to a conflict within the roots of American sociology between sociology in the service of social reform and as 'holding to a scientific purpose in the study of society, reflecting a continuity with the thought of Auguste Comte and Herbert Spencer' (Lemert 1972: 5). In fact these strands cannot be seen as distinct, for Comte advocated the reform of society along scientific principles. He is regarded as the founder of 'positivism', a view that the social world could be described and explained in general, unambiguous terms according to a set of social laws in the same way as the natural sciences (see Bryant 1985) and it seems that Söder is an inheritor of this tradition though I am not sure that he would self-label himself in this way.

It is this view of science which leads him into contradiction for it disables him from using the knowledge of his own experience or of recognising the significance of the experience of people with disabilities. Of course nobody's views are simple. In expressing his view of future research Söder calls for more 'analytical', and I take that to mean qualitative, interpretive studies. He also asks for 'much more research on the social meaning of disability'. If like Paul Abberley he were to discover that oppression is part of the meaning of disability in some cultures and subcultures would he continue to avoid commitment then?

NOTES

1   I know nothing about the reputation of this club for fairness and tolerance or otherwise.
2   The British National Front Party has a well-documented reputation for racism and bigotry more generally.

REFERENCES

Abberley, P. (1987) 'The concept of oppression and the development of a social theory of disability', *Disability, Handicap and Society* 2 (1), 5–19.

Bicknell, J. (1988) 'The psychopathology of handicap', in G. Horobin and D. May (eds), *Living with Mental Handicap: Transition in the Lives of People with Mental Handicaps*, London: Jessica Kingsley.

Bogdan, R. and Taylor, S. (1982) *Inside Out, the Social Meaning of Mental Retardation*, Toronto: University of Toronto Press.

Booth, T. (1981) 'Demystifying integration', in W. Swann (ed.), *The Practice of Special Education*, Oxford: Basil Blackwell.

——— (1988) 'Challenging conceptions of integration', in L. Barton (ed.), *The Politics of Special Educational Needs*, London: Falmer.

Booth, T. A. and Simmons, K. (1989) 'Learning difficulties, whose terms?', *Community Care*, October, 19–22.

Bryant, C. (1985) *Positivism in Social Theory and Research*, London: Macmillan.

Burt, C. (1937) *The Backward Child*, London: University of London Press.

Clarke, J. and Wrigley, K. (1988) *Humanities for All*, London: Cassell.

Deloach, C. and Greer, B. (1981) *Adjustment to Severe Physical Disability*, New York: McGraw-Hill.

Department of Education and Science (DES) (1978) *Report of Committee of Enquiry into Special Educational Needs*, London: HMSO.

—— (1981) *The Education Act*, London: HMSO.

Gove, W. (ed.) (1980) *The Labelling of Deviance: Evaluating a Perspective*, London: Sage.

Groce, N. E. (1985) *Everyone Here Spoke Sign Language*, Cambridge: Harvard University Press.

Higgins, P. (1986) *Outsiders in a Hearing World: A Sociology of Deafness*, London: Sage.

Lane, H. (1984) *When the Mind Hears*, New York: Random House.

Lather, P. (1986) 'Research as praxis', *Harvard Educational Review* 56 (3), 257–77.

Lea, S. J. (1988) 'Mental retardation: social construction or clinical reality?', *Disability, Handicap and Society* 3 (1), 63–72.

Lemert, E.M. (1972) *Human Deviance, Social Problems and Social Control*, New Jersey: Prentice-Hall.

Lynas, W. (1986) *Integrating the Handicapped into Ordinary Schools: A Study of Hearing Impaired Pupils*, London: Croom Helm.

Mercer, J. (1973) *Labelling the Mentally Retarded*, Los Angeles: University of California Press.

Nirje, B. (1976) 'The normalization principle', in R. J. Flynn and A. Shearer (eds), *Changing Patterns in Residential Services for the Mentally Retarded*, Washington: President's Committee on Mental Retardation.

Perrin, B. and Nirje, B. (1989) 'Setting the record straight, a critique of some frequent misconceptions of the normalisation principle', in A. Brechin and J. Walmsley (eds), *Making Connections*, London: Hodder & Stoughton.

Rieser, R. and Mason, M. (1990) *Disability Equality in the Classroom: A Human Rights Issue*, London: Inner London Education Authority.

Scott, R. A. (1969) *The Making of Blind Men*, New York: Russell.

Söder, M. (1984) 'The mentally retarded: ideologies of care and surplus value', in L. Barton (ed.), *The Politics of Special Educational Needs*, London: Falmer.

—— (1989) 'Disability as a social construct: the labelling approach revisited', *European Journal of Special Needs Education* 4 (2), 117–29.

Swann, W. (1985) 'Is the integration of children with special needs happening?', *Oxford Review of Education* 11 (3), 13–18.

—— (1987) 'Being with Sam', in T. Booth and W. Swann (eds), *Including Pupils with Disabilities*, Milton Keynes: Open University Press.

Wolfensberger, W. (1980) 'The definition of normalisation: update, problems, disagreements and misunderstandings', in R. J. Flynn and K. E. Nitsch (eds), *Normalization, Social Integration and Community Services*, Baltimore: University Park Press.

Part 6

Aspects of national policy

Chapter 24

Local management of schools and special education

Tim Lee

In this chapter Tim Lee describes the main features of local management of schools (LMS), brought into the education system with the passing of the 1988 Education Reform Act and its implications for special education. He outlines the constraints LMS places on local education authority spending, the systems LEAs devise to fund individual mainstream and special schools, the effect on local authority support services and on Statementing and integration policies. He argues that LMS changes the ground rules for funding education but does not represent a fall from a golden age.

1 INTRODUCTION

The funding and organisation of special education is in the process of being radically reformed, with all the opportunities and dangers that this implies. The local management of schools (LMS), a key policy of the 1988 Education Reform Act, is the dynamic for much of this change. According to the government, LMS is designed to give those in tune with a school's needs the authority and the money to manage that school. It is also seen as about ensuring that all schools are equitably funded. In both these ways, LMS is meant to be a protection for schools against the impositions of bureaucratic LEAs which are viewed as often wasteful and sometimes misdirected. Others are more cautious or indeed critical of aspects of LMS. They may applaud the handover of school management to heads and governors but may also fear that some of the positive developments in special education in recent years may be jeopardised or even reversed by LMS.

LMS was originally intended to give budgetary control to all secondary schools and all primary schools with over 200 pupils by 1993. Delegation to smaller primaries was allowed but left to the judgement of individual LEAs. Special schools were specifically excluded. Less than one year into LMS the Secretary of State made radical changes to these arrangements. From April 1994 all mainstream schools will be locally managed regardless of size. From the same date also, all special schools will be funded by a formula method – different to the mainstream formula – and they will be able to apply to become locally managed (DES 1990a).

What is LMS?

The overriding aim of LMS is the delegation of powers and resources from LEAs to schools to 'secure the maximum delegation of financial and managerial responsibilities to governing bodies' (DES 1988: para. 10). Schools receive a 'delegated' budget, calculated primarily according to the numbers of pupils on the roll for the head and governors to manage. The distinctive feature of LMS is the degree of control schools hold over how their budget is spent. For example, an LEA may calculate the incidence of non-Statemented pupils with special needs at the school. Using that calculation it allocates a specific amount to the school via the formula for calculating the share of the LEA budget which the school receives. But the governing body cannot be told by the LEA how much to spend on special needs provision. According to DES Circular 7/88, allowing governing bodies such unparalleled freedom to determine and act according to their own local 'needs and priorities' is necessary if schools are to become both more efficiently managed and also more responsive to what the circular calls 'their clients': parents, children, local communities and employers (DES 1988: paras 92 and 9).

A brief guide to LMS is not easy to construct for a number of reasons. The first is that the policy keeps changing. The basic framework of LMS was established by DES Circular 7/88 (DES 1988). However, by various means, particularly through regulations issued in December 1990 (DES 1990a), central government has made significant alterations to policy during its implementation. The second obstacle to offering a guide to LMS is that every LEA's scheme is unique in its precise character and content (Lee 1990a). Within the framework laid down by the DES each LEA's scheme for putting LMS into place is expected to respond to specific local 'needs and circumstances' (DES 1988: para. 11). In what follows it is important to bear in mind both the evolution of the policy and extensive local variations in its implementation.

2 FIXING THE LIMIT ON CENTRALLY CONTROLLED SPENDING

DES Circular 7/88 lays down the new framework for resource allocation that was introduced in April 1990. For the first time limits were imposed on the proportion of their budget LEAs could hold back at the centre to provide services to schools. There were three kinds of spending which LEAs were allowed to hold back, this being collectively known as 'excepted items'. *Mandatory exceptions* were items which LEAs were not allowed by the DES to delegate to schools. *Unlimited discretionary exceptions* were items which LEAs could hand over to schools if they wished, but if they decided to retain control of them there was no preset limit on the proportion of the LEAs spending on primary and secondary schools that these items could absorb. The third group was composed of *limited discretionary items*. These were items over which LEAs could retain control, but total spending on these items was not allowed to exceed 10 per cent of the LEA's total budget for primary and secondary schools. This group of items included most of the money that LEAs spend on centrally run special provision. It covered the following:

- Structural repairs and maintenance.
- Premises and equipment insurance.
- Statemented pupils and special units.
- Educational psychology services.
- Education welfare officers.
- Peripatetic and advisory teachers.
- Pupil support (uniform and maintenance allowances etc.).
- LEA initiatives (e.g. curriculum innovations).
- Teacher supply cover.
- Contingency reserves.

Meeting the 10 per cent limit necessitated reductions in central services in some areas, either through outright cuts or by delegating more money to schools. Services relating to special needs were on the whole unaffected. However, a survey of senior LEA staff in 1990 showed that a further restriction on the amount which could be spent on these items to 7 per cent of the General Schools Budget (GSB), originally planned by the DES for 1993, was likely to necessitate the delegation of at least some of the costs of special needs services, and their reorganisation (Lee 1990b).

A revised system

These arrangements, and the focus of LEA policy-making, were altered in mid-course by the regulations issued by the Secretary of State in December 1990 which made a number of major changes. These changes were designed to force LEAs further into 'shifting resources from administrative overheads and other central services to school budgets' (DES 1990a: para. 5). Ministers had not been satisfied that LEAs were delegating enough of their budgets to schools.

The reformed system envisaged in the regulations, and towards which LEAs now direct their attention, is summarised in Figure 24.1. The system works as follows. First, the LEA separates out the money that it spends on primary and secondary schools from other expenditure headings, such as special schools and nursery schools. The total sum it spends on primary and secondary schools is called the GSB. From this, it then deducts five items which it is not permitted to delegate to schools. These correspond roughly to the mandatory excepted items of the original plans. They are:

- Capital spending (i.e. the cost of new schools and other major building projects).
- Specific government grants (e.g. some funds for in-service training).
- Home to school transport.

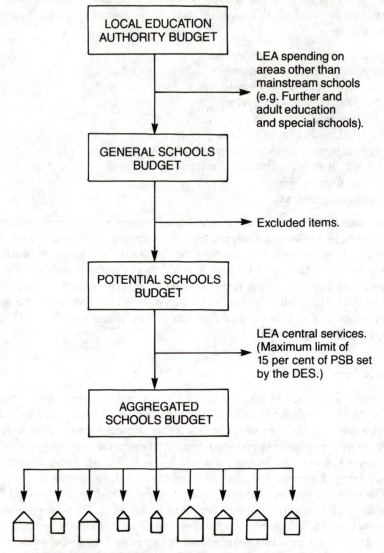

LOCAL EDUCATION
AUTHORITY BUDGET

LEA spending on
areas other than
mainstream schools
(e.g. Further and
adult education
and special schools).

GENERAL SCHOOLS
BUDGET

Excluded items.

POTENTIAL SCHOOLS
BUDGET

LEA central services.
(Maximum limit of
15 per cent of PSB set
by the DES.)

AGGREGATED
SCHOOLS BUDGET

Individual schools' budget shares allocated by
formula. 80 per cent of each school's budget
depends on the number of pupils.

Figure 24.1 LMS resource allocation

- School meals.
- Transitional exceptions (i.e. money used to smooth the process of transition into LMS).

What remains after these items have been deducted is known as the Potential Schools Budget or PSB, so called because it is the money an LEA can potentially delegate to schools. From its Potential Schools Budget the LEA can then deduct the cost of services which will be provided and controlled centrally. The money left after this stage of the process is called the Aggregated Schools Budget or ASB, so called because it is in effect the budgets for all the schools in an LEA aggregated together.

As from 1993, it is the duty of LEAs to delegate at least 85 per cent of their PSB to schools. (Inner London LEAs, created after the abolition of the ILEA, must conform to this limit from 1995 onwards.) Thus only a maximum 15 per cent of the PSB can be held back by the LEA. This is a substantial change from the original rules set out in Circular 7/88. Under that circular, there was a 10 per cent limit on some of the excepted items, and this limit was a percentage of the GSB. Now there is a 15 per cent limit which has to cover all the excepted items – a much larger sum of money – and this is a percentage of the PSB (a smaller amount than the GSB). Thus LEAs can now retain a lower proportion of a smaller total budget than the DES had at first allowed. The effects of forcing LEAs to delegate spending to this extent on services for children with special needs are considered below.

3 FORMULA FUNDING

The money available for each mainstream school from the Aggregated Schools Budget (ASB) is derived by a process known as formula funding. LEAs have to devise a formula for dividing up the ASB according to the needs of schools which are to be assessed according to 'objective and explicitly stated criteria'.

The DES does not prescribe a national formula and there is great scope for variations between schemes for various reasons. The DES does not specify precisely what the needs of different schools arise from. It presumes that needs vary from area to area. But schemes also vary because even where similar needs are recognised by LEAs there is no prescription for how they should be measured. All formulas are therefore LEA-specific, designed with particular, local needs and circumstances in mind, and reflect the idiosyncrasies and varying abilities of different LEA policy-making bodies. However, there are certain basic rules to which they must adhere (DES 1988).

- The calculation of school budgets must be based on objective assessments of need to ensure equity. Formula budgets should not be based on what schools historically received because past methods may have been incorrect.
- The 'central determinant of need' for all schools is defined as the numbers of pupils on the roll although adjustments should be made to take account of

variations in the cost of provision for different age groups. LEAs therefore refer to 'age-weighted pupil numbers'.

- The methods used to assess needs and allocate resources must be 'simple, clear and predictable'. Formulas should therefore not contain too many different elements since this is thought to make the process of budget calculation 'less intelligible without necessarily making it more equitable'.
- The Secretary of State expects all LEAs to recognise the costs of pupils with Statemented and non-Statemented special educational needs and protection for small schools in their formula.
- It is left optional for LEAs to take variations in the incidence of social disadvantage and gifted pupils into account in their formula allocation.

Funding must be primarily based on pupil numbers. This affects the potential of the formula to be genuinely equitable in its impact on schools whose needs may vary significantly in ways unrelated to pupil numbers, and to reflect the needs and circumstances of different areas as LEAs themselves see them. The first formulas applied by LEAs, as implemented in 1990, had to allocate at least 75 per cent of the ASB on the basis of age-weighted pupil numbers. In practice most LEAs devoted higher percentages to pupil-led funding. But the 75 per cent minimum restricted inner city LEAs, where high average levels of special needs tend to mask what are sometimes extreme differences between schools, their pupils and the communities they serve, which are unrelated to pupil numbers. Yet as a result of the changes in late 1990, the potential for LEAs to take account of such differences diminished further. From April 1993 (1995 in inner London), the minimum which must be allocated on the basis of pupil numbers is to be increased to 80 per cent (DES 1990a: para. 10). Counting towards this new total are two additional categories of pupil-led funding. The Secretary of State will 'look sympathetically' on LEAs wishing to provide extra funds via the formula for Statemented pupils in mainstream schools (on top of the relevant age-weighting for that child) and for pupils in nursery classes (DES 1990a: para. 41).

Measuring special needs and disadvantage

Apart from the stricture that they should be 'simple and objective', the DES has given very little guidance about how needs should be measured. This has led to tremendous diversity in the ways in which LEAs measure educational and social needs. The first generation of LMS formulas showed a broad agreement among LEAs that the distribution of resources should reflect the incidence of special needs. However, this consensus is in many ways superficial. LEAs work from different definitions of special educational needs and/or social disadvantage. Even where definitions are similar, the methods chosen to identify and measure needs vary in the relative priority which each gives to special needs. In 1990 the percentage of resources allocated through the formula specifically for special needs varied from none at all in the Isle of Wight to 12 per cent in Rochdale.

Lincolnshire was one of very few authorities which began LMS by funding special units via the formula. Schools were given extra allowances for each pupil attending a unit. The value of the allowance varied to reflect the type of unit and whether it was in the primary or secondary sector. In 1990/1 sums ranged from £680 for a secondary pupil in a moderate learning difficulties unit to nearly £3,400 for a primary pupil at a unit for pupils with sensory impairment, on top of the age-weighted per pupil allocation for these children. It is likely that many other authorities will adopt similar strategies as restrictions on LEA central spending grow. However, children do not fall into neat categories according to the units they attend. It is hard to fund the sort of provision individual pupils require solely via a limited number of lump sum allocations. In the case of children with severe learning difficulties the mismatch can be made good by the pupil's Statement; however the needs of non-Statemented pupils are less easy to protect. As with all formula-provided resources, in theory money allocated specifically to finance special units could be redeployed by heads and governors.

The vast majority of LEAs use their formula to allocate resources for non-Statemented special educational needs, social disadvantage or some combination of the two. In many cases the distinction is blurred. It is not clear whether LEAs view the funding of special educational needs and social disadvantage as similar or different. They might attempt a basic distinction between special educational needs as about individual pupils, and social disadvantage as associated with the general population of a school or the community it serves. There are obvious problems in carrying this distinction too far.

A survey of the LMS schemes implemented in 1990 showed that the numbers of pupils covered by different definitions of special needs varied from 'Statemented pupils' and the much larger 'Warnock 20 per cent' up to what can only be described as ridiculously huge groups such as all those children with 'below average' scores on an attainment test (Lee 1990a). Some LEAs were expressly targeting needy pupils, others needy schools or schools in needy areas (which may or may not be the same thing).

There has been controversy over the methods by which needs have been identified in schools and measured for the purposes of formula funding. Many LEAs rely on the basic information to guide their special needs allocation: the numbers of children who receive free school meals. Clearly, free meal data does not measure directly either learning difficulties or social disadvantage. *Eligibility* for free school meals, rather than receiving free school meals, would in any case be a better measure of the latter. Further it would be foolish to suggest that children never experience learning difficulties so long as they attend schools where a few or no children receive free dinners. For the LEAs concerned the advantages of using free meal data outweigh these doubts as well as the benefits of using other methods. Free meal numbers are easy and cheap to collect. They are routinely updated by LEAs and provide direct comparisons between schools. They also comply with DES demands for 'objective' criteria to be used in allocating money.

The DES sees professional assessments of children's needs as partly subjective, therefore forming an invalid basis for funding schools. The idea that subjectivity can be avoided rests on a misunderstanding of what social indicators such as free meal numbers can do. Even if they did provide a precise ranking of schools according to the incidence of pupils with learning difficulties or social disadvantage, these data cannot reveal other more important information such as the severity of pupils' needs or their duration. These affect the costs to the school if it provides adequate resources to the children in its care. In giving each free meal a cash value to the school, LEA policy-makers have to make judgements which cannot be as 'objective' as Circular 7/88 demands.

Various other social and educational statistics gathered in surveys have also been used to quantify special needs for formula funding. Data from the national census is problematic because it is always out of date, being only updated every ten years. Its use also assumes that the pupils at a school come from a clearly defined catchment area. Under open enrolment this will become less and less true. To get around this problem, some authorities trace each child individually by using the postcode of their home address, however this is a time-consuming exercise. Surveys by local authority planning departments or LEAs themselves can also be tapped for information such as the ethnic composition of a community, housing and employment conditions, and details on family formation.

At their best, these data can identify factors which affect schooling in a particular area, such as homelessness in London where annual pupil turnover reaches 200 per cent in one school (in *Westminster Independent* on Sunday, 12 August 1990), or language diversity and the needs of pupils for whom English is not their first language in Haringey, where a third of pupils have a first language other than English.

Results from verbal reasoning, cognitive ability, reading or mathematics tests are also commonly found as measures of special needs. Since test scores seem to reflect specifically educational matters rather than social circumstances, they do appear to hold a certain merit. The Standard Assessment Task scores seem set to become a popular indicator of special needs as formulas evolve. However, with all these methods it is less than exact to say that a child's low test score denotes that s/he has some form of learning difficulty. Also, there is concern that in allocating resources on the basis of low scores LEAs may actually be rewarding ineffective teachers or inefficient establishments. Educational statistics seem to score highly in terms of 'making sense'; however, any system which institutionalises and attaches financial value to the categorisation of the 'below average' child merits at least careful consideration before adoption since it may have negative consequences in terms of labelling children and schools.

Putting special needs and disadvantage into the formula

The simplest way to represent special needs and disadvantage in the formula for allocating school budgets has been used by those LEAs which have attached a monetary value to each and every pupil on free meals. Even so, the amounts allocated vary from less than £50 to several hundreds. The most complex methods rank schools according to a composite measure of needs employing many different types of data. Gateshead LEA's formula uses the incidence of large families and single-parent families, households without a car, overcrowding and unemployment. Some LEAs do complicated things with simple data. Stockport LEA allocates resources to schools 'in proportion to the number of children on roll and the square of the percentage of children entitled to free school meals averaged over the last three years'.

The majority of LEAs occupy the middle ground. They use a threshold to exclude schools with least needs or a system of bands of entitlement to make the allocation progressive. For example, in the first Devon scheme schools with under 6 per cent of pupils on free meals received no extra money. Those with between 6 and 18 per cent of pupils on free meals received £100 per entitlement, and schools with over 18 per cent of children on free meals received £300 per entitlement. Some LEAs give more money to primary schools. Others target resources according to school size because pupils in very small schools are presumed to benefit from lower pupil–teacher ratios.

Evaluating the effects of formulas

There are a number of questions that can be asked about the way need is represented in an LEA formula. To what extent does the formula distribute resources according to need? A crude assessment might consider whether schools receive roughly the same for special needs via formula funding as they did prior to LMS. But comparisons with the past contravene the philosophy if not the practice of LMS and will anyway become increasingly obsolete.

How closely does the distribution of funds achieved by the formula correlate with professional assessments of where needs lie? Many LEAs have done this to evaluate their formulas. Professional judgements cannot be used explicitly as a basis for allocating resources via the formula, but they may be used profitably to tell policy-makers which indicator best shows up variations in special needs and which specific method of allocating resources matches money most closely with needs.

To what extent are assessments of need understood and supported by teachers, parents and governors? There is aggressive competition for resources between different schools who argue for their extra budget share on the basis of such things as split site and the small size of their schools as well as deprivation of area and special needs. That measures of special needs make sense and command widespread support is essential if the size of the special needs allocation is to be protected against erosion.

LEAs have already found that governors and parents may see little or no link between what they define as special educational needs on the one hand and free school meal numbers on the other. Such doubts will be compounded if changes in social security benefits suddenly change the numbers of children in receipt of free meals and hence schools' special needs allocations. The last major reform to state benefits – the 1986 Social Security Act – took effect in 1988 and had an extremely varied impact on patterns of free meal entitlement in different schools.

What is the effect of the formula on schools' awareness of the needs of pupils? In the original Isle of Wight scheme the LEA estimated that the incidence of non-Statemented special needs was reasonably constant between all schools. Thus, a specific allocation for special needs in the formula was deemed unnecessary. However, there may be important tactical reasons why a specific element in the formula under the heading 'special educational needs' or 'social disadvantage' is important. Receiving £x because of y incidence of special needs, it is argued, may be necessary to make heads and governors aware of their responsibilities and to make them realise that they are increasingly expected to provide for children with special needs out of their 'overall resources', i.e. their delegated budget, rather than supplementary funding from the LEA (DES 1989: para. 12).

4 LMS IN SPECIAL SCHOOLS

The push towards local management in special schools came mainly from LEAs, many of whom took the opportunity of their first published LMS schemes to state their intention to extend delegation to special schools. Trafford and Birmingham LEAs, for example, stated plans to delegate management to their special schools in 1994 and 1995 respectively. These were local initiatives. Special schools were specifically excluded from LMS by Circular 7/88. Responding to such developments, and to their own policy agenda, the government commissioned management consultants Touche Ross to conduct a feasibility study into the local management of special schools (LMSS). The report noted that a somewhat different approach from mainstream LMS was needed but concluded that delegation was not only feasible, but also, 'since its greater flexibility will allow heads and governors scope to deliver better education, it is desirable' (Touche Ross 1990: 4). Amid the enthusiasm the report did warn that LMSS 'will only achieve its full benefits if it is implemented in the context of a well considered and up-to-date LEA policy for special educational provision' (Touche Ross 1990: 6).

The DES gave LEAs just over three years to implement these proposals and allowed for a two-year transitional period to ease the switch from historical to formula-calculated budgets (DES 1990a).

Formula funding for special schools

Six criteria were established to guide the new system of funding for special schools (Touche Ross 1990: 5):

- The formula must be based on a recognition of pupils' individual needs.
- It must avoid categorising pupils in a way which is unacceptable.
- Schools must be allowed to maintain provision during fluctuating rolls.
- The process should be 'open, explicable and not overly laborious in operation'.
- Where similar needs are being met the special school formula should reflect that of the mainstream.
- Schools must not be subject to financial pressures to either recruit or lose pupils.

The precise format of special schools formulas is up to individual LEAs to determine, however four elements must be included.

- The first is an allocation based on the number of places (not pupils) of a specific type at each school. The per place element of funding covers the costs of the staff maintained at the school and the specialist equipment required by children occupying places there.
- The second element allocates an amount per pupil to cover items such as books, general equipment and exam fees.
- There is a premises element similar to mainstream formulas.
- The fourth element is designed to compensate schools for the exceptional needs of some pupils, i.e. needs which cannot be adequately covered by sums allocated via the per place and per pupil elements of the formula.

Additionally, LEAs must ensure that both mainstream and special schools are adequately recompensed if they engage in 'collaborative arrangements'; and second, to include details of their plans to monitor special school provision in their LMSS scheme (DES 1990a: paras 91–2).

Delegation of powers?

Special schools will not automatically receive delegated powers in 1994 when their budgets become determined by formula. The DES states that it will be for LEAs to decide which special schools, either by type or size, should receive delegation and that authorities should set up their own phasing-in arrangements (DES 1990a: para. 86). All special schools will be allowed to request delegated powers from the LEA if they are not included in the authority's plans. If this request is denied, special school governing bodies will have access to the Secretary of State who may make an Order to force the LEA to comply with their wishes.

5 THE FUTURE OF CENTRAL SUPPORT SERVICES

Prior to LMS, many vital forms of support and provision for children with special needs were provided directly by LEAs and paid for from centrally managed budgets. These included the work of educational psychologists, peripatetic and advisory teachers, extra allowances for schools serving socially disadvantaged communities, funding the provision specified in pupil Statements and maintaining special units attached to schools. In the initial period of LMS there was relatively little change from this position, except in the case of allowances for social disadvantage and non-Statemented difficulties in learning which LEAs must now channel through their formula.

Long-term outcomes may be significantly different. As I have indicated, from 1993 LEAs are allowed to retain no more than 15 per cent of their Potential Schools Budget with which to 'discharge their statutory responsibilities and provide other essential LEA-based services', including those for special education (DES 1990a: para. 37). In 1990/1 only one in five authorities already delegated more than 85 per cent of the PSB. The implication that on the whole LEAs would prefer to hold more money back was taken by ministers as evidence of the reactionary nature of education authorities. However, many others have argued that 15 per cent is too low and that there are valid financial and educational reasons why LEAs should be able to hold on to direct control of services. Quite apart from mere tradition, a range of justifications are cited.

- Centralised provision allows LEAs to reap 'economies of scale'.
- Central services enable LEAs to coordinate standards authority-wide, in contrast to the piecemeal and varied provision which individual schools would arrange if funds were delegated.
- Some services are unsuited to delegation because they are 'client-based' – the individual child is the LEA's client and not the school.
- Central control enables resources to be targeted for specific purposes. Funds allocated through the formula:
    (i) cannot be protected from redeployment – there is no guarantee that specific support for pupils will materialise if funds are delegated.
    (ii) are limited in their redistributive impact – the bulk of the formula allocation is determined by pupil numbers, not specific needs that vary between schools.
- All LEAs have a statutory responsibility for the assessment and Statementing of pupils with special educational needs under Section 5(1) of the 1981 Education Act, therefore authorities cannot relinquish control of either the process or the funds to provide that service.
- The ambit of some services such as educational welfare extends beyond the school to the families of school children, and often calls for coordination with health and social services. This would be difficult and costly for schools to administer.
- The demand for certain services is irregular and the costs of provision un-

predictable. Therefore, holding on to a central pool from which to apportion staff and resources is often seen as the only feasible option open to LEAs if the diversity of needs is to be met.

The first, economic argument for central provision over delegation is difficult to evaluate and typically asserted rather than proved. The importance of uniformity of service provision, stressed in the second argument, is recognised by the fact that the DES has issued a circular on staffing for pupils with special educational needs which gives LEAs guidance on desirable staffing levels (see DES 1990b: para. 3). Such uniformity will prove extremely difficult for LEAs to achieve where funding and decision-making are delegated to schools. This does not mean that leaving LEAs as service providers rather than service sellers automatically ensures consistent standards for all pupils in an area. This was manifestly not the case prior to LMS. But central control does permit planning and it does enable a 'whole authority' perspective to develop. Delegation inevitably leads to variation which at best reflects a range of 'whole school' approaches.

The agency model

In many areas, significant changes to central services are needed if the 15 per cent PSB target is to be met. One or a combination of three basic options are open to LEAs:

- cutting services completely;
- reducing the size or scope of the service;
- reorganising individual services so that they are funded partly or primarily by schools buying the skills they need.

LEAs are actively pursuing the third option, developing plans for what is called an 'agency' model for LEA services. Key services such as educational psychology, peripatetic and advisory teachers and special support assistants may eventually be affected. In the agency model all or part of the budget for providing a central service is divided up and allocated to schools. Each school receives extra money instead of free services and is able to buy in help and advice from the LEA or 'alternative suppliers' as and when they are needed (DES 1990a: para. 61). This is intended to enhance the opportunities for schools to arrange provision to suit their specific requirements.

One of the first examples of this model came in 1990 when Cambridgeshire proposed to cut its central spending by half. For the county's educational psychology service the plan was for only a core of central funding to remain to cover statutory work, notably the assessment of pupils, with all other funds delegated to schools, allowing them to decide their own requirements for professional advice and support.

Agency arrangements introduce LEA schools to the conditions under which all opted-out schools operate and open up LEA services to market forces. This makes them attractive to Conservative ministers, one of whom commented: 'If the customer is willing to buy, LEA services will flourish' (Fallon 1990). But given the option to buy-in services, some heads and governors may decide not to. Schools may have different priorities to LEAs. A firm of management consultants commissioned by the government to report on LMS warned that there may be 'a tendency in schools to under-purchase . . . services and seek to make do with staff less qualified, perhaps at the expense of the pupil(s) concerned' (Coopers and Lybrand 1988: 17).

While the agency approach may reduce central spending, it may be less than effective in safeguarding special educational provision. Success or failure will hinge on two factors: the extent to which heads and governors accept the need to spend on special needs and understand the process of buying services from agencies, and whether LEAs are able to allocate resources equitably between schools.

A major change in educational culture is required if heads and governors are to see themselves as buyers of care for pupils. LEAs must make concerted efforts not only to explain the procedure and offer advice on suitable purchases, but also to remind governors of their statutory responsibilities for Statemented and non-Statemented pupils under the 1981 Education Act. In the best scenario, this combination of carrot and stick will lead to local managers being more responsive to their pupils' needs and achieving greater educational value for money. At worst, 'whole authority' approaches to special education will be made inoperable and vital LEA services will fragment if undersubscribed.

Any school's willingness to buy-in LEA services will be partly related to the size of its budget. As part of the agency approach to delegation LEAs must be able to find an equitable method of sharing out central funds among schools via the formula. This is not an easy task. It is extremely difficult to estimate with any degree of certainty the demands a particular school will need to make on central services from year to year or even from month to month. Detailed historical data on how each school used to use each LEA service probably does not exist. Even if it did, it is contrary to the aims of LMS to allocate resources according to past practice. Funds allocated via the formula must be calculated according to objective needs. In practical terms this leaves two options open to LEAs. Both rely on the LEA to hold back at least a safety net of funding to provide for contingencies. The first option is simply to boost the element of the formula linked to pupil numbers. The presumption would be that, all in all, demands for LEA services should broadly relate to pupil numbers. The central reserve would be used to give discretionary top-ups ensuring some form of equity between schools. In the second method resources would be channelled through the special needs element of the formula in an attempt to find a closer match between needs and resources. The stipulation that measures of need be simple may restrict the ability of LEAs to achieve the close match they seek.

6 LOCAL MANAGEMENT, STATEMENTING AND INTEGRATION

LMS rests on the presumption that governors and head teachers are uniquely placed to manage schools 'to maximum effect in accordance with their own needs and priorities, and to make schools more responsive to their clients' (DES 1988: para. 9). This commitment to promoting responsiveness in education augurs well if it is true. Yet LMS also encourages the cut and thrust of the market which, it is argued, leaves pupils with learning difficulties vulnerable because their needs impose extra costs on cash-limited schools trying to compete with each other.

If children with special needs do not bring with them extra income for schools via the formula, it seems that there are incentives for heads and governors to refer more children for Statementing. Statements are a means of generating extra income to provide support for the pupil, leaving more of the school's delegated budget for other spending. The effect of LMS on the Statementing procedure was already visible in 1990. Increases in referrals of over 50 per cent in some cases were witnessed in the year covering the introduction of LMS. Such increases cost LEAs money. They can also cause delays to children receiving support if educational psychologists are unable to keep up with the demand for assessments. Since central budgets are cash limited, the more that is spent on assessment the less remains for supporting pupils. The limit on central budgets may also restrict LEAs in giving support to non-Statemented pupils. More than before, it seems, educational psychologists will be required to act as gate-keepers to the limited resources available for pupils with Statemented needs. They will be expected to tailor their professional recommendations to the provision which the LEA makes available rather than that which the pupil requires.

Under LMS, schools may attempt to limit the intake of pupils who are potentially 'expensive' unless they are specifically and adequately funded by the LEA (Evans and Lunt 1990, DES 1990c). However, as I have argued, even if the formula provides generously for special needs this does not guarantee that children's particular needs will be met because those funds cannot be earmarked by the LEA for specific purposes.

The ultimate impact of LMS on moves towards integration is difficult to predict. Much depends on the policy of individual LEAs and the standard of provision they offer in their special schools, rather than LMS *per se*. However the integration of special school pupils into the mainstream may be restricted by LMS. The process is usually expensive, demanding substantial classroom support, and LEAs will be forced to evaluate whether resources are sufficient or sufficiently protected (if delegated via the formula) to support pupils in the mainstream, or whether those pupils will not be better provided for in the guaranteed special school environment of specially trained staff, low teacher to pupil numbers and enhanced funding.

7 CONCLUSION

There are fears that the Education Reform Act will lead to a degeneration of special provision. However, when critics say that LMS arrangements are likely to 'fail' children with special needs, it is as well to remember that the old system, as familiar as it was inequitable and ineffective, was also guilty of 'failing' those very same children and their communities in many cases. LMS did not cut short a 'golden age' of special education and it does not suddenly eradicate all possibility of providing quality education for all. But it does substantially alter the rules by which the education system is governed, and particularly the relationship between LEAs and schools. LMS will place the onus for determining and arranging provision more and more on the individual school rather than on the education authority. However, under the new system of school management, LEAs still retain their responsibilities for pupils with special educational needs as defined by the 1981 Education Act. The effect of LMS on special education – the development or degeneration of provision, whether children's needs are met or ignored – is a vital litmus test for the whole delegation experiment. The evolution of special education provision will highlight both the value and the limitations of delegated management in schools.

NOTE

The research reported in this paper was supported by the Economic and Social Research Council project *Social Disadvantage and LEA Resource Allocation to Schools* (grant number R000 232504), directed by Tim Lee.

REFERENCES

Coopers and Lybrand (1988) *Local Management of Schools*, London: HMSO.
Department of Education and Science (DES) (1988) *Education Reform Act: Local Management of Schools*, Circular 7/88, London: DES.
—— (1989) *Assessments and Statements of Special Educational Needs: Procedures Within the Education, Health and Social Services*, Circular 22/89, London: DES.
—— (1990a) *Local Management of Schools: Further Guidance Regulations*, London: HMSO.
—— (1990b) *Staffing for Pupils with Special Educational Needs*, Circular 11/90, London: DES.
—— (1990c) *Special Needs Issues*, London: HMSO.
Evans, J. and Lunt, I. (1990) *Local Management of Schools and Special Educational Needs*, London: London Institute of Education.
Fallon, M. (1990) 'Downwardly mobile', *Times Educational Supplement*, 7 December.
Lee, T. (1990a) *Carving Out the Cash: LMS and the New ERA of Education*, Bath: Centre for the Analysis of Social Policy.
—— (1990b) 'A cash flow that is likely to leave little in reserve', *Times Educational Supplement*, 29 June.
Touche Ross (1990) *Extending Local Management to Special Schools*, London: HMSO.

Chapter 25

Special education funding for children with severe disabilities in Alberta

Nancy Marlett and Denise Buchner

In this chapter, Nancy Marlett and Denise Buchner discuss an aspect of the changing funding policies towards special education in the province of Alberta in Canada. They outline how in the late 1970s pressures from parents coincided with the availability of funds to force the inclusion of all children with severe disabilities within local systems of education. The funding formula adopted by Alberta provided an incentive for this inclusion to be within neighbourhood mainstream schools. The mid-1980s witnessed a change in funding prompted by the recession, a decline in service, and a change in attitude except in small authorities who had taken on a culture of 'inclusion'.

1 CANADIAN EDUCATION SYSTEMS

Canada is a country with a population the size of Greater London, spread out the distance from London to Moscow and divided into ten interdependent provinces and two territories. Unlike Britain, the Canadian Federal Government has virtually no control over education. The Canadian system is decentralised at many levels. Each province has full jurisdiction over educational matters, including the processes of taxation, curriculum, teacher training, school leaving standards, etc. But most provinces delegate considerable authority for taxation and resource allocation to local authorities serving a city, county or district, containing from 50,000 to a million people. Provinces retain responsibility for maintaining curriculum standards, and, in some cases, set provincial school leaving exams. The size of local authorities is determined both by population and geographical area. Some remote local authorities might include 15–20 schools with several thousand children whereas metropolitan school authorities oversee the education of several hundred thousand children. Most large cities have both secular and Catholic school authorities.

Some provinces, like Alberta, support private schools with provincial tax dollars. In Alberta there is no impediment to private schools but they represent only a very small percentage of the total. Most reflect religious or ethnic alternatives although a few offer alternative education for children with 'learning disabilities' – mainly reading difficulties.

Educational authority for aboriginal peoples has been a federal responsibility but now tribes and bands are forcing decentralisation for both curriculum decisions and resource management to the local band.

The diversity that results from education decentralised and administered by twelve autonomous authorities with their own systems of delegation can lead to inequality of educational opportunities (of service or qualifications) between provinces or even from city to city. For example, teachers trained in one province often have to requalify in order to teach in another province. Students moving between provinces may find themselves in a different grade upon arrival, and programmes taken for granted for children with special needs in one city may not exist in a neighbouring city.

Nevertheless, local responsibility leads to community involvement and commitment to their education systems. Education in Canada reflects the character of the region and tends to respond to local needs. The diversity in programmes has provided a unique opportunity to innovate and to study educational alternatives. It has created a climate wherein changes can occur in small, relatively simple systems where the risks associated with change that often immobilise large and complex structures are limited.

Education in Alberta

The population of Alberta has doubled since 1950 and is now almost 2.6 million. Alberta has developed a reputation as a province where change occurs quickly, if not at times in haste. This was particularly true in the 1970s, which marked a time of unprecedented, oil-based wealth and prosperity for Alberta. Provincially funded education programmes flourished. During the recession of the 1980s the Alberta government decentralised educational decisions and funding in an effort to make local authorities accept fiscal responsibility. In many ways this experience closely parallels current decentralisation of financial management in Great Britain. The story which follows catalogues the effects on children with severe disabilities of this expansion and contraction of funds.

2 A PERIOD OF EXPANSION

Prior to the 1950s children with a wide range of disabilities in Alberta were sent for their education to provincially funded, residential 'school hospitals' (institutions). Then, during the 1950s, parents began to join together to operate their own local 'special schools' so families would not have to send their children great distances to be educated. These 'special schools' were gradually accepted into local educational authorities when they proved successful and this alleviated the financial burden for parent groups.

In 1969 Albertan funding patterns changed to recognise the inclusion of children with special needs in the public school systems. Special education teacher grants supported peripatetic and part-time and full-time classroom teachers. An Educational Opportunities Fund provided resources for innovative programmes to support children in regular classes – enrichment centres, catch up programmes, resource classes. Funds were also available to provide school psychologists to conduct pupil assessments, and large numbers of children with specific learning disabilities were 'discovered' and classified as eligible for special grants. In some ways this is similar to the effect of the British 1981 Education Act's introduction of Statementing.

It was not long before Alberta school authorities were using these Educational Opportunities Grants to serve children with an increasing range of learning difficulties. In large urban centres, the focus shifted from using specialised resources to support children in regular classes to the provision of highly specialised and segregated special education classes.

Amid this rush in the early 1970s to label children and gather them into special classrooms Mrs Carrier emerged. She had a daughter who was labelled as being best served in a special class in a distant city because of her cerebral palsy. Mrs Carrier became the symbol for parents and parent associations who did not want their children to have to live away from the family to receive education. Mrs Carrier took her concerns to the press and publicised them during the election campaign of 1975.

The Programme Unit Grants

In response to such pressures from parents and supportive professionals the provincial politicians announced the formation of the Programme Unit Grants (PUG) which would provide resources to local education authorities to educate children with 'high needs' within their home communities. While officially these grants were to be available from 1981, they were started earlier in some regions. The grants were based on a unit of six children who were 'legally blind, clinically deaf, dependent handicapped, multiply handicapped or severely behaviourally disordered and whose needs were beyond the services provided by the existing special education programs' (Barnsley 1986). They could be used to hire specialised personnel such as physio, occupational and speech therapists, sign-language interpreters, psychologists and to purchase capital equipment, materials, and cover in-service and administrative costs.

While the grant was intended for a group of up to six children (from £11,900 for two students to £19,800 for six) with £3,700 for each additional child, the major impact of the grant came when it was applied to individuals. In areas where only one child was eligible the school board was entitled to £10,000 per year. The money provided from PUG grants followed individual children regardless of where that child received his education. The net result was a dramatic reversal – from congregating children into special classes to widespread dispersal of funds and integration of severely handicapped children throughout small communities.

Local authorities were responsible for identifying children whose needs were not being met locally and then they could apply to the province for the grants. In most authorities, a wide range of students were identified as eligible. In the large authorities only those with the most severe disabilities were 'outside of existing programs'. These were children who, because of the financial incentive, were welcomed into public education for the first time. The province set standards for the services, e.g. the adult/child ratios, equipment, mandated programme of studies because of their direct involvement in the funding.

The impact of the grants

By 1984 there were 1,044 children receiving education through the PUG system, with a fully developed therapy service (Alberta Education 1984). In just four years, the educational landscape of Alberta schools had changed dramatically. Children once institutionalised had become part of the community schools. Alberta had become, almost accidentally, the Canadian pioneer in provision of publicly supported educational services for all children when it produced the first Canadian curriculum designed to encourage integration of children with profound and multiple disabilities into schools and communities.

Figures from the city of Calgary from 1976–80 – the lead-up time to the official availability of the PUGs – illustrate the extent of change. Calgary is one of the two large cities in Alberta and is highlighted here because of the existence of a unique community census of people with disabilities which allowed year by year tracking of children. Calgary was in a unique position during this time as it was home to the provincially run institution for the profoundly handicapped. As many of the children were wards of the state, Calgary had an inflated proportion of children of school age with profound handicaps on its registers. Whereas in 1976, there were only eleven persons with severe and profound disabilities in educational programmes, by 1980, 287 were involved in a variety of alternatives. Of these 146 children had entered the state-supported school programmes, 85 in programmes run by voluntary associations, and 56 in educational programmes operated by state-run residential institutions for people with profound and multiple disabilities. Some were in regular school with individual support, others in specialised classrooms in regular schools, and some were preparing to enter a specially adapted school for children with profound disabilities.

Alberta was in a strong position to respond to the incentive of the PUGs because in the mid-1970s there had been a shift in funding for families with children with profound and multiple disabilities. In 1976 the province had introduced the Handicapped Children's Services programme which negotiated an individual social contract with families – both natural and foster families. It provided money for relief, medical needs, adaptations and in-home support for children who would otherwise have been institutionalised. Figure 25.1 shows the very rapid change that occurred in just four years in Calgary.

In 1975 only 12 per cent of medically dependent young people were in their own home or community alternative. By 1977, 81 per cent were living with fami-

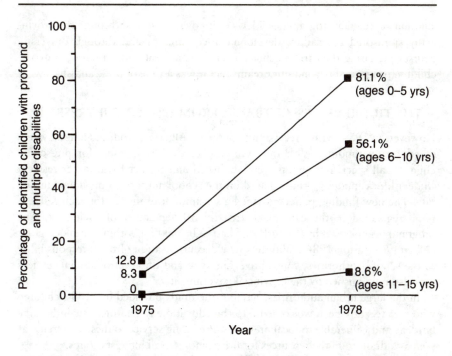

Figure 25.1 Percentage of children with profound and multiple disabilities at home or in families (the remainder live in group homes or institutional settings)

lies, only 19 per cent required institutionalisation. This programme has virtually eliminated institutional placement of children with disabilities and learning difficulties. When the school programmes came into being it seemed to be a natural extension of a community response to support families who were keeping their children at home. It became a circular process – schools felt obliged to serve children living in their neighbourhoods and family support programmes mobilised to help the children in schools. Today there are only twenty-five children in institutions run by social services and most of these are in their 20s.

In the early stages of the PUG the provincial government already had an effective process of curriculum development underway, with staff and local committees devoted to development of special education curricula. The granting process piggy-backed onto these committees and government staff. Those involved became the channel for introducing change, to LEAs, schools and teachers while continuing to work with the development of curricula that could support the changes that were underway.

Serendipity struck with the PUG grants – not only was there a centralised response but also the granting system accidentally involved an incentive that encouraged innovation. Because of the flexibility of the grants, LEAs were motivated to identify children in need and there was a financial benefit for individual solutions in regular programmes. News of innovation spread through the provincially sponsored curriculum development committees and through university courses preparing the early teachers. There was a great enthusiasm because the children progressed beyond our dreams and it was a time of pride and sharing.

3 THE TIDE REVERSES: CUTBACKS FROM 1984 TO THE PRESENT

However, in 1984, with a recession under way, Alberta introduced a new system of education funding. With the exception of the PUG grants for pre-school children, all specialised grants were abolished and replaced with a per resident student block funding formula based on the school authority's previous funding rate. The new funding policy provided a set amount of money for each resident pupil registered in the catchment area on 30 September of each year. Any programmes operated by the authority had to be paid for within that block grant (Alberta Education 1984). With this new decentralisation of fiscal responsibility to the school authorities, control over the type and duration of special services was also relinquished by the provincial government.

In the large urban authorities, without the funds provided by PUGs, children who had recently been welcomed into the education system once again became burdens and vulnerable to local pressures. Providing service to these children was seen as a drain from the resources for other, more vocal interest groups.

Parents who were organised and militant were more successful in securing funds for their children. The difference is dramatically apparent when we look at two identified groups – parents with children who had specific learning disabilities and parents whose children had severe disabilities ('PUG' parents). A large number of children were identified as 'learning disabled' (specific problems such as reading delays), and their families were well organised. These families and their associations were able to lobby the local school authorities for increased funding. Within a four-year period their efforts resulted in an increase from approximately 35–40 to 141 classes for learning disabled children in one school authority.

Parents with children with severe disabilities lost ground. As their children had just recently gained entry into the school system their parents were less familiar with the politics and organisation of the school system, they had not formed lobby groups and their children's needs absorbed most of their spare energy. In the same four years class sizes for children with severe disabilities jumped from 6–8 children per class to 18 children per class, teachers were replaced by assistants, and therapists were asked to fill in as teachers.

As school authorities struggled to manage capped funds, escalating demands and inflation, children with severe disabilities continued to be a target for cuts. When it was no longer possible to water down services for children with severe disabilities, pressure was exerted on the Provincial Minister of Education to have children with 'high medical needs' and 'severe cognitive disabilities' declared uneducable, and therefore in need of services outside of the school mandate.

These proposed revisions in the Alberta School Act of 1988 were greeted with international outrage and concerted political pressure by parents' groups, disabled people and professionals. In one of the rare occasions in Alberta history, the government was forced to withdraw a section from the proposed legislation, but the concerns still remain.

In the smaller or more dispersed authorities, the PUGs had seeded a school-based response and therefore school-based responsibility for local children. The individual PUGs created a culture for handling special needs within the school and when the province decentralised, the response in the more remote areas was to establish a *de facto* school-based authority and thus these schools allocated priorities as if there had been no change.

In 1989 Alberta Education interviewed twenty school-based special education administrators and seven education consultants for their opinions on what they perceived to be the major issues in special education in Alberta (Premier's Council 1990). In every case, the issue of funding programmes for children with severe handicaps was identified. It was felt that the funding available to school districts was insufficient to provide for comprehensive programmes and services and most of them wanted a return to PUGs.

Amid this uncertainty, the Programme Unit Grants for pre-school children continue to exist. During the pre-school years, specialised services are available to promote integration and expectations and hopes. These expectations fall quickly when the child enters grade one where services for high needs children are much more limited due to the block funding structure (Barnsley 1986).

4 CONCLUDING REMARKS

The story of funding policies for special education had a number of distinct phases. At the end of the 1970s, because of the ready availability of funds, a number of groups had a coincidence of interests which enabled everyone to be 'winners'. Children won because they gained access to education and responded by learning and growing. Parents gained strength in the acceptance of their children by the educational authorities and their communities. Teachers and schools discovered that they could create learning environments for all children, and, finally, politicians won because they became inadvertent pioneers for the rest of Canada.

The financial solution provided an incentive for local education authorities to find locally based solutions. However the mid-1980s saw a reduction in funding levels with the onus placed on individual authorities to dispense a fixed budget according to need. The education of children with severe disabilities and difficulties in learning was no longer protected and this group sometimes lost out to the stronger voice and organisation of the specific learning disability lobby. Innovation has remained most stable where the funding has been most decentralised. Many communities and individual schools have taken over responsibility for their children with disabilities.

No funding system is immune to change and each carries its particular pressures. Voucher systems have been used in the USA to decentralise funding to the level of the consumer. They have led, also, to the separation and stratification of students according to parental commitment and belief. Parents committed to integration apply pressure for their children's inclusion in neighbourhood schools, parents in favour of segregation apply pressure to develop or maintain separate facilities. Parents who weren't involved, or were not informed, might leave their children in inappropriate situations. Devolution of decision-making to the level of the child's family relies heavily on the family or designate to advocate appropriately on behalf of the child.

The implications of Albertan experience accord with current rhetoric elsewhere in North America where 'mainstreaming' and 'integration' have been replaced by the concepts of 'neighbourhood schools' and 'full service schools'. Individualised funding builds on the strength and creativity of the small community school. It allows the school and community to take pride in handling problems within the school instead of removing problem children to special programmes in designated schools.

As we have seen in Alberta, when funding changes those children who have been welcomed and properly included find that they have advocates within their schools. While it remains doubtful if most schools will persist with inclusive policies without the security of resources for 'exceptional' children, some will find a way and it is from these schools that we will learn.

These have increased, dramatically, the responsiveness of the education system to individuals.

REFERENCES

Alberta Education (1984) *Annual Report (1984)*, Edmonton: Queen's Printer.
Barnsley, R. H. (1986) 'Special education finance: then and now, teaching atypical students in Alberta', *Special Education in Canada* 15 (1), 15–22.
Premier's Council (1990) *Action Plan*, Edmonton: Queen's Printer.

Chapter 26

A curriculum for all
A hard task for some

Margaret Peter

Margaret Peter is the editor of the British Journal of Special Education *and early in 1989 she was asked to coordinate the production of the National Curriculum Council's guidance for schools on special educational needs in the National Curriculum as consultant editor. This chapter tells the story of putting together a document which had to blend and fuse the views of a large disparate group of people and steer a path between differing voices in the National Curriculum Council (NCC), Department of Education and Science (DES) and the School Examinations and Assessment Council (SEAC). The report* A Curriculum for All *(NCC 1989a) to be circulated to every school in the country was put together in just a few breathless months.*

1 JOINING THE TEAM

Late in February 1989 a call came from the National Curriculum Council. The Council's newly appointed task group would be producing guidance on special educational needs in the National Curriculum. It might look for help in drafting and editing it. Would I be available if the need arose?

The call, brief and exploratory, came only a few days after the task group had first met. Chaired by Dr Ronald Davie, a member of the National Curriculum Council (NCC), it consisted of fifteen members and its creation had come none too soon. Kenneth Baker, then Secretary of State for Education, had turned down requests for special educational needs to be specifically represented on the subject working groups who were recommending programmes of study and attainment targets for core subjects in the National Curriculum. The groups' reports, so far, had contained few paragraphs on pupils with learning difficulties and disabilities and the National Curriculum Council's non-statutory guidance on the three core subjects being prepared at the time did not offer detailed advice on special educational needs. The Education Reform Act, passed the previous July, had given *all* children the right to a 'balanced and broadly based' curriculum including the National Curriculum. So much for entitlement, what about the means?

Every day the National Curriculum Council had been receiving telephone calls and letters from teachers asking 'What should we do about special needs?'

Anxiety was running high. The Council had decided that its fifth circular, and the second in its series of *Curriculum Guidance*, should concentrate on pupils with special educational needs. Consequently, the task group had been formed and had met for the first time on 24 February. Its members, who included several teachers and many others with past teaching experience, had already begun work on the circular *Implementing the National Curriculum: Participation by Pupils with Special Educational Needs* (NCC 1989b), subsequently published in May 1989, and had started to plan its curriculum guidance for schools.

When the circular was in its final draft two months later, and the first papers were being put together on curriculum guidance, Helen Carter, then NCC's professional officer for special educational needs, rang again. Would I join the group as editorial consultant to work on the first draft. It would be needed by the end of May.

The challenge was irresistible. I was committed to the principle of access to the National Curriculum for pupils with special educational needs – despite misgivings about the potential use of a national and narrowly conceived curriculum to stimulate divisiveness among schools, which I had worked with others to oppose when the Education Reform Bill was going through Parliament. The National Curriculum was now law; it was unavoidable. It must be made to work for children and for teachers, not to shackle them. Whatever could be done to reassure teachers that pupils with special needs would not be stranded on the sidelines of change was worth doing. The size of the challenge was not yet clear.

2 PUTTING THE REPORT TOGETHER

The first drafts arrived from the National Curriculum Council by mid-May. An array of papers from individuals and from clusters of task group members discussed general principles like entitlement and access, and dealt with issues, practical advice and examples in the core subjects of English, Mathematics and Science. It was a promising start but it had as yet no clear conceptual framework nor the depth and breadth to respond to teachers' needs. By the time the remaining drafts arrived there were only eleven days left to write, rewrite, edit and circulate a first full draft of the booklet planned at that stage to run to about 10,000 words.

Where should work begin? Clearly the array of papers needed a title and a structure. For a while a title was elusive. Suggestions tended to founder on length and impact ('special educational needs' is enough to choke the digestion of almost any title). 'A Curriculum For All' came to me suddenly. It was a title intended to be taken at several levels: a statement of equal rights; a declaration of intent; a challenge to be critically examined, with an unseen question mark hovering on its right. Reference to 'needs' could go into the subtitle instead.

Deciding a structure was harder. While the overall structure was quickly rearranged into five chapters, through general principles (Chapter 1) and school policies and practices (Chapter 2) to chapters on each of the core subjects in turn, a common conceptual framework for Chapters 2 to 5 was attempted several times and later cast out.

The size of the challenge now hit me. There would be only 10,000 words (later extended to 12,000) to cover a much wider area than in other NCC publications. *A Framework for the Primary Curriculum* (NCC 1989c) and the non-statutory guidance in the core subjects had narrower remits and many of those contributing had been given more time together to discuss and plan the contents. Our project, *Curriculum Guidance 2*, would need to cover the whole ability range, all ages from 5 to 16, all three core subjects and two school systems, special and mainstream. It seemed, as everyone kept saying, an 'impossible task'. How could adequate guidance be compressed into thirty printed pages of A4? On the other hand, schools were still grappling with the small print of programmes of study and statements of attainment. Advice would be premature and hard to formulate; the statutory orders for the first core subjects, Mathematics and Science, had only recently been laid before Parliament. It was still three months before the National Curriculum would formally begin in ordinary schools and fifteen months before special schools would be required to introduce it. Could good examples of National Curriculum practice yet be found? Wasn't it a year too soon?

The question of to whom the advice should be directed also arose. Was it intended for newly qualified teachers in primary and secondary schools, working with pupils who had mild learning difficulties, or for specialist teachers with twenty years' experience and qualifications in teaching the hearing or visually impaired? If it was to be for both – and all teachers in between – it would be necessary to decide where the main emphasis should lie.

Questions like these had already been raised by the task group at its earlier meetings. They came up again when I joined members for the first time at their meeting on 24 May. Opinions wavered on the framework of the guidance to be offered but on the main aims members were unanimous: guidance must promote access for all pupils, it must be based on existing good practice and, above all, its message must be positive. Members also agreed that the guidance should be addressed primarily to teachers of the estimated 20 per cent of pupils with special educational needs in both special schools and the mainstream, but should also be relevant to all teachers and of interest to school governors, parents and other groups.

At the same meeting new frameworks for individual chapters were discussed and additional materials sought from the task group's science, mathematics and English specialists who were working with the NCC's professional officers for the subjects concerned. More than anything, examples were needed of how the programmes of study and statements of attainment could be made accessible to pupils with learning difficulties and disabilities and, predictably, they were proving hard to find. If pockets of advanced practice had developed three or four months in advance of the statutory introduction of the National Curriculum, it would have taken longer than the task group's tightly drawn timetable to trace them. There were only seven days to go before the deadline for the drafts of all five chapters at the end of May.

Over the next week as drafts of the core subjects and general sections of the guidance were discussed with individuals in the task group, and edited, drafted or redrafted, earlier questions began to recur more often to me.

What did 'access to the National Curriculum' mean? Did it mean that all pupils could take part in all or most programmes of study and meet attainment targets at Level 1 or above, or should access also be defined as participation by some children in activities leading into programmes and statements of attainment at Level 1?

Access for whom? Should it extend to children with profound and multiple learning difficulties for whom learning how to chew and swallow independently would take priority over questions of food and digestion in Science, Attainment Target 3?

Access to what? This was a curriculum which, when the Education Reform Bill was being debated at Westminster, critics had condemned as a strait-jacket for pupils with special educational needs. Now that this curriculum had become compulsory they were only too eager to ensure access, however awkwardly it might fit. At the same time the curricular content was still unclear. Programmes of study and attainment targets for only the three core subjects had been proposed; there were still another seven to go and the shape of the Standard Assessment Tasks (SATs) was not yet known.

Access by what means? Was the National Curriculum to be set in motion by teachers not yet trained in teaching it, by dwindling numbers of support and advisory staff, by schools with diminished funding under schemes of local management and without the means to buy enough books or even sand trays?

Most of all, why? Was it because of a commitment to equal rights, to a National Curriculum which, through its time-consuming demands, could lead to *unequal* opportunities to experience the wider curriculum of Section 1(2) of the Education Reform Act, and thereby to less adequate preparation for adult life? Could we end up by doing pupils with special educational needs a disservice by discouraging 'exceptions' to the National Curriculum? It might be wiser to look for imaginative alternatives to unrealistic attainment targets, alternatives which might give greater flexibility and a better fit.

Given all these questions, it seemed frivolous to preach 'maximum participation' when the fragile foundations for it were in danger of being undermined by LMS, open enrolment and other provisions of the new Act – it was like dancing on eggshells. 'But how do you know,' responded one member of the task group, 'that the eggshells are not broken already?'

Nor did the questions end here. Access, yes, but what about *progress* within the National Curriculum? The issue of progress was crucial for a much larger number of children than those with severe to profound learning difficulties or with physical or sensory disabilities. The 'framework for progression' offered by the National Curriculum was one thing, progress was another. A structured sequence of learning was essential but it was not sufficient to guarantee progress.

Other necessary conditions for pupils' progress seemed in jeopardy under the Education Reform Act. There would be, for instance, unprecedented pressures on teachers to teach to a wide range of levels – perhaps five or six within the National Curriculum – and to get caught up in inter-school rivalry for pupil numbers and national assessment results. Local management of schools could encourage school governors to reorder spending priorities. Under such conditions the progress of pupils with mild to moderate learning difficulties, or with emotional and behavioural difficulties, might be endangered.

This issue of ensuring progress as well as access is touched on briefly in Chapter 1 (para. 6) of our report which refers to 'achieving maximum access and subsequent progress'. A year later it is more widely addressed as local education authorities and schools re-examine the challenge of responding to pupil diversity within a new curricular context, and as conferences, books and materials on 'differentiation' begin to multiply. Given the National Curriculum Council's deadline for publication and the task group's resolve that the curriculum guidance must be positive and practical, questions like this were not explored.

The deadline for a first draft of the complete guidance was now only two days away. Helmeted messengers arrived more frequently from the NCC's London office (since closed) in Notting Hill Gate. When the Council had first suggested 'biking up' the scripts to Hampstead I had thought it quaint, but environmentally sound. Expecting a junior clerk panting up the foothills on a pedal cycle I had been caught unawares by the roar of the 500 cc engine, the screech of brakes and the flying dust as the first messenger hurtled towards the front door.

When 31 May came, most – though not all – chapters were ready to be circulated to the task group to consider at its meeting on 7 June before going to members of the National Curriculum Council for their approval a few days later. The chapters were still far from offering adequate guidance. Chapter 2 was lifeless and, in parts, simplistic. The subject chapters needed more coherence and less overlap. They continued to be short on examples of how the core subjects could be opened up to pupils with learning difficulties or disabilities, which was not surprising. Task group members were having to project themselves, at speed, into a curricular context in which neither they nor anyone else had yet worked.

Nine more days, I calculated, would give time to trawl teachers' centres, curriculum working parties and subject specialists for examples of translating attainment targets and programmes of study into classroom practice. There might have been a worthwhile catch. But it became clear, at the task group meeting on 7 June, that this would not be possible. The National Curriculum Council wanted guidance to reach schools from mid-July, before the end of the summer term. There were only six weeks to go.

The NCC's three professional officers for English, Mathematics and Science, who had already been working with other groups to produce non-statutory guidance in the core subjects, were asked to redraft Chapters 3 to 5, working closely with subject specialists on the task group. I returned home after a seven-hour meeting to work on yet another draft of Chapter 2, with a new deadline twelve days away. It still lacked a context-specific focus and the 'punch' that task group members felt it needed, and platitudes in both Chapters 1 and 2 pleased no one. Final drafts were now due to go to the National Curriculum Council on 19 June for its approval.

Then came a temporary reprieve. After discussions between the National Curriculum Council and the Department of Education and Science (DES), the date for publication was changed to the autumn term. This gave everyone a chance to look at chapters again. During a meeting with the chairman and three other members of the task group on 27 July a new framework was sketched out for Chapter 2 which included the controversial issues of national assessments and pupils 'excepted' from the National Curriculum. The chapter was torn apart and rewritten for the fifth time.

The additions to Chapter 2 on exceptions to the National Curriculum and on assessment arrangements replaced earlier references by the task group and came direct from the DES and the School Examinations and Assessment Council (SEAC). Both issues were controversial, particularly the question of modifications and disapplications of the National Curriculum under Sections 18 and 19 of the Education Reform Act. The task group's interpretation of the legal provisions had been wider and the group decided to distance itself in the report from the DES advice by placing the latter in italics. It also added a sentence to discourage the possibility that pupils working on National Curriculum levels below those of their peers might be taught with younger children as an option that 'will not often be practical or educationally desirable'. *The Times Educational Supplement*, reporting the publication of *A Curriculum for All* on 13 October, speculated about a 'rift' between NCC and DES, in line with earlier allusions to the predictable tensions between two bodies where one, while set up as an independent statutory body, is funded and has its members appointed by the other.

With the reprieve now over, circulating revised drafts to task group members was more difficult than before. Lists of holiday dates (but fewer holiday addresses) were sent round and far into August the work went on: adding to and subtracting from sentences and paragraphs as telephone calls, letters and scribbled notes in the margins of the final drafts rushed in. With fifteen members on the task group, about as many members of the NCC, senior staff in NCC, SEAC and DES, and a wide range of individuals and groups associated with the National Curriculum Council, I estimated that between 60 and 100 people saw one or more of the drafts.

Time-lines had been revised again. The final re-editing of *Curriculum Guidance 2* was completed on 21 August. Two days later I passed the page proofs for the next issue of the *British Journal of Special Education*, on which I had continued to work throughout the period, checked the publishing timetable for *Special Educational Needs: Towards a Whole-school Approach*, a book based on articles from the journal, and caught the next plane to Budapest. I set off for ten days' holiday in Hungary, having lost four pounds in weight and the larger part of a long, hot summer.

When I returned to London, publication of the draft, with minor changes, had been approved by NCC and final work on preparing copy for the printers began. Later in September there were proofs to check and details of typographical design to be decided but the work was almost over. Four weeks later, on 5 October, at a press conference in York, *A Curriculum for All* was launched. Soon afterwards the first of 150,000 copies came off the presses and in November began to find their way into schools.

3 REFLECTIONS

Looking back on it all a year later, I recall the feverish pace, the pain and the exhaustion of those five months attempting to do the impossible. (It was both consoling and daunting to be constantly reminded of the impossibility of what one was trying to do.) But mostly I remember the excitement of the unexpected twists and turns of progress towards publication, the pleasure of working with a group of people both in the task group and the National Curriculum Council who gave time so generously to turn visions of *Curriculum Guidance 2* into reality, and the lessons I learnt from colleagues who widened my understanding and encouraged me to re-examine my own writing for negative overtones, often unintended.

Terms like 'a history of academic failure' were struck out of references to pupils. The abbreviation for 'special educational needs' was deliberately printed in lower case as 's.e.n.' so that visually, and unlike the capitalised form, it would not dominate 'pupils' or any other noun it qualified, putting conspicuous emphasis on the needs rather than the child. Even the choice of a preposition could be critical. Changing 'movement *from* special schools to ordinary schools' to 'movement *between*' would, some members suggested, more accurately reflect practice and avoid causing concern to a number of teachers in special schools.

Coming from a training in journalism, I was accustomed to expressing critical views without having them scrutinised by at least sixty people in advance. I found consensus drafting hard to take, although the insights gained into Civil Service styles of working and the internal tensions within the DES, were compensating. One of President Bush's speech writers, Peggy Noonan, reported in a BBC broadcast that her drafts for major presidential speeches were circulated for comment to fifty officials in the White House and elsewhere. The process, she said, was not unlike feeding a bunch of fresh vegetables into a meat grinder and watching them come out at the other end as a tasteless purée. Although the flavour of the task group's message was preserved, colour and texture disappeared. Metaphors and similes were prised out like blemishes from carrots and very few stayed ('bedrock', in the opening paragraph of Chapter 2, is one of the few to survive).

The extent of the scrutiny was self-inflicted however. The aim of 'maximum participation' stressed in Circular Number 5 (NCC 1989b) and in our report was carried through the drafting of the advice as well. It would have been quicker, less strenuous and, at times, less demoralising to have produced a literary *fait accompli* with less full and frequent consultation, but it was not the way I saw the role of editorial consultant, nor did my professional experience fit me for it. It was important that the sense of ownership should be widely shared and, to a greater extent than might have been expected, I think this probably occurred. If at times consensus proved difficult it was not surprising. The task group members had a range of views and professional backgrounds: from mainstream and special school heads and teachers to advisers, educational psychologists and teachers in higher education, from those working in LEAs and post-school education to those in voluntary bodies. There was also a representative from the DES and one from HM Inspectorate among the members.

Was it all worth while? A year later the feeling of 'dancing on eggshells' lingers. I became editorial consultant for *A Curriculum For All* because of my conviction about the needs for access and progress within the National Curriculum for children with special educational needs. I agreed fully with the task group's determination that the message should be positive but in doing so found I had cast myself in the role of a public relations officer for a national curriculum which I supported, within the wider context of government reforms which I opposed. The Conservative government's strategy could be seen as nationalising the curriculum in order to privatise education, leaving special education on the margins of change.

Training as a journalist breeds a critical and questioning approach (or feeds a predisposition to it). It leads to identifying wider issues, not leaving them unexposed. At times during the five months I felt that my energies would have been better spent in raising issues about special educational needs in the *British Journal of Special Education, The Times Educational Supplement*, and in pressure groups as I had been doing previously. While I continued with many of these activities during work on *A Curriculum For All*, the time available for them was lessened. To keep them all going at the same time as working with the task group often meant beginning work at 7 a.m. and finishing after midnight.

Working more closely and continuously than anyone else on *A Curriculum For All* I was also more aware of what it did not do − or could not do in the time available. Critics have referred to its neglect of pupils with profound and multiple learning difficulties, its underemphasis on pupils with mild learning difficulties, and its need to do a 'salvage job' because special educational needs had been neglected in previous guidance from the National Curriculum Council. Others have seen its examples of classroom practice as unreal and its advice as superficial, unaware of the limits on its length and its time-line. The pace of government reforms was requiring bodies like the National Curriculum Council and its hardworking but voluntary committee members to move at indecent speed. To outsiders like me it seemed to be a situation of 'act now, think later'.

Given that the National Curriculum was not yet in place at the time *A Curri-*

culum For All had to be published, expectations were unrealistic. Members of the task group were not a troupe of magicians pulling instant solutions out of hats (although, at times, meeting precipitate deadlines seemed to demand nothing short of sorcery). It was too soon for do-it-yourself conjuring tricks and those, anyway, were a feat that could confidently be left to publishers with varying degrees of skill.

It *was* worthwhile. What *A Curriculum For All* has succeeded in doing for many teachers is to reassure them that pupils with special educational needs are not being left out, that *all* children share the right to a balanced and broadly based curriculum including the National Curriculum and that, as the opening sentence of Chapter 2 says, 'Translating the principles of entitlement and access to the National Curriculum into daily provision ... begins with existing good practice'. It has offered schools a starting point, and checklists, for merging past and future practice, taking into account the school's curriculum development plan, its schemes of work, learning environment and pupils' teaching needs. It has been seen as relevant to all pupils and all schools. If it also enables schools to remove the invisible question mark from its title it will have more than met its aims.

NOTE

The views expressed here are those of the author and do not represent those of the National Curriculum Council or the task group.

REFERENCES

National Curriculum Council (1989a) *Curriculum Guidance 2, A Curriculum for All; Special Needs in the National Curriculum,* York: NCC.
—— (1989b) *Circular 5, Implementing the National Curriculum: Participation by Pupils with Special Educational Needs,* York: NCC.
—— (1989c) *Curriculum Guidance 1, A Framework for the Primary Curriculum,* York: NCC.

Chapter 27

A union view of special education policy

Shirley Darlington

Shirley Darlington is Assistant Secretary – Equal Opportunities, with the National Union of Teachers. In this chapter she discusses the involvement of the union in special educational policy. She provides background details about the effort union officials make to establish credibility with their members and assess the possibilities for influencing the education system. She discusses the complexities of the role of the union in integration policy, matching a principle of integration with negative views and reports of some members. The ambivalence about integration is contrasted with the straightforward support that the union has given to arguing for equality of access for people with disabilities into the teaching profession. She documents the efforts the union made to mitigate what it saw as the retrograde effects of the 1988 Education Reform Act on children and young people who experience difficulties in learning in schools.

1 THE UNION CONTEXT

A teachers' trade union has an important role to play in influencing policy-making on educational issues. Teachers' unions are voluntary bodies: teachers join them through choice, partly for self-protection but also because of a perception of the power they have to express the collective voice of teachers on matters affecting the development of the education service.

I write from the perspective of someone who has worked in the Education Department of the largest and most influential teachers' union – the National Union of Teachers – for the past twelve years. I have held responsibility for various policy areas, including special educational needs, and race equality. In 1988 the department was reorganised to encompass equal opportunities as well as education. At that time I became responsible for Equal Opportunities in the widest sense; gender, race, disability and 'inequalities from whatever cause that may arise', including the education of children with special educational needs. For me special education is very much an equal opportunities issue. This is a philosophical stance which, perhaps, distinguishes NUT policy-making from that of other educational organisations. It has a long-held belief in providing equality of opportunity for *all* children and their teachers. It has never adopted a narrowly protectionist stance on behalf of its members, but has sought to promote what it sees as desirable objectives both educationally and in wider social terms. It believes that winning support for good educational practice, and especially the support of parents, can only be good for teachers and children.

The NUT fought for comprehensive education, where every child could attend his or her chosen local school, for adequate resourcing for education, smaller class sizes, professional salaries for teachers, an all-graduate profession with the enhanced status quality teacher education brings, and a common examination at 16+ (now the GCSE). It has supported teacher appraisal on the professional development model, and fair appointment and promotion procedures for teachers.

I would characterise these policies as progressive and egalitarian. They seek to improve conditions of learning and teaching, thereby enhancing the quality of educational experience for everyone involved.

Establishing credibility

It is very important for a union officer working at headquarters to consult widely and to learn from the direct experience of people 'at the chalk face'. In addition to our advisory committee and conferences, I regularly meet members in local associations which I visit to speak about policy and listen to their concerns. The union's training courses, on which I have taught, provide a valuable forum for exchange of views. Members of our executive have had experience of children with special needs in mainstream schools, but very few have taught in special schools. As an officer I therefore have to listen to ordinary union members' concerns, liaise with voluntary bodies, attend specialist conferences, read the specialist journals, and generally keep abreast of thinking in order to be able to brief executive members effectively and inform policy discussions and decisions. Contacts with university departments, the Select Committee and the DES and HMI are all important.

Unless one has a good grasp of all the current issues in a particular policy area, it is impossible to play a leadership role for the profession. It is very important that members can have confidence in the judgement of their full-time officers.

Points of influence

It may be asked at this point: who are you trying to influence? Who makes things happen in education, and who promotes change? It used to be said that education in England and Wales was 'a national system, locally administered'. The balance in this equation seems now to be tipping to the centre as the present government introduces a national curriculum and assessments and seeks to encourage schools to opt out of local authority control. The government claims to be giving power to the people while using its new powers to enforce national 'standards'. The image of a hub at the centre of a wheel with spokes linking to the outer rim is popular with Conservative politicians: schools are at the rim, with strong fixed links to the central powerhouse.

The NUT has always sought to influence central government, local education authorities, and of course the teaching profession itself. In the wider sense it also tries to influence public opinion – the voters, who elect the government and county councillors who control the purse strings – though it recognises local control over finance is diminished after rate and poll tax capping. There is now even a suggestion of taking education spending out of local control completely, which would weaken union influence at local level.

2 SPECIAL NEEDS POLICY

The thread which runs through developments with which I have personally been involved is that teachers, pupils and parents have a common interest in ensuring that each child receives the best possible quality of education suited to their individual needs. Of course, there can be tension between the needs of parents, children and teachers. But we have always sought to resolve those tensions in the most constructive way, and in addition to seek the support of voluntary organisations, parent and governor organisations which are powerful allies in the field of special education. We also try to make links with those in higher education, teacher education, and advisory services who wield influence.

Supporting integration?

The debate about the integration of children with special educational needs provides a good example of how the NUT tries to influence central government and local education authorities, to gain support from parents, governors and voluntary organisations, and to provide leadership for the teaching profession itself. After submitting a major piece of evidence to the Warnock Committee of Enquiry, the NUT warmly welcomed the report which emerged in 1978 (DES 1978) and supported most of its conclusions and recommendations. Strong lobbying took place as the 1981 Act, which was meant to embody the Warnock principles, went through Parliament. We were extremely dismayed that the government did not allocate additional resources to local education authorities enabling them to implement the Act, since there was no financial memorandum attached to the Bill.

The NUT produced a guide to the 1981 Act (NUT 1984a) in which it warned about the dangers of unplanned and under-resourced integration as LEAs interpreted their duty to educate children with special needs in ordinary schools 'wherever possible'. The union's national Advisory Committee for Special Education insisted that there should be a continuing commitment to special schools. The tension between the views of members working in special schools, who saw the value of favourable staffing ratios, expert teaching and ancillary staff, and specialised buildings and equipment, and those who favoured integration on ideological grounds was apparent.

A similar debate took place over proposals to end specialised initial teacher-training courses and replace them with a model which provided general training first, post-qualification experience and then specialised training. This model fitted with an integration philosophy, but loss of specialist initial courses was deplored by some of those working in special schools.

The union's Annual Conference in 1982 passed a tough resolution setting out a list of demands and guarantees before integration was contemplated. These included adequate 'human and material resource provision' such as a teacher with responsibility for special needs in schools where pupils were integrated, improved staffing and ancillary assistance, adapted premises, medical and paramedical support, and in-service training covering special needs. Another aspect of concern was the Act's failure to do anything for the wider range of children with special needs, the so-called 18 per cent of The Warnock Report's 20 per cent of children who might have special needs at some time during their school career.

Concern was also expressed about possible closures of special schools, and loss of teaching expertise if special school teachers were redeployed on a piecemeal basis. The idea of special schools as resource centres and curriculum development centres was floated. The twin concerns of the interests of special education teachers and the progressive development of the special education service were held paramount in union thinking at that time. The NUT also recommended that LEAs train their governors about their responsibilities under the 1981 Act, and provide clear information for parents in the form of a handbook.

Such a wide-ranging change in special education provision obviously aroused fears as well as interest. The NUT tried to address these fears through dissemination of information and advice, by holding a major national conference on 'The Future of Special Education', and through regular discussion of the issues in its other activities such as its annual education conference, and in branch meetings at local level.

A further publication in 1984, *Meeting Special Educational Needs in Ordinary Schools* (NUT 1984b), took the debate forward by advocating a whole-school approach to meeting special needs, and aimed to provide practical support and an 'integration checklist' for schools which were considering integrating pupils with special needs.

The *opportunity* presented by the 1981 Act for LEAs to review their provision and adopt a planned approach was stressed. As experience of the Act in operation was gained, the union was critical of the use made of the Statementing process by LEAs to fit provision to resources available, and to produce a Statement only for those pupils who would previously have been in special schools. The assessment process was seen by the NUT as having the potential to provide important safeguards for pupils and as a means of securing the resources required to meet their needs. Teachers were urged to work in partnership with parents to secure that provision.

But already a backlash was occurring. The delicate balancing act between support for the principle of integration – which was felt to be a right for children and which would enable them to integrate more easily into adult life – and the fears about under-resourcing continued, and were borne out in the experiences of schools during the 1980s. Children were being placed in mainstream schools without adequate planning and preparation, and cuts in resources generally made for a hostile climate to successful integration. Members who had been looking to the union for advice and support became angry at what they saw as a confidence trick played by the government on children with special needs, their parents and teachers. We received many complaints about under-resourced integration which over-burdened teachers who were not adequately trained to deal effectively with pupils with disabilities and learning difficulties, previously found in special schools.

Sometimes a desperate teacher would phone headquarters: 'They are asking me to have a spina bifida child next week. I am in favour of integration, but we have no proper toilet facilities and no ancillary help, what shall I do?' This was a common kind of call, as was the complaint about class sizes being too large to give sufficient attention to a child with special needs. The advice was 'Get your school representative, local secretary or regional office to press the LEA to provide the necessary resources for successful integration of the particular child or children in question.'

The 'casework' approach was successful in some cases, but not with unsympathetic LEAs who were using integration as a means of saving money without adequate safeguards for teachers or pupils. Anger was expressed in such LEAs (for example, Bradford) which moved towards integration on the cheap – not just on behalf of overstretched teachers, but on behalf of children with special needs who were being sold out.

We asked our divisions to urge LEAs to bring forward coherent plans for special education, and to consult teachers in the process. We urged more secondments to in-service training, posts of responsibility for special needs in all schools, and effectively coordinated support services.

In 1987, the Annual Conference passed a resolution calling for additional resources for integration and action to prevent closure of special schools if the union's demands were not met for 'acceptable alternatives which will meet the curricular and social needs of pupils with special educational needs without adversely affecting mainstream education'. Here was a dilemma for the union's executive: were they to encourage 'action' (i.e. strikes) against closure of special schools? Did this not fly in the face of their positive policy on integration? Firm and tactful interpretation of this resolution by the union's leadership was required.

The result was a very successful pamphlet *Guidelines on Negotiating for Special Needs* (NUT 1988) which formed part of a high profile campaign on special needs by the NUT and secured favourable media coverage. A poster and pamphlet were sent to every school, and divisions were asked to go and negotiate with their LEA on a clear shopping list of items to be included in their special education plan. This pamphlet, which I drafted in conjunction with a small executive working party and the Advisory Committee for Special Education, pulled together our thinking and experience of the operation of the 1981 Act and also drew on our evidence to the House of Commons Select Committee which was investigating the implementation of the 1981 Act.

The advice contained in the guidelines was very well received by our members. It was not as discursive as earlier pamphlets and laid out a clear set of requirements, which enabled divisions to go and negotiate with their LEAs and report back to us. The conclusion very firmly stated that we were asking for a planned approach from each LEA, including whole-school policies which treated children and young people with disabilities as 'full members of the community, with equal rights of access to the whole range of educational opportunities available to all'. This made integrated special education an issue of equal rights, but did not neglect the very proper concerns of teachers of pupils with special needs.

Equal opportunities for teachers with disabilities

Connected with equality of opportunity for pupils with learning difficulties and disabilities was a campaign for teachers with disabilities. The union had strongly developed policies on equal rights for women and Black teachers (NUT 1990a), and wanted to extend its equal opportunities policies to include support for disabled teachers. There were many barriers to equality of opportunity for disabled teachers, including prejudice and ignorance on the part of employers, and the reluctance of teacher-training institutions to take students with physical or sensory disabilities. Our Working Party on Disability, formed in 1989, included teachers with disabilities, one of whom uses a wheelchair following a climbing accident, another who suffered polio as a child, and a blind woman head of an English Department. We were joined later by a deaf deputy head. We wanted to show positive images of what disabled teachers could achieve with support and encouragement, in order to dispel the myth that disability equals inability. The links between integration of pupils with special needs and successful disabled teachers working in schools are clear: with a change in attitude, good will, improved access, support and resourcing, disabled children and adults can participate fully and effectively at all levels of an integrated education service. The union held a consultative conference of disabled teachers in 1990 and published guidelines on teachers with disabilities in 1991 (NUT 1991).

3 THE 1988 EDUCATION ACT

The union's depth and breadth of knowledge and influence became vitally important when the government introduced its Education Reform Bill, later to become the 1988 Education Reform Act (ERA). One of the functions of a teaching trade union is to monitor the likely impact of legislation, to seek to amend it where necessary, and then to comment on the ensuing regulations and circulars.

The ERA is the biggest piece of education legislation since the 1944 Act. When I read it, it was with anger and some amazement that I realised it contained just three and a half lines which related to children with special needs, to the effect that a Statement might mean exemption from National Curriculum requirements.

The NUT, along with other educationalists, expended a great deal of energy – to very little effect – commenting on consultative documents which preceded the Bill. The competitive 'market forces' ethos of the Bill was anathema to us, and we campaigned very hard against the Bill and sought to have amendments tabled. I wrote a campaigning leaflet entitled *Government Proposals and Special Educational Needs* which started with the words 'Government proposals for education, which have been brought forward in the name of improving parental choice, increasing diversity and raising standards could do quite the opposite for children with special needs and their families' (NUT 1987). In particular we highlighted opting out, LMS and open enrolment as factors which could work against the 1981 Act and destroy careful links built up between mainstream and special schools, and support services. The government proved vulnerable on how the National Curriculum would be made accessible to children with special needs, and was forced to bring in some rather clumsy and bureaucratic amendments and modifications to the Bill to meet criticism. The NUT's statement in that leaflet: 'the Union believes all children should have access to the whole range of the curriculum, adapted or modified if needs be, and that assessment should be used for diagnostic, not competitive purposes' stands as NUT policy today.

I am sure that by focusing on how the Bill failed children with special needs, we highlighted weaknesses in the legislation which are now becoming apparent and affect all pupils. We also predicted that

> the pressures created by the proposals to record and publish achievements so that schools may compete for popularity will lead to schools being unwilling to take pupils with special needs and learning difficulties. Open enrolment too will lead to covert discriminatory selection as schools seek to attract high achieving pupils to stay viable. This could force pupils with special needs back into a segregated system ...
>
> (NUT 1987)

Indeed there are signs that this is now beginning to happen.

A major success in relation to the Bill (and there were very few because of the government's large majority and disinclination to listen to educationalists) was in relation to the financing of pupils with special needs in relation to local management of schools (LMS). With intensive lobbying and working with other concerned organisations we managed to get an amendment on the face of the Bill to the effect that LEAs must make provision in their budget formula for special education provision. This is a weighting which can be given to schools according to how many pupils they have with special needs, including the wider range of pupils without Statements. I feel some personal satisfaction over this because I wrote countless letters and lobbied very hard for this amendment. On a subsequent deputation to the DES about the LMS circular, I made sure that the wording of the circular included children with the wider range of special needs but no Statements, and also contained provision for a weighting for social deprivation.

The union produced a detailed pamphlet giving guidance on LMS and special needs, and suggesting criteria for additional weighting in the formula (NUT 1990b). We also produced a shorter version for schools with a checklist for monitoring to ensure that the additional money is reaching the children for whom it is intended.

There is always an uneasy relationship between being opposed to a particular piece of legislation and then, when it becomes law, doing your best to mitigate its effects or use it to advantage. That is the situation which now faces us as a union over the Education Reform Act. We have a duty to our members not to put them at risk through encouraging them to break the law, and also to support them in trying to make sense of the new arrangements. A pamphlet on the National Curriculum and special educational needs was written in that spirit (NUT 1990c).

4 ALL OUR FUTURES

Morale in teaching unions, as well as the teaching profession at large, is at an all-time low. It seems a very long time since we had a government that wanted to listen to what teachers had to say. The unions have become associated with the educational establishment which the Radical Right so deplores. Over the past few years, 'egalitarianism' has become a pejorative term. Our allies in the beleaguered LEAs seem to have a short shelf-life ahead; but I remain surprisingly optimistic. There *are* chinks in the armour. Special education (and equal opportunities in its widest sense) is one such chink. After all, I am sure we are on the side of the angels.

REFERENCES

Department of Education and Science (DES) (1978) *Special Educational Needs* (The Warnock Report), London: HMSO.

National Union of Teachers (NUT) (1984a) *The Education Act 1981: A Union Guide*, London: NUT.

—— (1984b) *Meeting Special Educational Needs in Ordinary Schools: A Union Guide*, London: NUT.

—— (1987) *Government Proposals and Special Educational Needs*, London: NUT.

—— (1988) *Guidelines on Negotiating for Special Needs*, London: NUT.

—— (1990a) *Fair and Equal: Union Guidelines on Equal Opportunities in the Appointment and Promotion of Teachers*, London: NUT.

—— (1990b) *Local Management of Schools and Special Educational Needs*, London: NUT.

—— (1990c) *Special Educational Needs and the National Curriculum*, London: NUT.

—— (1991) *Teachers with Disabilities: An Equal Opportunities Issue*, London: NUT.

Chapter 28

Empowering the voluntary sector
The campaign for policy change

Mairian Corker

Mairian Corker, who at the time of writing this chapter was the Education Officer for the National Deaf Children's Society, starts by outlining a set of principles on which to base the activities of voluntary organisations of and for deaf children, young people and adults. She then provides a detailed case study of the educational work of the National Deaf Children's Society. She goes on to examine some of the conflicts of interest which may impede voluntary societies in living up to their principles.

> The truth is: we do need you, not to be 'experts' or managers of our lives, but to be friends, enablers and receivers of our 'gifts' to you.
>
> (Mason 1990: 45)

1 INTRODUCTION

The organisation which is the subject of the detailed case study is, at the time of writing, my employing organisation. There are inherent difficulties in writing a completely open account about the functioning of one's employers. The activities of all organisations and institutions show examples of good practice and bad practice. What follows should not be taken as advocacy for this organisation *per se*, but as an essentially honest attempt to look at the pros and cons of providing services from the perspective of one individual working in the voluntary sector. What must be stressed, however, is that as a deaf person I am aware of being unable to move outside the perspective of a person with a disability.

The role and power of the voluntary sector

The voice of the voluntary sector has become progressively powerful over the last ten years or so, for a number of reasons. The voluntary sector has become more wealthy as a result of effective campaign management and fund-raising activities, which merge private sector technique with political know-how. In the United Kingdom, charities, collectively, are now the second biggest employer after the statutory sector (Mason 1990). There are now a larger number of services which are provided by the voluntary sector because they are not provided by the state. There are an increasing number of umbrella voluntary organisations which act as a forum for cooperative and multidisciplinary activity. There is a growing recognition of the professionalism of voluntary sector activity. Finally, the increase in voluntary sector activity can be directly related to the increase in the need for the particular services that it offers.

2 FINDING PRINCIPLES FOR ACTION

The current confusion between what the state should provide and what it is able to provide has paralleled an increase of clarity of aims and objectives within voluntary organisations which has allowed them to identify areas of need and respond appropriately. However, services provided by voluntary organisations are based on a broader concept of need and policy than that which is evident within the statutory sector. There are a number of principles which I feel underpin this broader concept.

The recognition and promotion of natural rights and human rights

Within the voluntary sector, there is a greater recognition that consumers of state services have *natural rights* and *human rights* as well as legal rights. For example, parents are seen to be uniquely knowledgeable about their own children, and are often the only people who see their child as a whole, and over time (Madden 1989). It is therefore their right to have their feelings and perceptions taken seriously. There has also been an attempt within the voluntary sector to invert the legislative pyramid which places children and parents at the bottom and resources and 'the system' at the top 'wherever possible'.

Dilemmas of charity and rights

Mason (1990) has argued that charity law is very different from laws which govern state spending. She says that it is illegal for the 'beneficiaries' of voluntary sector services to be involved in the management of those services in order to safeguard against vested interests affecting decisions.

If we look at voluntary organisations concerned with deafness, we can see a clear division between those which work *for* deaf people (for example, the Royal National Institute for the Deaf) and those which are organised *by* deaf people (The British Deaf Association, the National Union of the Deaf, the Deaf Broadcasting Council). There are others which presently employ a high quota of deaf people, but have very few deaf people on the council of management (the National Deaf Children's Society). Charities organised by deaf people are frequently hampered by limited funds, some would say because of the negative stereotypes used by the 'giants' to raise funds.

Countering disabling policies and attitudes

Disabling policies (Fulcher 1990) are those which focus on *dis*-ability and place undue emphasis on learning *difficulties*. They stem from lack of knowledge, skills and understanding on the part of policy-makers, and stereotyped dispositions to view disability as the responsibility of the 'sufferer'. Examples of disabling policies can be seen in the major contradictions between the declared intention that the National Curriculum is an entitlement curriculum for all children and policies which allow exemptions, modifications and disapplications of the National Curriculum for pupils with special educational needs (DES 1988), and prevent disability equality in the classroom (Corker 1990a, 1990b). This is one of the ways in which the 1988 Act and the 1981 Act diametrically oppose each other, because implicit in the 1981 Act was the use of the Statementing machinery to make appropriate educational provision to allow a child's access to mainstream education.

Disabling policies also stem from the prioritising of resources over and above need – sometimes called resource-led thinking. Such thinking leads to the provision of inadequate services to the minority under the guise of providing 'efficient' services for the majority. It is inherent in the contradictions between the financial delegation of budgets (see Chapter 31) and the powers of head teachers to request Statements for children they feel have special educational needs for whom in theory the resources are open ended. The National Association of Head Teachers (House of Commons 1989) recently estimated that the education of around 80 per cent of children in special schools is determined by the LEA's resourcing policies rather than the child's needs.

In practice it is difficult to separate disabling policies from disabling attitudes. One leads to the other. Disabling attitudes can be observed in the use of language which reinforces negative stereotypes of disability as seen, for example, in the use of the term 'the deaf and dumb' in preference to the term 'deaf people'. They can also be seen in a refusal to acknowledge that people with disabilities like Black people or women may have a particular perspective on the world. This attitude leads to the generation of policies which are based on the needs of people with disabilities as defined by people without disabilities rather than themselves. Such policies can force people with disabilities into the benefits system as opposed to education and training commensurate with their ability and potential.

Promoting the social/functional model of disability

Some voluntary organisations respond to need in a way which perpetuates the 'medical model' of disability by delivering services which aim to 'cure' deaf people of their 'affliction', or 'prevent' that affliction happening. The medical model therefore assumes that human beings are flexible and 'alterable' while society is fixed and unalterable. Adaptation is the responsibility of the individual and not of society. Other organisations respond to need within the framework of the 'functional' or 'social' model of deafness, which values deaf people for the unique contribution they can make to society and as equal participants in the framework of that society. Rieser and Mason (1990) describe the social model of disability thus:

> Disabled people's own view of the situation is – that whilst we may have medical conditions which hamper us and which may or may not need medical treatment, human knowledge, technology and collective resources are already such that our physical or mental impairments need not prevent us from being able to live perfectly good lives. It is society's unwillingness to employ these means to altering *itself* rather than *us* which causes our disabilities.
>
> (Rieser and Mason 1990: 15)

For further discussion of the medical and social models of deafness, see Corker (1990b).

Promoting equal opportunities

Many of the issues I have discussed are concerned with restoring the balance of power between disabled children, young people and adults and their non-disabled peers. Use of medical models of disability, disabling policies and attitudes, promoting charity as opposed to rights, all serve to keep disabled people locked in a dependency culture and prevented from contributing fully to society on their own terms. It follows from this that perhaps the most fundamental principle which should underpin voluntary sector activity is promoting equal opportunities both within the voluntary sector and at all levels in society.

3 THE NATIONAL DEAF CHILDREN'S SOCIETY – A CASE STUDY

The National Deaf Children's Society (NDCS) has an approximate annual turnover of £850,000 (in 1990). It cannot claim to compete with the giants – the multi-million pound charities such as the Spastics Society, the Royal National Institute for the Blind, and the Royal National Institute for the Deaf. It has a local membership of about 12,000 plus a national membership of 125 (this is a new category of membership), but membership patterns are changing with the introduction of direct mailing. These figures in any case belie the total number of people using the organisation's services. The NDCS typically receives 100 individual requests for information per week plus many more which require more than one contact.

As from 1 November 1990, the NDCS will employ thirty staff in three offices. Within the last two years there has been a fundamental change of ethos within the organisation which has led to the creation of a completely new multidisciplinary structure which aims towards a whole-child approach to services.

The NDCS refuses to be drawn into debates concerning 'correct' terminology. It prefers to see the term 'deaf' as meaning 'the full range of hearing loss' and rejects the professional's term 'hearing impaired' because of the negative connotations of the word 'impaired'. The NDCS is an equal opportunities organisation and this is reflected throughout its services and in staff training. It is also committed to child-centred practices, informed choice and creating positive images of deaf children. The organisation is constantly evolving to meet changing needs and the last five years have been a time of rapid growth.

The Society is one of four major charitable organisations concerned with deafness (the Royal National Institute for the Deaf, the British Deaf Association, and the British Association of the Hard of Hearing are the other three) and is also part of a consortium of organisations such as SENSE, the National Deaf–Blind Rubella Association. There are also other smaller organisations such as the Breakthrough Trust for deaf–hearing integration, and Friends of the Young Deaf. The NDCS is, however, the only charitable organisation concerned solely with deaf children and young people from birth and throughout compulsory education.

THE NDCS's activities in education

NDCS's education services are presently delivered by two officers and two administrators/secretarial staff. There are an estimated 65,000 deaf children in Great Britain who are considered to be educationally disadvantaged by their deafness. This represents the potential caseload which is the focus of educational services. The work of the department is overseen by the NDCS Education Subcommittee which consists of up to twenty parents of deaf children and professionals working with deaf children in the educational setting. The membership of the Subcommittee reflects the equal opportunities commitment of the Society, including deaf and hearing people and people from ethnic minorities. The Subcommittee is itself responsible to the NDCS Management Committee and through them to the NDCS National Council.

Challenging disabling attitudes and policies is the central core of the activities of the Society's education services. I believe that disabling attitudes in education result from the widespread philosophy which utilises the medical model of deafness in the assessment of need. This model, which was discussed in the introductory section, is strongly connected to 'normalisation' approaches to integration in education, which concentrate on making deaf children as like hearing children as possible. The medical model is prevalent throughout the Health Service, which is the diagnostic centre, and often the first point of contact that parents of deaf children have. It is also prevalent throughout teacher-training courses leading to the specialist qualification of teacher of the deaf, where audiology and remedial speech and language teaching take priority over communication skills, deaf awareness and equal opportunities.

At the 12th biennial convention of the American Society for Deaf Children in Vancouver, Canada, 1990, it was generally acknowledged that Britain lags about ten years behind other more advanced countries such as the USA, Sweden and

France with respect to communication approaches used in deaf education. Success can be clearly measured in terms of results – the number of deaf school-leavers progressing to further and higher education and occupying professional positions in employment. It is also striking that at this conference, audiology was hardly mentioned. The attitude was that the use of hearing aids and other aids to hearing was acknowledged and understood. The real task was to look at the children and young people between each pair of ears, because there lies the key to unlocking the disablement – an understanding of deaf experience and the deaf identity. The USA, Sweden and France have been adopting the 'functional model' of deafness for many years now, which is based on the acceptance of difference. It is this model that the NDCS uses to challenge the widespread paternalism within deaf education in Britain.

The educational activities of the society are summarised in Table 28.1 and I will give a little more detail on those concerned with influencing policy.

Table 28.1 Activities which influence policy change within the National Deaf Children's Society

---

- Involvement in the consultation machinery when Education Bills are passing through the enactment process by parliamentary lobbying, giving evidence to all-party select committees, involvement in parliamentary groups responsible for developing policy.
- Involvement in the consultation process for the development of non-statutory guidance and DES circulars relating to the implementation of education law.
- Direct action and indirect action through parents' groups, individual parents and sometimes professionals to effect local policy changes and variations in the way that education law is interpreted.
- Research and monitoring of the implementation of education policy as it relates to the education of deaf children and young people, and the dissemination of up-to-date research findings to the Department of Education and Science, Her Majesty's Inspectorate, local education authorities, school governing bodies, schools and units for deaf children and the NDCS membership.
- Promoting the parent–professional partnership by empowering parents to become informed, active partners with more enlightened, more aware professionals.
- Advocacy and counselling work with individuals.
- Promoting access and entitlement to the National Curriculum for all deaf children.
- Development of and wide dissemination of internal policy on different aspects of deaf education, e.g. communication, integration, school transport, Statementing and recording, speech therapy, local management of schools, pre-school education.

Involvement in legislation

The NDCS uses its knowledge of Parliament and its committees in its campaigns to change policy as it is being enacted. We lobby Members of Parliament who have relevant experience and involvement in both parliamentary and extra-parliamentary activities to do with education and disability. Such involvement can be anything from personal experience of disability, to being a member of a voluntary organisation or an ex-head teacher of a special school. The all-party approach is always used, but problems are encountered because, for example, there are currently many more Members of Parliament who themselves have a disability in the Labour ranks than there are in the other political parties. What does this say about the pressure on the voluntary sector to remain politically impartial, or about the representation of disabled people in Parliament?

The NDCS has met with some success by utilising these channels fully. But it is also true to say that any amendments of legislation achieved have been minor, particularly in recent years. One of the frustrations of parliamentary lobbying where a government has a massive majority is that it is known from the outset that an enormous amount of hard work will be largely ineffective, except in the amount of awareness that is generated by campaigns. It is here that voluntary sector activity generates its real power, power which leads for example to the report from the All-Party Select Committee on the implementation of the Education Act 1981 recommending stronger cooperation between the voluntary sector and local education authorities, some five years *after* the implementation of the Education Act 1981. The value of the voluntary sector voice is recognised, but sometimes it is only recognised after a great deal of damage has been done.

Targeting non-statutory guidance

With non-statutory guidance, DES circulars and consultation on matters concerning the school curriculum, we find a completely different story, however. It is in this area that the Society's activities frequently meet their objectives. For example, a number of the recommendations made in the Society's publication *A Mockery of Needs* (NDCS 1989) are reflected in the final draft of DES Circular 22/89.

The NDCS, along with other representations from the voluntary sector and the statutory sector, drew attention to the risks facing many thousands of deaf children in mainstream schools without Statements of special educational needs. Conceivably, without the protection of a Statement, these children would be deprived of access to appropriate support when needed because of lack of resources. DES Circular 22/89 recommends that the needs of these children are acknowledged and that LEAs make use of the scope to target resources within their proposals for local management of schools. The latter recommendation echoed the Society's recommendation in their survey report on local management of schools (NDCS 1990).

Within the National Curriculum Council's consultation process, the NDCS successfully demonstrated some of the dilemmas surrounding access to the curriculum. The Society did not share the Council's optimism that curriculum modifications and disapplications and the powers of head teachers to effect temporary exceptions would only be used 'sparingly' or 'rarely'. Our view was backed by the increasing number of enquiries received by the Society from parents who are being told that their children need to be Statemented and exempted from the National Curriculum. This is also the experience of the Advisory Centre for Education (ACE 1989).

In order to strengthen the argument for curriculum access we have tried to show that many deaf children have special educational needs because resources are insufficient to provide appropriate support over a sustained period of time. We provided suggestions as to how access could be facilitated, for example, by proper attention to, and understanding of, different approaches to communication with deaf children and to the training of teachers, both in-service and specialist.

We have drawn attention to the issues which surround the use of British Sign Language (BSL) by pupils. The crux of the matter is that BSL is not recognised as a language by the Department of Education and Science. This means that deaf children who have BSL as a home language are not given the same rights as other children who are bilingual in two spoken languages. The use of BSL tends to be seen as special educational provision rather than as the use of a minority language. Assessment arrangements under the National Curriculum are not sufficiently flexible to allow for BSL to be used as the language of assessment. A video recording might need to be made of BSL-using pupils to replace some oral or written assessments, since very few teachers of the deaf are sufficiently proficient in BSL to understand fluent users. Few native users of BSL have sufficient educational knowledge and understanding to participate in the assessment arrangements for the National Curriculum.

Our influence here is qualified if we remember that these documents are for the *guidance* of LEA administrators, teachers, school governing bodies and others involved in special education. It is not compulsory that such guidance is followed. Moreover, guidance rarely comes with facts and reasons. It is assumed that in digesting guidance, there is a fundamental awareness of the issues involved. It is the Society's experience that this is not the case. The NDCS's activities therefore centre around making sure that accurate and contemporary information is fed from consumer groups (parents and young people, primarily) and 'aware' professionals to the policy-making body.

Research and monitoring

A good example of effective monitoring can be seen in the work of the Joint Monitoring and Study Group on Training of Teachers of the Deaf (JMSG). This group was set up by the NDCS primarily to monitor the number of teachers of the deaf being trained and how this compared to DES figures of the number that were needed. It consists of representatives from the teacher-training colleges offering courses leading to the specialist qualification of teacher of the deaf and from voluntary organisations of and for deaf people. It has also been concerned with looking at the DES bid system for LEA secondments. Each LEA is allocated a certain number of secondments for trainee teachers of the deaf for which it can bid. In practice, the system has not worked because the total number of secondments available nationally is fixed, as are the regional allocations. LEAs who do not take up their quota of secondments cannot direct these secondments to areas of need. This had led to services in some LEAs being seriously depleted.

The JMSG has finally convinced the DES that the bid system for the allocation of secondments for training as a teacher of the deaf is a shambles and has contributed to the current shortfall in trained teachers of the deaf. However, it is disappointing that related issues have not been tackled by the JMSG. These include the content of specialist teacher-training courses and the access of deaf people to specialist teacher training. The neglect of these issues is one of the drawbacks of 'partnerships' between the voluntary and professional sectors, as we shall see later.

Empowerment, advocacy and the parent–professional partnership

At the heart of the Society's activity is the empowerment issue – putting power where it is most needed, in the hands of children and their families. It is here that the *independence* and *neutrality* of the NDCS is to the forefront. And it seems that there is a need for these qualities. A report by Her Majesty's Inspectorate concluded:

> From the psychologist's point of view there were often tensions between acting as an advocate for a client and carrying out LEA policy. From the education officer's point of view there could be the decision as to whether to uphold publicly expressed opinions and thereby unduly strain existing resources.
>
> (DES 1990: 26)

The Society has recognised for many years now that the parent–professional partnership as advocated in The Warnock Report (DES 1978) would only work if both parents and professionals respected each other and had a mutual commitment to the same ideals. To achieve this parents need information about their rights and either training or independent advocacy which helps them to express their wishes. Professionals can be prevented from developing partnerships with parents because of conflicts of professional interest fuelled by LEA policies about placement and resources. The NDCS's advocacy services have enabled more parents to use the legal machinery effectively in cases of dispute with LEAs. This success is reflected in the increase in the number of successful local appeals involving parents of deaf children lodged under Section 8 of the 1981 Act in the period 1987–90, and in the number of successful appeals lodged with the Secretary of State under Section 8(6) of the Act for the same period. The figures for successful appeals are shown in Table 28.2.

It should be noted that the two successful appeals recorded in the second cate-

Table 28.2 Successful appeals by parents of deaf children against LEA decisions, 1987–90

	1987–8	1988–9	1989–90
Local appeals	2	6	9
Appeals lodged with Secretary of State under Section 8(6)	1	0	2

gory for 1989–90 represented cases where for the first time parents had fought all the way to the DES with the NDCS's help and won. In 1987–8, the appeal that was won was settled by the LEA before the Secretary of State made a decision. All appeals were with the DES for more than eighteen months before a decision was made, and at least one other case remains with the DES.

Many of the professionals working with deaf children have no specialist expertise in this area. This group will, in the majority of LEAs, include county or borough councillors, Statementing officers, educational psychologists, chief education officers, assistant education officers (special needs), head teachers and mainstream teachers. In short, major decisions are made about the future education of a deaf child by professionals who lack sufficient awareness of deafness and who, at best, have generic experience of special needs. It is necessary to empower parents and others to effect local policy changes by issuing challenges based on real understanding of the issues involved. But it is also necessary to issue direct intellectual challenges to professionals in order fully to achieve the aims and objectives of the voluntary sector. I believe that a two-pronged approach such as this is the foundation of special education policies that work for the interests of deaf children.

4 CONFLICTS OF INTEREST IN THE VOLUNTARY SECTOR

The Society has had success in achieving policy change but it has not been successful in identifying and addressing all the issues, nor has it been able to totally embrace the principles outlined in the introductory section. One of the difficulties in being employed by an organisation which calls itself 'The National Deaf Children's Society' *and* claims to be a parents' organisation is that it can be difficult to look at conflicts of interest between parents and children. It would be completely wrong to assume that all parents are beyond criticism and that they always have the best interests of their child at heart. Within the Society's practice, there are cases where the parent's interests may have been placed above those of the child. Occasionally parents do deny the implications of deafness for their child, and this can set into motion a chain of events which leads to the child being placed in inappropriate educational provision for life. In empowering parents we are not always ensuring that deaf children and young people are themselves empowered.

Facing up to controversial issues about language, communication, the deaf–hearing power imbalance, and the dynamics and problems of integrated education, would all yield valuable information as to how children can be empowered. The NDCS, in common with other voluntary and statutory bodies, remains shy of these issues because it is more important to try to please all of the people all of the time.

There is also a tendency to encourage employees of the organisation to act as if they can be all things to all people. Frequently, generic skills have been promoted at the expense of specialist expertise. Recently, there has been more emphasis on teamwork; but what of that well-known proverb 'too many cooks spoil the broth', or the possibility that there may be very real conflicts in ideology between people from social services and education backgrounds, and between deaf people and hearing people?

I noted earlier that there are a number of major organisations concerned with deaf people. It is heartening to see that there is so much cooperation between these organisations. But there has been confrontation in the campaign for policy change, particularly over approaches to communication. Organisations have attempted to discredit each other's approach in general rather than to explain the merits of individual approaches for individual children. This has worked against the interests of deaf children because policy-makers are unable to make decisions when so many professionals are telling them that their approach is the *only* right one.

There have been continued attempts by the National Aural Group (who promote natural auralism) to discredit BSL as advocated by the British Deaf Association. Neither organisation has publicly recognised that there may be a valid case for both approaches to communication depending on the individual deaf child. The NDCS, as the organisation which advocates individual needs, has been caught in the middle of this debate, and is privately, if not publicly, labelled as an 'oralist' organisation because it represents 'hearing parents'. The politics are complicated, but they are based on one organisation spreading misinformation about another in order to gain support for its own cause, a practice which is discouraged at some – though certainly not all – levels of the NDCS. My feeling is that the education services of NDCS were firmly based on the principal of individual needs but that the voluntary section of the organisation (which includes the Management Committee) found it extremely difficult to recognise equal opportunities or to be objective on the subject of communication.

5 CONCLUDING REMARKS – THE FUTURE

Many disabled people *do* become dependent on charity because fundamental human rights are not recognised. They are viewed as sick rather than different, and penalised by a free-market ideology and by policy decisions. Tokenism is widespread within voluntary organisations of and for disabled people and power games are played which are designed to maximise the non-disabled voice at the expense of the disabled voice. Divisions are rife within voluntary organisations, which weakens their voice.

Policy is never likely to be in the hands of the voluntary sector, which is limited to *influencing* the way that policy is formulated and implemented. As the voluntary sector becomes more 'professional' in its moves to change the balance of power and to counter disabling policies, it is itself becoming involved in the same market philosophy which has led to existing policy. Voluntary sector activity is becoming competitive, almost to the point where aims and objectives disappear. In a time where hope is needed where there is no hope, it is sad to see the life force of the voluntary sector flickering in uncertainty over whether it can embrace principles which amplify the much-needed, independent voice of disabled people. Ultimately, they will have to accept that the empowerment of disabled people may lead to the demise of the voluntary sector.

REFERENCES

Advisory Centre for Education (ACE) (1989) *Bulletin 32*, London: ACE.

Corker, M. E. M. (1990a) 'Communicating the curriculum', *Special Children*, March, 21–3.

—— (1990b) *Deaf Perspectives on Psychology, Language and Communication – A Series of Six Discussion Papers*, London: NATED/SKILL.

Department of Education and Science (DES) (1978) *Special Educational Needs* (The Warnock Report), London: HMSO.

—— (1988) *The Education Reform Act*, London: HMSO.

—— (1990) *Education Observed: Special Needs*, London: HMSO.

Fulcher, F. (1990) *Disabling Policies – A Comparative Approach to Educational Policy and Disability*, London: Falmer.

House of Commons (1989) *Minutes of Evidence to the House of Commons Select Committee on the 1981 Act Implementation*, London: House of Commons.

Madden, P. (1989) 'What Katy Did', *Special Children*, April, 10–11.

Mason, M. (1990) 'Charities v. Rights', in R. Rieser and M. Mason (eds), *Disability Equality in the Classroom: A Human Rights Issue*, London: ILEA.

Rieser, R. and Mason, M. (eds) (1990) *Disability Equality in the Classroom: A Human Rights Issue*, London: ILEA.

The National Deaf Children's Society (NDCS) (1989) *A Mockery of Needs: Parents' Experiences of Assessment, Statementing/Recording and Appeals under the Education Act 1981 and the Education (Scotland Act) 1981*, London: NDCS.

—— (1990) *Local Management of Schools – A Survey Report*, London: NDCS.

Chapter 29

Settling the score: responses to young deviants

Mel Lloyd-Smith

Mel Lloyd-Smith reviews the complex system of provision that has developed to respond to children and young people whose behaviour is viewed as unacceptable by those in authority. This system, which has expanded rapidly in the past twenty years, is composed of educational provision such as special units for disruptive children, provision run by social services departments such as Community Homes, and the juvenile justice system. These diverse institutions reflect equally diverse professional and lay attitudes towards the treatment of deviant young people. Mel Lloyd-Smith argues that concerns about the detailed operation and effects of different forms of provision should not obscure the general risk of increasing deviance by placing children and young people in special provision.

1 INTRODUCTION

The opening of the final decade of the twentieth century brought with it some indications of changing attitudes to the treatment of those who transgress society's laws. Evidence about inhumane and counterproductive features of the penal system had been mounting up. A series of riots and demonstrations in English and Scottish prisons received extensive public exposure and the judicial enquiry which followed the Strangeways riot in 1990 was highly critical of government policy, and set out a comprehensive and radical agenda for penal reform. There was growing concern about the number of suicides among young prisoners on remand; almost fifty were reported in 1990 alone. Some of these remand prisoners were as young as 15 years and were awaiting trial in over-crowded adult prisons, sharing cells with older prisoners who were experienced criminals. The Prison Inspectorate noted that opportunities for juveniles to engage in purposeful education, work or recreation were extremely limited and there was concern about bullying and intimidation.

In February 1991 the government responded by introducing legislation to end the imprisonment of 15 and 16 year olds on remand. This was one of a series of reformist policy changes. Also planned was an increased use of cautioning by the police in order to divert some young people from a court appearance, the use of more non-custodial sentences, and increased funding for the probation service to facilitate more extensive and effective supervision in the community.

These overdue reforms could be characterised as attempts to counteract the tendency to criminalise youth. They seem to be an acknowledgement that the systems set up to deal with young offenders have not only been unsuccessful, but also harmful. These systems reflect the way deviance among the young has been regarded in society in general. As Cohen (1972) showed there has been a recurrent tendency in post-war Britain towards 'moral panics' about perceived threats to social stability from what are seen as the deviant values and behaviour of certain groups of young people. The mass media are particularly significant in raising these groups to the status of 'folk devils'. Football hooligans, drug abusers and 'joy-riders' were high-profile examples in the 1980s. A number of less dramatic, though none the less disturbing phenomena such as solvent abuse, vandalism, classroom disruption and bullying, likewise provide the stimulus for continuing debates about their causes, the apparent increase in their incidence, and how to respond to them.

Broadly speaking, these debates reflect two competing standpoints on deviance among the young. Deviance is either perceived as evidence of insufficient enforcement of law and order, or it is seen as the result of social and economic decline and conditions such as deprivation and unemployment. Variations in the nature and severity of court sentences reflect these shifting standpoints. In the 1980s especially, an emphasis on punishment and deterrence led to calls for the 'short, sharp shock'. At other times the alternative perspective encouraged responses in which treatment, resocialisation and rehabilitation have been the overriding aims. Similarly, in the case of disruptive school pupils, differing interpretations of the meaning of this behaviour have led to different formal responses to it. Thus in the regimes of disruptive units it is possible to discern differing emphases on the aims of care as against control.

There has been a steady increase in the number and range of services catering for deviant young people. This trend is quite independent of the prevailing ideology, whether emphasising punishment or reform, control or care. This fact raises the important question of whether the expansion of provision for deviant youngsters has itself contributed to the increased incidence of deviance. Superficially, the expansion would seem to be a simple response to increased demand, but there are three ways in which the reverse might be the case. First, the very existence of a form of provision, coupled with increasing capacity, creates a process of formal identification. Therefore the statistics of deviance reflect changes in provision, not necessarily an increase in the incidence of deviance. Second, provision may discourage the use of alternative ways of responding to the problems. Third, the facilities themselves may be part of a socialisation process which confirms and strengthens a young person's deviant identity and makes further deviance more, rather than less, likely.

In the light of possibilities such as these, arguments have been developed asserting the need to decriminalise youth. One early exponent of this view was Schur (1978) who advocated what he termed 'radical non-intervention' as a means of reducing the problem of delinquency. This requires a basic change in social values: less fear of youthful 'misconduct', greater concentration on socio-economic reform and less on measures designed to force individuals to 'adjust' to allegedly common standards of behaviour. In practice it would mean that only in very extreme cases would young people be allowed to become enmeshed in the juvenile justice system.

Although this is so fundamentally divergent from traditional approaches, it has been reflected in some recent changes of policy, such as the various forms of community service introduced as alternatives to custodial sentences for young offenders. Enthusiasm for these policies has been greater in America than in the UK (see Bakal 1973) and lessons can be learned from experiences there. Scull (1984) has subjected the approach, which he refers to as 'decarceration', to critical scrutiny. He concludes that in the case of juvenile justice, the provision of community-based correction programmes can ironically lead to heightened, not reduced, control.

These conclusions should inspire scepticism when trying to assess the relative merits of different responses to deviance. This is an attitude which Topping (1983) also encourages, having reviewed the literature evaluating a range of provision for disruptive adolescents. He argues that very few responses to disruptive behaviour can lay claim to spectacular success. Indeed some forms of intervention would seem to make matters worse. In general, the more elaborate and expensive the intervention, the less effective it is likely to be. Such reservations should be borne in mind in the constant debates about how to increase the effectiveness of the various regimes. We should not obscure fundamental questions about the unintended, negative consequences of *any* form of intervention.

2 LEA PROVISION

In education labels abound. In institutions with rule systems, transgressors of the rules can become labelled and 'typed'. A label may be a simple description based on observed behaviour, such as 'truant' or 'disruptive', or it may be a judgement inferred from observed behaviour, such as 'disaffected' or 'emotionally disturbed' (but see Chapter 23). One purpose of labels is to give meaning to the behaviour, another is to ascribe deviants to groups seen as requiring schooling in establishments separated from mainstream provision. The most common forms of segregated provision for pupils seen to be deviant in their behaviour are special schools or units for pupils with emotional and behavioural difficulties and off-site units for disruptive pupils.

Special provision for pupils with emotional and behavioural difficulties

Since the rejection of the old statutory categories of handicap by the Education Act 1981, the term 'emotional and behavioural difficulty' (EBD) is now widely used in preference to the term 'maladjustment'. It is, however, a notoriously vague concept. Criteria for allocation to this category are wide-ranging, theories about 'causes' and philosophies of treatment are likewise diverse (see Ford *et al.* 1982, Laslett 1983). This, however, has not been an impediment to the development and expansion of provision for pupils so labelled.

'Maladjustment' was first brought into the vocabulary of statutory provision by the 1945 Regulations relating to the 1944 Education Act. During the Second World War, 'unbilletable evacuees' had helped to bring the problem of 'difficult' children to the fore and a new category for children who were seen as not well adjusted to their social environment was included in the framework for 'special educational treatment' (Bowman 1981).

There was a remarkable rise in the population of special schools from about 500 in 1950 to more than 13,000 in 1983. The sharpest increase came in the period from the mid-1960s to the mid-1970s, when numbers increased by a factor of four.

Pupils are supposed to be placed in these special schools following formal assessment and completion of a Statement under the Education Act, 1981. This procedure usually follows a history of disturbed and disturbing behaviour and in most cases it is initiated by teachers in the mainstream school which the pupil attends. The majority of these children are of secondary school age, about three-quarters are boys, and almost all come from working-class families.

The schools themselves are small, with an average of between 40 and 50 pupils, and they have a high staff–pupil ratio, 1 teacher to 6 or 7 pupils is typical. In 1983 there were 89 day schools and 131 residential schools in England and Wales.[1] Increasingly, attendance at the latter is on the basis of two-weekly or weekly boarding.

It is difficult to generalise about the nature of the pupils' problems or about educational approaches adopted in the schools. Despite many sophisticated analyses of the nature of emotional and behavioural difficulties, a simple typology persists in the literature: children are seen as experiencing either acute emotional disturbance or severe behavioural problems, or a combination of the two. Accordingly, treatment is often assumed to occupy a place on a continuum ranging from psychotherapy for emotional disturbance to behaviour modification for behavioural problems. This, however, does not seem to be reflected in practice. The last large-scale surveys (Wilson and Evans 1980, Dawson 1980) found that teachers agreed on the six most effective features of treatment: warm, caring attitudes in adult–child relationships, improvement of self-image through successes, firm consistent discipline, a varied and stimulating educational programme, continuity of child–adult relationships, and individual counselling and discussion. In this sample of schools, methods based on psychotherapy, group therapy and behaviour management were low on the list of treatments used.

These features of treatment are clearly echoed in the methods advocated for 'disruptive pupils'. This is not surprising since the only clear division between the two groups is an administrative or legislative one. Whether a pupil is labelled

EBD or disruptive and whether he or she is sent to a special school, a special unit or remains in a mainstream school can depend on arbitrary factors (Galloway 1985).

Off-site units for disruptive or disaffected pupils

The 1970s saw the sudden advent of the special unit as the preferred solution to the problems posed by pupils whose attitudes and behaviour were regarded as unacceptable. The proliferation of units, with their wide range of euphemistic titles, was a striking development during that decade. Since there has been no routine, centralised collection of statistics on these units, it is difficult to obtain accurate figures. Some indication of the rapid growth can be seen in the findings of a series of national surveys. In 1977, the DES found that in 69 local authorities there were then 239 units, with a total population of 3,962 pupils (DES 1978). In 1980, the Advisory Centre for Education published the results of its survey which indicated a unit population of 5,957 (ACE 1980). Ling and Davies (1984) found a population of about 7,000 pupils in off-site units in England and Wales. The majority of unit pupils were in the final two years of compulsory schooling, boys outnumbering girls by 3 to 2.

It is becoming evident that this new form of provision has not had the benign influence on behaviour in schools which many had hoped for. It has not, for example, reduced the use of the sanction of suspension even where units have been set up with this intention (Lloyd-Smith *et al.* 1985). This evidence, together with other evidence of the lack of effectiveness of units (Topping 1983) and arguments in favour of helping schools themselves to accommodate and deal with disruption (Steed 1985), are leading to a change of emphasis. There are signs that many local authorities are developing strategies for dealing with problem pupils which do not rely on removal to an off-site unit (Lloyd-Smith *et al.* 1985, Coulby and Harper 1985, Drew 1990).

The 1988 Education Reform Act is likely to have a significant effect on future policy. With schools effectively competing with each other for resources, the need to keep as many children on roll as possible may discourage schools from referring their problem pupils to other establishments. The increasingly popular strategy of peripatetic support teams would then become an attractive option. On the other hand, the complexities of local management of schools mean that finding funds to pay for such services will be problematic (see Chapter 31). An alternative response would be for a school to create its own on-site unit or special class in which the National Curriculum could be temporarily disapplied under Section 19 of the Act, thus allowing the operation of special, intensive programmes for disruptive or disaffected pupils. In the competitive education market, however, the existence of a unit for deviant pupils might be seen as undesirable by prospective parents.

As I write, it is too early to say what the precise effects of the Reform Act will be; though the new legislation does contain elements which are potentially harmful to children with special needs (Lloyd-Smith 1991, Swann 1991, and Chapter 31 of this vol.). Policy changes elsewhere can also conspire to put extra strains on educational provision for children labelled EBD or disruptive. In Birmingham a sudden and drastic reduction of social service day provision led to the influx into the LEA's suspension and guidance centres of young people with more serious problems than they were used to. In another authority, the closure by Social Services of all children's homes has been accompanied by increased admissions to residential special schools (Cliffe 1990).

3 COMING BEFORE THE COURTS

The minimum age of criminal responsibility in England and Wales is 10 years; the juvenile justice system makes a distinction between 'children', aged 10–14, and 'young persons', aged 14–17. The courts have a number of sanctions at their disposal, including various non-custodial orders: absolute discharge, conditional discharge, fines and deferred sentences. The custodial order now available is detention in one of the young offender institutions, which in 1988 replaced the former detention centre order and youth custody centre order. Other sanctions include the requirement to spend time at an attendance centre, the supervision order, which may involve attendance at an intermediate treatment centre, and the care order, which may entail removal to a foster home or community home.

The tension between care and control referred to earlier can be clearly seen in the operation of this system. In 1969 a new Children and Young Persons' Act was introduced with decriminalisation as one of the government's intentions. It shifted the emphasis in juvenile courts from criminal to care proceedings, it introduced a greater stress on preventive measures, and it opened the way for the greater use of community-based measures for young offenders. The Act was received with suspicion; it was criticised as being 'too soft' and some of its key provisions have never been implemented. Its effect on the sentencing policy of the magistracy was the opposite of that intended by its sponsors. The number of custodial sentences meted out in the 1970s rose more sharply than the number of offences. It led to increasing numbers of younger children being identified as 'at risk' and subsequently drawn into the juvenile justice system.

The backlash against the ostensibly liberal and reformist features of the 1969 Act found strong expression in the Criminal Justice Act, 1982. Although it encouraged the use of non-custodial sentences for young people, the Act also shortened the length of custodial sentences. The purpose of this was to make more places available in the overcrowded detention centres and borstals, which the Act renamed youth custody centres.

Initially there was a fear that shorter sentences, as little as three weeks in the case of detention centre orders, would lead to an increased use of custody as a sanction. Muncie (1984) predicted that 'the 1980s are likely to see more working-class young people having a "taste" of custody, as welfarism recedes and state authoritarianism becomes more strident' (Muncie 1984: 155). In the event the reverse trend became evident (see Table 29.1).

A number of factors are involved in this trend, including a reduction in the population aged 10–17 and a fall in the juvenile crime rate during the past decade: from 3,233 per 100,000 in 1978 to 2,878 per 100,000 in 1988. The new statutory criteria for the award of custodial sentences set out in the 1982 Act and clarified in the 1988 Criminal Justice Act, did eventually have the desired effect of encouraging the courts to seek non-custodial alternatives. The marked drop in the last five years reflects the improving access to such alternatives through the work of new interagency committees, schemes such as the DHSS Intermediate Treatment Initiative, and the extension of community service orders to 16 year olds (NACRO 1990). A further factor has been the increased use by the police of cautioning rather than prosecuting young offenders, particularly in the 14–16 year old range, a policy which was encouraged by Home Office Guidelines published in 1985. In a White Paper in 1990 (House of Commons 1990a) the government noted that the increased use of non-custodial sanctions had not been accompanied by an increase in offending by juveniles. It proposed to extend similar statutory guidelines for the sentencing of adult offenders.

4 NON-CUSTODIAL MEASURES

Attendance centres

As part of the trend towards community-based and preventive measures, the network of attendance centres has expanded. In 1988 there were 137 in England and Wales, 111 junior centres for 10–16 year olds and 26 senior centres for 17–20 year olds. The junior centres include thirteen for both boys and girls and seven for girls only. An attendance centre order can only be made on an offender who has not previously served a custodial sentence. It specifies a number of hours, usually 12–14, which have to be spent in a series of Saturday afternoon sessions consisting typically of physical education followed by recreational activities. The

Table 29.1 Juvenile offenders in custody, 1981–8

Year	No. in custody	Year	No. in custody
1981	7,900	1985	6,200
1982	7,400	1986	4,500
1983	6,900	1987	4,100
1984	6,900	1988	3,400

Source: Prison Statistics, England and Wales, 1988 (Home Office 1989b).

centres are run by police officers in their own time who attempt to 'strike a balance between the punitive and rehabilitation objectives of the attendance centre order' (Home Office 1984a: 55).

Intermediate Treatment

Intermediate Treatment (IT) came into existence as a result of the Children and Young Persons' Act, 1969, providing a court sanction which was 'intermediate' between supervision at home and custody. The term 'treatment' implied a move away from punishment, though the validity of the concept of treatment in view of what is actually carried out has been questioned (McCabe and Treitel 1983). IT is often included as a condition of a supervision order, in which case the duration of attendance is determined by the court, generally on the advice of a social worker. It will usually last for the equivalent of thirty days; the time in some cases may involve attendance in out-of-school hours, while in others day-time attendance is required.

Many young people are referred by agencies other than the courts: by schools, education welfare officers, the police, the probation service. In many cases, school-related problems feature as important reasons for referral. Kenny (1981) found in a survey of IT centres in the London Boroughs that underachievement, non-attendance and behaviour problems at school were commonly cited criteria for IT. The increasing use of these centres as an alternative to mainstream schooling has been noted and they have been criticised for their limited educational programmes and for the possible effect they have of drawing attention away from fundamental problems in schools (Beresford and Croft 1981, 1982).

Although IT can contribute to the reduction of care and custody, concern has been expressed at the 'net-widening' effects of preventive work which draws into the juvenile justice system young people who would not otherwise be involved (House of Commons Social Services Committee 1988, see also McMahon 1990). Young people who later appear before the courts may ironically be disadvantaged if they have formerly taken part in an IT programme. Their 'failure to benefit' may count against them, resulting in the process known as 'raising the tariff' when sentences are determined.

IT centres are in the main run by Social Services departments and the form the 'treatment' takes can vary greatly from one centre to another. It is essentially community-based, the main emphasis being on 'constructive activity'. This will typically take the form of activities which confront the offenders with their behaviour and enhance their understanding of its effects on others. The development of social skills, personal responsibility and the constructive use of leisure are sought through group work and individual counselling. It may also incorporate trips to pursue activities of the outward bound type.

The reconviction rate of young offenders participating in IT schemes is considerably lower than that of their peers who undergo custodial sentences. NACRO (1989) refer to monitoring at several local centres where reoffending rates of 35–

50 per cent have been recorded. These contrast with reconviction rates of 70–80 per cent among male graduates of young offender institutions.

5 CUSTODIAL MEASURES

Community homes

In 1987 there were 69,400 children in England and Wales who were in the care of a local authority. There had been a steady decline in the previous five years: the figure for 1982 was 93,200. This partly reflects the fall in the child population though the rate per thousand shows a significant drop from 7.4 in 1982 to 5.9 in 1987. About 20,000 of these children were in some form of residential provision though the policy of fostering or 'boarding out' in preference to institutional care continues to grow. In 1987 53 per cent of children in care were placed with foster parents, as compared with 42 per cent in 1982.

The majority of children in residential care are in community homes (CHs) which were created following the Children and Young Persons' Act, 1969, to replace the old 'approved school' system. Most of these children receive their education in ordinary schools but those considered to need care and control twenty-four hours a day will attend a 'community home with education on the premises' (CHE). The respective populations of CHs and CHEs in England in 1988 were 11,100 and 1,600. Despite the direct descent of community homes from the pre-1930s juvenile reformatories, via 'approved schools', only a minority of their combined population is admitted as a result of criminal proceedings: less than 10 per cent in the case of CHs and 50 per cent in CHEs. As Muncie (1984) indicates, there are problems in determining suitable aims and regimes for the mixed occupants of these institutions. A 1984 report says that CHEs 'seem uneasily poised between their essentially punitive past and their supposedly therapeutic future' (House of Commons Social Services Committee 1984: lxxxvii).

The more disturbed and disturbing children in residential care are likely to be found in the CHEs. An HMI survey of 15 boys' and 6 girls' CHEs (DES 1980) found a high incidence of health and behaviour problems, emotional disturbance and violent disruptive behaviour; almost all the children were said to be under-achievers. The most common age of entry was between 14 and 15 years and the average length of stay was from 10 months 2 weeks to 2 years for girls and from 14 months to 2 years 11 months for boys. Return to ordinary school was rare; schools were reluctant to readmit pupils.

Observation and assessment centres

Observation and assessment centres were also set up in response to the 1969 Act. They were planned as a means of carrying out a multiprofessional assessment of juvenile offenders, before making a decision about placement. The centres are also used for non-offenders for whom a place of safety order has been made (for a maximum of 28 days). Though the intention was that attendance at these centres would be short-term, many young people remain for longer than the period required for assessment. It has been suggested that observation and assessment centres have become dumping grounds for young offenders regarded as unacceptable by other institutions (Taylor *et al.* 1979). A major government report commenting on these centres and their 4,500 occupants, remarked that 'Observation and Assessment Centres are in a sense the waiting-rooms of care: too often they have become the sidings' (House of Commons Social Services Committee 1984: 1xxxvi).

Young Offender Institutions

In 1988, Home Office Prison Department provision for young offenders was unified. The former detention centres, first introduced in 1948, and youth custody centres, which began in the 1920s as 'borstals', were redesignated Young Offender Institutions (YOI). This change was connected with the trend towards shorter sentences and the fall in numbers of young people sentenced to custody. It enabled the Prison Department to 'make better use of the prison estate' (Home Office 1989a), such as converting youth custody centres into training prisons to take pressure off the acutely overcrowded adult sector of the service.

The change also simplified the sentencing of young offenders. Formerly there were two separate sentences. A detention centre order was for a minimum of three weeks and a maximum of four months. It would be served in either a junior detention centre, for 14–16 year olds, or a senior detention centre, for 17–20 year olds. The second sentence, passed on more serious offenders aged between 15 and 20, was the youth custody order where the court would fix a sentence within the range of four months to one year. The new sentence has a maximum length of 4 months for 14 year olds, and 12 months for 15 and 16 year olds. The sentence for young offenders aged 17 to 20 can vary; the average in 1989 was 12 months.

There are forty Young Offender Institutions; thirty-five are for male and five for female offenders. The average populations of different types of establishment in the year 1989/90 are shown in Table 29.2.

The total number admitted to Young Offender Institutions during 1989 was 17,674, a drop of 18 per cent on the previous year. This continued the series of annual reductions since the peak in 1985 when there were almost 30,000 admissions.

The efficacy and desirability of keeping juveniles in custody in Prison Department institutions have frequently been called into question. The evidence of success in deterring young people from further unlawful behaviour is far from impressive. The reconviction rate – that is, the proportion of those released from custody who are reconvicted within two years – is high, both for detention centres and youth custody centres, generally in the 70–80 per cent range.

Table 29.2 Young Offender Institutions, 1989/90

| Type of establishment | Closed | | Open | | Total |
	Male	Female	Male	Female	
Number of establishments	27	3	8	2	40
Average population	5,496	87	972	37	6,592

Source: Home Office 1990.

Measures such as shortening sentences or making the regimes more rigorous and demanding – the so-called 'short, sharp shock' approach (Home Office 1984b) – appear to have made little difference.

The failure of imprisonment to change the behaviour of most delinquents is one factor behind the changing sentencing pattern referred to earlier. There are further steps which could be taken to divert even more offenders away from custody. One is contained in a Bill in 1990 (House of Commons 1990b) which proposed to abolish the sentence of detention in a Young Offender Institution for boys aged 14 (the minimum age for girls is already 15). The National Association for the Care and Resettlement of Offenders (NACRO) has put forward a strong case for the next stage: a 'phased removal of 15 and 16 year olds from the custodial net' (NACRO 1989: 11).

Secure accommodation and youth treatment centres

There are some children and young people in residential care or in custody who are regarded as being so disturbed or disruptive that normal forms of residential provision are considered inadequate or unsuitable. Those who are severely emotionally disturbed, who exhibit extreme anti-social behaviour, who repeatedly abscond or who are thought to be a danger to themselves or others, are likely to be admitted into 'secure accommodation'. This is provided in certain local authority social services establishments: selected community homes with education for longer-term placements, and some observation and assessment centres for shorter periods.

In 1988 there were 41 such units in England with a total of 306 places. During the year ending in March 1988, 1,826 children had been held in secure accommodation (1,129 boys and 697 girls). The majority of the placements were for short periods – 64 per cent for less than one month – and the average age of the young people committed was 15.

In addition to these units, there are four 'youth treatment centres' administered by the DSS. These establishments, the first of which was opened in 1971, are for the long-term care and treatment of boys and girls between 12 and 19 who are severely disturbed or who have committed grave crimes.

Serious concern has been expressed about the growth of secure accommodation. A DHSS research report in 1979 pointed out that there was no evidence of an increase in disturbed or violent behaviour among children in care and no evidence that secure units were effective in reducing such behaviour (Cawson and Martell 1979, see also Muncie 1984). Despite this, and despite allegations that their use may sometimes infringe children's rights (Children's Legal Centre 1982), and also despite the extremely high cost of such provision – as much as £1,200 per inmate per week in a youth treatment centre in 1985 – the creation of more places was recommended by a House of Commons Committee (House of Commons 1986).

6 CONCLUSION

The growth in recent decades of this diverse system for dealing with young people who attract labels of deviance is striking. Although the incidence of certain forms of deviance may have increased, the capacity of the social institutions for care and control has grown at a faster rate, in a seemingly ineluctable trend. Attempts to reverse this and divert deviants into less stigmatising and more constructive forms of treatment and training are beginning to make an impact on some areas but there remain many signs of the stubborn gulf between the rhetoric of reform and the practical achievement of its aims. The rhetoric of prevention has not reduced the numbers of young people coming within the ambit of welfare and justice agencies, the system has merely expanded to accommodate new clients (those 'at risk'), who then have an increased likelihood of promotion in a deviant career. The rhetoric of care has not succeeded in decriminalising juvenile offenders, the new strategies have been grudgingly used. Measures have continued to emphasise punishment and deterrence, despite evidence of the failure of these methods. The rhetoric of 'special' provision for disaffected pupils has sometimes been a thinly disguised justification for ridding schools of their most troublesome pupils.

There has been constant questioning and argument about the various programmes and institutions provided for young deviants. The debate has principally been concerned with issues such as working philosophies, types of regime, duration of intervention, location and resourcing. The pursuit of these surface issues can easily cause us to overlook a fundamental truth, the implications of which are seldom explicitly recognised. Each of these forms of social control, however justified or necessary – whether punitive or caring, custodial or community based, segregated or integrated, preventive or deterrent, long term or short term – constitutes a stage within a deviant career. It can never be an alternative to such a career and rarely an escape route from one.

NOTE

1   Since 1983, following the implementation of the 1981 Education Act, the DES has
     not published statistics showing the population of different types of special school;
     later figures are therefore not available.

REFERENCES

Advisory Centre for Education (ACE) (1980) 'Disruptive units – ACE Survey', *Where*,
     no. 58, 6–7.
Bakal, Y. (ed.) (1973) *Closing Correctional Institutions*, Lexington: Lexington Books.
Beresford, P. and Croft, S. (1981) 'Intermediate treatment, special education and the
     personalisation of urban problems', in W. Swann (ed.), *The Practice of Special
     Education*, Oxford: Basil Blackwell.
—— (1982) *Intermediate Treatment: Radical Alternative, Palliative or Extension of
     Social Control?*, London: Battersea Community Action.
Bowman, I. (1981) 'Maladjustment: a history of a category', in W. Swann (ed.), *The
     Practice of Special Education*, Oxford: Basil Blackwell.
Cawson, P. and Martell, M. (1979) *Children Referred to Closed Units*, DHSS Research
     Report no. 5, London: HMSO.
Children's Legal Centre (1982) *Locked up in Care*, London: Children's Legal Centre.
Cliffe, D. (1990) 'An end to residential child care? The Warwickshire direction', Paper
     delivered to a conference of the National Children's Bureau, 11 October.
Cohen, S. (1972) *Folk Devils and Moral Panics*, London: MacGibbon & Kee.
Coulby, D. and Harper, T. (1985) *Preventing Classroom Disruption*, London: Croom
     Helm.
Dawson, R. (1980) *Special Provision for Disturbed Pupils: A Survey*, London: Macmillan.
Department of Education and Science (DES) (1978) *Behavioural Units: A Survey of Special
     Units for Pupils with Behavioural Problems*, London: DES.
—— (1980) *Community Homes with Education*, London: HMSO.
Drew, D. (1990) 'From tutorial unit to schools' support service', *Support for Learning 5*
     (1), 13–21.
Ford, J., Mongon, D. and Whelan, M. (1982) *Special Education and Social Control*,
     London: Routledge & Kegan Paul.
Galloway, D. (1985) *Schools, Pupils and Special Educational Needs*, London: Croom
     Helm.
Home Office (1984a) *Report of Her Majesty's Chief Inspector of Constabulary*, London:
     HMSO.
—— (1984b) *Tougher Regimes in Detention Centres*, London: HMSO.
—— (1989a) *Report on the Work of the Prison Service 1988–1989*, London: HMSO.
—— (1989b) *Prison Statistics, England and Wales, 1988*, London: HMSO.
—— (1990) *Report on the Work of the Prison Service 1989–90*, London: HMSO.
House of Commons (1986) *Social Services for Children in England and Wales, 1982–1984*,
     HC90, London: HMSO.
—— (1990a) *White Paper: Crime, Justice and Protecting the Public*, London: HMSO.
—— (1990b) *Criminal Justice – A Bill Session 1990/91*, London: HMSO.
House of Commons Social Services Committee (1984) *Session 1983/84 2nd Report:
     Children in Care, Vol. 1*, London: HMSO.
—— (1988) *Children in Care (Memoranda)*, London: HMSO.
Kenny, D. (1981) *Intermediate Treatment: Review of Policies and Practices in the London
     Boroughs*, London: GLC.

Laslett, R. (1983) *Changing Perceptions of Maladjusted Children, 1945–1981*, Portishead: AWMC.

Ling, R. and Davies, G. (1984) *A Survey of Off-Site Units in England and Wales*, Birmingham: City of Birmingham Polytechnic.

Lloyd-Smith, M. (1991) 'The Education Reform Act and special needs education – conflicting ideologies', in N. Jones and J. Docking (eds), *The National Curriculum and Integrated Pupils*, Lewes: Falmer.

——, West, J. and Richmond, J. (1985) *A Review of Suspension and Guidance Units in Birmingham*, Coventry: University of Warwick.

McCabe, S. and Treitel, P. (1983) *Juvenile Justice in the UK: Comparison and Suggestions for Change*, London: New Approaches to Juvenile Crime.

McMahon, M. (1990) ' "Net-widening" – vagaries in the use of a concept', *British Journal of Criminology* 30 (2), 121–49.

Muncie, J. (1984) *The Trouble with Kids Today*, London: Hutchinson.

National Association for the Care and Resettlement of Offenders (NACRO) (1989) Policy Paper 1 – *Phasing Out Prison Department Custody for Juvenile Offenders*, London: NACRO.

—— (1990) *Criteria for Custody (NACRO Briefing)*, London: NACRO.

Schur, E. (1978) *Radical Non-Intervention – Rethinking the Delinquency Problem*, Englewood Cliffs: Prentice-Hall.

Scull, A. (1984) *Decarceration – Community Treatment and the Deviant*, 2nd edn, Cambridge: Polity Press.

Steed, D. (1985) 'Disruptive pupils, disruptive schools', *Educational Research* 27 (1) 3–8.

Swann, W. (1992) 'Hardening the hierarchies: the National Curriculum as a system of classification', in T. Booth, W. Swann, M. Masterton and P. Potts (eds), *Curricula for Diversity in Education*, London: Routledge.

Taylor, L., Lacey, R. and Bracken, D. (1979) *In Whose Best Interests? The Unjust Treatment of Children in Courts and Institutions*, London: Cobden Trust/MIND.

Topping, K. (1983) *Educational Systems for Disruptive Adolescents*, London: Croom Helm.

Wilson, M. and Evans, M. (1980) *Education of Disturbed Pupils*, London: Methuen.

Part 7

Local authority?

Chapter 30

Voices behind the statistics
Personal perspectives on special education in Cornwall

Christopher Onions

Cornwall has the lowest proportion of children in special schools of all the LEAs in England. This fact was the starting point for this chapter, in which Christopher Onions has collected together the views of six professionals in the county: an advisory teacher, an education officer, an educational psychologist, two head teachers and a class teacher. Together they present a picture of a system of special provision that is the result of many factors that developed over a long period of time. The low level of special school placement has been influenced by geography, limited money, community minded schools and low levels of awareness of learning difficulties, but is not the result of a planned policy. Professionals also discuss Statementing, support services, in-service training, the process of making policy in Cornwall, and the impact of the 1981 and 1988 Education Acts.

1 INTRODUCTION

In 1989 the Centre for Studies on Integration in Education (CSIE) published the results of a survey carried out by Will Swann (Swann 1989). This survey compared levels of segregation in different local education authorities (LEAs) between 1982 and 1987. It revealed considerable differences between LEAs in the numbers of children being educated in separate special school provision. The county of Cornwall achieved the distinction of having the lowest percentage of children placed in its own, or out-county, special schools, of any authority in England and Wales. This fact attracted national attention at the time and caused one educational administrator to remark that their special provision was either the poorest or the best in the country, depending on how one chose to look at things. It was suggested by some that the only reason for the figures achieved by Cornwall was that being a relatively poor LEA, historically it had spent relatively little on special education compared to other authorities and that a low percentage of children in special schools should not be confused with good mainstream provision; it simply meant very little provision. A recent update of the CSIE survey, providing comparisons from 1982 to 1990, shows that Cornwall has maintained its position relative to other LEAs, with only 0.66 per cent of its children being educated in special schools (Swann 1991).

These figures raise some interesting questions. How can one LEA achieve such a low level of separate special school placements while some comparable shire authorities place two to three times this proportion of their pupils in such provision? Are children with special needs in Cornwall really receiving the provision they need? Are mainstream schools suffering undue pressure as a result of stretching their resources to maintain children with special needs in the mainstream, possibly at the expense of other children? How does a county with a large geographical area, poor road networks and a widely spread population deal with special needs which have a very low incidence, such as those of children who are blind? What are the factors that have maintained the low percentage of special school placements? Has a low educational budget led to a high demand for Statements from hard-pressed schools?

What follows is not claimed to be definitive research, it is simply the personal perspectives of people currently working in different parts of the educational service in Cornwall.

2 CHARLES: AN ADVISORY TEACHER FOR SPECIAL EDUCATIONAL NEEDS

Charles has worked for the authority for over twelve years. He came to Cornwall to work in a secondary school in an area which had a high proportion of children with special needs. He had previously worked in a special school for children with moderate learning difficulties in another part of the country. Charles moved from the secondary school to become an advisory teacher for special educational needs shortly before the implementation of the 1981 Act.

Most of the kids in the special school I came from wouldn't have appeared to have special needs put alongside the kids I was being asked to teach in mainstream when I first came to Cornwall. The expectations of some village children are still very low. You still hear people say 'He'll be all right, he'll go to work on the farm.'

I was the brand new special needs adviser – a one man band – the only contact point for the whole county. I think it's fair to say, that on the whole, awareness about special needs was pretty low. In the west of the county we had a residential school for children with moderate learning difficulties and two schools for children with severe learning difficulties. There were also some units for children with moderate learning difficulties and there was some additional staffing for primary and secondary schools who were providing for children with special needs.

If you had severe learning difficulties and you lived in the east of the county you went to a friendly local primary school, you went out-county, or you didn't go to school at all. There were a number of these children in rural areas who simply stayed at home.

The service for children with a hearing impairment was very well organised with virtually all of these children being educated in units integrated in mainstream schools. The county was very proud of its achievements in this area and was always ready to support developments of this service. In the main it's a nice, clean handicap with clear definitions and margins.

Prior to the 1981 Act there were officially only three children with visual impairments in Cornwall. One adviser for children with visual impairments was appointed and at the end of twelve months the number of children with visual impairments had grown to sixty.

Children with severe physical disabilities tended to be educated at out-county schools. Some village schools are very good at mopping up their own problems; they tend to see it as part of their community responsibility, but the local community is not always a positive factor. Children with special needs are known about well in advance of entering school and some schools take very early steps to indicate to the parents and to the authority that they are not an appropriate placement for the child. It works both ways; it's the attitude of the head teacher that is the crucial factor, and possibly how the child and his or her family are regarded in the community.

When the 1981 Act first appeared on the scene, the initial reaction of the education committee was one of shock horror at the possible financial implications – they almost declared UDI! As a relatively poor local authority, operating in a climate of financial restraint, significantly increasing the educational budget was not possible. With virtually no special schools there was not even the possibility of switching money from special schools to mainstream, as has been done in some other LEAs. Any money had to come out of the mainstream budget and this initially caused some feelings of resentment, both from teachers in mainstream and from council members. Another aspect of having very little special school provision was that there was a very small pool of expertise within the county on which to draw for developing support teaching and carrying out in-service training. The LEA had to look to bring in additional expertise from outside the county.

In 1985 the awareness of special needs within the county was very low. Apart from the service for hearing-impaired children, I think it's fair to say that the rest of the special needs provision was a bit of a jumble, with what happened to any particular child largely depending on where he or she lived in the county. Prior to the Act, some organisational improvements had been made. A divisional structure had been established with a team of advisory teachers for special needs in each division. This corresponded to the structure of the School Psychological Service. With more advisory teachers and the publicity given to the Act – both nationally, and locally through in-service training – a lot more children were thrown up as having special needs. Underresourced schools saw the Act and Statementing as a good way of getting extra resources so they started referring more children. Initially Statements were a way of throwing money at problems without any real, overall, long-term policy or planning. It was just an extension of what had existed before with a bit more money being found each year. There were schools that demonstrated very good practice and those that just didn't want to know. We had got the organisational structure for the advisory staff across the county and we had a budget that enabled us to direct training where we thought it was needed and that we could use to 'reward' good practice.

The county started to realise that simply allowing things to grow just couldn't go on so there has been a fundamental review. Up until three years ago special education had its own separate committee, but then it became a sub-committee of the education committee. There was a plan to gradually increase the number of support teachers by ten a year but all this was overtaken by LMS. As an advisory service, we've lost control over in-service training money; schools now hold their own in-service training budgets and identify their own priorities. The money for non-Statemented special needs has been devolved to the schools and we can't any longer reward good practice. I spend a lot of time dealing with formal assessments and reviews, and I'm not sure where we go from here.

3 TOM: SENIOR EDUCATION OFFICER

Tom has worked with Cornwall for the past five years. Before this he worked for an LEA which had a considerable number of special schools.

Since the 1981 Act was implemented there has been a steady growth in the number of requests for formal assessments. At first we were carrying out 250 assessments a year but currently we have 550 on the go; not all of these will result in Statements being made. We maintain Statements on about 2.4 per cent of our children. For the first three years after the Act was implemented the authority simply dealt with each case as it arose, without any overall planning, by appointing an ancillary or allocating additional teaching hours and advisory help. Where there were schools with high numbers of special needs we were able to help by improving their staffing rather than attaching help to a particular child. This was paid for out of an annual overspend on the special needs budget that was simply rolled over to the following year. In 1986/7 we got agreement for planned growth but, without any additional funding, this was still on the basis of rolling the annual overspend forward each year. We intended to add ten support teachers a year to the teaching establishment, eventually aiming to have one support teacher to every three schools but we only achieved one and a half years of this planned growth. Moves towards LMS meant that the books had to be balanced so by 1990/1 the possibility for any overspend was gone and along with it the planned growth. In fact it caused major problems. In June and July 1991 we had to review all our allocations and reduce our budget. This meant taking teaching and ancillary hours away from some children. It wasn't *just* a cost-cutting exercise however – we did find some children who we felt deserved more assistance than they were getting and where this happened we put in additional help.

We do take our review procedures for Statements very seriously. It is very well organised in Cornwall with full participation from all the relevant parties. I actually think that the review procedure is probably more important than the original Statement. You have the evidence of experience as to whether each child's needs are being met or not and overall it allows for good management of resources and planning of future needs within the education system. At first, in allocating provision through the Statementing procedure, we were able to trust to the professional judgements of the people involved. If they said a child had a particular requirement then, by and large, it was provided for. We always had a certain flexibility but with LMS that has now gone. All the money for special needs, other than the budget for Statements, is now devolved to the schools. We have to keep within our budget which means that professional judgement is no longer enough – we need to produce facts and figures to show members if we are to obtain the budget we require. Many teachers and advisers find this irksome I know, but if we can produce the information I am sure we can manage to achieve planned growth.

We are also having to introduce some control over requests for Statements. Most of our head teachers have been extremely responsible over requests for Statements but there are always one or two cynical individuals who see getting a Statement for a child as a way of getting extra resources for their school. The financial pressures on schools have perhaps been one of the reasons why this sort of request has been increasing. In future there is going to be an informal pre-assessment procedure that will have to be followed by everyone.

Cornwall is still bottom of the league table when it comes to spending on special needs but then its pretty near the bottom of the table when it comes to spending on education in general. It is essential to link the budget to planning and a key element in this is the education of elected members by demonstrating to them exactly how resources for Statemented children produce progress. It's also important for them to understand that while a child's needs may change over time, most children with Statements continue to require resources to maintain progress – they don't get better by and large. We have worked very hard to get political commitment to planned growth. We have in fact just got agreement to the planned expansion of resources for children with special needs and we hope to maintain this growth over the next few years. The attitudes have been very positive and in all the time I've been here hardly anyone has ever raised the question of special schools. People fight for their children and there is very much an attitude amongst county councillors that we should care for *all* our children.

The very small number of special school places that exist in the county (and their location) has undoubtedly influenced the way our policy towards special needs has evolved. In my previous authority you automatically thought in terms of special schools as a way of meeting a child's needs because they were there. Here that is not part of the tradition. Quite a high proportion of our special school placements are out-county. In the past the majority of these out-county placements – approaching 60 per cent I think – were children with severe physical disabilities. There were one or two children with sensory impairments whose parents wanted them to be educated at a separate special school and the rest were children with emotional and behavioural difficulties. I think that now the proportions have been reversed, with the majority of children who are placed out of county being those with emotional and behavioural difficulties. Interestingly, members have often been very keen to provide additional support for a child with emotional and behavioural difficulties to stop other children's education being disrupted; it is only in extreme cases that anyone suggests the alternative of removing the child.

I know that primary schools are feeling the increased pressures of implementing the National Curriculum and the Standard Assessment Tasks but there do seem to be far more very difficult children about at a very much younger age than there used to be, and at the moment we have no real answer. There have been some moves to get the school for children with moderate learning difficulties to take more children with behavioural problems.

Historically, children with physical disabilities have always been difficult to provide for within the county. Many of our older schools – and we have a lot of them – have very poor physical facilities in the first place: small rooms, steep stone steps, different levels, outside toilets, etc. There is also the problem of getting Health Service back-up to some remote parts of the county – physiotherapists, speech therapists, for example – but I think that in virtually all cases where parents have wanted it we have provided the facilities and staffing to enable the child to attend his or her local school – at primary level that is. We have spent as much as £20,000 to alter a school for a single child and some children have an ancillary and additional teaching time. While we do have a lot of old schools, we have built quite a few new ones and all of these have been built with access for children with disabilities in mind. We do have problems at secondary level – often a child who has been supported at the local primary school has to travel a considerable distance to a different secondary school because of access problems.

We have units for children with severe learning difficulties at primary and secondary level and there are a number of children with severe learning difficulties who attend their local schools with additional ancillary and teaching support. We also have quite a lot of unit provision for children with moderate learning difficulties throughout the county at primary level – area special classes – and rather less at secondary level and not so evenly dispersed. We also allocate support teaching – on average 0.1 of a teacher – and additional ancillary time to children with moderate learning difficulties in mainstream primary schools. Again, secondary aged children with moderate learning difficulties do rather less well with, on average, an extra hour of teaching time per week.

I think that most children for whom the LEA maintains a Statement get a good deal. We do try very hard to tailor the provision to their individual needs. The ones I am most concerned about are the children with moderate learning difficulties at secondary level. We really need to do more for them but that will require considerable extra resources. Then there are those children with behavioural and learning difficulties, who do not warrant a Statement but who nevertheless have special needs which currently the schools have to meet as best they can from within their own resources. LMS means that money for non-State-mented special needs, that we were previously able to direct towards particular schools with perhaps more than their fair share of problems, is no longer available – it's all out there and they have to make the best of it. The special needs services were not happy about this. They are worried that schools will not give children with special needs sufficient priority given all the other pressures. The next question is whether we devolve Statement money to individual schools? Philosophically the answer has to be 'yes', but there are considerable practical difficulties to be sorted out.

4 SIMON: AN EDUCATIONAL PSYCHOLOGIST

Simon has worked in three other LEAs before returning to Cornwall in a senior position.

As a Cornishman I can say that we have a saying in Cornwall: 'You look after your own'. This is very much the attitude of the members of the Education Committee. They genuinely believe that we must care for all our children and that we should care specially for our handicapped children. They are very proud of the service for children with impaired hearing and have always given a lot of support. It hasn't been too difficult building on this and getting support for children with clear handicaps and we're now getting to grips with enlisting a similar level of support for children with moderate learning difficulties and those with emotional and behavioural difficulties.

Historically, Cornwall is a poor county; there are no major industries or companies paying large rates. Amenities and facilities in many areas are limited so rateable values were low. Because there wasn't a lot of money there was never any real interest in spending it on building special schools; Cornwall invested in people rather than plant because it was seen as a cheaper way of providing. Schools here tend to be very much part of the communities in which they are based and traditionally they too have seen it as part of their role to 'look after their own'.

There have been more head teachers appointed from outside of the county but this does not seem to have made any real difference. The culture *is* changing slowly, perhaps more so in the towns than in the villages. This is partly due to people moving in from outside the area – in some parts of the county we have had considerable influxes of overspill families from the big cities up country – and partly due to changing parental styles in the country as a whole. There *is* some evidence that we are starting to get more pressure in the area of children with emotional and behavioural difficulties. Children with these problems, that can't be contained within mainstream schools with additional ancillary and/or teaching time, tend to end up going out-county. We certainly need some provision for 'emotional and behavioural difficulty' (EBD) within the county but we are not sure what is the best way to provide this. In some ways a residential special school might be the best solution but I can't see it being taken seriously.

We already had the established model of the service for hearing-impaired children which has educated children within units at mainstream schools for many years. All the children with hearing impairments are educated in mainstream schools apart from one or two where parents have specifically requested that they learn signing; the tradition here is heavily oralist. Even before the 1981 Act Cornwall had developed a lot of special unit provision within mainstream schools for children with moderate learning difficulties. We have steadily expanded this provision since the Act was implemented, not particularly because we are committed to a policy of integration but because it seemed to be the most appropriate way to provide for the needs of the children concerned. I think that given the size of the special needs budget in this county, it would have been virtually impossible to get anyone to commit the amount of money that would have been required to build a new special school. The amount of functional integration that is achieved varies from unit to unit depending upon the people involved.

I'm not committed to total integration. I think we need appropriate facilities for individual children and that we have to allow for parental choice. Many parents of children with severe learning difficulties, for instance, prefer their children not to be in mainstream secondary schools, even within unit provision, similarly with some parents of children with physical disabilities – and we do place a considerable number of children with physical disabilities out-county. I know the disadvantages of out-county schools but for some children they do have a lot to offer. One advantage is that it is possible to pick the school to match the needs of the child. In the previous authority I worked in, on more than one occasion, a child ended up going to the LEA's special school that was not as appropriate a placement as it might have been, whereas when you have virtually no special schools you have a choice of a range of out-county facilities.

We have political commitment to the planned growth of the special needs budget and the extra money that is in the pipeline has been earmarked for Statemented children with moderate learning difficulties, particularly those at the secondary level. At the moment a secondary age child with moderate learning difficulties receives, on average, one hour extra teaching a week. We're looking to increase this to two hours. It doesn't sound a lot but if you have, say, fifteen children in a secondary school it's an increase from 0.5 of a teacher to a full-time teacher and that makes quite a lot of difference.

The size of the county and the spread of the population does cause problems, as does the poor road system. You have to remember, it's further from the southwest to the north-east of the county than it is from London to Birmingham and there are no motorways. It means that support staff spend a lot of time in the car, perhaps two hours a day or more. It makes specialisms for educational psychologists across the county difficult; people really have to work on a patch basis. It does mean that support services have to organise their priorities very carefully and children with Statements will obviously tend to come first.

5 TOBY: A COMPREHENSIVE SCHOOL HEAD TEACHER

Toby took up an appointment as head of a secondary modern school in 1977 and supervised the transition to a comprehensive school in September 1978.

I inherited a good secondary modern school with an identified group of children with special needs. The head of special needs argued strongly for retaining the separate group because of the level of needs; they were certainly much greater than anything I had encountered within mainstream school before. I was very keen to see the breaking down of the grammar/secondary modern boundaries and wanted to see mixed-ability teaching, particularly in the first year, as did the majority of my staff. It was the head of special needs who argued that the children with special needs required protection and that they would be lost in mixed-ability groups. These were children with moderate learning difficulties and they would certainly have been in special schools in my previous authority. Here it didn't really occur to me to think in terms of special school placement, although undoubtedly I might have done if there had been one just down the road.

In 1978 I was challenged by parents asking for two children with Down's Syndrome and a child with brain damage to attend the school. Parental choice was the important factor, not lack of alternative provision and the authority provided the support they needed. It increased the pressure on us to have a special group alongside the mixed-ability classes. The parents of these children felt far happier with this arrangement, as did my head of special needs. We made a virtue out of necessity and it has provided benefits for some other children who we have been able to withdraw for particular subjects over given periods of time.

We tried to move towards greater functional integration of these children – including them in the mixed-ability teaching groups with extra support – but it caused considerable parental anxieties and we reverted to the separate class. Unfortunately, this experiment served to rather upset things. The children with special needs themselves felt they had failed in some sort of way and returning them to the special class somehow served to make them more visible and less integrated than they were before within the school. With hindsight I think we should have persisted with trying to make it work. The mainstream staff were very positive about the experiment and we very much want to move towards mixed-ability teaching for all. It is perhaps those with the special needs background and the parents of the children who have the greatest reservations, but I think that we should make another attempt next year.

The 1981 Act caused us no particular anxieties; we felt we were already doing what was required. We had people coming to visit us from other authorities to see how children with heavy special needs were coping in a comprehensive school. The Act really didn't bring about any major changes for us. There were rather more formalities and perhaps a little less flexibility in getting resources but where the children with clear special needs were concerned – those who warrant a Statement – we have more or less been given what we need. We have 4 per cent of the children in this school with Statements and for them we get reasonable provision. It's the next 5 to 10 per cent who are suffering – the children who display difficult behaviour and low attainments. Obviously they do benefit from the extra provision given to those children with Statements, but without specific recognition and provision for these children it is very difficult to plan ahead. What do you do when the child to which the provision is attached moves? How can you commit some of the provision to help with other children if the needs of the child for whom it is provided vary from day to day in an unpredictable way?

In Years 10 and 11 we have been able to achieve quite a bit – practical work, small teaching groups, adapted curriculum that kind of thing – as a result of Technical and Vocational Educational Initiative (TVEI) money but Years 6 to 9 we don't have this flexibility and with all the other demands our budget is fairly tightly stretched.

6 ROBERT: A PRIMARY SCHOOL HEAD TEACHER

Robert is the head teacher of a primary school in a small town. The town has in the past taken its share of overspill families from London and Birmingham. His school is in an area that has a relatively high proportion of children with special needs. He has worked in Cornwall since 1971 and has been head of his current school since 1977.

Prior to the 1981 Act I wasn't conscious of children at this school having particularly severe special needs – possibly there weren't the problems then or perhaps our awareness was lower and we didn't focus the same degree of attention upon them. Basically, in those days, if you bent the Educational Psychologist's ear long enough you'd get ancillary provision. This caused a considerable unevenness of provision between schools – the arbiters were the head teacher's views, the test results and the budget. One or two children went to the Area Special Class but in the main, prior to the 1981 Act, responses tended to be informal and flexible.

At the time the Act was implemented I had anxieties that it would slow things up – which it did – I also thought that we couldn't have any more special needs than we already had. I think we do take more children with special needs now. It is more clear cut in the case of the physical and sensory disabilities, the assumption was that children with learning difficulties were what you dealt with anyway so it is more difficult to say for them.

After the Act there were a considerable number of training courses relating to special needs and this certainly raised people's awareness about children with special needs and I think that this put them under more pressure. Whereas before people had assumed that they would have these children in their classes and that they would get along as best they could, the post-Act awareness raising made them feel guilty about things that they weren't providing. We've certainly had more of the hard handicaps than we would otherwise have had but the Statement has provided the resources and support to enable us to feel we are coping and giving these children a good deal.

The staff certainly feel under more pressure – whatever the truth of the matter they perceive that they are being asked to handle more children with more difficult behaviour now than before the Act was implemented. Whether this is as a result of the Act or whether there are just more difficult children in the system is hard to say. Perhaps too, the increased sensitivities of teachers to criticism and the demands being placed upon them by the National Curriculum have made them more aware of children who interfere with the teaching process.

Certainly the lack of special school alternatives has meant that teachers have battled more valiantly than they might otherwise have done with children with behavioural difficulties. I don't think that we would have tried so hard with some children if we knew that a separate system existed. If it isn't there you don't think about it, you think about what you need in order to be able to cope. These children cause staff the greatest concern.

In the past, we have had quite a good relationship with the authority and the needs of the school have been recognised in the staffing and ancillaries provided. We've appreciated the support we've started to get from the special needs advisory teachers – regular contact with someone from outside helps people to feel that they *are* doing the right thing.

Local management of schools, the introduction of the National Curriculum, the Standard Assessment Tasks (SATs) have all served to heighten confusion and worries. The allocation of funds under LMS is causing great concern. Will it be fair? What about contingencies? When it comes to the National Curriculum when should it be disapplied? We have children for whom completing the SATs would present major difficulties, for them and their teachers, but it seems we can't exempt them from the SATs without disapplying the curriculum. But if the children undertake the SATs and don't do terribly well how will that be seen by others outside the school? All of this is making teachers very unsure about the future.

7 RACHEL: A PRIMARY SCHOOL TEACHER

Rachel is a teacher in a village primary school which has its share of children with social problems and children with moderate learning difficulties. She has worked in Cornwall for three years. Before that she worked in a number of special schools in another authority.

A lot seems to be done for children who have Statements and clear disabilities: specialised equipment, alterations to buildings, extra teaching time, additional ancillary hours. I'm not sure that the authority has really got itself organised in what it does about the children who have ongoing learning difficulties. Specialist teaching time is all very well but it's not what I really need. You only get this help for part of the time. What tends to happen is it just leaves you feeling more helpless because you feel that you can't really do anything for the child when the help isn't there. I would much rather have a full-time ancillary and someone who visited the school on a regular basis to help me plan what to do with the child over the next week or fortnight and with whom I could discuss any problems that had arisen. I could use the ancillary as an extra pair of hands in the classroom either to supervise the work of the child or to supervise other children while I worked with him or her. That way the child has continuity of support and provision as well as the professional input.

I think that the lack of special schools makes us think about special needs in a different way: because they aren't there you aren't tempted to think that a child might be better off elsewhere. On the other hand, in my previous authority the special schools provided a pool of expertise on which mainstream schools could draw. They provided a sort of Portage Service[1] for schools, with a teacher from the special school visiting on a regular basis to help with ideas and materials. There have to be clear goals and it has to be clear that the responsibility for the teaching of the child remains with the class teacher, otherwise there is a danger that you simply create another 'hit and run' peripatetic service like the old remedial teachers.

I think that the children with a visible disability, whether it's sensory or physical, do very well out of being integrated into mainstream schools, as do the children with severe learning difficulties. They all gain so much from the social contact and the incidental learning that goes on in a mainstream environment. The authority seems to be prepared to put in the money that is required to make it work. It is the children with the less clear-cut problems that concern me. I've got a boy in my class at the moment who is going to be formally assessed. Apart from the fact that it will take nine months and he needs the help now I'm not sure that I am going to get the help that I need. I know what I need. He has considerable learning difficulties but his behaviour is also extremely difficult and the two needs are interrelated. I need a full-time ancillary because his behaviour is so unpredictable and disruptive to other children and for much of the time he can only do something if there is an adult nearby. I have some idea of how to teach him, as I have considerable experience of working with children with special needs. Even so, I feel I need regular support and back-up from someone else who knows about children like this to help plan his work. I shouldn't be left on my own. In a small school everyone now has so much to do there is no real time to get regular support from another member of staff. If I feel like this I wonder how other teachers feel who have less experience of teaching children with these sorts of problems.

Of course, here there isn't a special school base to draw on, but I wonder whether something could be set up, based on the school clusters with a teacher attached to the staff of a school so they had a base, but supporting teachers and children in other schools.

8 REFLECTIONS

Pinning down exactly how one LEA manages to provide for special needs without resorting to separate special school provision is far from easy. What follows are my own personal views as a parent of children attending Cornish schools, as a husband of someone who teaches in a Cornish primary school, and as an independent child psychologist and educational adviser who has worked with children with special needs and their parents and who has also undertaken in-service training in the area of special needs with teachers from Cornish schools.

It is not my impression that there is a burning commitment to some ideal of integration, either within the Education Committee or amongst the Education Officers. Although there are some individuals who believe that it is no longer morally defensible to segregate those with special needs, there are others who genuinely believe that if more money was available in Cornwall that some additional segregated special provision should be created, notably for children with emotional and behavioural difficulties. Certainly the relatively limited amount of cash available within the county for capital projects has served to limit the development of separate special schools. Geography has also played a part. Faced with limited funds and the choice of building three separate special schools to cover the county (and even then transport for some children would still have been difficult) or developing units attached to existing mainstream schools, it made practical sense to develop unit provision. Once you have geographical integration, social and functional integration at least become possibilities.

Old ideas of community and 'looking after your own' which are still very strong in many parts of Cornwall (although not all) have helped. It was relatively easy for people to extend this philosophy to accept the idea of a child with major special needs attending a local school. At the same time, the lack of any tradition of special school provision in the county has meant that there has been a very limited pool of expertise on which to draw to build up support services. The limited finance available to the LEA has meant that developing these services has been a slow process. Other demands for educational change, not to mention the need to improve school buildings have also meant that the competition for the available funds has been high.

How well does it work? This is very difficult to assess. What criteria does one use? Some children may not receive physiotherapy or speech therapy as regularly as they might do in a specialised school, but they have access to a mainstream curriculum and all the stimulation of a mainstream school and contact with their neighbourhood peer group. Certainly those children with major special needs seem to be very well provided for. The LEA takes provision for these clearly definable children very seriously, Statements are genuinely tailored to the needs of the individual, and the wishes of the parents and child are given a high priority. For those children with less clearly defined disabilities the provision appears to be much more hit and miss. These are the children with moderate learning difficulties and those children who display difficult behaviour. It is becoming increasingly difficult to obtain Statements for these children. At primary level the provision is much better than it is at the secondary level. The LEA is aware of this and is attempting to improve the provision at secondary level. At the same time, local management of schools has meant that the LEA's central resources have had to be devolved to schools and the limited facilities that the special needs support services had available to provide support for these children have been further eroded.

As in most areas of the country it is the children with emotional and behavioural difficulties who present the greatest challenge. For those with Statements the choice is usually additional ancillary and/or teaching time and if this is not sufficient, out-county placement. Again, the difficulties of making provision become greater at secondary level and there are some children who complete their secondary education on home tuition; it is too late for out-county placement and without local facilities there is currently no other choice.

Certainly, special needs has a high priority in Cornwall both with members and officers within the LEA. It is clear from Cornwall's experience that integration is not simply a matter of resources: attitudes and geography play a major role, but the severe financial constraints under which the LEA has to operate have made it increasingly difficult for it to improve the provision for those children who do not have clearly definable disabilities. What further pressure will be produced by LMS, the implementation of the National Curriculum and the Standard Assessment Tasks remains to be seen.

NOTE

1   The Portage Service is a method of providing home-based support to parents of children with learning difficulties and disabilities. A teacher visits parents on a regular basis and provides teaching programmes for the parents to use with their child between visits.

REFERENCES

Swann, W. (1989) *Statistics of Segregation: LEAs Reveal Local Variations*, London: Centre for Studies on Integration in Education.
—— (1991) *Variations between LEAs in Levels of Segregation in Special Schools, 1982–1990*, London: Centre for Studies on Integration in Education.

Chapter 31

Reviewing provision for special education in Avon

Tony Kerr

In this chapter Tony Kerr describes the review of special education provision in Avon, which he coordinated in 1990/1. He provides details of the background to the review, the terms set by the Education Committee, the establishment of eleven task groups to produce reports on aspects of special education, and the outcome of the review process.

1 PROLOGUE

For years we had been discussing the possibility of a review of special education yet somehow the time was never right. Every new change in the agenda provided good reasons to let things settle down before trying to look too far ahead. It seemed wasteful to invest time and money devising plans when new demands always loomed on the horizon. In any case, with only a single officer to oversee the whole system, there was plenty to do just keeping it all running.

Yet, I suppose I should have seen it coming. Grumbling about the confused state of special education was such a comfortable routine for us in Avon – like chatting about the weather – that we took it in our stride when, in 1990, the new Director said he was going to sort things out. New Directors always say those kinds of things, after all. It's expected of them. I even joined in enthusiastically when he led a planning seminar of senior officers and we all spent an enjoyable day identifying vital but impossible tasks for someone else to do. As the list got longer, I began to get uneasy. Was this what he had in mind when he said he might be releasing me from some of my normal duties to spend more time on the review? A fortnight later I was seconded to coordinate the task, and the phone was already hot with people wanting to know when they would see some results.

2 BACKGROUND

Avon is a large shire county with a bit of everything. Rich farmland below the Mendip hills, huge chemical industries by the Severn, Bristol's urban sprawl reaching out to the high-tech corridor near the M4 and M5, nearly linking up with Bath's Georgian splendour – all this provides a background for growing prosperity as new industries and tourism replace traditional aircraft, shipping and tobacco.

At the time of writing, in May 1991, Labour is just the largest party on the hung council, where a handful of Democrats hold the balance between two strongly conflicting philosophies. Last year's charge-capping debate put on the agenda such major cuts as closing all nursery provision, and this year's process has been just as difficult.

Education in Avon

The education system embraces two-teacher village schools and huge urban comprehensives, with 127,000 pupils in over 450 maintained schools, and 70,000 students and adults in the eight FE Colleges.

In the 1970s and 1980s the Special Education Sub-committee oversaw a development programme generous compared with the other nine authorities in our audit 'family', a situation which has left some scope for redeploying resources but which has also attracted the attention of the accountants. September 1989 saw £25 million spent on special educational provision, including the thirty-one special schools and about sixty special units. In addition there are still special classes, and eight forms of further education provision, as well as a dozen or more different support services, yet in September 1989, 225 children were placed in out-county residential schools at a cost of £3.5 million. Overall, the county's provision was very uneven and still reflected some aspects of the different systems we inherited from Bristol, Somerset and Gloucestershire after local government reorganisation in 1974.

Together with the two universities, the polytechnic and a college of higher education, the county has developed a wide range of in-service courses relevant to special educators, but taken as a whole the in-service training available in the county was not coherent.

There has been a real will to change, and to develop policy jointly with the major partners in health, social services and the voluntary sector. This led to the county being chosen as one of three authorities by the DES/London University project 'Developing Provision for Special Educational Needs'. Avon's experience of this project provided a useful basis for the present review, since some of the key issues had already been identified.

Why review?

There were four reasons why it became important to conduct a review of special educational provision and services in the county. First, there have been enormous changes since 1983, the year that the 1981 Education Act implemented just a few of the Warnock proposals. The Education Acts of 1986 and especially 1988 have knocked us sideways. The 1986 Disabled Persons Act has added yet more duties though without much publicity. There is a vast agenda introduced by the

Children Act 1989, which will include education supervision orders for truanting pupils, a register of all children with disabilities, the inspection of residential schools and a joint review with the social services department of all county services to under fives. We were attempting to respond, piecemeal, to a flurry of DES circulars on special schools and Statementing procedures and on the implications of the National Curriculum and financial delegation. As a recent House of Commons Select Committee noted:

> Some of the effects of the 1988 Education Reform Act on the 1981 Education Act are as yet uncertain and not recognised. There is no guarantee under the 1988 Act that children with the wider range of special educational needs in mainstream schools will receive the support and extra provision they require to gain access to the National Curriculum.
>
> (House of Commons 1990)

Second, just like other LEAs, we have experienced problems which have shown us that our provision wasn't meeting some of the most acutely felt needs. There were increasing demands for support to deal with behaviour problems, repeated failures to release resources from the boarding schools' budget, a rising demand for Statements, and mounting administrative burdens for everyone.

Third, the pattern created by fifteen years of *ad hoc* response was so confusing that no single person understood all aspects – certainly not those who oversaw the whole rich tapestry. Most of the provision was excellent in itself, but as a whole the pattern represented a set of solutions to separate problems, some of which had long since changed. There was growing confusion about what was available for particular children and young people. The local authority policy on integration was neither clear nor widely known.

Last, we had to do it anyway. There is a legal duty for LEAs to review their arrangements for special educational provision, though little guidance had been available on what this should involve. DES Circular 11/90 has now rectified this. It mentions some general issues that 'LEAs will wish to look at' – the overall balance of provision, the level of in-service and other training necessary for all maintained schools to respond effectively to the needs of children with SEN, the impact of the National Curriculum and of the LEA's curriculum policy statement, the broad range of staffing appropriate to pupils with different degrees of learning difficulty. It also gives some quite specific aims: 'to move towards a coherent pattern'; 'to secure that every county and voluntary school is able to call upon a teacher with specific responsibility for advising other members of staff on pupils with special needs' (DES 1990a).

The pressures, then, for a coherent review of policy and provision were building up from the beginning of the 1980s. By the end of the decade they were overwhelming.

3 1989: GATHERING MOMENTUM

At the end of 1988 the Policy and Service Review Sub-committee made special education one of two priorities for 1989, which moved the subject up the officers' crowded agenda. Representatives from the Schools and Post-schools branches, the Advisory Service, Psychology and other support services, met to draft some principles. These were adopted in June 1989 by the sub-committee as a basis for further planning. They weren't perfect but represented a great step forward from the passing mention of integration in the general booklet for parents that was all we had to go on previously.

In September 1989, the same committee had a lively cross-party debate, and accepted that new support systems would be needed before any savings could be made by more efficient use of the resources devoted to out-of-county placements and other reductions in the use of segregated provision. Their priorities for review included:

- better support in mainstream schools and colleges;
- reorganising into six support-service areas (sectors) with more mainstream units;
- rationalising special school provision, paying particular attention to boarding schools, the primary/secondary split, and a unified hospital/home tuition service;
- better administrative systems;
- partnership with health, social services and parents' organisations.

In November 1989 a new Director arrived with a strong commitment to developing coherent policy in special education (and in many other areas). He announced a stop to *ad hoc* reorganisations and called for a single coherent philosophy for special education, properly linked to the wider work of the department, before any major decisions were made.

Early in February 1990, the Director led a seminar at which a dozen senior officers and a seconded head drew up an outline plan for the next stage of the review. A new brief was developed and approved in March by the Policy and Service Review Sub-committee. One of the members expressed both the need for action and the prevailing mood by saying 'I've been asking for this for eight years, and I must say the plans all look very interesting – I do hope I live to see the results.'

Setting the terms of the review

The official purpose of the review was 'to achieve the best match between needs and resources in the area of special education in Avon'. The end result was to be 'a system of provision which meets special educational needs as effectively as is possible within the framework of policy and resources decided by the County Council'. These are succinct long-term aspirations but are hard to measure precisely, so we needed to specify some of the more tangible outcomes the committee wanted to see. They asked for:

- a statement of Entitlements to put alongside the Principles for meeting special educational needs;
- clear recommendations for the development of services and provision;
- outline implementation plans with options where appropriate.

They also agreed that officers would need to:

- establish a more complete picture of the scale, scope and nature of the need for special education over the next ten to fifteen years;
- chart the scale, scope, nature and quality of current provision, and identify the strengths, the key factors that underlie them, and the main obstacles to more effective provision;
- describe a realistic system of possible provision in the light of best practice elsewhere, of the aspirations of those who provide the services, and of the expectations of those for whom they are provided;
- draw up a menu of costed options for change, based on feasible schedules for implementation, and specify the benefits and risks of each option.

All the above were to be carried out 'in such a way as to generate and build on the widespread support necessary for sustained and effective development of Avon's practice on special education', an important recognition of the need to avoid DES-style, top-down change.

4 THE REVIEW STARTS

Despite our pleadings that it was impossible, the Director of Education wanted results to be delivered by the end of October 1990, because the budget process would need to start in November, and preliminary thoughts would be needed by then or another year would go by without action.

The review was to be very open. A poster setting out its structure and the mechanisms for consultation was sent to all schools shortly after the sub-committee meeting in March 1990, although within a couple of months the possibility of charge-capping affected our timetable and a new poster was circulated.

As the review developed it had four distinct phases. March to August 1990 involved gathering information and preparing initial proposals. This was the stage for which I was the coordinator. The proposals were to be refined in the autumn of 1990, then sent out for consultation together with a detailed review of special schools in early 1991 with the final implementation phase starting in April 1991.

We started by setting up a steering-group of a few officers. We wanted to have a broad group to gain widespread support, commitment and credibility, but with only seventeen weeks to the summer holidays we couldn't see how to do it. It was difficult enough getting officers to postpone other work so that they could contribute, and we never saw as much of the advisers as we would have liked because of all their new commitments to school reviews. So we settled for about half-a-dozen people, and this team took on the job of setting up the task groups, agreeing their briefs, identifying links and overlaps in their work and finally combining their proposals into a coherent whole.

Next, we had to find the right 150 people quickly for the eleven task groups. This was frantic, but very rewarding because so many of those we approached said 'great – at long last, I'm with you, let's get going'. The teacher unions were helpful in suggesting interested and knowledgeable practitioners. Finding officers and advisers able to commit time at such short notice was much harder and several groups had to cope with changes of group leader as people were pulled off to deal with plans for charge-capping. We had hoped to use as leaders people trained in a particular groupwork approach ('Coverdale') that was beginning to be adopted widely throughout the authority, but the timescale made this impossible.

The task groups

We set up eleven multidisciplinary task groups to work on tasks established by the Education Sub-committee. These covered the following areas:

- Policy.
- Assessment.
- Units and mainstream support.
- Out-of-school provision.
- Day special schools.
- Residential provision.
- Under fives.
- Management of special educational needs services.
- Information technology.
- Curriculum and professional development.
- Monitoring processes.

They are widely felt to have been very successful because of the enormous efforts put in by all the teachers, lecturers, parents, governors, officers, psychologists, welfare and careers officers, health and social services colleagues and others too numerous to mention. Once people realised that there really was no preconceived agenda, and that the authority was completely dependent on them for a high-quality product, people rolled up their sleeves and got to work with incredible energy. I found it an exciting and satisfying process to coordinate.

The first group worked on broad issues of policy and definition. They provided a statement of intent on equality of opportunity and entitlement for all, a policy for integration, a definition of special educational needs. They produced an interim policy paper for the Policy and Service Review Sub-committee in June

1990, in which members were asked to choose one of three options so that further plans could be prepared with this in mind:

- Full integration by the year 2000:
  An uncompromising commitment and a clear timetable.
- The consumer/market led approach:
  Providing what parents and young people ask for, as far as resources permit. Members were reminded that this could be an expensive strategy, and the implications were spelled out: parallel systems would be required for most types of need, with separate special schools, mainstream units and in-class support; planning would be difficult in a system where an advance in the field of treatment or provision could lead to very large swings of demand. The approach, however, would clearly be in line with the trend to consumer-led services which has been supported by the county council.
- 'Think total – build piecemeal':
  An intermediate strategy, where the assessed need of the child, young person or adult would always be the starting point, but officers would be constantly alert for opportunities to redirect resources to integrated placements. The aim would be to move as rapidly towards an integrated system as is compatible with the clear approval of those who use the services involved, or, in the case of children, of their parents.

The committee's discussion made the contradictions of the second option clear. Members chose the third option.

The Policy Task Group also produced a definition of special needs as gaps between what is and what ought to be, and they prepared a consultation paper on Entitlements which was distributed to all heads, governing bodies and members of the Reference Group in June 1990 for comments by November.

A second group addressed the issue of assessment, and was both swift and practical in producing some long-needed drafts of suggested criteria for beginning a Section 5 assessment, of forms to bring the informal stages up to date, and of ways of handling the Statement process more smoothly. They were helped in this work by strong links with the local umbrella group Supportive Parents for Special Children (see Chapter 17).

Another cluster of tasks concerned special educational provision. Separate groups worked on units and mainstream support; residential special school provision; day special school provision; out-of-school provision and provision for under fives. These were the groups producing the meat of the proposals. They were encouraged to be open and honest, even if that meant they didn't reach consensus, or their proposals were uncomfortable for the LEA. They took advantage of both these freedoms.

A further cluster of tasks was about the Education Department's role in managing, monitoring and developing education: management of the education service; information technology; monitoring processes, curriculum and professional development. These groups had to have one eye on what the previous four were developing, and the other on developments in the department or the DES – such as the constraints of restructuring, the cuts in government training grants, the National Curriculum assessment arrangements. The Information Technology Task Group decided to focus on curriculum aspects, since the broader LEA-wide ones depended on so many factors outside the review, and they were pleased to see that their own suggestions matched so closely those of HMI when they produced their booklet on special educational needs in the 'Education Observed' series (DES 1990b).

The Reference Group

We compiled a Reference Group to receive draft proposals from the task groups and to subject them to informal scrutiny at an early stage. The group consisted of people in schools, colleges, university departments, education support services, special classes, voluntary organisations, parents' groups, teachers' organisations and community groups. Unfortunately this did not work as well as we had hoped because the new timetable forced on us by charge-capping made it harder to find time to consult.

Pulling it together

We were fortunate that a new Assistant Director joined the authority in July 1990 to take joint responsibility for the previously separate branches of Schools and Colleges. As the restructuring had been delayed, he was able to devote more time than would otherwise have been possible to the review, and chaired the steering group. As a result we avoided producing the kind of document that makes sense to a small group but doesn't fit the overall priorities of the department, and our report had much greater authority and a higher profile than would otherwise have been possible. As I watched it being sold to heads by key members of the management team, instead of special education 'specialists', I was sure it would avoid the fate of some other reviews where an intellectually impeccable glossy document has gathered dust because it isn't owned by people with the power to implement it.

5 OUTCOMES

In the spring of 1991, a summary of the proposals from each task group was collected and circulated (Avon County Council 1991). Rather than list the proposals from each group in detail I will discuss some of the more fundamental policy issues which emerged. Inevitably the final report represented a compromise between the views of the various people involved in the task groups. For example, the definition of special educational needs that went into the final report had a more traditional flavour than some of us had intended. It was regarded as a broad concept relating to a student's disability of mind or body and to behavioural, emotional and learning difficulties.

Entitlements

The Principles and Entitlements paper was written during the course of the review and had received broad support. It started with general principles or 'assumptions' which included:

- a right of access for all people to equivalent learning opportunities regardless of race, gender, disability, class, religion, creed, age, sexual orientation, stage of development or other personal circumstances;
- an equal esteem for all people as learners, regardless of race, gender, disability, class, religion, creed, age, sexual orientation, stage of development or other personal circumstances;
- an assumption that children learn better and develop more fully if parents and professionals work in partnership on a basis of equality, and that all students should be involved in negotiating their own learning, either directly or, if necessary, through advocates.

It went on to specify what various constituencies in education such as children and young people, adult students, teachers, parents and governors, could expect from the education service 'relating to Special Educational Needs in the county of Avon'. For example, children and young people are entitled to prompt and appropriate assessment and where relevant 'a Statement of Special Educational Needs which always considers the appropriateness and availability of main-stream provision'. They are entitled to expect a whole-school policy and a desig-nated teacher with expertise. Teachers were entitled to 'resources and support ... to provide high quality learning experiences for students'. Parents have a right for their preferences to be 'seriously considered' and to expect 'support and assist-ance in advocating for their child's needs'. Governors were entitled to 'support and guidance', access to information and training and adequate funding. Given the flavour of these proposals it is not surprising that the review document noted 'widespread support ... provided resources could be made available'.

Integration policy

Early in the review process the Education Committee adopted the 'think total – build piecemeal' approach to integration. We asked for a reduction in special school placement but anticipated the retention of some special schools. The special school task group agreed that:

- integration was desirable but, in any scheme moving towards integration, the provision for the pupil should be demonstrably as good as currently provided by Avon special schools;

- special schools should be the agencies through which resources (finance and some staffing) are delivered. They should be centres of curriculum expertise.

Pupils with Statements would normally be on the roll of a special school and resourced through it. Between the ages of 3 and 7 they would attend a local mainstream nursery or infant school with a resource base. From 7–16 a mainstream school would be the place for children who could follow 'a mainstream curriculum with support', otherwise they would attend a special school.

It was felt that some residential provision would be retained for children with physical disabilities and sensory impairments and severe learning difficulties, though the amount could be reduced by local hostel arrangements to allow students to attend day-special and primary and secondary schools. It was felt that the four residential schools for emotional and behavioural difficulties should be retained.

Devolution

The task group on units and mainstream support proposed that special education policy should be based on five levels of provision across the county. These would be:

- School.
- Network/cluster (containing one or two comprehensives and feeder primaries).
- Sector (containing resource bases and day-special schools).
- Combined sector (containing resource bases for two or three sectors).
- Whole county (to cater for low incidence special educational needs).

The devolution of resources is a central part of our strategy to meet needs with a minimum of fuss and bureaucracy. We want to move away from the centralised allocation of relatively small amounts of money by those who cannot know the children in question, to a system under greater local control but subject to central monitoring for quality and meeting of agreed targets. This is easier to envisage than to create, and we realise that much detailed negotiation remains to be done.

Assessment procedures

We need to streamline our systems radically if we are to get anywhere near the six-month target mentioned in Circular 22/89 (DES 1989), let alone promote the kind of genuine partnership we and the parent organisations all agree is necessary. We hope to promote a shift away from assessments which are little more than requests for funding to those which focus on overcoming barriers to learning and achievement. A computer system is long overdue, and will be essential to the coordination with health, social services and the voluntary bodies.

Support services

The review did not develop detailed proposals for support services. Some realignment will be required and they have been asked to show how they can provide some services (such as those which are non-statutory) financed more directly from school or college budgets.

6 REFLECTIONS

The review achieved its key aim of devising and gaining support for a new integration policy framework. We achieved the main tasks we had been set despite the impact of major educational changes during the work of the review. We convinced people that the review was valuable and the process was widely owned within and beyond the Education Department. People from very different backgrounds came together, established understanding and developed concrete proposals. Members supported our process and were realistic in what they expected from us. In the end we gathered much useful information about our special education service which we had never previously pulled together and which was a necessary basis for policy decisions.

We feel we managed successfully the handovers between phases of the review from information gathering to eventual implementation. The material from the first stage is still being used in the third and fourth stages. Those who started the process are able to see their contribution used and built on.

We provided a structure that enables special school heads to show that far from being diehard opponents of all integration they have some radical ideas for change, and will carry them forward if the authority does its bit too. It was noteworthy that the proposal to amalgamate three hospital schools, and transfer two of their special needs units to mainstream sites, came from three heads. Two of them were only acting heads, and all three were aware of the difficulties for their careers that would follow from their own proposal. Likewise, it was the governors of a school for pupils with severe learning difficulties who wanted to move their assessment nursery to a mainstream site to ensure both maximum integration and better opportunities for thorough assessment.

The review process did run into a number of difficulties. We had to change the whole basis of the review in mid-stream and rewrite the timetable which was very trying. We didn't find the officer/adviser time to do the tasks as planned. However hard I cajoled and however clearly the Director expressed his support, people were very overcommitted in the education service. Much of the data we needed was impossible to obtain. The mass of figures we did have were not always reliable and were hard to process. Coordination with other key tasks for the department such as restructuring, charge-capping, reorganising into sectors, took much time and energy. I felt it was important that correspondence was answered promptly, but the volume meant that I was sometimes diverted from more central tasks. It was hard to incorporate the FE perspective fully, despite having several FE people contributing.

We are now busy consulting on some parts of the plan and filling in the details on others. We had to balance our desire to tie up loose ends and produce a comprehensive review document with the reality that in a time of rapid change politicians want broad answers immediately. There is no point spending another few weeks fine-tuning the figures or getting yet more views if it means you miss the budget deadline.

It is very encouraging that one of the two key Principal Education Officer posts in the new departmental structure has a main responsibility for leading the implementation of the review recommendations, as well as for overseeing the production of more detailed plans.

REFERENCES

Avon County Council (1991) *The Review of Special Educational Needs Provision in Avon*, Bristol: County of Avon.

Department of Education and Science (DES) (1989) *Assessments and Statements of Special Educational Needs: Procedures within the Education, Health and Social Services*, Circular 22/89, London: DES.

—— (1990a) *Staffing for Pupils with Special Educational Needs*, Circular 11/90, London: DES.

—— (1990b) *Education Observed: Special Needs Issues*, A Survey by HMI, London: HMSO.

House of Commons (1990) *Staffing for Pupils with Special Needs*, Education, Science and Arts Committee, Fifth Report, London: HMSO.

Chapter 32

Integration policy in Newham, 1986–90

Linda Jordan

Linda Jordan is chair of the schools' sub-committee in the London Borough of Newham council. In this chapter she describes the attempts in Newham to introduce a clear policy on integration and to link it with an analysis of and developments within mainstream primary, secondary and further education. She discusses the emergence of a group within the council after the local elections of 1986 who were able to agree on policy guidelines and make considerable progress in ending segregation in the borough.

1 INTRODUCTION

Looking back to May 1986 and thinking about the council elections and the Labour Party's election manifesto, dramatically brings to my attention how much change has taken place in education over the past four years. Of course much of the change has been as a result of the 1988 Education Act. No one in the borough who is in the slightest way connected with the education service has been untouched by the implementation of the Act. However, the Education Committee has addressed many local issues which are not directly related to government legislation but which are the preoccupations of people in the borough.

Nowhere have the changes been more significant than in the provision of special education. In 1986 there were eight special schools in Newham which were attended by 700 children with a further 100 pupils receiving separate special education in residential schools outside the borough. At the time of writing there are less than 400 children attending six special schools and less than twenty-five attending special residential schools. More than 400 pupils who have Statemented educational needs attend mainstream schools, with support. There is a borough development plan for special education which shows how to achieve the end of segregated schooling for children and young people with disabilities and learning difficulties. The integration of special education into the mainstream is now a firm borough policy with widespread understanding and support.

There *are* some people in the borough who are opposed to the integration policy. These include some members of the local Conservative Party and some staff who work in special schools. However, the opposition is stated to be against the speed of integration, rather than the principle. There has been no opposition whatsoever from parents of children who do not have Statemented educational needs, or from any pupils. There have been some protests over school closures, but it must be emphasised that the numbers involved have been very small – in each case the lobby has consisted of three or four parents in very close association with some teachers. A year after the first group of secondary-age special school pupils had gone to a mainstream secondary school, the parents who had been involved in the lobby were saying that it was the best thing that had ever happened to their children.

I still have a sense of impatience about the progress of the special education policy, but I am aware that change is difficult to achieve quickly. This has been the hardest lesson for me to learn as a politician.

2 THE CONTEXT FOR THE DESEGREGATION POLICY

When the new Education Committee was formed after the May 1986 elections we set out a number of priorities for action. The overriding priority was to do something abut underachievement in the borough. Newham is part of the 'East End' of London and has always suffered from problems of poverty and class prejudice. On league tables of examination results Newham has always appeared either at, or close to, the bottom of the league along with the other East London boroughs and Knowsley.

It is no surprise that Newham and these boroughs are always in these positions. The populations are almost entirely working class and therefore have a mass of obstacles to break through in order to have an opportunity of achieving educational success in the sense of exam results and entry into higher education equal with the populations of the boroughs who appear at the top of the league tables. Time and time again, educational research has shown that social class is the single most influential factor affecting levels of achievement, in terms of examination passes and participation in further and higher education.

The Education Committee realise that the young people in Newham have the same abilities and potential as young people anywhere and that the quality of education was probably equal to any in the country. We believed, however, that it must be possible to improve achievement levels and increase the number of people participating in further and higher education, against the odds.

One of the first decisions taken by the Education Committee was to set up two independent inquiries to examine reasons for underachievement in Newham and to make recommendations to the borough. Both reports achieved many of the aims for which we hoped and were welcomed enthusiastically by the council.

The first inquiry (LBN 1990a) looked into reasons for underachievement in schools. It was chaired by Seamus Hegarty of the National Foundation for Educational Research and consisted of four other members. The inquiry lasted for eighteen months and was a unique piece of research in that pupils, parents, teachers, head teachers and members of the community were interviewed as well as officers of the education department and members of the Education Committee. It made 121 recommendations which advised the local education authority about how improvements could be made in the education service. The recommendations can be summarised by saying that they are about breaking a cycle of low expectations and introducing rigour into every aspect of the service from the way the education office is run to ensuring that schools are taking measures to stop non-attendance and bullying. The members of the inquiry team have gone to great lengths to point out that Newham's problems of under-achievement are shared, to some extent, by every local education authority in the country. This has been borne out by the requests to buy the report. The recommendations have been discussed throughout the borough and adopted by gover-nors as the basis for their schools' development plans. The borough inspectors have also used the recommendations to form an important part of the criteria which are used when schools are visited, surveyed and inspected.

The second inquiry (LBN 1990b) was into the reasons why Newham people do not go on to higher education and was chaired by Professor Peter Toyne of Liverpool Polytechnic. It made recommendations along similar lines to the first but also made recommendations to institutions of further and higher education and to local industry, to get out into schools and to make relationships with schools and the population. The message again was that there is untapped poten-tial in the borough.

A second strand to the strategy for tackling underachievement was to reorga-nise secondary education. There was a great need to remove surplus places from secondary schools, not least because government funding was going to be allo-cated on the assumption that spare places had been removed. But just as import-antly the school sixth forms were in the main very small, with only a handful being anywhere near to a respectable size.

We firmly believed that the restricted staffing and provision for sixth formers was failing to attract many students and not providing relevant courses for others. A large number of 16 year olds were already transferring to Newham Community College. After a long consultation period the council decided to close one secondary school, to reduce the size of another and make all the secon-dary schools 11–16 with a break at 16, and to create a sixth form college, along-side Newham Community College, for post-16 education. This plan will come into being in September 1992.

Equally important for the Education Committee was to further develop equal opportunities policies. Anti-racism, anti-sexism and the integration of special education had all been central to the two independent inquiries and to the plans for secondary reorganisation.

3 THE DEVELOPMENT OF THE POLICY

Following the formation of the new Education Committee in May 1986, I was elected as chair of the schools' sub-committee. When the chair and vice-chair of the Education Committee and the chairs and vice-chairs of the sub-committees met to discuss the way in which we were going to work, we decided that as well as taking the usual responsibilities for all matters relating to schools, I would be the 'lead member' for special educational needs.

The local Labour Party manifesto had committed the new council to pursuing a policy of integrating special education, but this had not been straightforward. Throughout the writing of the manifesto, integration had been, as usual, an area of controversy. Many members of the Labour Party were vehemently opposed to integration, others were sceptical, while others were passionately committed to it. For many people, including myself, it would have been unthinkable to claim to be committed to comprehensive community education, while excluding from one's definition of 'comprehensive' and 'community' a small number of children, young people and adults into segregated institutions. The discussions and arguments which took place within the Labour Party were crucial in bringing out the important issues and bringing together people who would later be involved in making policy decisions. The supporters of integration, then, argued that desegregating special education was a structural change necessary in the development of comprehensive education. They also argued that the quest for improvement in the quality of education in the borough would be helped by the introduction of the expertise from special education into the mainstream. But, perhaps most importantly, the proponents argued that fundamental human rights are denied if people are segregated on the basis of arbitrarily chosen characteristics.

No one said they were against the principles as such, just about technicalities, such as the timing and pace of change yet some people proposed that there should be a commitment to retain some special schools so as not to alarm people or appear too radical. However, eventually the Labour Party manifesto included a commitment to integration.

After the elections of May 1986 we had many discussions with the officers of the Education Department who had previously been involved with the integration working party, and decided on a short policy statement and to set up a small steering group of councillors and officers, literally to steer the policy along. The steering group consisted of five elected members of the Education Committee, two of the parent representatives from the Education Committee and a teacher representative from the Education Committee, all as full voting members. All steering group minutes and decisions are reported to the Education Committee. Officers attend the meetings of the steering group as and when necessary. The difference between this steering group and the earlier integration working party which met between 1983 and 1985 is that now all of the members of the group are committed to integration and were determined to make a policy into a practical reality.

The policy statement was accepted by the Labour group without dissent and then by the Education Committee and full council:

THE LONDON BOROUGH OF NEWHAM
SPECIAL EDUCATION POLICY STATEMENT

The London Borough of Newham believes in the inherent equality of all individuals irrespective of physical or mental ability. It recognises, however, that individuals are not always treated as equals and that young people with disabilities experience discrimination and disadvantage. The Council believes that segregated special education is a major factor causing discrimination. We therefore believe that desegregating special education is the first step in tackling prejudice against people with disabilities and other difficulties. They have been omitted from previous Equal Opportunities initiatives, and it is now obvious that our aim of achieving comprehensive education in Newham will remain hindered while we continue to select approximately 2% of school pupils for separate education.

It is also the right of pupils without disabilities or other difficulties to experience a real environment in which they can learn that people are not all the same and that those who happen to have a disability should not be treated differently, any more than they would be if they were of a different ethnic background. It is their right to learn at first hand about experiences which they will possibly undergo in future, either themselves or as parents.

Desegregating special education and thus meeting the needs of Statemented children in mainstream schools will also contribute, by the entry of expert qualified staff into mainstream schools, to improve provision for the considerable number of children who already experience difficulties.

Looking back, that policy statement was the most important part in developing integration. The message was clear, and whenever anyone said 'Does that mean that you will be closing special schools?' there was only one answer. There would no longer be the pretence that integration and segregation could both exist at the same time.

Following the adoption of the policy statement, we had to tackle the difficult task of deciding how much could happen at the same time, and where to start. Despite my impatience, I realised that changes need officer and councillor time and that there would have to be a fairly gradual implementation over about five years. I had also learned by this stage that if we had produced a plan which showed what we would be doing in two or three years' time it would cause unnecessary alarm and rumours would flourish.

Our next step was to appoint a coordinator for all of the integration work which was already going on in the borough. This person would also act as a focus for training teachers and ancillary staff. It was also agreed that every school had to designate a member of staff to be responsible for special needs and to act as a link with the coordinator. Each governing body was asked to nominate a governor who would be the link for special educational needs. Both the designated staff members and the link governors received training.

The steering group tried to ensure that every development in special education in the borough would be towards integration. We agreed that every phase of education should begin to address the issue of access for pupils and students with disabilities and learning difficulties. The first major developments were, however, in the pre-school and post-school sectors. During the 1987 budget-making process the council agreed to spend an extra £90,000 for Newham Community College to develop a special needs department, and an extra £50,000 on ancillary staff to support nursery and infant-age children who experience difficulties in mainstream schools.

At that time (early 1987) it became clear that our secondary school for children with emotional and behavioural difficulties was floundering. There was a roll of about forty, but on any one day there would only be about half that number at the school. The staff were having great difficulties with a number of the pupils and morale was very low. We decided to take the positive move to consult on the possible closure of the school and suggest the relocation of resources into alternative provision. We consulted the parents, staff and governors of the school and then went ahead and published the official notices to close the school. We grappled with ideas about how best to meet the needs of the young people at the school and those who might have been placed there subsequently. By the time that consultations began in autumn 1987 the roll of the school was down to less than thirty. No new placements had been made for some time, and a significant number had left school in the summer.

We considered putting resources into two mainstream secondary schools to enable them to meet the needs of young people with emotional and behavioural difficulties, but this plan was abandoned after consulting the governing bodies of the two secondary schools. Both meetings were extremely unpleasant, with governors speaking in graphic detail about the horrific things that would go on in their schools if 'these pupils' were allowed in. In fact there was a very small number of students remaining at the school that we were planning to close and some of those would be leaving before it closed. The governors could not grasp that they were being offered extra staffing to support pupils who were experiencing difficulties in their schools. They could not get rid of the notion that somewhere we had hidden away hordes of young people who would come into their schools and cause havoc. Amazingly, none of the governors took up the offer to visit the special school. Their arguments were reminiscent of arguments against immigration. The alternative proposal, which was the one which was agreed in the end, was to use the resources of the special school to create a support team of teachers who would be able to work with all of the secondary schools. The young people remaining on the school roll began to be supported in mainstream by the support team (see Chapter 33).

During 1989, consultation was carried out on the proposal to close a second special school. This school catered for children with a range of learning difficulties. This time the solution did result in resourcing mainstream schools to meet the needs of a specific number of pupils. As from September 1990 one secondary school and two primary schools in the borough will have received relocated resources.

This closure did not happen without protest; there was a core of stable staff, many of whom had worked at the school for a number of years. Some parents felt that their children would not be able to cope if they went to mainstream schools. There were lots of meetings with parents and governors, with time spent explaining the council's policy and how positive the experience of integration had been for many children in the borough. There were lobbies at the Education Committee and council meetings. Those of us who were closely involved in planning the arrangements after the school had closed were able to explain carefully to colleagues and people who had come to hear the debate that we wanted to close the school for the best possible reasons and to give details of the alternative arrangements of mainstream education where we would provide experienced staff.

As structural changes were made and resources reallocated from special to mainstream schools, more and more children were being placed in their local mainstream schools with support. We brought this support together to create a learning support team of teachers.

In March 1990, there was a fire which resulted in the total destruction of the school for children with physical disabilities. There had been plans to amalgamate the school with a primary school on same site and to relocate the secondary pupils into a local secondary school. The fire was a very traumatic experience for the children and staff at the school who have been temporarily housed in a vacant school building. The insurance money will be used to make a primary school which is being built in the borough totally accessible for up to thirty-five primary aged pupils from the school, and to adapt secondary schools. A second new primary school is being built, designed and planned to include children with disabilities.

A number of other policy initiatives are at various stages of development. They will greatly increase the momentum towards the end of segregated special education in the borough. We plan to bring together the disparate services for children and young people who are deaf and hearing impaired. As in many authorities, the services comprise a special school, special units, a peripatetic service and out-borough placements. These services will be brought into one coherent service based on equality of opportunity and bilingual teaching of English and British Sign Language (BSL), and changes based on integrated provision will be in place by September 1992.

The Sixth Form College, also due to open in September 1992, will be fully accessible, and from then all students who continue their education after 16 will either go there or to Newham Community College.

From September 1990 the staffing of special education will be on the same basis as it is for nursery, primary and secondary: that is, according to pupil-teacher ratios. The learning support teams are staffed on a pupil to teacher ratio of 6.5 to 1, as are the special schools. This enables resources to be moved around on a rational basis.

4 CONCLUDING REMARKS

Much has been said about special education in relation to the local management of schools, the National Curriculum, assessment and testing and other contemporary political issues such as poll tax capping. The will to stop segregating children, young people and adults who have disabilities and learning difficulties is not dependent upon technical issues such as these. If anything is used as an argument against desegregating special education, it is just an excuse.

During the period 1986–90 the council's budget had to be reduced by at least £30 million, half of which was from the Education budget. When the Education Committee decided on how the cuts would be made, over the last four years, none were made to the Special Education budget. There have been areas of growth, such as the new department of Newham Community College, additional ancillary staff for nursery and primary aged pupils, and building works to improve physical access to schools and the college. These have been paid for by making cuts in other areas of the Education and council budget. But people's feelings, beliefs, attitudes and behaviour are more important than money.

I sometimes find it hard to believe how much has changed during the past four years. Consulting governing bodies and others about integration still sometimes has difficult moments, but it is a long time since I heard someone say something like, 'But we don't want those children here!' Schools that have taken disability on board as an equality issue, and as part of treating children as valued human beings whatever their situation, are much nicer places. There is no one way to integrate special education. In Newham, we are in the process of changing from one way of special education to another. We are learning from our experiences and from having a mixture of resourced schools and children individually placed and receiving support from central teams. As has often been said, integration is a process, not a state. Closing special schools is only the start of the process and the plan for integration. The entire education system gradually has to change if special education is desegregated. For example, if deaf children are going to start attending mainstream schools, then the implications for those schools are enormous. BSL will have to be part of the curriculum for everyone, there will be more adults in classes in the form of interpreters, facilitators and support teachers, and all teachers will have to work together much more closely.

In Newham, we believe that schools need to change and we are pleased that desegregating our special education is one of the ways to spearhead change.

REFERENCES

London Borough of Newham (LBN) (1990a) *Boosting Educational Achievement*, Report of the Committee of Inquiry into Educational Achievement in the London Borough of Newham, Chaired by Seamus Hegarty, London: LBN.
—— (1990b) *Higher Education for Newham*, Report of the Committee of Inquiry, Chaired by Professor Toyne, London: LBN.

Chapter 33

Challenging behaviour support

Paul Howard

Paul Howard is head of the support service set up in the London Borough of Newham to help pupils identified as a focus of concern because of emotional or behavioural difficulties. He describes the establishment of the service following the closure of a secondary special school in the borough and the broadening of the notion of support from a concern with labelled and Statemented pupils to a wider group who experience difficulties and their interaction with their teachers and curricula.

1 INTRODUCTION

The decision of the London Borough of Newham, in 1988, to set up a support service for secondary school pupils with 'emotional and behavioural difficulties', was in itself unremarkable, for a number of other authorities had established, or were introducing similar provision. However, the fact that Newham's plan also entailed the closure of its secondary special day school for pupils categorised as emotionally and behaviourally disturbed may have generated more interest and concern than did otherwise comparable schemes.

In this chapter I wish to set out the changes which have taken place within this provision and to examine the implications of our experience for future developments. In the first section I provide a brief outline of the provision in the borough prior to September 1988. In the second section, I turn my attention to the impact of the authority's policies on that provision, while the third section focuses on the changes which have been effected since 1988. My final section addresses the lessons we have learned and the way these are being used to inform future practice.

2 PAST PROVISION

Prior to September 1988, the bulk of Newham's response to pupils whose behaviour was a focus of concern to schools was made in two day-special schools, one secondary, the other predominantly primary, though with the flexibility to work with pupils of lower secondary age. Of the two schools, the latter had a strong reintegrative tradition and, since 1984, had released an increasing amount of staff time to support pupils in the primary sector and around transition to secondary school. This proved to be both a spur to the reintegration process and a means by which some pupils' removal from the mainstream could be prevented. In addition to its own schools, the authority made use of a number of residential schools. The roll of the secondary special school, which had been decreasing, continued to decline, but more steeply, once its closure had been mooted. Numbers remained constant at the other special school, while the general trend in out-borough placements was downwards.

Within the context of these largely segregated arrangements, the use of the term 'emotional and behavioural difficulty' (EBD) as a label for schools and pupils was assumed to be unproblematic and was, therefore, largely unchallenged. It could reasonably be assumed that placement in any of the special schools was indicative of the pupils' special educational needs. However, with the shift of provision towards mainstream settings, such assumptions were to be increasingly questioned. Yet even before the introduction of new models of provision, there was a degree of rejection of the EBD label in the borough's Home Tuition Service (providing mainly for permanently excluded pupils), and the Secondary Support Centre which offered part-time off-site placements for lower secondary pupils to prevent exclusion or truancy. Indeed, some saw these facilities as alternatives to the traditional EBD special schools.

3 INTEGRATION: POLICY INTO PRACTICE

The publication, in February 1987, of Newham's policy statement on integration produced an agenda for accelerated but more carefully planned change. Previously, change had tended to be arbitrary and cyclical but the unequivocal policy commitment to 'desegregating special education and thus meeting the needs of Statemented children in mainstream schools' (LBN 1987) lent a clear sense of direction to subsequent developments.

There was nothing unique about Newham's policy document. Indeed, occupying less than one side of an A4 sheet of paper, it could be described as concise to the point of being uninformative. However, like an iceberg, the small, visible portion of policy plans – the political rhetoric of the policy statement – gave little evidence of the scale of what was hidden. Newham's policy statement was only a starting point for the movement of resources away from the segregated special education sector and into mainstream schools.

The replacement of the secondary special school (EBD) with a support service was, then, one of a number of integration initiatives which have emerged since the policy document. However, I do not wish to give the impression that translating policy into practice was straightforward. The move towards a support model of secondary provision was complex, and, in common with much educational development depended on expediency and circumstances as much as on the enactment of principles.

Had the special school concerned established a reputation for successful reintegration and outreach work, it is questionable whether the belief, that many pupils with 'emotional and behavioural disturbance' could be more effectively educated in the mainstream, could have alone prompted a major shift in such a short space of time. In the event, the school was experiencing a 'Catch 22' crisis. The problems associated with teaching disturbed and disturbing pupils in segregated settings, which are widely recognised, if not well documented (Topping 1983, Galloway and Goodwin 1987), necessitate a stable and consistent staff, yet in Newham these difficulties had created pressures on staff retention that proved irresistible. Turnover of teachers was high and dependence on a large proportion of temporary staff, however competent, tended to exacerbate the situation. The closure of the school, and the shift to providing support in the mainstream, was one evident solution to difficulties at the school.

Given the fears, suspicions, prejudices and vested interests involved, the consultations over the special school closure and support service development were understandably protracted and complicated. As a matter of principle, it was vital that the new provision be established on the firmest possible footing. However, the authority was working within certain obvious constraints, not least the need to develop the support service from resources saved from its precursor's closure. In short, the service had to be in place in September 1988, just six weeks after the closure of the special school.

Although the authority had consulted widely over the shift in provision, as a matter of expedience, I, as head teacher designate, was not involved in the appointment of the service's initial teaching complement, while the lack of time between appointments and the start of service delivery precluded extensive dialogue in advance, within the service, or with schools and other agencies over the service's principles, practices and procedures. There was a basic agreement – over the move to a support model of secondary 'emotional and behavioural difficulty provision – but some of the key features of the service, as described in the details for applicants, had not been approved by the time my colleagues and I took up our posts in September 1988. First, the plan to concentrate two support teachers in each of two schools, as an enhanced support facility for up to 8–10 Statemented pupils, foundered on the resistance of these schools to becoming what they perceived as a particularly unattractive variety of magnet. Second, the objective of deploying the remaining five teachers in a support centre, where they would work flexibly with individuals and groups on a part-time or short full-time basis, and from whence they would visit schools to offer help and advice to teachers was affected by the collapse of the 'enhanced provision' idea and further undermined by the lack of suitable premises. Finally, the intention to incorporate the Secondary Support Centre and Home Tuition Service within the new service, as the basis for a coherent and comprehensive provision, was hampered by the three service elements being located in different parts of the borough.

Consequently, on taking up our posts, my colleagues and I discovered that the structure of service envisaged in May 1988 by the LEA bore little resemblance on paper to what was being required of us. It was ironic that the only available and suitable [sic] premises were on the site of the special school which was closing. We inherited from the school the first pupils to attend the service's centre – a hapless group, for whom arrangements had not been made when the school closed. At a time when we needed to establish the principles of our relationship with the education service as a whole, we were confronted with the more pressing, expedient task of negotiating a range of provision for these young people. Without effort, the new service was in danger of becoming little more than a minuscule version of its predecessor, thus jeopardising the aim of refo-cusing provision into the mainstream.

The further assessment and subsequent placement of these pupils was completed by January 1989, yet the impact of the initial arrangements for the service left its mark on morale and relationships long after we had managed to reassert our founding principles. Furthermore, the continuing attempts by the LEA to locate enhanced staffing provision in two schools remained unsuccessful. This latter difficulty appears to have been compounded by the absence, during the planning stages, of a contingency model for the service. While it was clear that schools did not want an enhanced facility, an acceptable alternative was not obvious.

In the final analysis, the authority could not continue to resource an undeliver-able model, and by the end of 1988 had approved the development of the service along peripatetic lines. The peripatetic model was to make support equally avail-able to all schools thus avoiding the magnet effect. It strengthened the idea that mainstream schools were to be the focal points in the response to emotional and behavioural difficulties. However, the change of model reduced the level of staffing available for the service's off-site centre role, an issue I will discuss in greater depth towards the end of the chapter.

4 THE EFFECT OF CHANGE

How has the switch in policy affected provision for pupils? In general pupils are less segregated, schools as well as pupils are seen as the focus of intervention, support is given outside of the Statementing process, and a unified service for responding to challenging behaviour is evolving. I will examine these in turn.

The movement from segregated to integrated practice

At the risk of stating the obvious, the principal change in Newham's EBD provi-sion has been the transfer of resources from segregated special to mainstream contexts. The possibility of placing pupils long term on a separate site has been swapped for a capacity to respond to emotional and behavioural difficulties at, or closer to, their source. Acceptance of the change has not been automatic or universal. Although we have experienced little direct resistance to the new service, some mainstream schools have been less adept than others at casting off their previous perceptions of how the service would respond. Expectations remain that the appropriate responses to the most difficult pupils are withdrawal within school or removal from school.

Some of these expectations have persisted because those that hold them are resistant to change but in part, they can be attributed to weaknesses in communicating the practical implications of the new policy. Newham's special educational need support services have evolved from the borough's unequivocal integration policy, without a comparably clear explanation of the support process. Responsibility for this has tended to be devolved to the support services themselves, which has proved to be a mixed blessing. It has created opportunities for us to be involved in the development of support principles. Yet we have little real power to overcome the resistance of schools to accepting our new roles.

Underlying the change had been the conviction that most of the pupils involved could be more effectively educated in the mainstream than in a special school and that the minority who could not be thus educated was very small. Our experiences seem to confirm that position, though until, to use Dessent's (1987) phrase, ordinary schools are 'made special', there will continue to be pressure to adopt traditional solutions. There is little evidence that the closure of the special school has caused a flood of exclusions. Patterns of suspension and demand for the Home Tuition Services remain as unpredictable as in the past. However, there has been a slight increase in referrals for out-borough placements and trends in this area need to be monitored closely. Its significance in relation to the changes in local provision has yet to be fully established.

Developing institutional support

As the focus of our interventions has moved into mainstream schools, we have extended our practice beyond an individualistic view of special educational need in some of the borough's schools. Direct support of individual pupils may be favoured by schools because it is seen as a guarantee that individual needs will be respected and met. But this sound rationale is open to misunderstanding or abuse when it is assumed that difficulties are exclusively located within the pupil rather than in teacher–pupil and curriculum–pupil relationships, that the support service has a monopoly of expertise and that it should take responsibility for the problem. This can and does create conflicts between support teachers and teachers in the schools.

However, we are developing varied ways of broadening our interventions in a number of the schools. In one, we are embarking on support contracts, which set out the school's as well as the service's responsibilities in a given support situation which may become a model for the service's work elsewhere. Another school is utilising service staff as facilitators of a support group, similar to those described by Hanko (1987), geared towards helping teachers develop their own strategies for addressing disturbing behaviours. In an increasing number of schools, in-service training is being requested of the service, which is a further indication of those schools' commitment to integrated practice.

The development of non-statutory support

Before the establishment of a support service, provision in Newham was characterised by a preoccupation with those pupils for whom a Statement of special educational needs had been issued. The Secondary Support Centre and Home Tuition Service worked predominantly with pupils without Statements, but these provisions amounted to a small fraction of the total 'emotional and behavioural difficulty' resource allocation. However, in addition to meeting the needs of pupils with Statements in the mainstream, Newham's policy emphasised the possibility of creating 'improved provision for the considerable number of children (without Statements) who already experience difficulties' (LBN 1987). This theme was developed when staff were being appointed to the new service, which was to provide for 'pupils, both Statemented and otherwise, with learning difficulties particularly related to EBD' (LBN 1988).

While our statutory obligations under the Education Act (DES 1981) necessitate that support in respect of Statemented pupils takes priority, every effort has been made to deliver non-statutory support wherever possible. This has not only proved beneficial in promoting greater involvement of 'whole schools' by stimulating collaborative work with individuals, groups and classes, it has also helped avoid the degeneration in relationships which can accompany a lengthy (from six months to two years) assessment and Statementing process, and in some cases may have precluded the need to embark upon the process at all.

The development of a unified emotional and behavioural difficulty support service

In October 1989 the three existing service elements of the service – Home Tuition, Secondary Support Centre and the SEN Support Service (EBD) – were located in shared premises. Up to that point the process of unification had been a paper exercise. One year into our locational integration, we have produced a framework for the single service structure, which both preserves the distinct features of each element's practice and identifies a common body of practice. Moreover, the extension of a unified approach is underwritten by a development plan, drafted in October 1990, which will inform our practice for the foreseeable future.

5 THE IMPLICATIONS OF THE CHANGE

What lessons have we learned during the first two years of Newham's 'emotional and behavioural difficulty' support service? I will not dwell on those for the lead-in period which are mainly concerned with the need for a clear break from

preceding provision, for the emergence of an agreed model prior to implementation, and for sufficient time for service preparation. I am principally concerned
here with the implications of the work since the inception of the service in relation to the 'emotional and behavioural difficulty' label, the purposes of support
and the effect these have on the relationship between school and service and the
extension of integration.

The EBD label

Our experiences in Newham have demonstrated the ease with which the nomen-
clature of special educational needs can become an unquestioned currency for a
trade in problem-diagnosis and cure. It is not uncommon for pupils to be
described as 'EBD children', 'being EBD' or 'having EBD' in much the same way
as they might be noted as being ill. When the main emphasis of special educational provision is in segregated settings such constructions are relatively
problem-free. Indeed, in that context, identifying the difficulties of individual
pupils is an essential part of the process of selecting which pupils should be
educated outside the mainstream. When the focus of special education shifts to
the mainstream, as it has in Newham, there is a danger that traditional assumptions about EBD will be replicated. There is an obvious tension between integrating pupils with special educational needs and concurrently continuing to
describe their difficulties as if they necessarily stemmed from something pathological within them which seems to imply that they require separate treatment as
a group.

It will not have escaped the reader's notice that Newham's service carries the
EBD epithet. While this serves to distinguish it from an equivalent service for
learning difficulties, perhaps we should search for a less pejorative title. Alternatively, we have to ensure that our concerns are with the full range of factors which
produce or compound what may be described as 'emotional and behavioural
difficulty'. In other words, if the label is to have enduring use in mainstream
settings, a greater understanding of what it means needs to develop, along with
an appreciation that it is subjective not objective, relative not immutable, as
concerned with classroom management and the curriculum as with problems
within the pupil or his/her background.

The purposes of support and relationships with schools

Views of the way pupils are labelled have a significant bearing on constructions
of support. A narrow definition of pupils as having 'emotional and behavioural
difficulty' is likely to mean that support is confined to enabling young people to
adjust sufficiently to survive in ordinary school. A broader definition demands a
more expansive view of support as a means by which schools can be helped to
develop their practice so as to accommodate the needs of a wider range of pupils.
As a consequence, tension between our perceptions of support and that of others

may be heightened. In these circumstances, staff of the support service need to provide clear information and education about their new roles in supporting pupils and groups, teachers and whole schools.

If support is to have a significant impact on the education of pupils who experience and/or present difficulties, and on the school's capacity to accommodate them, the relationship between school and service must be an energetic partnership to which both are fully committed and within which both are engaged in pursuit of common goals. I would suggest that, of these goals, the extension of integration is the most important.

The extension of integration

The pressure to restructure the Newham service along peripatetic lines has limited its capacity to operate off-site support systems. It has never been disputed that a very small minority of pupils may be unable to cope with ordinary school (or vice versa) but the provision of extensive off-site facilities is bound to undermine integration policies in two ways. The number of pupils requiring placements is likely to expand to fill the available number of places. Further, the more a school articulates its special need practice in terms of displacement, the less likely it is to develop the conditions in which those needs could be met. So, our restructuring has enabled us to do rather more to focus the service's resources on pupils integrated in mainstream schools than may have originally been envisaged.

However, we do need to think critically about integration. If integration is only concerned with individual pupils, then the need for support from outside the mainstream will continue for as long as pupils who experience difficulties are identified. If, on the other hand, integration is about the development of schools to meet the needs of all their pupils then we may see the eclipse of external support as one of the goals of a support service.

REFERENCES

Department of Education and Science (DES) (1981) *Education Act, 1981*, London: HMSO.

Dessent, T. (1987) *Making the Ordinary School Special*, London: Falmer.

Galloway, D. and Goodwin, C. (1987) *The Education of Disturbing Children*, London: Longman.

Hanko, G. (1987) *Special Needs in Ordinary Classrooms*, Oxford: Basil Blackwell.

London Borough of Newham (LBN) (1987) *Special Education in Mainstream Schools: A Policy Statement*, London: LBN.

—— (1988) *Secondary SEN Support Service (EBD): Service Specification*, London: LBN.

Topping, K. (1983) *Educational Systems for Disruptive Adolescents*, London: Croom Helm.

Chapter 34

A changing learning support service

Mary Newton

Mary Newton is head of the learning support service in Staffordshire. In this chapter she describes the changes that took place in the service during the 1980s from peripatetic remedial work within individual pupils to a service offering curriculum support and development, collaborative teaching and encouraging parental involvement. She takes a critical look at the impact of the 1988 Education Reform Act on the work and the inadequacies of funding following LMS. She argues strongly for the retention of local education authority wide support services against the trends to devolution.

1 THE OLD MODEL

The last decade has created interesting times for teachers who work as members of LEA support services. Nowhere has this been felt more keenly than in the field of special education. In my own county, Staffordshire, a large service flourished before the 1981 Education Act, largely working with pupils who, at 7, had been identified as having a reading difficulty. All pupils who had a reading quotient of 85 or below were systematically followed-up by a 'remedial advisory teacher'. These pupils were given further, diagnostic assessment and an individual programme of work. The remedial teacher's role was to work with the pupils to improve their reading. Often, this did not involve the class teacher and was done away from the classroom. The approach became affectionately known by those working in support services as 'the stock cupboard syndrome'.

While many teachers enjoyed the private nature of their work, there were growing numbers who felt that what they did ought to be more closely related to what the class teacher did. It was also becoming apparent that pupils identified as having a reading difficulty at age 7 were not going to be 'cured' quite so quickly. There seemed to be a naïve assumption by policy-makers that a team of peripatetic teachers, armed with a bag of tests and a collection of books, could reduce the incidence of reading failure by themselves. The reality was that many of these pupils did not accelerate their learning in response to remedial teaching. They needed consistent teaching, reinforcement and consolidation in all aspects of the curriculum, which could only be provided by class teachers.

Very soon the teaching resources of the service were exhausted but the numbers of pupils who were identified by the county's regular reading survey continued to grow. The service had become fully committed to a relatively small number of schools who believed that pupils' progress in reading was the responsibility of support teachers.

2 THE NEW SERVICE

The 1981 Education Act and the spirit of integration which it promoted provided the opportunity for the rethink which the support service badly needed. The concept of special educational need in the Act allowed for a much broader definition of the role and responsibilities of the support service. The notion of the 20 per cent of pupils or The Warnock Report's 'one in five' (DES 1978) who, at some time, could have a special educational need, was also helpful to the process of redefining its role.

A new order of LEA special educational needs support services was created in the 1980s to help schools to provide for a potentially more diverse group of pupils than they had previously taught. Many of these services were created from existing LEA provision (DES 1989a). It was easy to change the name of a support service but not easy to change its operation. Changes of attitude, approach and delivery of services were required.

The rebirth of Staffordshire Remedial Service was heralded by a change of name and a redistribution of staff and posts of responsibility. The new service comprised sixty teachers; fifty-three full time and seven part time. They served 566 schools, concentrating their efforts in the 423 primary schools. The service was organised into nine area teams each with a minimum of six full-time equivalent teachers. A head of service post was created to provide coherence. The new Special Educational Needs Support Service emerged with a commitment to the notion that pupils who are experiencing difficulties in learning should have access to a broad, balanced and relevant curriculum which has been differentiated to take account of their individual learning needs. The service extended its professional interest to preventing as well as ameliorating learning difficulties. It supported the view that one can reduce difficulties in learning by reducing the mismatch between pupils and the curriculum.

Changes in practice

A review of the activities of area teams in September 1988 revealed similarities in practice across the county, although this was more by accident than by design. All teams provided in-service training for mainstream schools to raise awareness about pupils with special educational needs without Statements. Schools needed help to record pupils' strengths and achievements systematically in order to measure progress. All too often, the schools' assessments had tended to highlight the pupils' 'can't do's'.

The teams were beginning to extend below the junior phase into work with infants and their parents. The development of shared/paired reading schemes was becoming common. Schools were keen to involve parents in their children's education, especially if they felt that they were struggling with reading, though many wanted the support services to promote the programme and help parents to support their children's reading.

The teams were also becoming more involved with secondary schools. Many of these had appointed their own special educational needs coordinators, who were often heads of remedial departments known by a new name and who were still coming to terms with the new demands being placed on them. They felt that they needed help from the support service to implement the 'whole-school approach' for which they had been given responsibility. Support service teachers could be the ambassadors of this new approach by working alongside subject teachers, helping to develop appropriate curriculum materials, and deliver lessons. This new style of working was directed more at the subject teacher than at individual pupils, with the intention that the subject teachers would adopt the methods and materials themselves and learn to be more confident and effective with pupils who experience difficulties.

In primary schools, work with juniors was gradually shifting from withdrawing pupils to working in the classroom with individuals or groups and even sharing responsibility for the whole class with the class teacher. In the best examples of collaborative teaching, both teachers were jointly planning and teaching, exchanging roles regularly to ensure that the class teacher had as much experience of working with the pupils who were having difficulties as did the support teacher.

Some teachers in the service still believed in taking the children out of the classroom and working with them in the privacy of 'the stock cupboard'. Indeed, many were convinced that this was in the best interests of the pupils, who could concentrate far more easily when all the distractions of the classroom were removed. For those teachers, the move to closer contact with class teachers had to be more gradual. It is important that support teachers are not deskilled by any changes to their pattern of work. Where teachers are convinced that they are working in the best interests of the pupils by taking them out of the classroom, they are encouraged to liaise with the class teachers about their work and ensure that it is related to the rest of the curriculum. In this way the class teacher is able to build upon their work in the classroom.

Today, only a fraction of a support teacher's time is devoted to teaching individual children. Without all the careful preparation and support for the class teacher and parent the impact of any intervention would be limited. For many support teachers, direct teaching has become a vicarious activity, most effective when delivered by the teachers who are responsible for the child day by day.

The service has recently invested a great deal of time and energy in the production of high quality, reasonably priced resources to support the National Curriculum. Teachers and parents need practical help in interpreting the National

Curriculum for pupils who experience difficulties in learning. Teachers need help in presenting materials which are accessible to pupils. All the resources produced by the service offer suggestions as to how the curriculum can be differentiated for individuals within the class. In this way, the message of the service – *include all pupils in the curriculum* – is reflected in its material resources.

Reflecting all these changes, the service objectives are now:

- to enable ordinary schools to cater more effectively for pupils who are experiencing a greater difficulty in learning than the majority of pupils in their age group;
- to encourage a whole-school response to meeting the needs of pupils who are experiencing difficulties in learning;
- to provide a programme of in-service training opportunities to further assist teachers in their delivery of the National Curriculum to pupils with special educational needs;
- to involve parents in the education of their children from the early years through to the secondary phase;
- to liaise with special schools and other support agencies to ensure a consistent and coordinated approach to working with schools;
- to cater effectively for those children whose schooling has been interrupted.

Self-appraisal and professional development

Support teachers need to know what is expected of them. Some teachers in Staffordshire support service were not given job descriptions when they first joined the service. As a first step towards self-appraisal, job descriptions were drafted, outlining the roles and responsibilities of team members. Each teacher received a copy of their proposed job description and was given the opportunity to discuss it with their professional associations as well as with their immediate line managers before accepting or rejecting it. Teachers who held incentive allowance posts had their duties added to those included in the job description shown below. This explicit role provides the basis for self-evaluation and an assessment of how teachers may need to develop in order to be more effective.

A job description for a main professional grade teacher takes the following form:

Members of the Support Service are engaged as teachers and, as such, carry out the professional duties of a school teacher as circumstances may reasonably require.

As a member of the Support Service you may be involved in some, or all, of the following activities during the course of your work:

- Teaching to meet the needs of pupils within a classroom/school context.
- The development of appropriate methods/materials to ensure that pupils' needs are met across the curriculum and that access to the curriculum is enhanced.

- Teaching individuals as a corporate part of a broad integration project.
- Contributing to the development of the in-service training programmes offered by the team in response to the perceived needs of teachers and the Authority.
- Deployment of collaborative teaching approaches to enhance the learning experiences of all pupils.

NB Because of the varying nature of our commitments it may be that a member of the Service will not spend the whole of a morning or afternoon session in any one school. Such an arrangement would be clearly specified at the outset of any intervention programme.

A coherent approach to service delivery demands a shared philosophy among the team members. In a large county service it is possible that teachers from different teams will never have the opportunity to meet unless this is planned. In Stafford-shire service there is a comprehensive programme of staff development comprising a three-hour session each week and two fixed training days per year.

The creation of twelve coordinator posts for areas of curriculum responsibility has provided another effective means of linking the area teams. These coordina-tors are recruited from their area teams to spend a proportion of their staff deve-lopment time devising strategies and resources to support the work of their colleagues in the different subject areas. These posts have been useful in estab-lishing the service as an agent of National Curriculum development and linking team members with subject initiatives.

Distributing the service

The service evolved systematically throughout the mid-1980s, working with an ever-increasing clientele of schools, governors, parents and pupils. A service handbook set out what could be offered to these different client groups. A copy was taken into every school by a member of the team. This same team member would then offer to talk to staff, parents and governors about its contents, about the philosophy which underpinned the work of the team, and about the range of ways in which the service could help the school to meet the needs of pupils exper-iencing difficulties in learning. The way in which support was provided was a matter for negotiation between the service and the school, often in consultation with the pupils and their parents. Commitments were made and reviewed by those concerned and a written record was kept.

Raising the profile of the service in this way increased the demand for its work in developing broadly based curricula for all pupils. The teachers who had worked with a relatively small number of schools now needed to be spread over many more schools. The service had to consider the deployment of staff carefully. Each teacher was allocated to a 'pyramid group' of a high school, all its feeder primaries, and any local special schools and units. They became the 'named teacher' for the schools in this group throughout the year. As each teacher would have an average of ten schools, time had to be allocated carefully.

It was important to recognise and encourage those schools who were helping themselves but needed an injection of support from the service in order to launch a particular initiative. If support teachers shared their time evenly between all schools then each would get approximately one visit per week irrespective of their needs. If, on the other hand, support teachers shared their time unequally, they could be more responsive and make a greater contribution to some schools' priorities. After initial visits to schools each support teacher determines the amount of time that each school will be allocated during a particular term. A school which received a lot of time in one term will automatically have less in the following term, to enable the support teacher to increase support elsewhere. All schools are given a programme of their visits at the beginning of each term. This pattern has helped a number of collaborative ventures between schools to develop and has provided an effective means for disseminating good practice within the county.

3 LIVING WITH LMS

The moves to broaden the work of the support service in Staffordshire were well underway when the 1988 Education Reform Act came on to the statute book, requiring the centralisation of the curriculum and the decentralisation of funding. The service to schools had to be reviewed in the light of this Act, under which schools, not LEAs, became the prime managers of their budgets.

The introduction of the National Curriculum with its related assessment arrangements encouraged teachers working in support services to think positively and creatively about how children with special educational needs are to be given access to this curriculum and have their achievements recognised. But the effects of devolving funding to schools could stifle their ideas before they have had time to put any of them into practice.

Support service work has largely been directed at pupils in mainstream schools who experience learning difficulties of a mild, moderate or temporary kind who are not usually the subjects of Statements. However, local management of schools (LMS), with its need for simple formulas, encouraged a focus on separate funding arrangements for children with Statements in mainstream schools. Some LEAs have delegated funding to schools on the basis of the numbers of Statemented pupils which they have on roll (see Chapter 24). Statemented pupils are generally worth more than non-Statemented pupils. In Staffordshire's mainstream schools, a Statemented pupil is worth two non-Statemented pupils. The LEA is still responsible for providing what is written into a child's Statement; therefore the cost of additional welfare or teaching support will continue to be borne by the LEA, despite schools' extra money. This could have the effect of redirecting the support services to cater for the 2 per cent of identifiable children for whom the LEA is directly accountable. It might also give rise to an increase in the requests from schools for formal assessments under the 1981 Education Act.

If Statements become the only way to get resources, then who can blame schools for seeking them for their pupils?

For teachers working in support services this could herald yet another change of role, one in which they are 'attached' to particular Statemented pupils for specified amounts of time with very little opportunity to help develop curriculum differentiation or to improve the learning environment. This would be a retrograde step for both pupils and support teachers. It would marginalise them both from the mainstream of activity and planning. It is difficult to envisage how an informal advisory role, which is highly valued by teachers (Richmond and Smith 1990) could continue to operate if support teachers were attached to individual pupils. In order to be credible in offering advice, the support teacher needs to be involved in the classroom and should be able to respond flexibly to identified needs and priorities.

Before LMS, schools were usually happy to accept a free service and to respect its way of working. If they were paying for a service then they might want more say in what the service does. Some schools might even want to see a return to taking children out of classrooms for their dose of remedial teaching. One can imagine a situation where teachers group pupils according to their level on National Curriculum attainment targets and identify them with a command such as, 'Level Ones, off you go to see Mrs Brown and take your reading books with you.' Giving pupils access to the full curriculum could become increasingly problematic as schools struggle to maintain 'a good average' in the national assessment league table. Support teachers could find themselves in the unhappy position of having to comply with a school's wishes or withdraw their support from the school. This has always been a dilemma for the support teacher. Now, if schools choose not to pay, it could mean that teachers' jobs will disappear. This will test the integrity of support teachers who are there to act in the best interests of the pupils, while at the same time taking account of their pay masters.

Resisting the pressures

In order to resist any move to redirect the work of the service to a smaller, elite group of Statemented pupils, a support service has to show that it is working effectively with existing client groups. It is relatively easy to categorise the amount of time each teacher spends either in the prevention (before Stage 1 of an informal assessment) or the amelioration of learning difficulties (Stages 1 and 2 of The Warnock Report's informal assessment procedures). Each teacher records the amount of time spent each week under these two headings. At the end of each term, a record is made showing how much service time was allocated to particular groups of pupils. An analysis of these time charts reveals that the greater part of service time is spent on prevention or at the early stages of identification. The data suggest that the learning difficulties experienced by large numbers of children are resolved by these early interventions. Only a tiny minority are subsequently referred for formal assessment with a view to a Statement. If the allocation of teaching resource had to wait on Statements then pupils' difficulties would become more severe and complex, there would be a dramatic increase in the number of referrals, and a speedy resolution would be less likely. The preventive work of the service would cease because the demands of the Statemented pupils would exhaust all available time and the circle of events would continue. Keeping accurate time records to present to policy-makers might prove to be one way to resist such a manoeuvre.

A second way to preserve existing good practice is to give publicity and encouragement to those schools which recognise their responsibility for pupils with special educational needs and use support service time to ensure that all pupils are included in their curriculum. A newsletter is an excellent vehicle for this. It can promote the views of parents, pupils, teachers and governors and is more persuasive because it reflects personal rather than official views.

Schools are increasingly conscious of marketing themselves to their local communities; many are very aware of initiatives being developed by neighbouring schools. Support services can turn competition between schools to the advantage of pupils with special educational needs by publicising their parental involvement projects. In Staffordshire, all teams keep a record of in-service training delivered in their area and each teacher provides a breakdown of the team's commitments within each pyramid group of schools. If schools see that others are offering workshops for parents in maths, science, play, reading, spelling and writing then they are more likely to be interested themselves. This might be one way of preserving the in-service training role of the service while keeping parents as clients.

The governors of every school have the responsibility to ensure that the special educational needs of all pupils in their charge are being met (DES 1989b: para. 24, 1989c: paras 15 and 16). So it is reasonable to think of governors as clients of the support services. They need to know what the service has to offer. Does it represent value for money and does it satisfy their perceived needs? The head teacher, class and subject teachers continue to be important clients. They need to be persuaded and supported to create the enabling structure for pupils with special educational needs within the school so that supplementary advice and support can be effective.

4 THE FUTURE OF SUPPORT SERVICES

Do support services, then, have a place in the new order? Teachers who work in support services enjoy a unique status within the profession as a result of local management of schools – that of being a 'discrete exception'. The trouble with exceptions is that they are often not considered when the rules are made. This has happened with monotonous regularity to teachers who work in support services. Entitlement to National Curriculum and Assessment INSET programmes is very often denied to support service teachers. Perhaps someone somewhere has assumed that they don't need it in order to do their jobs properly.

The insecurity this generates is compounded by the treatment which they receive from national bodies. The National Curriculum Council, the School Examinations and Assessment Council and the Department of Education and Science all fail to send documentation to those teachers who are working in support services even when it is considered to be essential reading for all school-based teachers. Knowledge is enabling, and lack of it potentially disabling, so it is particularly disconcerting to find oneself denied so much information despite continued efforts to be included on mailing lists. Support teachers have been 'excepted' at the 'discretion' of these national organisations either because of a policy decision or because, in the government's bid to empower schools, only establishments with a DES number qualify for the documentation.

The Special Educational Needs National Advisory Council (SENNAC) recently sponsored a survey of LEA support services in England and Wales. Although only fifty-five out of a total of 114 LEAs responded, their findings indicated that 80 per cent of LEAs would 'wish to retain support services as a central resource, available equally to schools and able not only to assist existing integrated children with special educational needs but also able to respond to any increase or change in demand' (Garner *et al.* 1990: 7). Yet a study of schools' perceptions of support services by Lincoln (1991) found that schools expressed serious doubts about their long-term survival. If schools had to buy in support services they would look for in-service training, assistance with whole-school initiatives, and consultancy. They would not buy in tuition for individuals. The head teachers who were interviewed considered individual tuition to be a fairly low-level activity; many said that they would buy in cheaper non-specialist help. Does this assume that anyone can teach pupils with special educational needs? It will be interesting to see how closely the practice matches these intentions if schools are given the option of buying or not buying support services.

Support services can play a vital role in improving the education of children who experience difficulties in learning. They can survive despite financial restrictions, but they will need to be accountable, promote their role, and demonstrate their effectiveness with a far greater sense of urgency. Her Majesty's Inspectorate has examined 'the ways in which the contribution of support services affected the standard of teaching'; it concluded that 'service provision does make a difference to the schools and pupils receiving it' (DES 1989a: paras 5 and 59). This has helped to raise the profile of support services and has provided a sound basis for a review of services' objectives.

A new professional organisation of SEN support teachers (SENSSA) was launched in 1990 as a self-advocacy group providing information and guidance for its members, and as a national pressure group. This organisation could help support teachers to respond to any proposed changes of their work which might have detrimental effects on the education of children who experience difficulties in school.

Support services for children with special educational needs may be facing lean times. They are being forced to review their roles. In 1991 over 100 managers of support services demonstrated their concerns to the Secretary of State in a letter outlining their current role and asking for some reassurances that delegation of funding to schools will not result in pupils' special educational needs being ignored. Support services are agents of positive discrimination for minority groups; they are a way of ensuring equality of opportunity for children with special educational needs. Central control of a service in an LEA is a major asset. Teachers learn from each other and the collective expertise of large numbers of specialist teachers can be made available to every school within the LEA as and when it is needed. There is not a more cost-effective or efficient way to organise resources and, at the same time, ensure that pupils with special educational needs are given additional support to help them to realise their potential.

REFERENCES

Department of Education and Science (DES) (1978) *Special Educational Needs* (The Warnock Report), London: HMSO.
—— (1989a) *A Survey of Support Services for Special Educational Needs* (75/89), London: HMSO.
—— (1989b) *Education Reform Act 1988: The School Curriculum and Assessment*, Circular 5/89, London: DES.
—— (1989c) *Assessments and Statements of Special Educational Needs: Procedures within the Education, Health and Social Services*, London: DES.
Garner, M., Petrie, I. and Pointon, D. (1990) *Survey of LEA Support Services for Meeting Special Educational Needs*, London: Special Educational Needs National Advisory Council.
Lincoln, C. (1991) 'An evaluation of special educational needs support services', Unpublished thesis, University of Birmingham.
Richmond, R. C. and Smith C. J. (1990) 'Support for special needs: the class teacher's perspective', *Oxford Review of Education* 16 (3), Oxford: Oxford University Press.

Chapter 35

Working as an educational psychologist

Tim Jewell

Tim Jewell is the principal educational psychologist in the London Borough of Southwark. He has collected together reports of aspects of the work of five educational psychologists who work with him. They are in note and diary form and do not pretend to give a full account of the background to each of the reported tasks. We do not place a value on them as practice by their inclusion in this chapter but they indicate the variety of work undertaken by psychologists in one local authority. Tim Jewell provides an introduction to the chapter.

1 INTRODUCTION

The reports cover many of the different aspects of an educational psychologist's work. As our responsibilities are to children and young people between 0 and 19, psychologists need to draw on many different psychological themes to inform their work.

If a psychological service wishes to work in a preventive way it must put aside time to carry out such tasks as the in-service training of teachers and working with schools on their development plans. Overall, about 60 per cent of our time is taken up by individual casework. The remaining 40 per cent consists of in-service training, group work, our own professional development and contributions to other aspects of local authority policy such as responses to the Children's Act 1990.

Future developments in educational psychology practice will depend on decisions made by schools under local management of schools. If equality of access for all pupils is to be protected then most educational psychologists (EPs) would support the continuation of a centrally based local authority service providing the wide range of services illustrated in these reports.

Each of the reports is by a different psychologist and they include a home visit, office work and work in a special school, an infant school and a secondary school.

2 HOME VISIT

No office this morning. After dropping my children at school, I am going straight to a home visit at 9.00 a.m. to meet 2-year-old Sarah James and her parents.

Sarah is one of approximately 120 pre-school children 'notified' annually by the two local health authorities. 'Notification' is the term used when the Health Authority alerts the Education Authority that a child might need special help when they start school or nursery. A copy of the notification is sent to the Educational Psychology Service. The family is then linked to an educational psychologist who will offer advice.

Sarah has been 'notified' because she has cerebral palsy. This is one of the most common disabling conditions of childhood. It results in the loss of coordinated movement. Motor development and speech may be affected in varying degrees. Physiotherapy and sometimes occupational and/or speech therapy may be needed regularly.

I have already talked to Sarah's mum, Sue, on the phone when we arranged today's meeting. She and her husband would like to begin a full assessment with a view to providing a Statement for Sarah.

Visiting parents of pre-school children provides an opportunity to work with parents as real equals for the benefit of their children – and we see children do things at home that they don't do anywhere else. Today's meeting will be a time for introductions and exchanging initial information. I shall begin to learn about Sarah and how her condition affects both her and her family.

Arriving at the house, Mr James introduces me to Sarah and I play on the living-room floor with her while he makes coffee. Even in this relaxed setting, my training and experience in observation and child development means that I am immediately beginning to assess Sarah's behaviour in a positive way by noting what she can do.

Sarah can stand with some support. She moves by either rolling or dragging her body sideways using her stronger and more coordinated right arm. She is an alert little girl. She has no speech yet but uses her body movements and facial expression to communicate very effectively and I can easily understand her simple demands. There is no sign at the moment of the frustration and temper which can develop as a result of communication difficulties. Sarah draws me spontaneously into her play, offering me the ball which is part of her toy and indicating that she wants me to post it as she has been doing. She then deliberately rolls it across the floor and wants me to retrieve it so that she can do it again. Her use of this particular toy (which I recognise from my own children's infancy) is age appropriate.

On hearing her name mentioned, Sarah responds immediately to the sound of her father's voice from the kitchen by looking in that direction. She smiles and uses body language to greet her mother when she enters the room but does not demand further attention, content with me as a playmate.

When the adults gather to talk, Sarah continues to amuse herself passing between us and her toys like any other 2 year old and more self-sufficient than some! The only real difference is that Sarah cannot get to us on her feet. Her actions show that she understands each of the simple requests made by her parents during the course of our conversation.

Mr and Mrs James are currently working closely with the occupational therapists and physiotherapists, both of whom I also know, on an individual course of treatment to develop Sarah's muscular control. They work together as a team and will shortly be joined by a speech therapist to start focusing on developing muscles used for language.

At the moment, Sarah attends a private nursery while her parents are at work. This has been working well as the nursery is also fully involved in her therapy and has a very good staff–pupil ratio which enables them to give her all the special attention she needs. However, the situation will change shortly when Sarah moves to the older age group. She will be with much bigger and more active children and will also have to negotiate stairs, so her dependence on adult help will increase. Sarah's older brother attends the local primary school and it would be possible for Sarah to transfer to the nursery class there when she is 3.

Sarah's parents have two concerns. They want a Statement for Sarah to make sure that her needs are catered for when she begins school. They also want help to decide whether her present school can meet her needs until she is 5 or if she should transfer to the local nursery class using the assessment to establish what her needs will be in that setting. Factors such as Sarah's need for local friends and family arrangements for after-school care are as important as the details of educational provision.

By the end of my visit, we have arranged a list of actions. I will complete the form which triggers the full assessment, listing the professionals we have agreed will need to be consulted. I will also send a copy of the guidelines we have which help parents to write their advice for the assessment. Mr and Mrs James will talk to the head of the local primary school about Sarah and establish whether there is likely to be a full-time place available for her when she is 3. I will make enquiries when I visit there as I am also the psychologist for the school. I will ring Mr and Mrs James after the school holiday to arrange a visit with them to Sarah's nursery for further discussions with staff there and to continue my observations and assessment in that setting. By that time I should also have received the first official letter from the Education Authority to the parents confirming that the assessment is to take place and asking for their advice.

Team work

Over the period of assessment, there will be other meetings with the parents, myself and all the other professionals involved including the head of the local school to help Mr and Mrs James reach an informed decision about the kind of education they want for Sarah. My assessment will look not only at Sarah as an individual but also at environmental factors such as the existing expertise and resources available in each nursery.

Through discussion and observation, we shall build up a detailed picture of her needs in nursery/school. Where there are gaps in our information I can turn to a range of checklists to investigate aspects of her development in more detail. We often use the Portage checklist which gives detailed sequences of skills in the main areas of child development. These are valuable in working with children at home, with a trained visitor helping parents to plan a home teaching programme for the week. The Portage checklist covers the areas of language, movement, cognitive and self-help development. I find it useful in establishing what skills and concepts a child has developed. I am then able to plan with the parent what to teach next and also keep a record of progress. Working with parents in this way builds up a continuous record of the child's development and helps to place parents at the centre of the process of planning.

Working together as a team, we shall all contribute to the assessment from our own particular area of expertise but it is important that we agree on general principles. At the moment, Mr and Mrs James hope that Sarah will be educated in the mainstream school and not a special school. As this is also the policy of the local authority, every effort will be made to achieve this.

3 A MORNING IN THE OFFICE

Arrive at the office at 8.45 a.m. Look at my diary. Remind myself of the week's plan. Transfer this information to the office diary. (Office staff need to know where I am to advise others of the best time to contact me, or in case of an emergency.)

Collect typing. Check for errors. Two letters, a school visit record and my report for a child's full assessment of special educational needs. I carefully read my psychological report as it is likely to have important implications for the child's educational future and must be accurate. The child is of primary age. My report carries a brief history of my contact with her and her family and school. A record is then given of my assessment work which focuses on describing her behaviours and attainments in a wide range of teaching and social situations. This information has been gained from the teacher, the parent and from my observations in context and the individual work I have carried out with her. On the basis of this assessment I describe the child's needs from a psychological perspective. In my view she would benefit from a learning programme with clearly detailed objectives, daily recording of progress, a high level of success, regular review and updating of the learning targets. Parental involvement in the planning of this programme is particularly important since priority areas for development include self-help skills and language. The report concludes with a description of proposed provision, including daily individual teaching sessions under the management of her class teacher. This provision, I think, will mean that she will be successfully integrated within her mainstream class.

I receive a call from the Governor Training Officer seeking help from our service in organising and running a course on special educational needs. I agree to discuss this with EP colleagues and the Special Needs Inspector. I know the team will be keen to participate in this venture.

Weekly business meeting – 9.30 a.m. Team meetings at this point in the week work well. I check the rota and find I'm chairperson. Collect agenda from notice board. There are twelve items to discuss and these include aspects of the Education Department organisation, allocation of cases to individual educational psychologists and a sharing of general information including contacts on governor training, induction and matters relating to the Personnel Department. All are important issues generating lively discussion. To get through the whole agenda I work hard to maintain the focus of discussion. I ask the scribe to read back agreed actions as we go along.

Jobs I take away from this meeting are:

- To get back to the Governor Training Officer and to coordinate our input.
- To carry out the induction of our new colleague starting next week – this is the first chance to pilot our newly developed induction programme, which includes visits to mainstream and special schools, an introduction to key officers in the local education authority, and a treasure hunt where new members of the team are given a list of information to collect and have to find their way round all the offices and departments to collate it. There is no faster way to get to know the system.
- To meet with the head of Personnel Services. She works with all departments within the local council. She is leading a review of policy in relation to selection and recruitment of local authority employees. We are particularly keen to focus on the equal opportunities issues.

Coffee and chat at 10.30 a.m.

Team support meeting at 10.45 a.m. Colleagues bring concerns for joint discussion. One colleague has been asked to contribute to a learning programme for a child with a language disorder who is being supported in a mainstream school. In pooling our knowledge and experience we come up with a number of ideas she can take to a planning meeting involving the school, parents and speech therapist.

Another member of the team asks us to consider how to respond to a Black family's request for a Black EP. Our usual policy is for the patch EP to meet the family to explore the reasons for the request and to suggest the advantages of an EP with local knowledge. In this case the parents, head teacher and education liaison officer inform us that the child has been subjected to verbal and physical racial attacks from a group of local children. All are concerned about his increasingly withdrawn behaviour. This is most noticeable with White adults and children. We feel that a Black EP would be in a better position to get to know this child and this consideration should take precedence over knowledge of the local area.

Appointment with trainee at 11.45 a.m. Meet with trainee, whom I'm currently supervising, and his tutor. The aim of the meeting is to review Peter's practical placement. Like all trainee EPs, Peter has been a teacher and has a first degree in Psychology and is now seconded on to a training course. Peter has observed and worked with various members of our team and is now working more independently under my supervision across a range of ages and types of provision. He has concentrated on developing his skills in interviewing, assessment, and planning learning and behaviour programmes for children. We agree that during Peter's last few weeks with the team he will focus on extending his experience in the area of training.

The team has organised a workshop called 'Managing Behaviour Positively in the Early Years' for nursery nurses and teachers. This is due to take place next week. Peter expresses a wish to contribute. In addition, I invite him to a meeting to help plan the content of an assertiveness training course for senior teachers.

4 WORKING IN SPECIAL SCHOOLS

The emphasis within special schools has changed and developed over the last twenty or so years to increase the focus on the curriculum while maintaining a care ethos. This change has also involved changes in the approach taken by educational psychologists. Intelligence tests were used by EPs almost exclusively ten years ago to measure children's IQs. Educational psychologists now are less likely to collect this information because of concerns over its reliability and validity. Many educational psychologists feel that these tests are unfair to individual children because they may contain racial, cultural and class bias. Also it is felt that the information obtained from an intelligence test does not often help to develop a more effective teaching programme and learning experience for the child. An alternative approach emphasises the psychology of teaching rather than the psychology of individual differences between children. Assessment looks at what we are trying to teach and how it matches the pupil's current skills and concept development. This assessment also looks at the teaching method, the materials and the child's motivation to learn what is on offer.

For example, I'm helping to design a curriculum for David, aged 12, who attends a school for children with severe learning difficulties. The teachers have good skills in programme design – setting objectives, keeping a chart, writing down a teaching procedure. David has tubero sclerosis, a condition which can produce a range of effects from quite trivial signs to serious epilepsy. Unfortunately, David is suffering badly from the condition and seems to be deteriorating, experiencing more frequent fits in spite of medication and forgetting skills he has already learned rather than learning new skills. This is upsetting both his parents and his teacher. David has only a few words of speech and cannot express his feelings verbally, but he gives signs of distress. He likes the school swimming pool and mixes easily with other children when he is feeling well. When he is unwell he becomes withdrawn but with encouragement and guidance he will continue to work in school. The programme we design has three elements aimed at preserving the skills David has. First, overlearning continues the teaching procedure for skills David has already mastered, so reducing the probability of loss of skill. Second, maintenance activities exercise skills every day. Third, fluency activities help David to perform skills quickly and easily as well as accurately.

Another child, Binaben, experiences difficulties with learning and attends a school for children with moderate learning difficulties. She is happy in the school and works well. Her Statement of special educational needs is detailed and gives guidance about the curriculum she is going to follow.

The curriculum for Binaben is to be:

- modified from the National Curriculum so that she has a detailed learning programme on basic literacy and numeracy skills;
- extended to teach her key independence and self-help skills, e.g. crossing roads, shopping, combing her hair, choosing clothes for the day;
- adapted to give religious instruction in accordance with her parents' wishes in a form she can understand;
- otherwise based on the National Curriculum, so that she can integrate into mainstream classes for some of the week with the right kind of preparation.

Dividing time between special and mainstream schools

I visit my special schools for a morning every two to three weeks. Compared with large mainstream schools this may seem a lot, as most special schools are much smaller than mainstream schools. Only by allocating a lot of time to special schools can we begin to provide a real service to children and parents, rather than just a placement service. When an educational psychologist is known to the parents, some of the more sensitive issues can begin to be addressed which might otherwise remain taboo – for example, feelings of guilt or failure, 'blaming' the child, anxieties about assumed hereditary factors, worries about what will happen to the child as an adult, husbands opting out.

Allocating so much time to special schools does cut down the time we can spend in mainstream settings and one reason why parents sometimes ask for their children to go into special school may be the presence of visiting professionals, therapists for example. However, if a child *is* in special provision we feel that that child needs substantial support from all services including our own.

An EP with an awareness of equal opportunities who visits special schools has to face the fact that segregation and additional resources go together at the moment. Special provision is supposed to be intensive positive resourcing to help a child but segregation labels the child, and in some situations institutionalises the child.

Educational psychologists have to play their part in preventing conscious or institutional racism which can result in the disproportionate segregation of Black children in special schools or sexism which may involve directing special needs resources towards boys rather than girls.

Local management of schools (LMS) and the National Curriculum

My school for children with severe learning difficulties is looking at the National Curriculum, hoping to introduce much more Science, to promote integration in mainstream and to develop an overall curriculum structure that ranges from the Special Care Unit's initial sensory and physical skills to the published National Curriculum. A curriculum for all children was our aim and the work in this area has been invigorating for the school, bringing staff into closer contact with colleagues in mainstream and a broader range of inspectors.

Some teachers in special schools have commented that LMS has produced many problems for mainstream schools – for example, uncertainty about final budget figures, cuts in the special needs funding by the LEA, mounds of extra paperwork, and that these have led to an increase in the number of children whose needs are not being met. Teachers in special schools and units have said it's becoming more difficult to integrate children into mainstream, and that mainstream schools are reluctant to agree that children who have in fact transferred should appear formally on their rolls.

5 IN THE INFANTS

In office, 8.45 a.m. Making coffee. Phone rings. The interpreter for this morning is unwell. Call Talford Infant School with the bad news. The teacher has a good idea and agrees to contact parents suggesting they invite mother's sister along who apparently speaks fluent English. The morning might be saved. Under fives' Community Medical Officer returns my call to give relevant background details about a 2-year-old girl whose parents want help to assist her learning. Out of the door before phone rings again.

At Talford Infant School by 9.30 a.m. Meeting to review the progress of top infant, Inge. Present: parents, aunt, class teacher, me.

A learning programme to develop Inge's handwriting was set up two weeks ago when parents, school staff, physiotherapist, school doctor and myself first met. The teacher reports Inge has succeeded on two of the three set targets, drawing a circle and drawing a vertical line from top to bottom correctly. These are early steps towards the long-term aim of writing her name. The third target, drawing a horizontal line from left to right, didn't come on so well and needs further looking at. The teacher describes how the programme has gone so far. Inge enjoyed recording her own progress on the bar chart and even reminded the teacher on the two occasions when the daily activity had slipped her mind. Also, she needed no reminder to take the bar chart and the planned follow-up work home at the end of the week.

I think the teacher's ideas for incorporating practice of drawing circles and lines into everyday classroom activities are tremendous, I especially like the use of circles in the work on halves and quarters. On a more general note the class teacher contacted the Learning Resources Centre, this resulted in a visit the very next day and an easy-use keyboard will hopefully be delivered next week. In the meantime the class teacher has taken up the idea of encouraging Inge to use the school computer to record her written work. This enables Inge to produce legible work without the laborious effort and high level of frustration evident when she writes by hand. While using high tech in the short term we are teaching Inge writing skills. This is not only to help her feel less different from other children – you can't gamble that a child will have a word processor handy when she wants to write. As the parents and I agreed, we don't use high tech on the summer holiday beach – and we'd only get sand in the word processor if we did. Until Inge feels confident about writing her name the teacher has agreed to write Inge's name on sticky labels which she uses to identify her work. She is labelling enthusiastically at present!

The class teacher and parents tell us that Inge has worn her glasses to school every day since our last meeting – a real breakthrough! I tentatively ask about Inge's behaviour and it is great to hear that she has not scribbled on either her own or anybody else's work. Inge's mother comments that Inge has asked for pencil and paper to draw with several times, having not done so for several months before.

I check the time and suggest we explore possible alterations to the programme before time runs out. We agree steps to make the task of drawing a line from left to right easier. We will try a larger, different colour dot to indicate the start of the line and increase the length of the line to be traced. We talk about the clearest way of modelling the activity for Inge. We agree to meet again on my next regular visit in three weeks' time.

I came away feeling pleased about Inge's progress, but concerned about the lack of opportunity for Inge's parents to contribute equally in today's meeting. I was relieved when Inge's aunt stepped in at the last minute to act as interpreter. However, her own need to be actually involved in the meeting really stood in the way of her carrying out the interpreter's role. My repeated attempts to bring her back to this role were less than effective.

On balance I'm pleased the meeting went ahead, but *again* it has highlighted that sensitive, trained interpreters are essential if parents are to be fully involved in their children's learning.

6 WORKING IN A SECONDARY SCHOOL

I visit secondary schools for a morning and go in for half an hour or so the week before to finalise the schedule with the deputy head. We work out which members of staff I need to see, which parents and/or children I will be seeing and how much time will be allocated to discussions of policy and school development. Today we decide that I'll read the school files on three children and look at their work across all subjects with the form tutors but that the deputy head will have a look at the teachers' records before finalising my time with each teacher. The meeting is very brisk and tightly minuted. We work well as a team to sort out priorities. We try to make sure that the schedule is not dominated by boys.

An attendance problem

I'm seeing a parent today about her son's school attendance. The family have moved into the area recently and the son had home tuition for over a term in the previous area because of epileptic fits. However, medical advice says that the medication is now controlling the fits well and there is no reason why he should not attend school full time. His mother explains that her son is anxious about 'making a fool of himself' by having a fit in public and does not like to go out of the house. She thinks he is more likely to have a fit when he is anxious and would prefer him to have a home tutor. We discuss how the anxiety of a family can be transmitted to a child and how we can persuade him to attend without raising his level of anxiety.

Talking about 'eating disorders'

I talk to the teachers about eating disorders and provide an information package. These problems seldom come to educational psychologists. When they do the child is usually in a serious condition, perhaps in hospital. I stress to the school that the messages in the curriculum and hidden curriculum about food and body shapes, ambition and 'success' can either contribute to a solution to eating disorders or be part of the problem.

Learning about the work of colleagues

Today I'm also doing a joint visit with the school's general inspector. We've been trying to learn more about the day-to-day realities of each other's work. Last time, the inspector sat in on my visit and seemed very interested in the way I negotiated with the school about when direct involvement with a child was appropriate. This time I'm sitting in on the inspector's visit.

We start by seeing the head, and are then passed on to the head of Science. The inspector goes through a list of curriculum development questions and focuses on how the Science department could increase the number of examination choices, entries and passes by girls. Then we discuss the progress of a complaint against a teacher which has yet to be resolved. I am impressed with the organisation of the visit by the inspector who is clearly under a lot of time pressure.

Whole-school policies

I'm talking to the deputy head teacher this afternoon about our final arrangements for the school's internal review of behaviour management which will take place next term. We have planned that a colleague and I will spend a week in the school interviewing teachers and children about discipline using the questionnaire we worked out with the heads of year and pupil representatives last term.

The deputy head teacher will organise the timing of interviews.

The raising of pupil attainment is a core policy objective in this new education authority. We discussed a project for accelerating pupils' writing attainments and how we might select an appropriate method to help the school develop practice in this area. The project will take two terms.

An inter-agency meeting

We're having an inter-agency meeting in school at a time when as many key teachers can attend as possible. It concerns Peter, a 13-year-old boy. There are concerns about his behaviour towards girls in corridors. The head feels an exclusion is needed. The deputy and head of year were less sure. The school-based social worker said she'd counselled the child regularly but this had recently ended with the issue unresolved. The head expressed the concerns and complaints voiced by parents of other children in the school.

A series of suggestions was produced; the head of year would talk to the boy giving clear direction about behaviour and establishing a behavioural contact to specify the boundaries of behaviour. I felt there was a need for an active anti-sexist policy in the school. The situation would be reviewed at the next meeting in four weeks' time.

Chapter 36

Welcome to Newham!
Defining services to parents

Claire Debenham and Simon Trotter

Simon Trotter is Assistant Director of Education (Pupil Services) in the London Borough of Newham and Claire Debenham is the Assistant Education Officer (Pupil Services). This chapter consists of an exchange of memos between Simon and Claire in which they attempt to define Claire's position in the department, her work with parents, providing information and support through the assessment process and in dealing with complaints. They provide a basis for reflection on equality of opportunities for both staff and users of services. The chapter ends with a postscript from Andrew Panton, Deputy Director of Education (Pre-sixteen Service).

EDUCATION OFFICE MEMORANDUM 1

To: Claire Debenham

Date: 4.1.90
Ref: S-AD/ST/ET

Welcome to Newham!

This memorandum summarises a number of discussions we have had since you joined the Authority several weeks ago. It aims to set out some basic ways of working and some suggested constraints on how you should operate. I hope you find it helpful – if there are issues with which you profoundly disagree, please do not hesitate to comment.

I'm not going to look in detail at policy issues at this stage: we have had discussions on integration and its implications and we are both committed to furthering the policy. I want to focus here on some very mundane issues about working in a bureaucracy which is organised in a hierarchical fashion (what bureaucracy isn't?) with the intention that this may ensure your effectiveness within the Council structure. However good your ideas, if you can't get the bureaucracy to respond to them, you might as well not bother!

Names

First a very practical issue. Two points on names. I prefer to call councillors by their title in a rather formal way. You may wish to do likewise. It helps to remind everyone who is in charge.

Names within the department are less sensitive than they used to be. You as a professional assistant, can call everyone by their first names. I suggest that you assume that everyone should call you by yours. If you were a little more senior in the hierarchy, you might (at least, a couple of years ago) have encouraged junior staff to use your surname.

It is worth mentioning, though, that there is still a distinction in many educational departments (including this one) between staff with professional qualifications (mostly former teachers) and those without. Staff without such qualifications often see themselves (and are encouraged to do so by some) in a fairly subservient role, carrying out procedures without considering the end in view. As we discussed, it is important to encourage front line staff (those dealing with the public) to take more responsibility by discussion, training and delegation. I welcome your interest in this area.

Dress

I favour fairly formal dress – I always wear a suit. There are two main reasons for this. First, when you go out to meetings no one will know who you are. Few people in schools understand how the office works, so, if you look respectable and speak with authority, people will think you are important – and take more notice of what you say than they otherwise would. As a woman in a male-dominated hierarchy, you will have enough problems being taken seriously without being mistaken for my secretary.

The other reason is that, if you look respectable, you can be more radical in your arguments without being instantly branded as a trouble-maker.

There is a third, more personal reason. I like to put the job on and take it off with my suit. Changing out of work clothes helps me to leave work issues at the office – which is useful if things aren't going well. I expect that you CQWS-holders[1] have all kinds of sophisticated strategies for achieving this result, so my rather primitive one may not be much help.

Hierarchy

As you will already have observed, the education office is organised in a very hierarchical way. This is not, I hope, to say that decisions are taken in an arbitrary and unjustified fashion, or that staff at the bottom of the hierarchy are not valued. Nor should it mean that communication is necessarily top–down, and that the formation of project teams and support networks is undesirable.

It seems to me that there are clear benefits to hierarchical organisation systems, and that there are ways of overcoming their worst features. What I like about hierarchies is that everyone has (or should have) a good understanding of their responsibilities and, if they are properly organised, this makes for efficient management. The other side of this coin is that people may be encouraged to see their jobs in terms of duties rather than of responsibilities, and to refer any issue which falls outside a narrow perception of these duties up the line for action.

What are the intrinsic problems of operating a hierarchy? The first is, I suppose, avoiding the exercise of power in an arbitrary way. This is best overcome by encouraging open discussion within the hierarchy in order that decisions can be questioned – routinely (as opposed to reserving the right to question decisions only when they are thought to be wrong).

The second is the issue of promoting good communication. In their worst form, hierarchies encourage information to travel from the top downwards, from one individual to another, with distortion taking place at each transmission. Again, the solution to this seems to be to set up regular sessions in which discussion can take place: these kinds of staff meeting can then allow information to flow in both directions. There is obviously a balance to be struck in setting up patterns of meetings to avoid a situation in which people spend more time sharing information than actually formulating advice, contributing to policy-making or taking and implementing decisions. There is also a real issue about managers and staff finding these sorts of meetings fairly threatening, which brings me to my next point.

The third issue is one of support. I suppose the opposite of a hierarchy is a collective, and I also suppose (never having worked in one) that a collective in which responsibilities and decisions are shared may be a supportive place to work. Because of the way that hierarchies are organised vertically and that little thought is often given to horizontal links between people at similar levels in different areas, I think it is probably quite easy to feel isolated. This probably suits some people quite well (I am not a gregarious person by nature, for example, and like to think things through either on my own or with a very few others) but we all need support at times and many people perform best when the support is very much in evidence. At this stage, I think all I can do is agree that we need to do more work on setting up networks and identifying issues that are best handled by project teams drawn from different areas of the department.

The fourth issue relates to equal opportunities. I don't know whether organisations that are organised in a very hierarchical fashion create particular difficulties for disadvantaged groups, or whether it is simply very obvious in a hierarchy who has the status, money and influence and who hasn't. I suspect that it's a combination of both and that, in particular, hierarchical ways of working tend to suit those of us who are over-confident, pushy and self-opinionated and that those of us who fit this description tend to come from rather privileged (as opposed to disadvantaged) backgrounds. Local authorities in general, and Newham in particular, have a good record of developing policy and practice on the promotion of equal opportunities within their workforces, and these are written up in equal opportunities statements, recruitment manuals, etc. However, I remain concerned that these excellent policies and practices do not always result in workforces which reflect the communities they serve in terms of ethnic composition, gender and disability (especially at senior levels).

However, the hierarchical organisation of Council departments has the slightly curious result that, at meetings, the most senior person present from any department represents the Director. Thus, where you are representing the Department and the chair asks if the Director of Education has a view, you are required to state it. Not *your* view, but his view. This curious convention emphasises the fact that, as a bureaucrat, you are constantly representing the people to whom you are responsible. It also emphasises the need to ensure that you have talked through the possible options which may arise at a meeting in advance, in order that you can respond automatically. This will require, initially at least, some fairly careful preparation.

Obviously, as you learn more about the job, you will increasingly be able to judge for yourself how to respond to questions of this kind, and your pre-meetings will become less detailed.

I have written to you separately about your role with respect to parents, because it's so crucial to your job.

Best wishes and good luck!

Si—

Simon Trotter

EDUCATION OFFICE MEMORANDUM 2

To: Simon Trotter   *Date:* 8.1.90
AD (Special & Pupil Services)   *Ref:* S-PA/CD/EP

Thank you for your recent memorandum 'Welcome to Newham'. I found it a helpful and fascinating perspective on this organisation and cannot resist the urge to reply!

First of all, thanks for the tips on names and dress. I generally call people by their first names, since this has been the norm in other places that I've worked in – whatever your place in the hierarchy. It is as well to know that other people may have different ideas.

On the question of dress, I like to think I have looked fairly presentable since working here. I somehow absorbed the message at the interview that a woman in trousers would not be accepted easily in the post. Consequently, I have worn a dress or a skirt for the vast majority of the time despite the fact that this is not my usual mode. Your subsequent comments have told me that my first impression was correct.

You suggest that dressing in a 'respectable' and 'formal' way may help to ensure that people take notice of what I say, and that I am taken seriously and not mistaken for your secretary. I suppose you pick-up on this last point because you know it has happened quite a lot.

While there is something in what you say, I have two major reasons for suggesting that how I am perceived is only minimally affected by how I dress. To begin with, some of the best-dressed workers in this office (and indeed in most offices) are, in fact, secretaries. Secondly, more often than not it is people who are talking to me on the phone who make this mistake.

People make assumptions about my status and role without having set eyes on me. It is interesting to note that, other than referring to me as your secretary, their behaviour is affected. They speak in a tone and manner which suggests I am a 'minion'. On hearing my (female) voice they ask to speak to you in the belief you will have the answers I don't have, or persist in punctuating the conversation with 'dear', 'darling' or 'love'. This happens especially when I am asking for information they don't want to give, or asking them to do something they don't want to do. These responses have no gender or professional boundaries.

Imagine *yourself* on the receiving end of 'Well, Simon dear, I'll see what I can do for you. Don't think I can help though. Tell you what love, pass me over to Claire would you?' I imagine that most people sporting suits around here would be disconcerted by such unexpected intimacy!

One last point on the matter of suits. I think you are not specific enough on this issue. Not all suits convey the authority or anonymity you claim. The suits that do are suits for men (and in my experience they don't necessarily have to be very smart!). Are you advocating that I wear one? I think it unlikely to help me melt into the background. In fact, it's the kind of thing to *guarantee* me the label of 'trouble-maker'. You are right in suggesting that men in suits convey authority, however: but simply transferring the garb will not endow women with the same benefits. Besides, as I've already said, I've received a strong message about women in trousers. Perhaps this paradox conveys some of the confusions in attitudes to women in management positions.

I am aware that these kinds of issues come up for other people – not only women, who in any case are not a homogeneous group. For any one who is not of the dominant group in any organisation (especially at the top), daily, and often unconscious, decisions are made on the question of 'fitting in'. Important aspects of the 'self' are compromised, in my opinion resulting in a net loss to the organisation, including less effective service delivery in the long run.

So, therefore, I think there is a close link between these matters, and your later question about the intrinsic problems of operating a hierarchy in local government. Hierarchies in education services are here to stay, for all the reasons you describe, so from the point of view of service delivery it is important to ask the question, for whom do they work – and why. Perhaps particularly important when a stated policy objective is the implementation of Equal Opportunities in education. In Newham this policy is taken to encompass educating children with special educational needs in mainstream schools, and involving parents in the assessment process.

By your own description local authority hierarchies including this one, do not work for 'some groups' in the workforce (by which I assume you mean Black people, women, working-class people, people with disabilities, and gay and lesbian people), despite Equal Opportunities Recruitment Policies. It is hardly surprising, then, that such groups in the community feel that they are largely outsiders to these organisations; that they are not understood, and that services don't reflect or meet their needs very well. From this point of view, rather than being one in a series of problems thrown up by the operation of a hierarchy, Equal Opportunities is the central issue, which affects all the others you mention (communication, decision-making, support systems, and attitudes to work responsibilities and service delivery).

Why 'Equal Opportunities' Recruitment procedures 'don't work' – that is, don't result in a varied workforce from the top to bottom of the organisation – is a very complex issue. Some would say the answer is simple: policies only work if they are implemented, and this policy is unlikely to be implemented with enthusiasm by those traditionally in power in a bureaucracy, since it would disadvantage them. Individuals, usually in power, may have to make room for others.

I think the problem is to do with implementation, and much does depend on the values of people at the top. But others play their part too. As well as this, factors other than personal commitment come into play – usually 'efficiency' and 'cost-effectiveness'. I have no doubt that the relationship of 'Equal Opportunities' to efficiency and cost-effectiveness will be debated for a considerable time to come. Some will say that the terms are entirely synonymous, if effective service delivery is the goal, while others will put a quite different point of view.

It is worth remembering that 'Equal Opportunities' policies go beyond recruitment however. People have work practices which have grown and developed according to their view of the world. They are initially designed to maintain an order. The needs of service users, or the consumer's view of effective service delivery, may not coincide with an officer's view of what is orderly or efficient.

For example, I've often wondered what lies behind the name of the 'Authorised Officers' Briefing Meeting'. The inaccessibility of the name seems a curious anomaly in a Department committed to the involvement of parents in the assessment of the children's special educational needs.

From a parent's point of view there is a message in the name and that is that the organisation has a language and culture of its own that they are outsiders to. From the point of view of some officers, there may be some comfort in this! Language is a powerful defence, and more than just a way of defining 'us' and 'them'. In this instance, for example, what is being conveyed is potentially very undermining. 'You don't even understand the name of the body that is proposing a future for your child, and therefore, probably won't remember it properly and will feel silly saying it in case you get it wrong.' This undoubtedly serves to silence some people who might otherwise have made demands or asked questions. Try translating it into community languages for instance: the barrier to communication threatens to be insurmountable.

Arguably, here is an example of a work practice which serves the needs of the organisation, in terms of keeping service users in their place, and from the organisation's point of view it works well in terms of processing the work. However, in terms of developing the organisation's practice within the Equal Opportunities framework, it presents an obstacle. This kind of obstacle may affect officers and users, but is a more serious matter for users – in this case parents.

The question of language, communication and parents access to the Department is much broader than this, of course, and I am sure will provide more material for discussion between us. Could we possibly begin by discussing a new name for 'AOB' to be used by parents and professionals alike? How about the 'Special Needs Panel'?

Claire

Claire Debenham

EDUCATION OFFICE MEMORANDUM 3

To: Simon Trotter   *Date:* 5.2.90
AD (Special & Pupil Services)   *REF:* S-PA/CD/SD

Letters to parents

In reference to the subject above I wish to draw your attention to the density of prose frequently employed by administrative officers communicating, on your behalf, with parents. I note that the style of language is wordy and alienating, requiring several years of practice to refine. Having studied the method in detail, and worked hard to suppress the instinct to communicate, officers are reluctant to relinquish their style. Such language is considered a mark of 'professionalism', a display of specialist knowledge, and acquaintance with the power of legal processes. In short, the primary interest is not being understood.

This is my interpretation of why it is we issue so many letters which I find difficult to understand myself. I am learning the code, but I would prefer to work at changing the definition of 'professional' letter writing in the Special Education Section – with your support. As one starting point I have drafted a series of standard letters to parents whose children are being formally assessed. I have used 'everyday' language, and cut out unnecessary details. I would appreciate your comments on these.

In addition, I would like to do some work with the administrative officers on what the underlying issues are; why it is that using everyday language is preferable, and provides a more professional service. There are many letters they will continue to draft themselves. The work would be very boring if that was not the case. Moreover, they must be willing to use the standard letters, and experience has shown me that this will not happen unless the issues are understood.

In addition, and part of the same issue, is the question of using translations. I am doing some work on this at the moment and will write to you again. In the meantime, I look forward to hearing your comments on the letters and to agreeing a strategy for introducing them.

Claire

Claire Debenham

EDUCATION OFFICE MEMORANDUM 4

To: Simon Trotter   *Date:* 15.2.90
AD (Special & Pupil Services)   *Ref:* S-PA/CD/SD

Translated letters and information to parents

Thank you for your helpful comments on the letters to parents. I have had some productive discussions with the admin. section on the question on style and 'everyday language'.

Now, I would like your agreement to translating the series of standard letters to parents whose children are being assessed under Section 5 of the Education Act 1981, into the community languages recognised by the Council (i.e. Urdu, Hindi, Punjabi, Bengali, Gujerati, Malayam, Tamil, and Cantonese). It will also be necessary to develop a policy on their use.

Current situation

Whenever an administrative officer realises that a family may need letters in translation, they send each letter to the Council Translation and Interpreting Unit to be individually translated. This results in a long delay in sending letters out. A further consequence is that because officers find the process time-consuming and a nuisance, it will only be done if it is absolutely clear that no one in the family can understand what is going on. This generally means that some inconvenience has been caused to the Department. Even officers who are well motivated on this issue find the process irritating, and are more likely to use the facility reactively, rather than routinely.

I am concerned that families are being prevented from taking a real part in the assessment process because of this situation. Even where English language letters are apparently understood, it may be the case that parents are dependent on children for explanation, or one parent on the other. This may be partly the reason for the predominance of Asian children in Special Schools, for example. Despite our successful integration policy, there are relatively few Asian children with Statements in mainstream placements. Perhaps some Asian parents are being tripped at the first hurdle.

Development

We need to have a firm policy on sending information to parents in translation.

1   Information about home languages must be a matter of routine. At the moment psychologists usually supply the information, but where it is missing administrative officers must pursue the question with the child's school.
2   All the standard Section 5 letters and reply slips should be translated into the eight community languages above, and kept in printed sets in the Special Education Section for immediate use. It should be the responsibility of the Senior Administrative Officer to ensure new copies are printed as necessary.
3   If families require Section 5 letters in languages other than those I have mentioned, these can be ordered from the Translation Unit in the usual way, as can any individually composed letters.
4   Other information, for example the Parents' Booklet, should be translated into the eight languages for photocopying as necessary.
5   Letters should be sent out in English, and the language spoken at home. This will avoid:
     – offence, if the parents are fluent in English
     – too much confusion, if the wrong information has been given about the home language.
6   Also to avoid confusion, each letter should have a standard phrase in English

printed at its foot, listing the languages it is available in. Parents can request the correct language if we have got it wrong.

7   It should be stated that interpreters may be present at meetings with parents and children. The reply slip should have a space to indicate if this is desirable. If so, this information should be passed on to all professionals involved in the assessment, together with information about how to book interpreters through the Council Unit.

Conclusion

I hope you will agree with these suggestions. Once the bulk of work has been dealt with by having standard letters translated, I hope officers will find the process less frustrating and more a matter of routine. It may then be possible to generalise the principles to other communications with parents. The only drawback to standardising translation is that, unlike English Language versions, they won't be on a word processor, so cannot be 'mail-merged' for the personal touch. I think the benefits should outweigh this disadvantage.

If you agree, can we discuss implementing the system in the Administration Section? As with all changes in practice, evidence of your support will be crucial. You are not only 'Authority', but also have been here long enough to be seen as the 'Old Guard'. As you know, just telling people to change their practice is rarely enough, especially when there is not only resistance to change, but also to the issue.

Your support will be very important in motivating staff to carry this out.

Look forward to your reply.

Best wishes,

Claire

Claire Debenham

EDUCATION OFFICE MEMORANDUM 5

To: Simon Trotter   *Date:* 1.3.90
AD (Special & Pupil Services)   *Ref:* S-PA/CD/SD

Complaints

I should like to discuss with you how members of the public can make a complaint about services with particular reference to Mrs S mother of C.S. The Council's Equal Opportunities Policy Leaflet implies that there is a procedure for this, and this has not escaped the notice of Mrs S.

Mrs S as you know, is extremely dissatisfied with the history and progress of her son C's assessment, and the treatment he is getting at school, and she suspects she will be dissatisfied with the provision offered once the assessment is completed. Personally, I feel that she does have some cause for complaint on the first two issues, although not as much as she believes herself to have. However, whether she does, or does not, have legitimate cause for complaint is beside the point. The point is that she wishes to complain.

I know that you are aware of the issues and that you have spoken to her yourself. I won't go over them. Mrs S has asked repeatedly for an interview with the Director. The Equal Opportunities Policy Leaflet says that having taken her complaints to the Department concerned and not having obtained satisfaction, she should then put them in writing to the Director. This will obviously present a hurdle for some parents.

You have also suggested she should write to the Director, and he will pass the letter to you to deal with. Mrs S is well aware of this, and in her view this would not constitute progress.

The Director is willing to see her if you agree. He will, of course, be briefed by you, and no doubt his replies will be consistent with yours. I've no doubt he will also be sympathetic with her, as well as give her the impression that everything possible is being done. After all, it is. As we both know, the delays are by no means entirely the responsibility of this Department.

So, what is the problem?

Mrs S is furious, frustrated and feels powerless. Each subsequent contact she makes with this Department elicits, in her experience, an increasingly hostile and 'tight-lipped' response. This in turn confirms and intensifies her frustration, fury, and sense of victimisation. She feels powerless, and her instincts are correct. Once in open conflict with this office can the situation only get worse for parents?

It seems the only good parent is a quiet one, who offers comments when asked, in writing, and in fluent English.

I know I am offering an extreme view – I am identifying with Mrs S's sense of the 'Kafkaesque'.

To look at the matter more constructively; I have suggested to her that she should discuss the school-related issues with the Head Teacher in the first instance. Later she can take matters up with the Governing Body, if she wishes. She already has some contact with one of the Parent Governors. Secondly, I have told her about the normal procedures if she is not happy with the provision described on the draft Statement.

This leaves the matter of the process of the assessment itself, and this is where I have come up against difficulties. Mrs S wishes to pursue an interview with the Director. She knows she can also complain to her Ward Councillor, and I believe she may do so. I suggest that I draft a letter for the Director's signature offering an interview if she still wishes it, following completion of the assessment. Hopefully, in the process of discussing the provision, complaints about the other issues can be listened to and Mrs S will feel her views have been heard and noted thoroughly.

The issue will still remain, however, for other parents, if not for Mrs S. Whilst the Equal Opportunities Statement says that complaints can be made, it is not detailed in how they should be dealt with. Perhaps we might learn a lot about service delivery by monitoring the comments of consumers. Should we be actively seeking this information in a more routine way?

Your views on this last point will be welcome, as well as your agreement on how to proceed with Mrs S.

Look forward to hearing from you.

Claire

Claire Debenham

EDUCATION OFFICE MEMORANDUM 6

To: Claire Debenham

Date: 5.3.90
Ref: S-AD/ST/ET

Complaints

Thank you for your memorandum about Mrs S and the difficulties she has experienced with the Department. I think there is a general issue here about how we structure opportunities to make complaints and in particular how we respond to complaints about the processes as opposed to the outcomes that we administer.

There are various structures people can use to make complaints or seek remedies where they are dissatisfied.

Statutory procedures

The Education Act 1981, of course, sets out procedures for conciliation and appeal in cases where parents are unhappy about the proposals an authority is making for their children's education. There are other cases of such statutory procedures: the 1986 Act, for example, sets out in some detail the rights of parents and the responsibilities of governors, head teachers and local education authorities when children are excluded from school. These statutory procedures are generally intended to provide a framework for resolving disputes between parents and various parts of the education system.

Local authority procedures which are required by statute or which are the subject of recommendations by DES circular

The Education Reform Act 1988 requires authorities to set up procedures for parents to make complaints about curricular provision and arrangements for religious observance in school. These procedures have to be approved by the Secretary of State. To take a similar, but not identical example, a DES circular has recommended that authorities issue written procedures to facilitate the protection of children from abuse and the Secretary of State has asked for copies of these procedures although he has not formally taken the right to approve them. Again, these procedures have been concerned with remedies and outcomes rather than the processes through which authorities deal with people.

Other statutory routes

There are other general routes for complaining which are enshrined in statute. One is the right to complain to a local councillor, whose powers are determined by law; a second is to complain (in relation to an issue at school) to a school governor, who also has powers set out in law; a third is to complain via a local councillor to the Local Ombudsman who also has a form of statutory authority. These are all excellent routes for registering dissatisfaction or seeking redress: making a complaint to a councillor or the Ombudsman is a fairly serious step, however, and is unlikely to be taken except by someone with a serious grievance or who is seeking some significant form of redress.

Another external monitoring body

The local voluntary organisation which represents parents is also in a good position to pursue complaints. The Parents' Centre does not have any statutory duties or powers, but does have good links with many local parents and is in a good position to bring issues to our attention. They are particularly helpful in bringing to our attention emerging patterns of complaints. The complaints they tell us about may be about processes or outcomes but, generally speaking, I think people have to be pretty upset before they consider complaining through this route.

The missing links

There seem to be two elements missing from all this. The first is a guide to the public setting out the various complaints procedures that exist, and stating which of these procedures are appropriate to particular forms of complaint. Compiling this would be quite an undertaking, because the various kinds of remedy that exist which are dictated or administered by outside bodies are quite numerous and fairly complex.

The other missing element is a procedure for people to make complaints which are fairly low level but of which we ought nevertheless to be aware. Perceived rudeness of staff, unreasonable delays in responding to letters or phone calls, lack of positive helpfulness in explaining difficult issues – all of these must necessarily exist in any large organisation, but without a formalised complaints system we have no idea how much it happens, where it happens, and whether the situation is getting better or worse.

The two elements could be combined into a single guide setting out procedures and advising parents how best to approach making a complaint.

The main counter argument

The main argument against a formal guide of this sort seems to me to be that setting up a complaints system actually encourages complaints. If people are aware of the possibility of complaining, and if they believe that their complaint will actually be taken seriously, they are more likely to complain than otherwise. The possibility of complaining may even encourage people to raise their expectations of the service. Conversely, it is possible that, if complaints are handled well, dissatisfaction may be reduced and the number of issues which are referred to the outside bodies on statutory procedures set out earlier may actually diminish.

The next stage

I think the next stage is probably to draft some written policy and practices on complaints. This would initially refer to the area of special education only, but perhaps it should be cast fairly generally in order to allow its more general application. Perhaps you could let me have a first draft by half-term, please?

Perhaps I could finish by saying that, thanks to the intervention of yourself and the Principal Educational Psychologist, we have arrived at an agreement with Mrs S with which I think she is genuinely satisfied.

Many thanks for your help.

Si

Simon Trotter

EDUCATION OFFICE MEMORANDUM 7

To: Claire Debenham

Date: 7.3.90
Ref: S-AD/ST/ET

Your role with respect to parents

This is the most important part of your job and deserves a memorandum to itself. I have been somewhat slow in writing this, because we have had a number of discussions on the subject, and you have already raised some relevant issues. Perhaps I should start by answering, specifically, the points you have made on formal bureaucratic language and on translations into community languages. In the first case, please prepare in liaison with administrative staff some clearer standard letters – I agree the existing letters would benefit from rewriting. On the second issue, please go ahead and get translations of the redrafted letters (once I have approved them). I agree that we need to do some consciousness-raising work on the use of translators and you will have my full support. Your concern about these issues admirably illustrates both the need for your post and your competence in filling it. Thank you.

I think it might be helpful to take a historical approach to the genesis of your post. There has been a lot of loose talk since the Warnock Report[2] about the Named Person. The report saw the Named Person as someone who could 'introduce parents to the right service or ... ensure that any concern which there might be about the child's development is followed up' as well as offering 'expert counsel' (p. 157). The Report recommended that, for the parents of under fives, this person should be the health visitor. For the parents of older children, the Report recommends that the head teacher of the child's school should be the Named Person. They made these recommendations on the basis that it is to the health visitor and the head teacher that parents most naturally turn.

Where children are undergoing a multi-professional assessment, the Report recommended that the Named Person should be a member of the multi-professional assessment team – who should be an educationist but could be either from within the school or outside it. As children grow older and prepare to leave school, it is suggested that the careers officer or specialised careers officer should take over at least part of the Named Person role (p. 159).

However, the Report also recommended that, in the event of the Named Person arrangements being unsatisfactory, parents should be given the name of an officer of the local education authority whom they could contact (p. 159 again).

The Named Person was, therefore, someone with whom parents were to be in regular, perhaps day-to-day contact, and who could provide expert advice on their child's needs as well as offering guidance on access to a range of services. Your post is not a named person in this sense.

Since the Warnock Report, there has been concern that parents should have access to someone who can explain in a disinterested way the details of the multi-professional assessment (which has since, of course, become the statutory assessment as outlined in Section 5 of the Education Act 1981). It has also been suggested that parents may need someone to help them prepare for meetings with professionals and local authority officers and to accompany them to such meetings to provide support and to ensure that their views are heard. It is not your role to act as advocate in this way, either. The Authority funds a project at a local voluntary organisation to do this and it is very successful.

It seems to me crucial that parents have access to advice and support which is offered outside the structure of the local authority and which can be seen to be independent.

I think there is one area of possible overlap between your post and that of the voluntary organisation, and that is in helping parents to formulate their representations and evidence which they offer in the course of the formal assessment. I also think that there is an area of overlap between the voluntary organisation, yourself and the Named Person as described in the Warnock Report, and that is the provision of information about services which are available.

As well as these reasons for setting up your post which are probably applicable to all authorities, there were some quite specific issues we needed to address. As a result of informal feedback from parents and also following a survey of several authorities including our own by the Greater London Association for the Disabled,[3] we became aware that parents did not perceive the Department as helpful and informative at the outset of a formal assessment. At the same time, the Authority's policy of promoting the integration of children with special educational needs was creating the need for increasingly complex support packages and for a continuing dialogue with parents over their children's needs. The routine involvement of the Authority in a child's case is therefore potentially much greater, and it therefore became even more important that we should be able to offer advice which parents saw as helpful.

At the same time, we wanted to soften the distinction which I referred to in my earlier memorandum between administrative and professional functions. From the parents' point of view, it is important that they should be put in touch with someone who can advise them about both the administrative aspects of the procedure (what letter will be sent when, for example), as well as the possible outcomes. Up to now, they have been routinely put in touch with someone who can advise on the former but not the latter. At the same time, we wanted the administrative aspects of individual cases to be handled with a reduced input from the Assistant Director concerned, in order that I could spend more time on other aspects of the job (specifically, developing and implementing our integration policy).

The main responsibilities of your post, therefore are:

- To provide advice to parents from the point that we first write stating our wish to carry out a statutory assessment:
  - explaining the process,
  - outlining the likely outcomes,
  - helping parents to formulate their evidence, in liaison with Newham Parents' Centre.
- Attending the meetings of the special needs panel (which we in Newham call the Authorised Officers' Briefing Meeting), speaking to the parental evidence and playing a full part in the discussion which involves the Inspector for Special Educational Needs and the Principal Educational Psychologist and is chaired by the Assistant Director.
- To provide liaison with parents over their children's placements. Clearly, this will be particularly important where the initial view formed by the parent is at variance with the Authority's draft statement of special educational needs.
- To represent the Authority at review meetings and case conferences: generally this will only be required if a change of placement is likely to result from the meeting.
- To promote within the Special Section of the Education Department a way of working which is generally welcoming and supportive to parents. This is likely to involve assessing the need for training and support of staff, and linking with the Central Training Unit over meeting these needs.
- I would also hope that we could work together on developing the Authority's integration policy and ensuring that it is reflected in institutional change.
- To assist generally in promoting the Authority's policy on the integration of children with special educational needs into mainstream schools.

Best wishes,

Si

Simon Trotter

EDUCATION OFFICE MEMORANDUM 8

To: Simon Trotter   *Date:* 15.3.90
AD (Special & Pupil Services)   *Ref:* S-PA/CD/SD

My role with respect to parents

Thank you for your memorandum on this subject. I am glad to have the opportunity to discuss the issues.

Advocacy

As you point out the Parents' Centre Workers fulfil the role of independent advocates for parents very well, once parents have made contact with them. The various aspects of our work in relation to the concept of advocacy is something we often discuss. We are agreed that where there is a conflict with the

Department, or support is required at meetings, parents are most appropriately supported by the Parents' Centre. They are independent and are free to act and advise without the restraint of loyalties to an employer.

Not every parent makes contact with the Parents' Centre, however, even if advised to do so. I often attend meetings for the Department where parents attend without advocates, even though it may have been useful to them. This is of course sometimes a matter of choice, but not always. Even so, it is important to look at the concept of advocacy broadly as well as specifically.

In the sense that an advocate is one who supports another's cause, we agreed that it is true to say we all take on this role, sometimes in differing ways. I am not in a position to act as an independent advocate. However, I can act within the spirit of that definition in general and specific ways, and it is part of my work to do so.

Our roles in offering information to parents clearly overlap, and that is why both parties are named in letters to parents as potential sources of advice and information. As the GLAD report described, the method and attitudes adopted by an information giver are crucial in promoting or obstructing the cause of another.

We can also all help parents in constructing representations. Personally, I feel that the Parents' Centre Workers are in a better position to help more parents because they have more time to spend exclusively on this task and can offer facilities, such as word-processing the finished article. In recognition of this, we are organising a joint project: a monthly workshop, with the general aim of giving support to more parents, and generating a larger number of representations.

I will do the vast amount of work organising the workshop: supplying names, sending out invitations, organising interpreters, premises, etc. – and they will pick up most of the work which comes out of it. That will include helping parents put representations in a final form, getting them typed, giving further advice, etc. I think this division of work both recognises the responsibilities of the Department and promotes effective use of the independent advocates. Both parties will have a role in promoting the cause of parents in the Education Department, however.

I have written to you recently about the kind of language used in letters to parents and proposed a policy on the use of translated letters and information to parents. When I attend meetings I consider how parents are treated, how they are involved and listened to, and am concerned about promoting good practice in this respect. I would be interested in getting more involved in larger consultations with parents – for example, on proposed change to special schools – to facilitate greater parental involvement in the process of change and prevent increasing polarisation and confrontation.

This kind of work addresses parents' access to the Department, and in relation to the administration staff involves raising issues of attitudes and equality in communication. My work on the 'complaints' procedure will be another example of how I have a role in promoting the cause of the service-users, within the bureaucracy. It is difficult to change institutional practice from outside the organisation. This is a way in which my role is complementary to that of the Parents' Centre.

Also, as part of opening up the Department to parents, I have advocated the need for specific facilities for meeting with parents – a comfortable room, with decent furniture and play equipment, specifically set up for the use of people engaged in discussion with parents. This wasn't available when I came and this is an office building where space is at a premium. In fact, it has proved extremely important to myself and others enabling discussions to take place in an atmosphere which promotes a sense of equality and respect, and hence facilitates communication between all parties.

I am sometimes able to promote the cause of individual parents without compromising my loyalties to the Department on specific issues. For example, our discussion about Mrs S, and her complaints. As another example, I advise parents to use the Parents' Centre advocates when I can see conflict arising, as well as seek solutions within the Department.

Special needs panel

Again, there is both a general and specific advocacy role here. Whilst in a general kind of way all panel members have a sense of responsibility to parents, I often pick-up on issues when, for example, we are in danger of wandering into the realms of supposition and unsubstantiated belief, e.g. on the dynamics of family life. I would emphasise that I don't see this as a responsibility of my post alone, but I am aware of doing this.

Specifically, I promote individual causes by arguing a parent's case. What parents say can be misheard, misinterpreted, dismissed, or simply not read. The way in which comments are written can be the focus of interest, rather than their actual content. In my experience, the more literate and scholastically inclined a representation, the more likely it is to be taken seriously. Unless it is someone's job to speak on behalf of the parent's written case, no matter how well-disposed or skilled the panel, sometimes these factors will hold sway.

Therefore, even if in the end I am bound to represent a decision to parents which is not in their favour, at the point when I am speaking to their views and during discussion I am acting within an advocacy role.

This does not exclude any other panel member having similar interests and values. However, it is my role to emphasise that perspective.

Otherwise, why have me there?

Finally

There are different attitudes to my work within the Department. There will always be a conflict inherent in promoting the cause of another from within an organisation. However, I would like to clarify my position with colleagues and agree with you ways of positively promoting my work so that it is understood and seen as generally valuable and not threatening.

Look forward to discussing all this at our next meeting.

Best wishes,

Claire

Claire Debenham

Postscript from Andrew Panton

The need to accommodate educational services to the procedures of a large organisation is never a popular notion. This so-called 'bureaucracy' may be resented particularly in the field of special education, where the vulnerability of children and the legitimate anxiety of their parents can make such processes appear impersonal and insensitive. For the officers of local education authorities who are responsible for managing the statutory assessment of children's special educational needs and for making special educational provision which matches those needs, the requirement to operate within a framework of agreed policies and procedures, and within the constraints of available financial resources is unavoidable. At the same time it is of paramount importance to treat each child as an individual and to recognise the need to obtain the understanding and support of parents for the educational arrangements that are made. The professional conflicts which arise in this situation for officers cannot always be ultimately resolved, but they can be managed. This chapter by Claire Debenham and Simon Trotter gives an insight into such conflicts and the creative tension which they can engender. It testifies, too, to the priority which this inner city and culturally plural borough gives to working with parents for the benefit of their children.

NOTES

1 Certificate of Qualification in Social Work (CQSW).
2 Department of Education and Science (DES) (1978) *Special Educational Needs* (The Warnock Report), London: HMSO.
3 Greater London Association for the Disabled (GLAD) (1988) *A Joint Endeavour? The Role of Parents, Parents' Groups and Voluntary Organisations in the Assessment Procedure for Children with Special Educational Needs in Three London Boroughs*, London: GLAD.

Index

Notes: 1 Most references are to the United Kingdom, except where otherwise specified; 2 The words teacher, pupil *and* school *are generally omitted as they are implied throughout.*